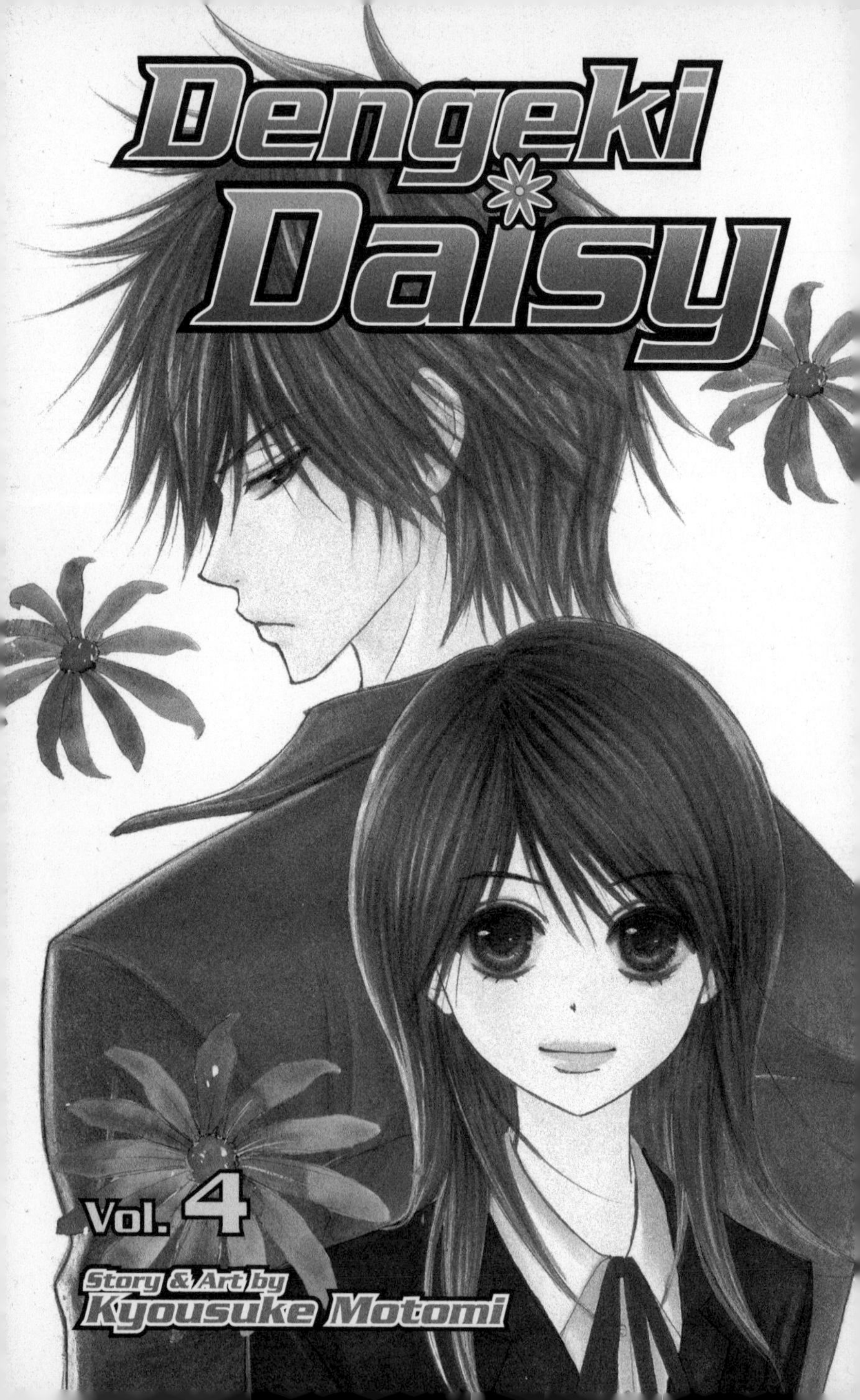
Dengeki Daisy
Vol. 4
Story & Art by
Kyousuke Motomi

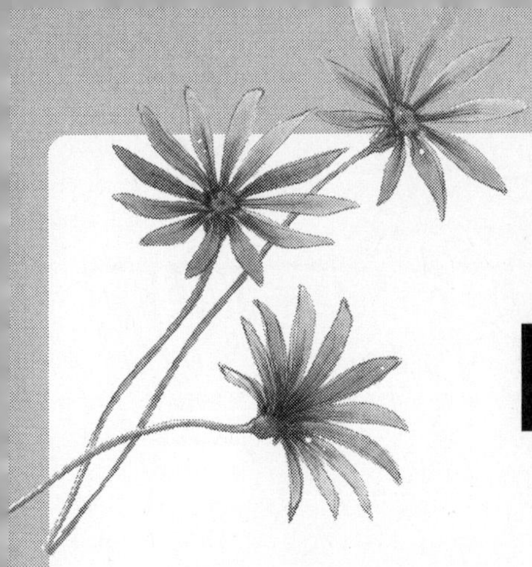

Dengeki Daisy

Volume 4 CONTENTS

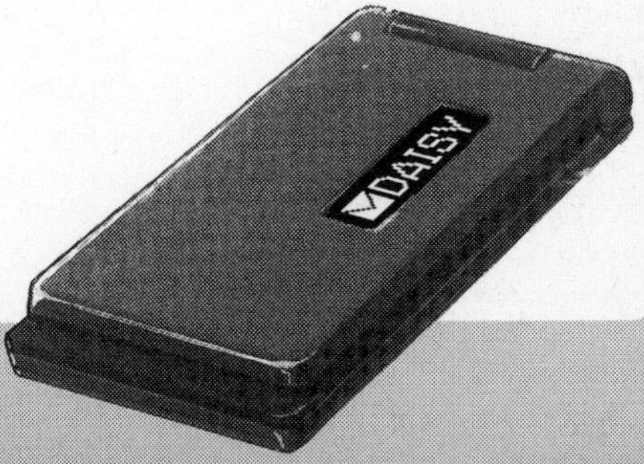

DAISY

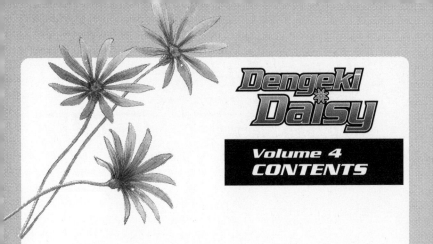

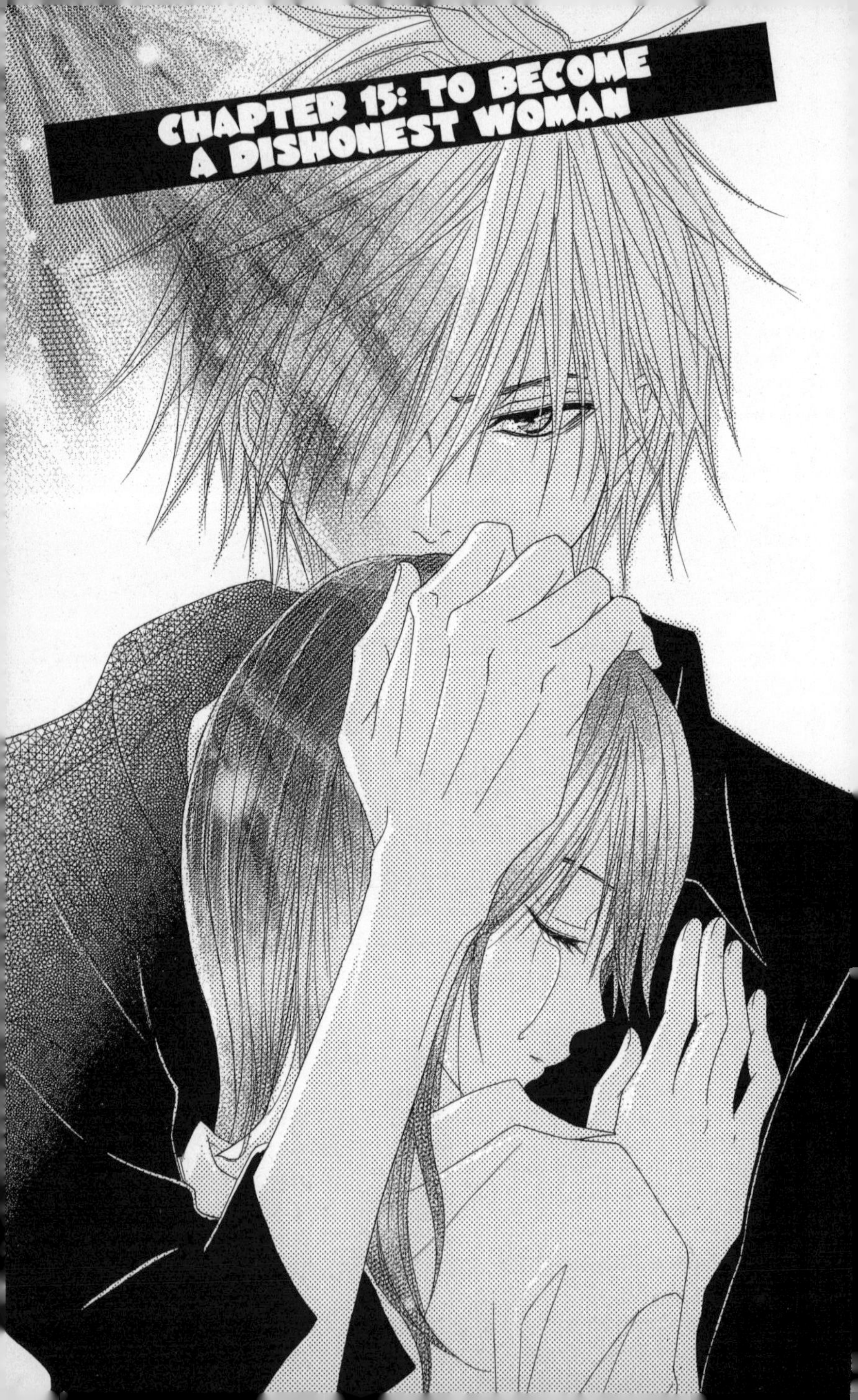
CHAPTER 15: TO BECOME A DISHONEST WOMAN

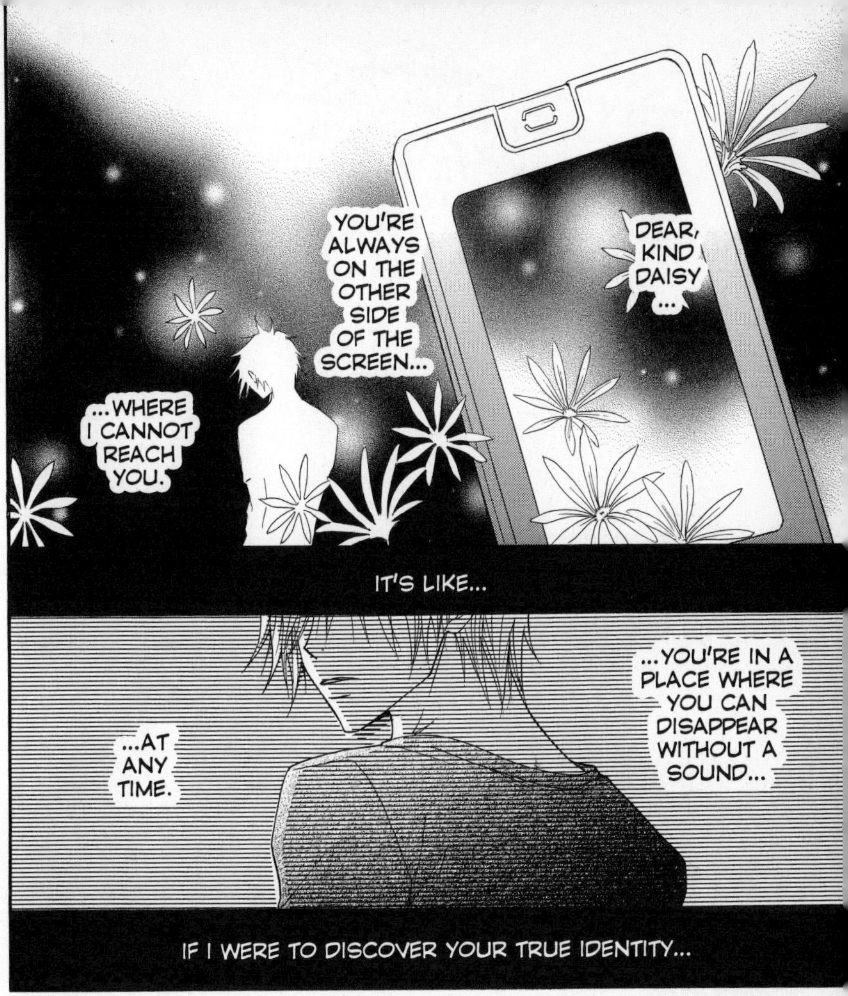
DEAR, KIND DAISY...
YOU'RE ALWAYS ON THE OTHER SIDE OF THE SCREEN...
...WHERE I CANNOT REACH YOU.
IT'S LIKE...
...YOU'RE IN A PLACE WHERE YOU CAN DISAPPEAR WITHOUT A SOUND...
...AT ANY TIME.
IF I WERE TO DISCOVER YOUR TRUE IDENTITY...

HELLO, EVERYONE. IT'S KYOUSUKE MOTOMI.

DENGEKI DAISY IS IN ITS FOURTH VOLUME. THAT MAKES ME, THE AUTHOR, HAPPY. *SHI* (FOUR) IS FOR "SHI" IN *SHIAWASE* (HAPPINESS). HURRAH. HURRAH. IF YOU ENJOY READING THIS VOLUME, I'LL BE EVEN HAPPIER.

NOW THEN, PLEASE READ ON.

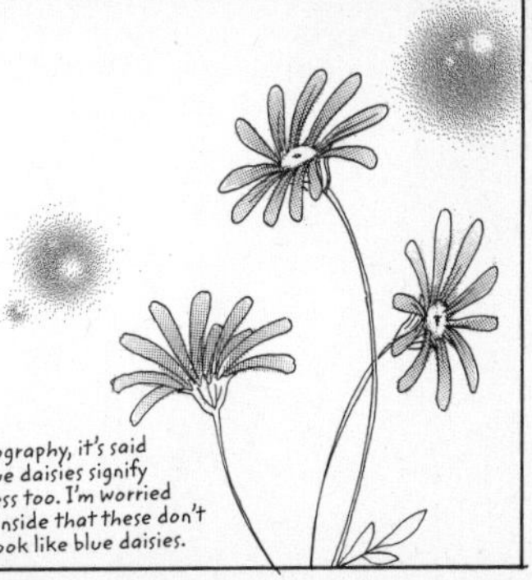

In floriography, it's said that blue daisies signify happiness too. I'm worried on the inside that these don't really look like blue daisies.

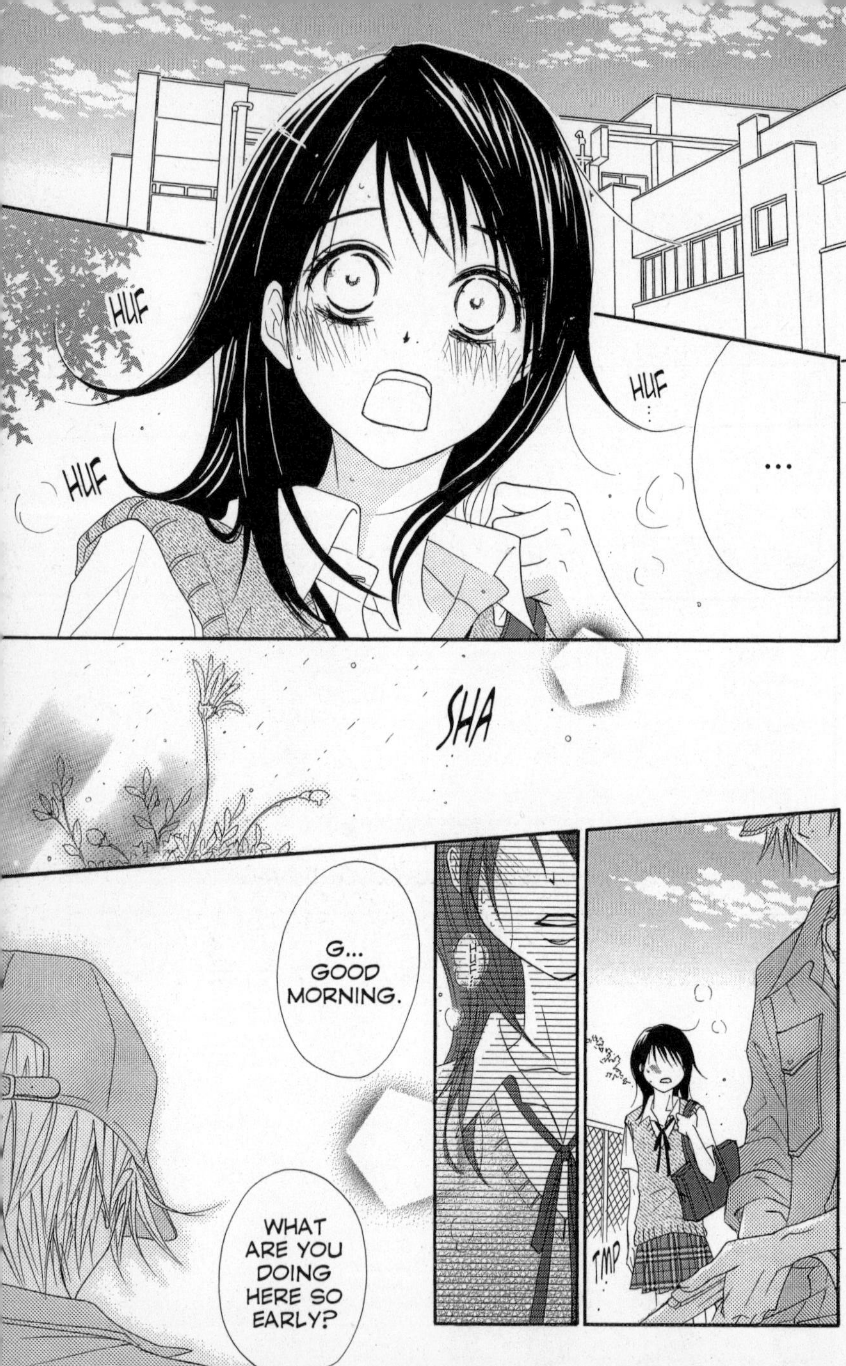
...
HUF
HUF
HUF
SHA
TMP
G... GOOD MORNING.
WHAT ARE YOU DOING HERE SO EARLY?

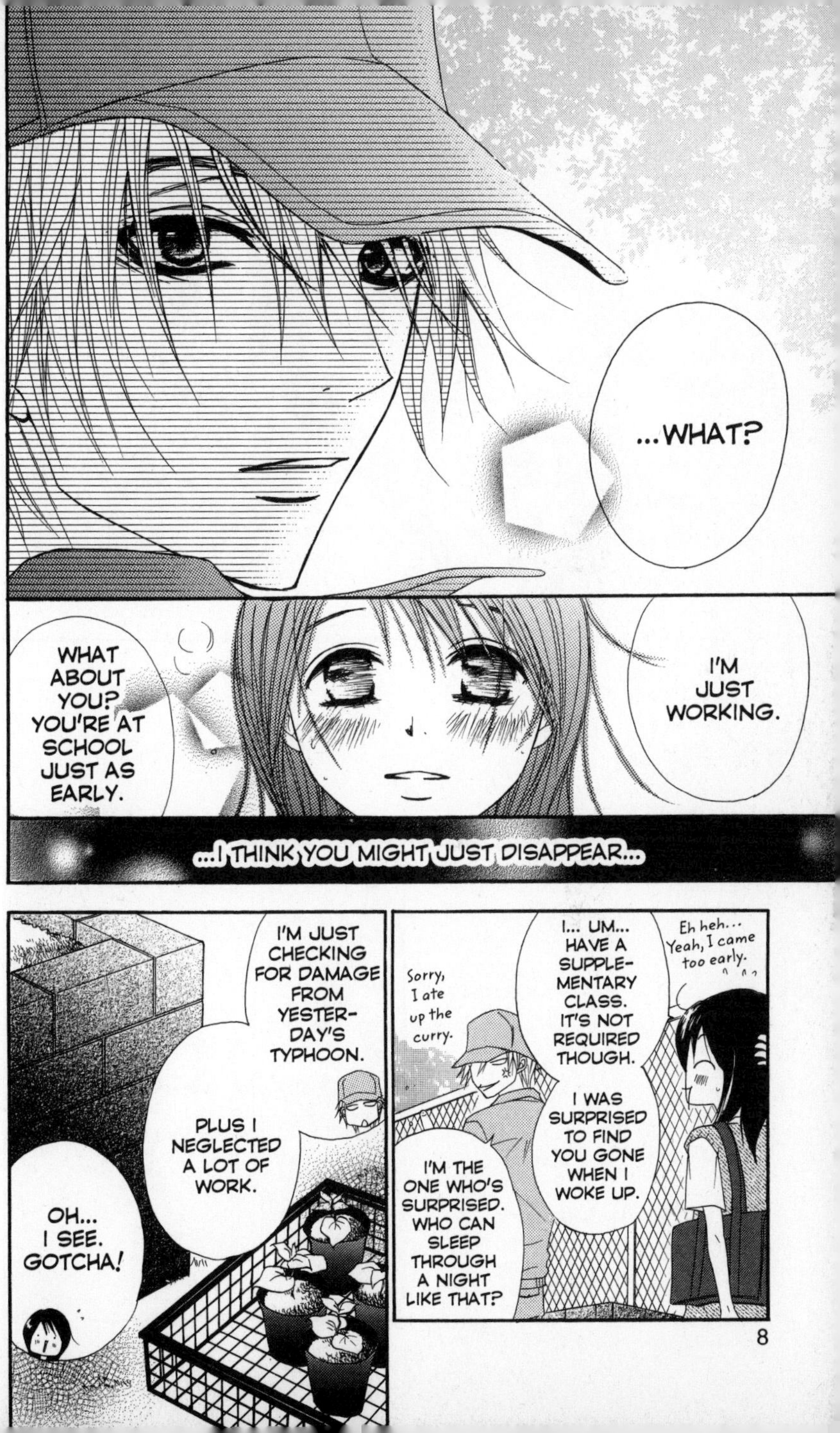
...WHAT?
I'M JUST WORKING.
WHAT ABOUT YOU? YOU'RE AT SCHOOL JUST AS EARLY.
...I THINK YOU MIGHT JUST DISAPPEAR...
Eh heh... Yeah, I came too early.
I... UM... HAVE A SUPPLE-MENTARY CLASS. IT'S NOT REQUIRED THOUGH.
Sorry, I ate up the curry.
I WAS SURPRISED TO FIND YOU GONE WHEN I WOKE UP.
I'M THE ONE WHO'S SURPRISED. WHO CAN SLEEP THROUGH A NIGHT LIKE THAT?
I'M JUST CHECKING FOR DAMAGE FROM YESTER-DAY'S TYPHOON.
PLUS I NEGLECTED A LOT OF WORK.
OH... I SEE. GOTCHA!

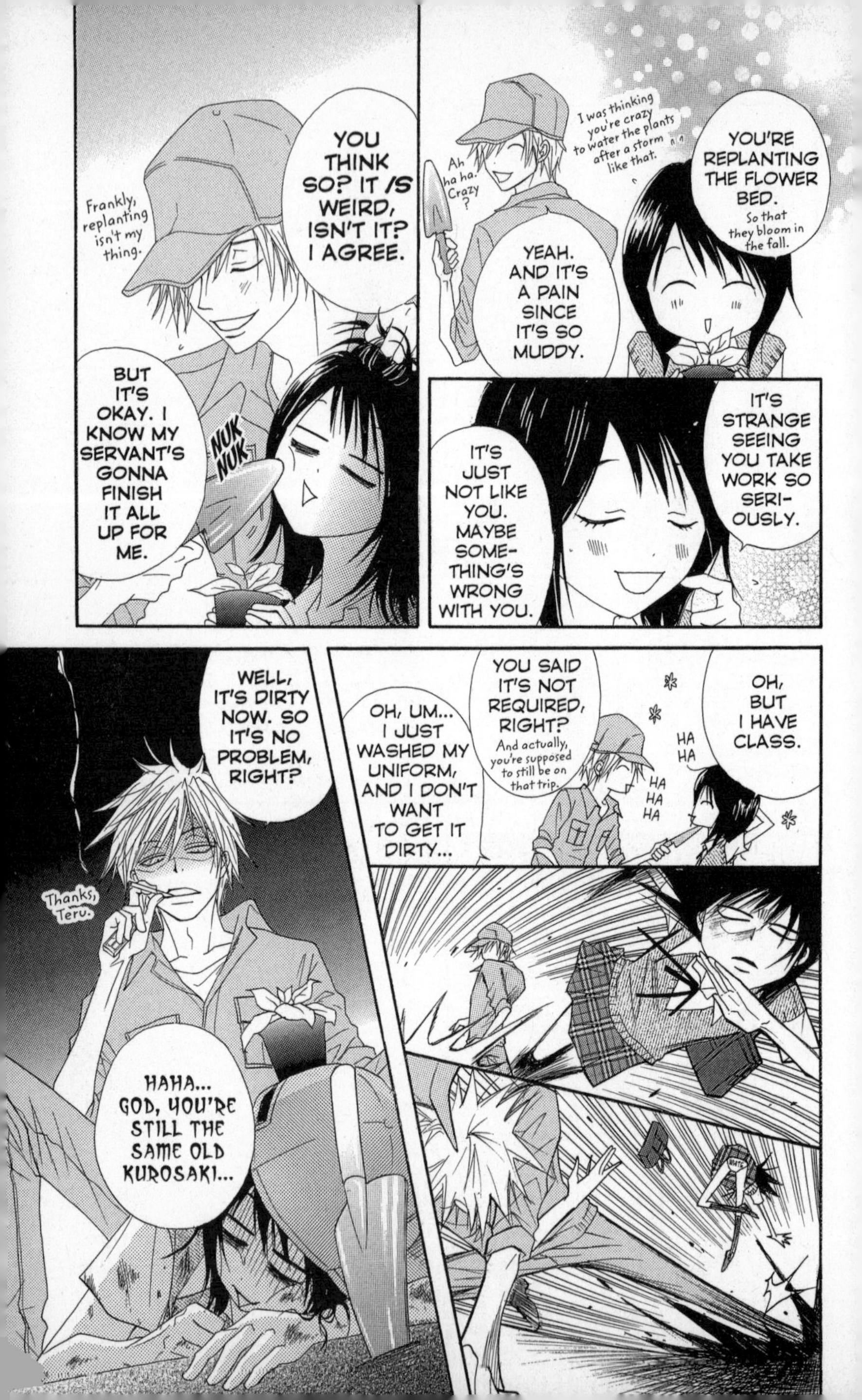
YOU'RE REPLANTING THE FLOWER BED.
So that they bloom in the fall.
I was thinking you're crazy to water the plants after a storm like that.
Ah ha ha. Crazy?
YEAH. AND IT'S A PAIN SINCE IT'S SO MUDDY.
IT'S STRANGE SEEING YOU TAKE WORK SO SERI-OUSLY.
IT'S JUST NOT LIKE YOU. MAYBE SOME-THING'S WRONG WITH YOU.
YOU THINK SO? IT IS WEIRD, ISN'T IT? I AGREE.
Frankly, replanting isn't my thing.
BUT IT'S OKAY. I KNOW MY SERVANT'S GONNA FINISH IT ALL UP FOR ME.
NUK NUK
OH, BUT I HAVE CLASS.
HA HA
HA HA HA
YOU SAID IT'S NOT REQUIRED, RIGHT?
And actually, you're supposed to still be on that trip.
OH, UM... I JUST WASHED MY UNIFORM, AND I DON'T WANT TO GET IT DIRTY...
WELL, IT'S DIRTY NOW. SO IT'S NO PROBLEM, RIGHT?
Thanks, Teru.
HAHA... GOD, YOU'RE STILL THE SAME OLD KUROSAKI...

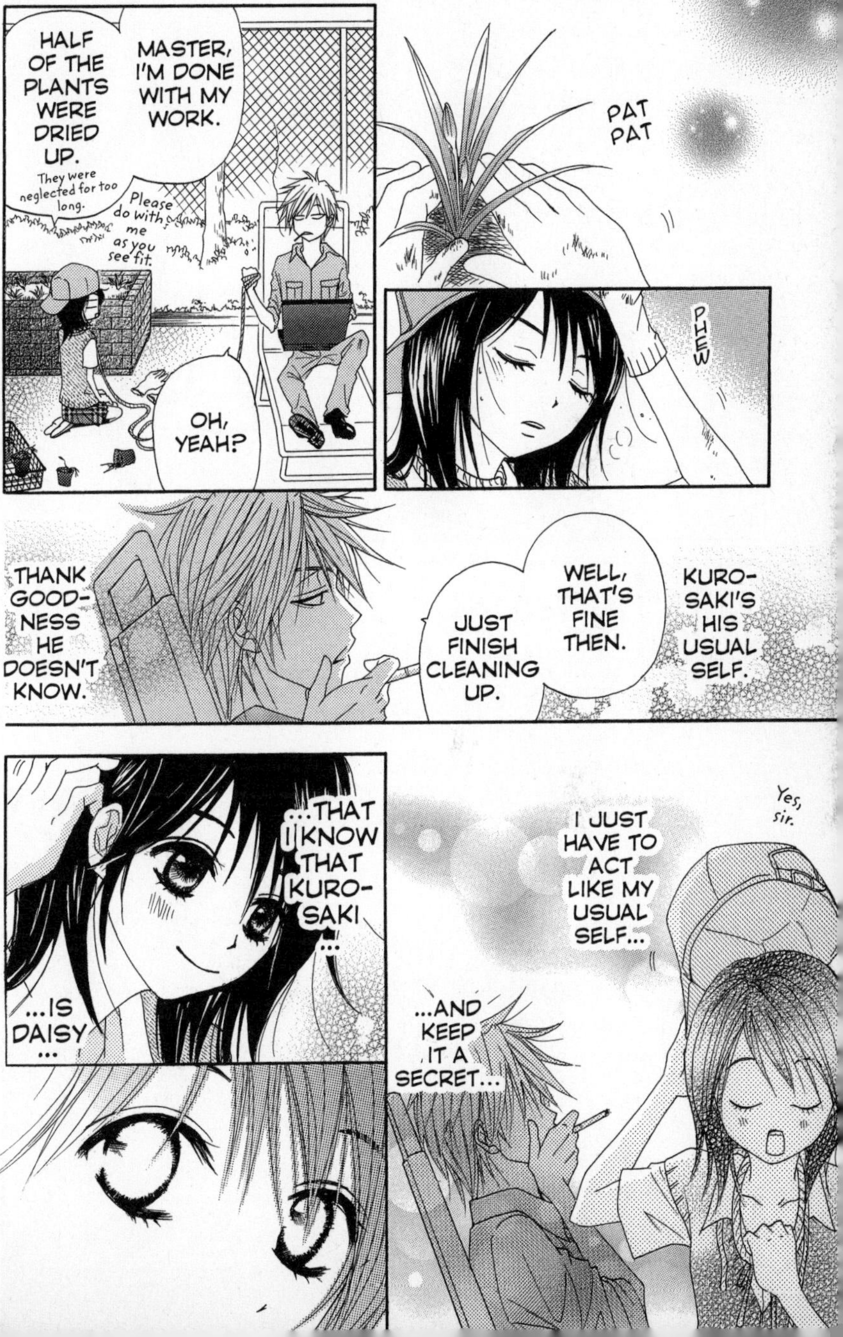
PAT PAT
PHEW
MASTER, I'M DONE WITH MY WORK.
HALF OF THE PLANTS WERE DRIED UP.
They were neglected for too long.
Please do with me as you see fit.
OH, YEAH?
KURO-SAKI'S HIS USUAL SELF.
WELL, THAT'S FINE THEN.
JUST FINISH CLEANING UP.
THANK GOODNESS HE DOESN'T KNOW.
...THAT I KNOW THAT KURO-SAKI...
...IS DAISY...
Yes, sir.
I JUST HAVE TO ACT LIKE MY USUAL SELF...
...AND KEEP IT A SECRET...

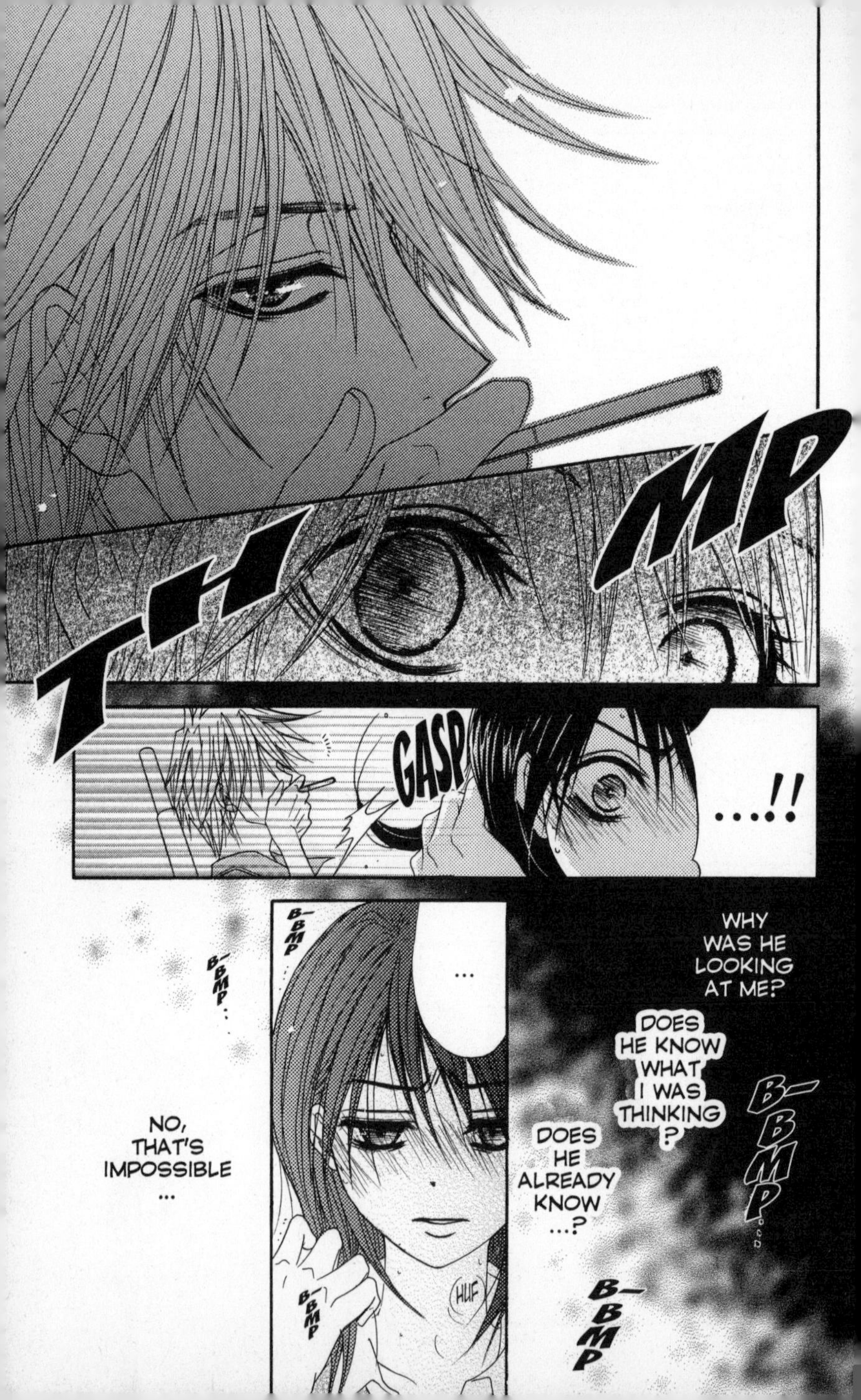
MP
T-H
...!!
GASP
WHY WAS HE LOOKING AT ME?
DOES HE KNOW WHAT I WAS THINKING?
B-BMP...
DOES HE ALREADY KNOW ...?
B-BMP
B-BMP...
...
HUF
B-BMP
B-BMP...
NO, THAT'S IMPOSSIBLE ...

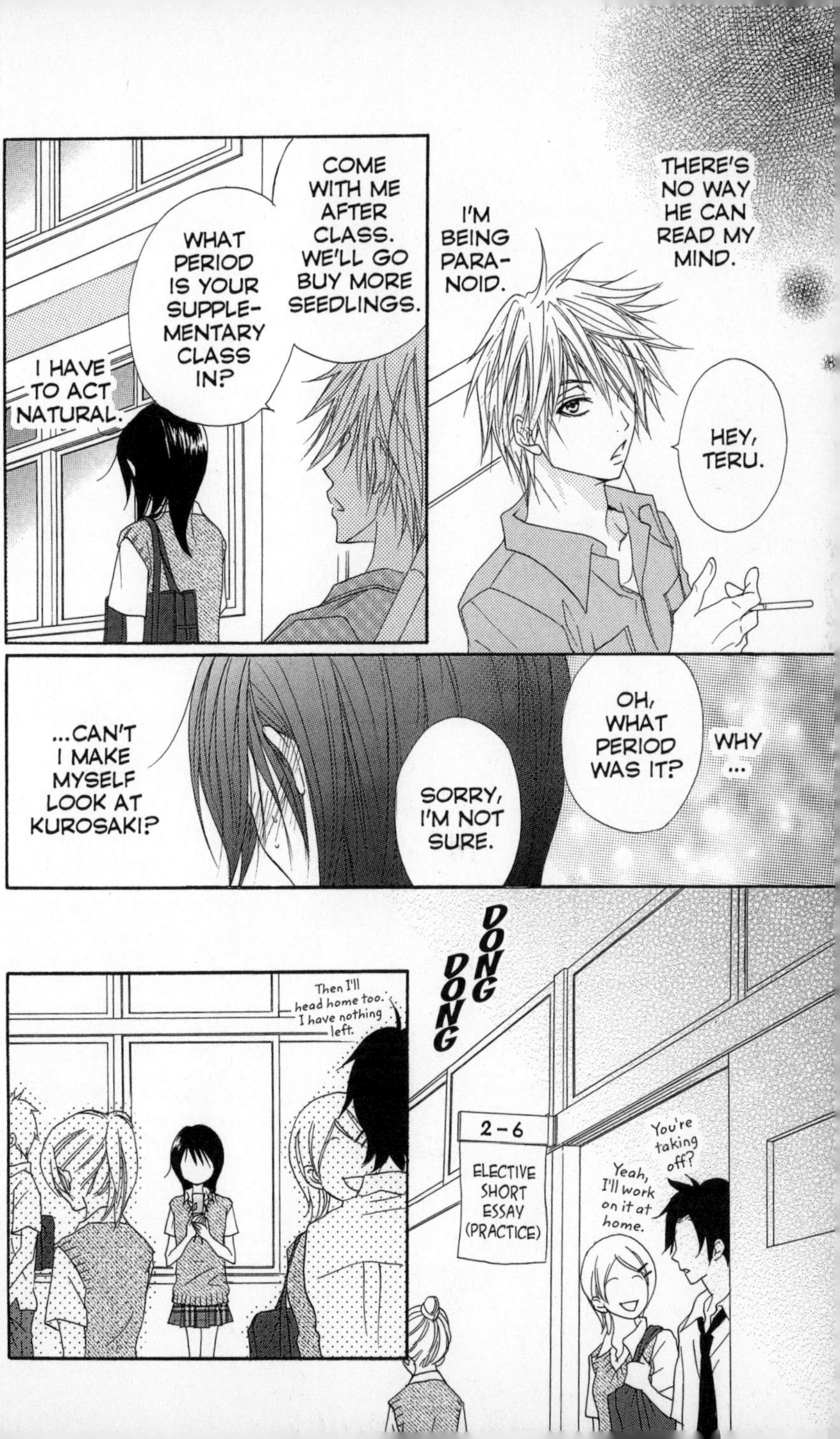
THERE'S NO WAY HE CAN READ MY MIND.
HEY, TERU.
I'M BEING PARA-NOID.
COME WITH ME AFTER CLASS. WE'LL GO BUY MORE SEEDLINGS.
WHAT PERIOD IS YOUR SUPPLE-MENTARY CLASS IN?
I HAVE TO ACT NATURAL.
WHY...
OH, WHAT PERIOD WAS IT?
SORRY, I'M NOT SURE.
...CAN'T I MAKE MYSELF LOOK AT KUROSAKI?
DONG DONG
2-6
ELECTIVE SHORT ESSAY (PRACTICE)
You're taking off?
Yeah, I'll work on it at home.
Then I'll head home too. I have nothing left.

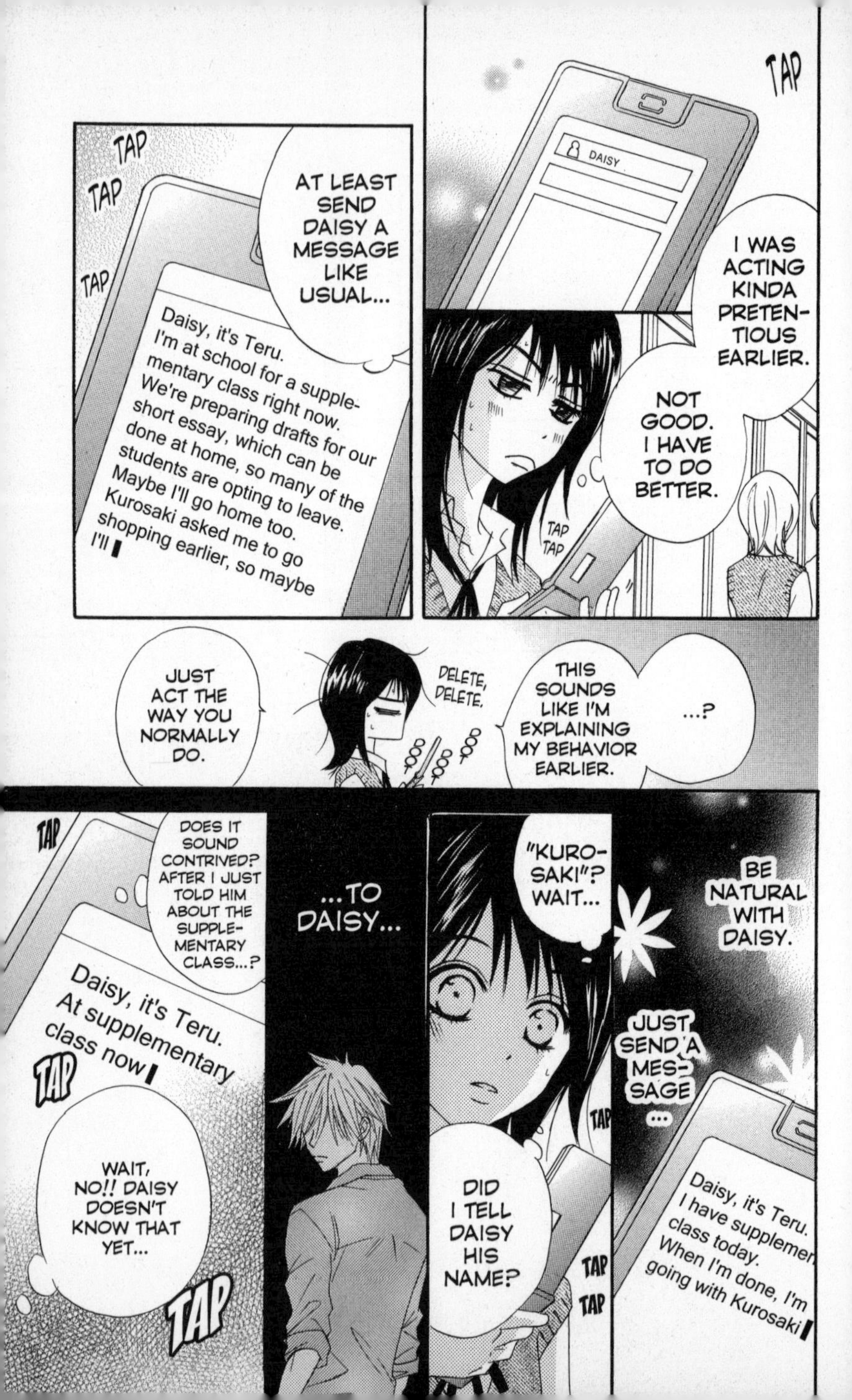
TAP
DAISY
I WAS ACTING KINDA PRETENTIOUS EARLIER.
NOT GOOD. I HAVE TO DO BETTER.
TAP TAP
TAP
TAP
TAP
AT LEAST SEND DAISY A MESSAGE LIKE USUAL...
Daisy, it's Teru. I'm at school for a supplementary class right now. We're preparing drafts for our short essay, which can be done at home, so many of the students are opting to leave. Maybe I'll go home too. Kurosaki asked me to go shopping earlier, so maybe I'll
...?
THIS SOUNDS LIKE I'M EXPLAINING MY BEHAVIOR EARLIER.
DELETE, DELETE.
JUST ACT THE WAY YOU NORMALLY DO.
BE NATURAL WITH DAISY.
JUST SEND A MESSAGE...
Daisy, it's Teru. I have supplemen class today. When I'm done, I'm going with Kurosaki
TAP
TAP
"KURO-SAKI"? WAIT...
TAP
DID I TELL DAISY HIS NAME?
...TO DAISY...
TAP
DOES IT SOUND CONTRIVED? AFTER I JUST TOLD HIM ABOUT THE SUPPLEMENTARY CLASS...?
Daisy, it's Teru. At supplementary class now
TAP
WAIT, NO!! DAISY DOESN'T KNOW THAT YET...
TAP

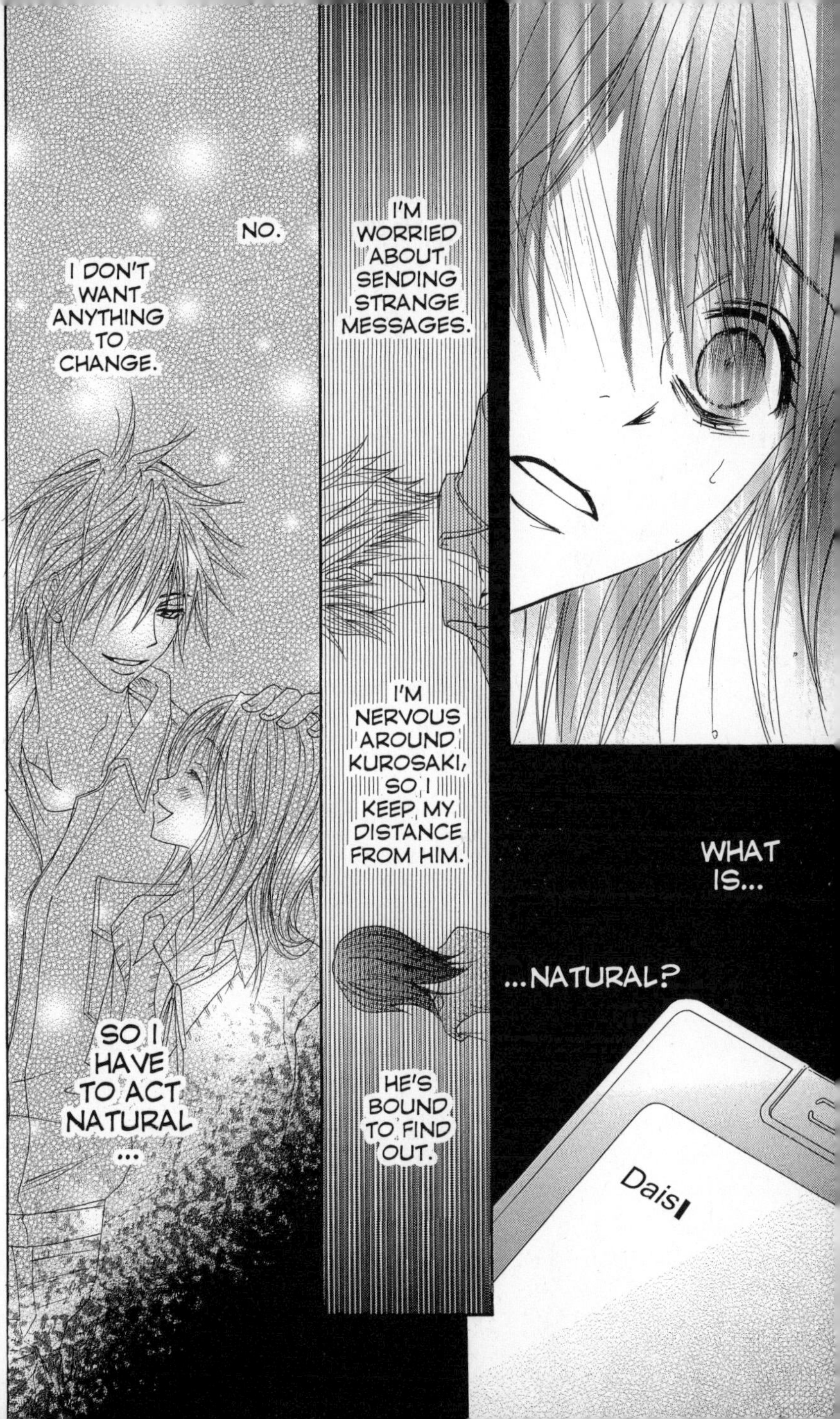
WHAT IS...
...NATURAL?
Dais
I'M WORRIED ABOUT SENDING STRANGE MESSAGES.
I'M NERVOUS AROUND KUROSAKI, SO I KEEP MY DISTANCE FROM HIM.
HE'S BOUND TO FIND OUT.
NO.
I DON'T WANT ANYTHING TO CHANGE.
SO I HAVE TO ACT NATURAL...

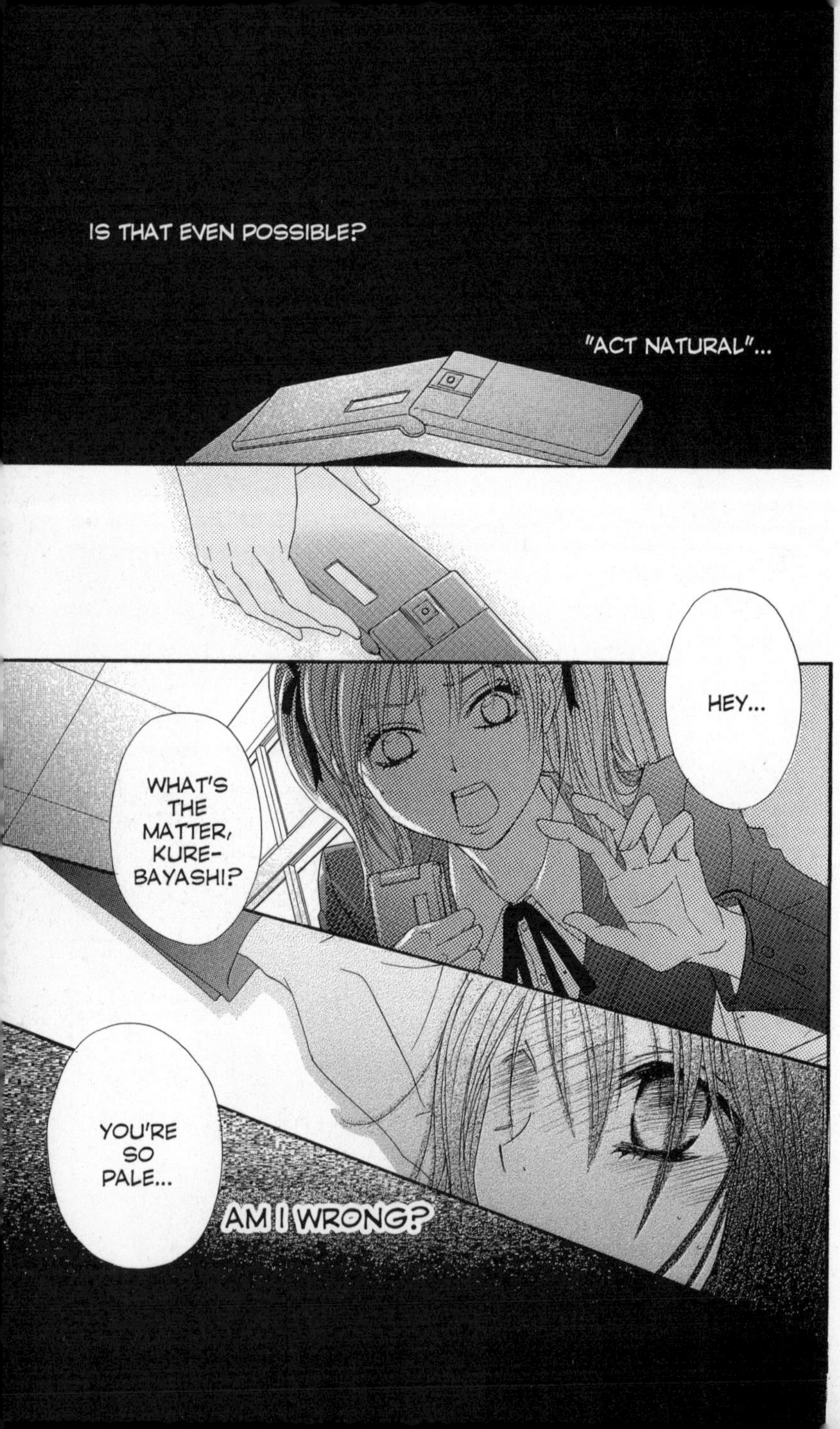
IS THAT EVEN POSSIBLE?
"ACT NATURAL"...
HEY...
WHAT'S THE MATTER, KURE-BAYASHI?
YOU'RE SO PALE...
AM I WRONG?

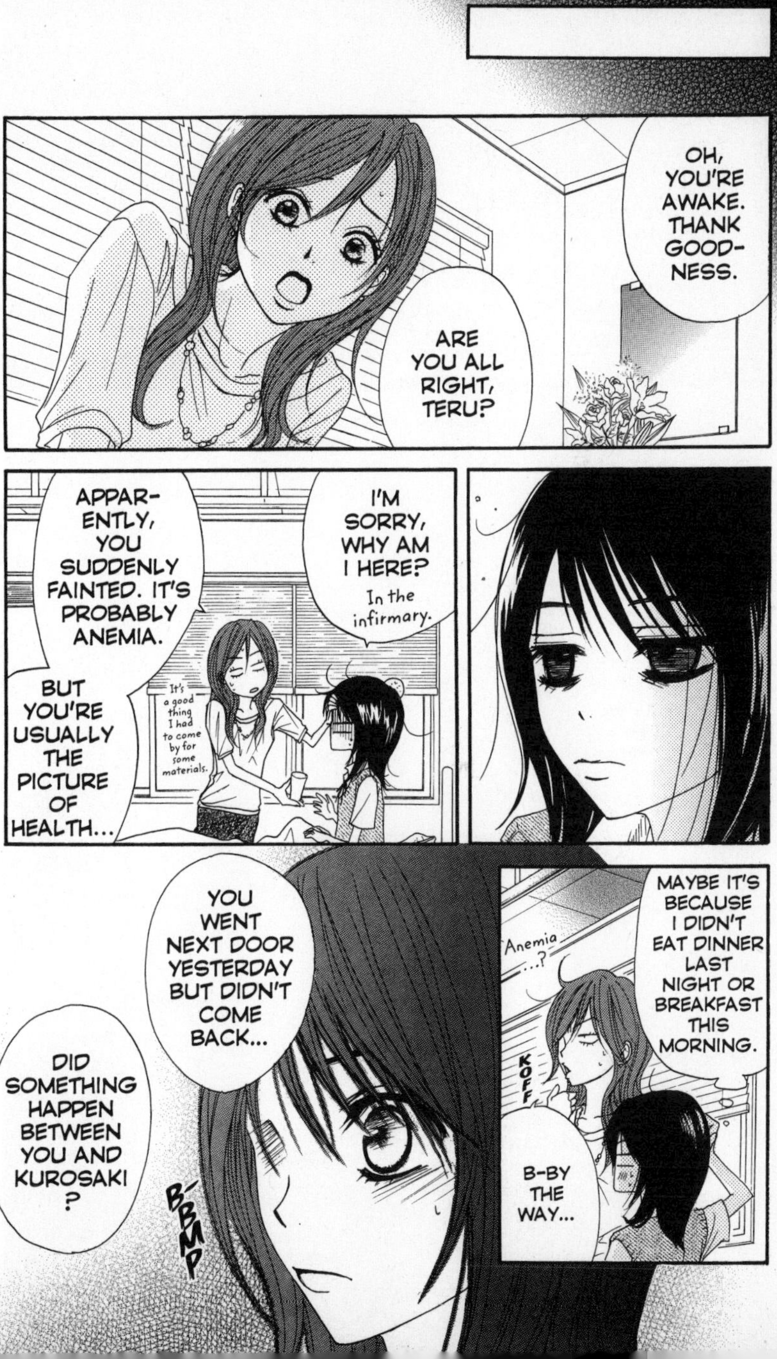
OH, YOU'RE AWAKE. THANK GOODNESS.
ARE YOU ALL RIGHT, TERU?
I'M SORRY, WHY AM I HERE?
In the infirmary.
APPARENTLY, YOU SUDDENLY FAINTED. IT'S PROBABLY ANEMIA.
It's a good thing I had to come by for some materials.
BUT YOU'RE USUALLY THE PICTURE OF HEALTH...
MAYBE IT'S BECAUSE I DIDN'T EAT DINNER LAST NIGHT OR BREAKFAST THIS MORNING.
Anemia ...?
KOFF
B-BY THE WAY...
YOU WENT NEXT DOOR YESTERDAY BUT DIDN'T COME BACK...
DID SOMETHING HAPPEN BETWEEN YOU AND KUROSAKI ?
B-BMP

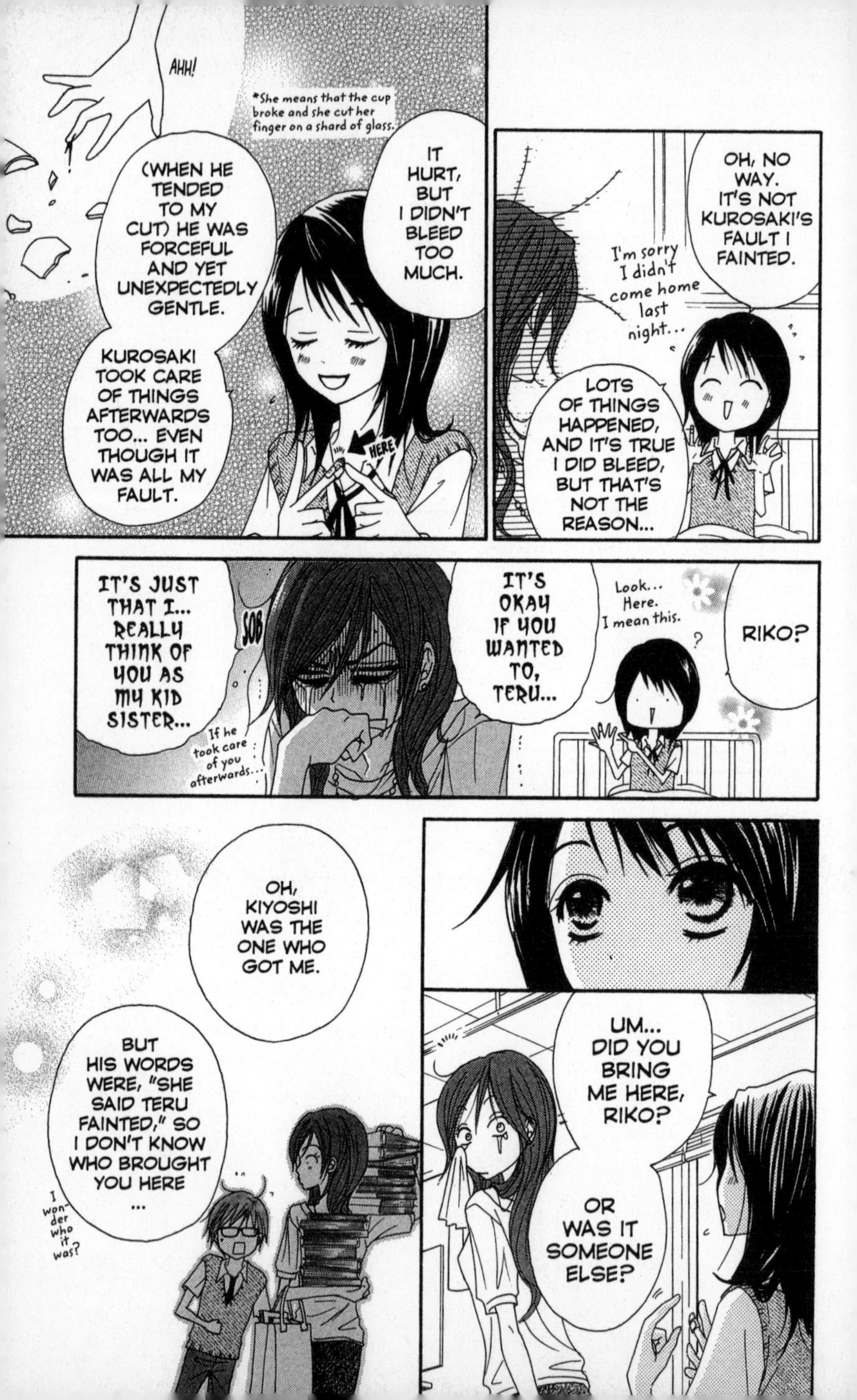
OH, NO WAY. IT'S NOT KUROSAKI'S FAULT I FAINTED.
I'm sorry I didn't come home last night...
LOTS OF THINGS HAPPENED, AND IT'S TRUE I DID BLEED, BUT THAT'S NOT THE REASON...
AHH!
*She means that the cup broke and she cut her finger on a shard of glass.
IT HURT, BUT I DIDN'T BLEED TOO MUCH.
(WHEN HE TENDED TO MY CUT) HE WAS FORCEFUL AND YET UNEXPECTEDLY GENTLE.
HERE
KUROSAKI TOOK CARE OF THINGS AFTERWARDS TOO... EVEN THOUGH IT WAS ALL MY FAULT.
RIKO?
Look... Here. I mean this.
?
IT'S OKAY IF YOU WANTED TO, TERU...
SOB
IT'S JUST THAT I... REALLY THINK OF YOU AS MY KID SISTER...
If he took care of you afterwards...
UM... DID YOU BRING ME HERE, RIKO?
OR WAS IT SOMEONE ELSE?
OH, KIYOSHI WAS THE ONE WHO GOT ME.
BUT HIS WORDS WERE, "SHE SAID TERU FAINTED," SO I DON'T KNOW WHO BROUGHT YOU HERE ...
I wonder who it was?

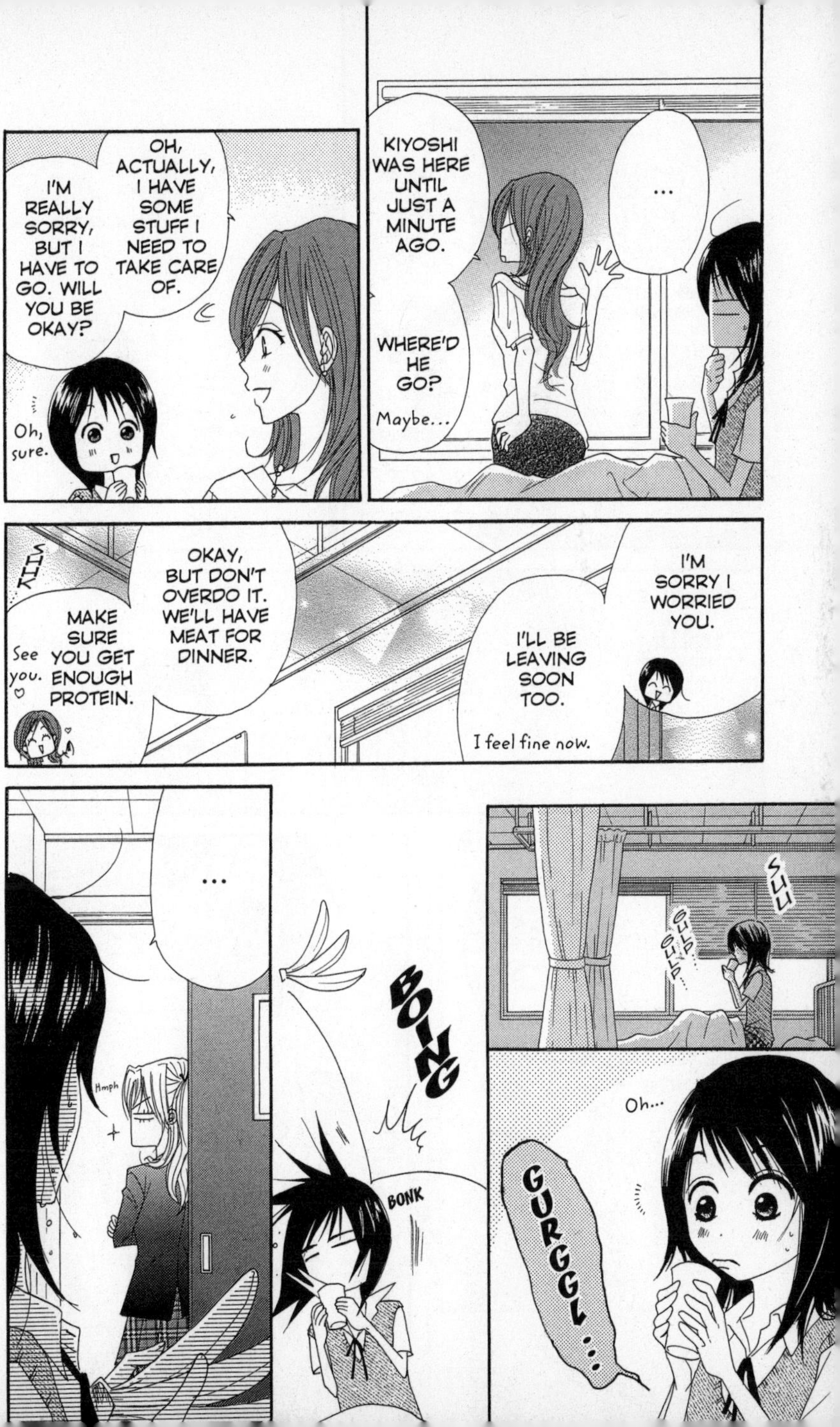
...
KIYOSHI WAS HERE UNTIL JUST A MINUTE AGO.
WHERE'D HE GO?
Maybe...
OH, ACTUALLY, I HAVE SOME STUFF I NEED TO TAKE CARE OF.
I'M REALLY SORRY, BUT I HAVE TO GO. WILL YOU BE OKAY?
Oh, sure.
I'M SORRY I WORRIED YOU.
I'LL BE LEAVING SOON TOO.
I feel fine now.
OKAY, BUT DON'T OVERDO IT. WE'LL HAVE MEAT FOR DINNER.
MAKE SURE YOU GET ENOUGH PROTEIN.
See you.
SHHK
SUU
GULP... GULP...
Oh...
GURGGL...
BOING
BONK
...
Hmph

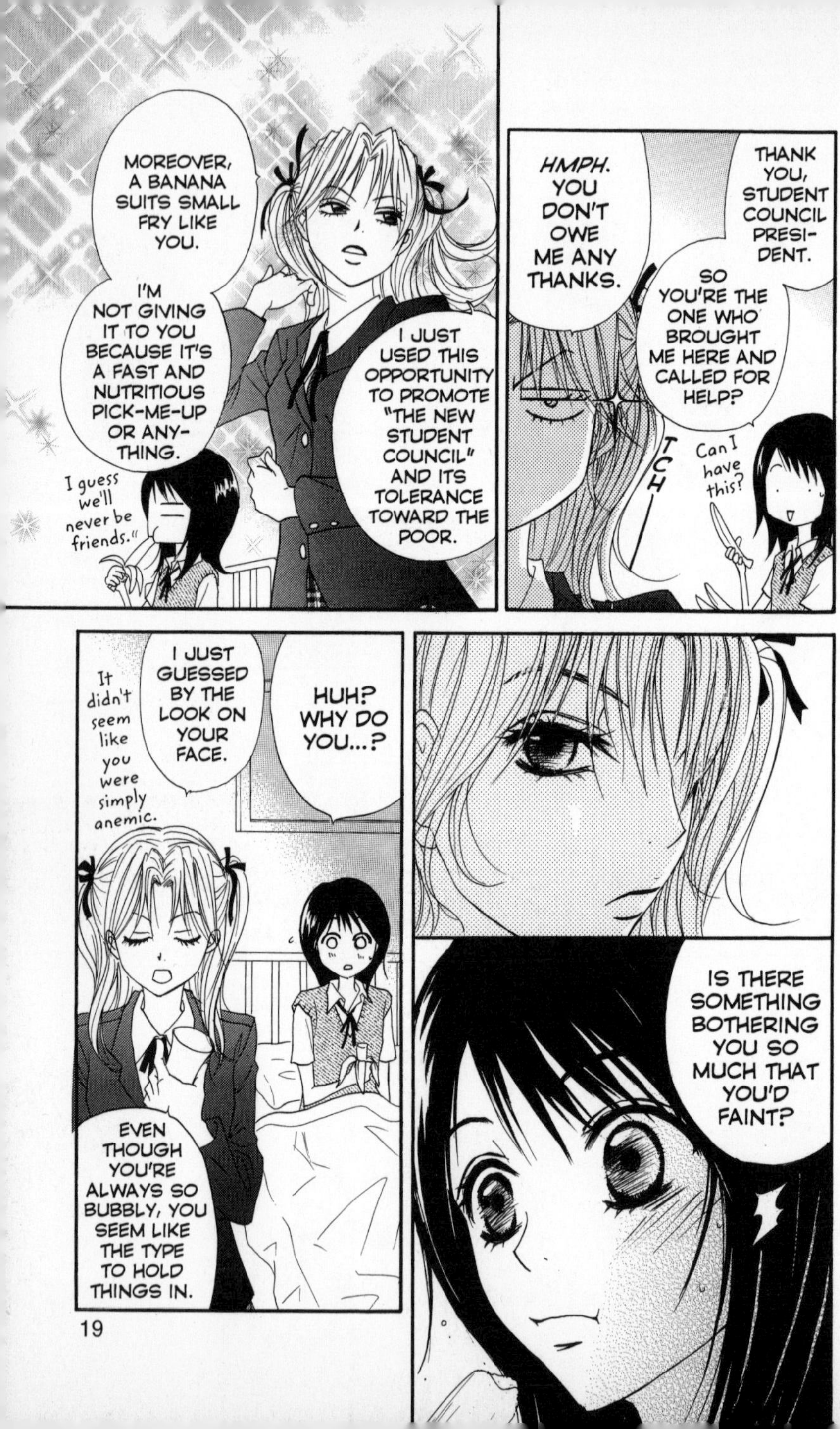
THANK YOU, STUDENT COUNCIL PRESIDENT.
SO YOU'RE THE ONE WHO BROUGHT ME HERE AND CALLED FOR HELP?
HMPH. YOU DON'T OWE ME ANY THANKS.
TCH
Can I have this?
I'M NOT GIVING IT TO YOU BECAUSE IT'S A FAST AND NUTRITIOUS PICK-ME-UP OR ANYTHING.
I JUST USED THIS OPPORTUNITY TO PROMOTE "THE NEW STUDENT COUNCIL" AND ITS TOLERANCE TOWARD THE POOR.
MOREOVER, A BANANA SUITS SMALL FRY LIKE YOU.
I guess we'll never be friends.
IS THERE SOMETHING BOTHERING YOU SO MUCH THAT YOU'D FAINT?
HUH? WHY DO YOU...?
I JUST GUESSED BY THE LOOK ON YOUR FACE.
It didn't seem like you were simply anemic.
EVEN THOUGH YOU'RE ALWAYS SO BUBBLY, YOU SEEM LIKE THE TYPE TO HOLD THINGS IN.

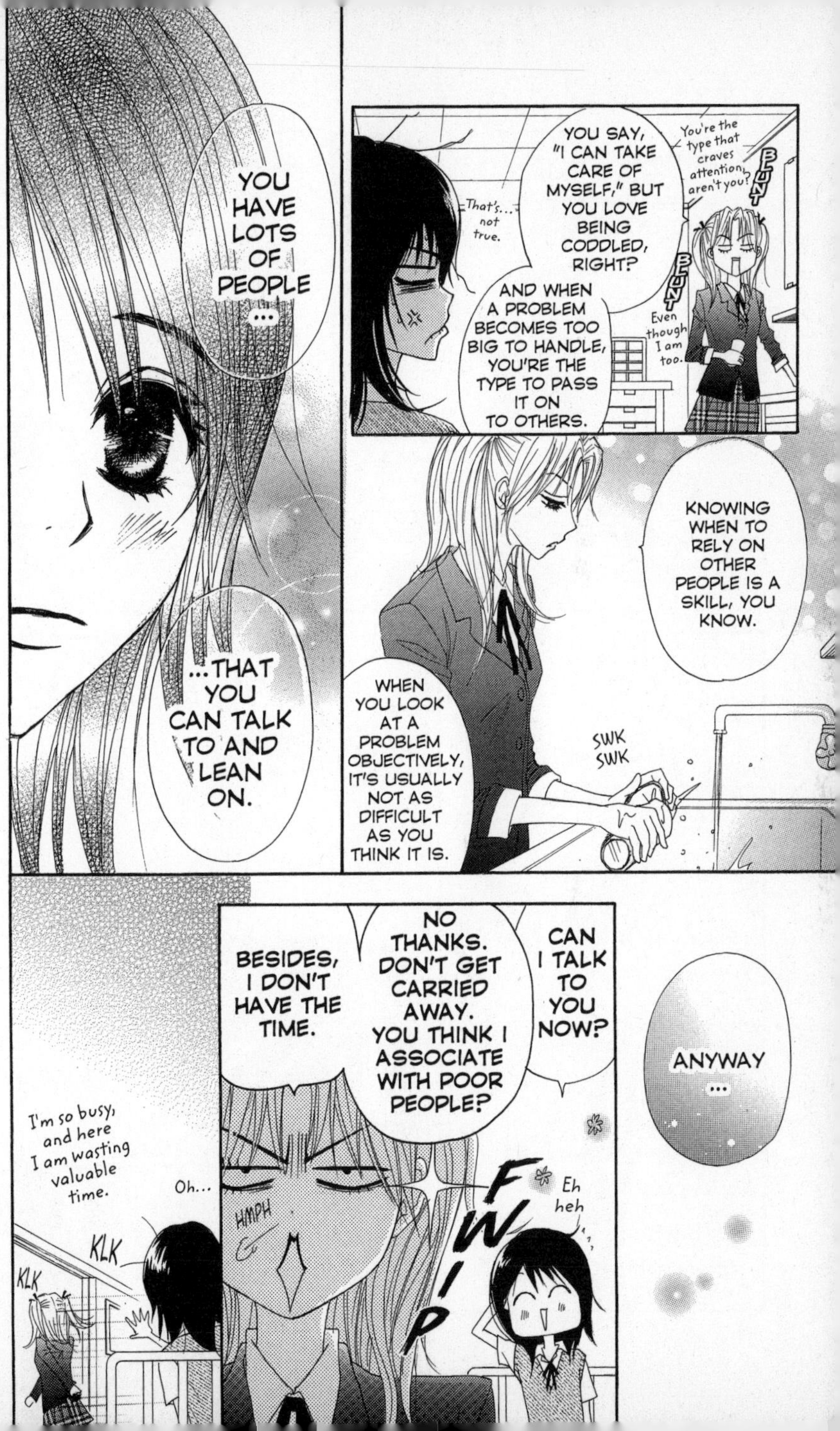
You're the type that craves attention, aren't you?
BLUNT
YOU SAY, "I CAN TAKE CARE OF MYSELF," BUT YOU LOVE BEING CODDLED, RIGHT?
That's... not true.
BLUNT
Even though I am too.
AND WHEN A PROBLEM BECOMES TOO BIG TO HANDLE, YOU'RE THE TYPE TO PASS IT ON TO OTHERS.
KNOWING WHEN TO RELY ON OTHER PEOPLE IS A SKILL, YOU KNOW.
SWK SWK
WHEN YOU LOOK AT A PROBLEM OBJECTIVELY, IT'S USUALLY NOT AS DIFFICULT AS YOU THINK IT IS.
YOU HAVE LOTS OF PEOPLE...
...THAT YOU CAN TALK TO AND LEAN ON.
ANYWAY...
CAN I TALK TO YOU NOW?
Eh heh
FWIP
NO THANKS. DON'T GET CARRIED AWAY. YOU THINK I ASSOCIATE WITH POOR PEOPLE?
BESIDES, I DON'T HAVE THE TIME.
HMPH
Oh...
I'm so busy, and here I am wasting valuable time.
KLK
KLK

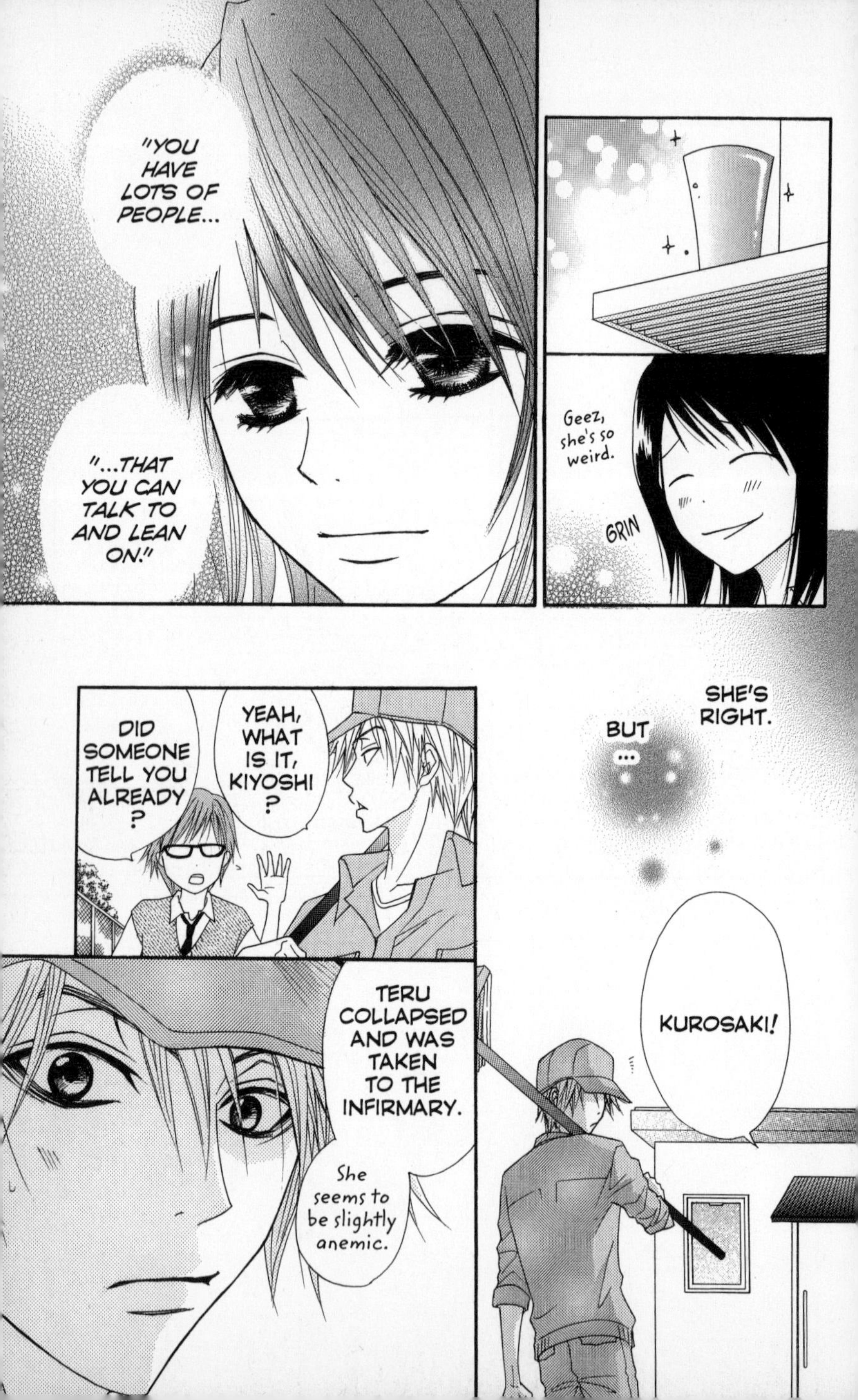
Geez, she's so weird.
GRIN
"YOU HAVE LOTS OF PEOPLE...
"...THAT YOU CAN TALK TO AND LEAN ON."
SHE'S RIGHT.
BUT ...
KUROSAKI!
YEAH, WHAT IS IT, KIYOSHI?
DID SOMEONE TELL YOU ALREADY?
TERU COLLAPSED AND WAS TAKEN TO THE INFIRMARY.
She seems to be slightly anemic.

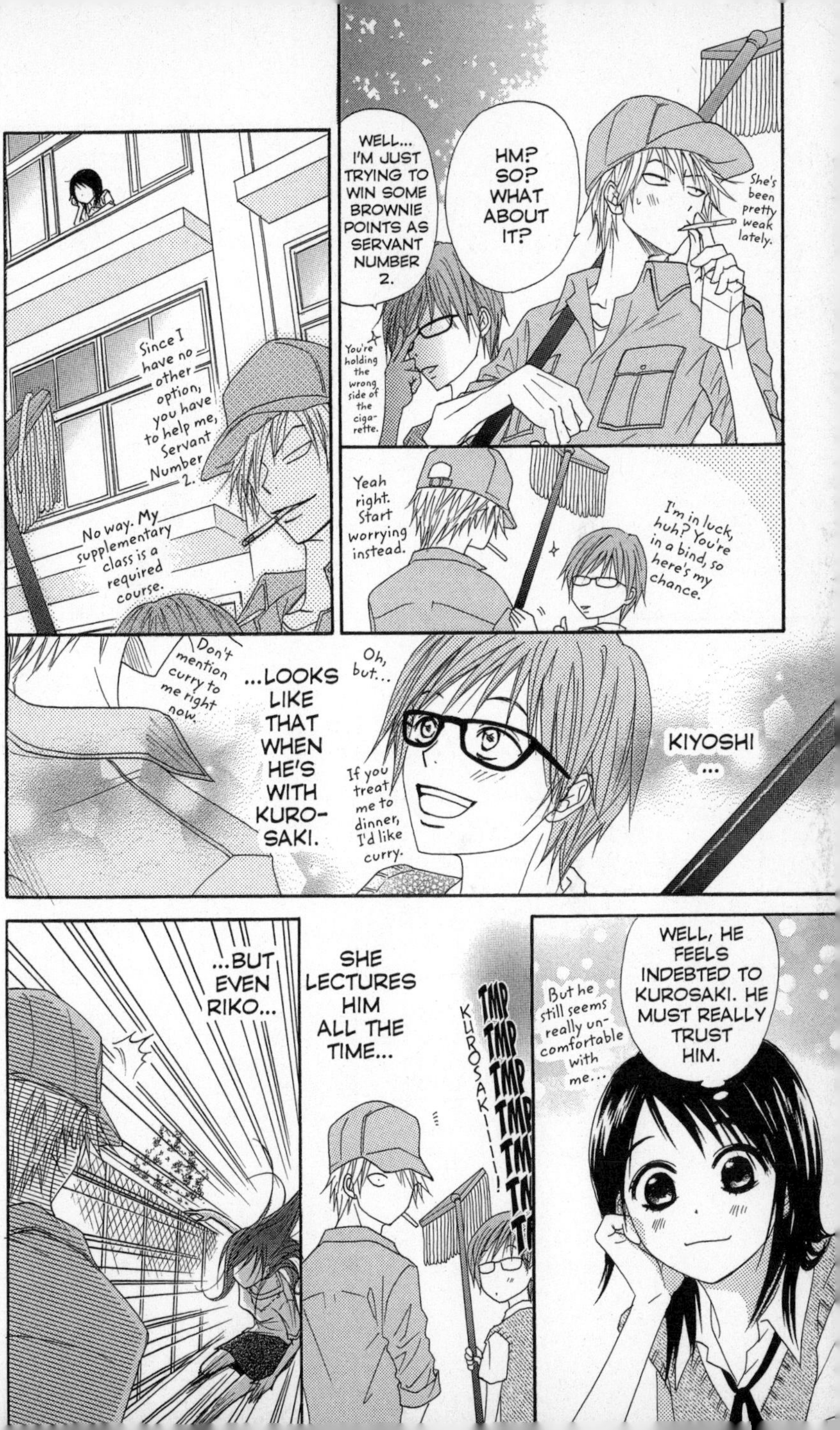
She's been pretty weak lately.
HM? SO? WHAT ABOUT IT?
WELL... I'M JUST TRYING TO WIN SOME BROWNIE POINTS AS SERVANT NUMBER 2.
You're holding the wrong side of the cigarette.
I'm in luck, huh? You're in a bind, so here's my chance.
Yeah right. Start worrying instead.
Since I have no other option, you have to help me, Servant Number 2.
No way. My supplementary class is a required course.
KIYOSHI ...
Oh, but...
If you treat me to dinner, I'd like curry.
...LOOKS LIKE THAT WHEN HE'S WITH KUROSAKI.
Don't mention curry to me right now.
WELL, HE FEELS INDEBTED TO KUROSAKI. HE MUST REALLY TRUST HIM.
But he still seems really uncomfortable with me...
TMP TMP TMP TMP TMP TMP TMP
KUROSAKI!!!
SHE LECTURES HIM ALL THE TIME...
...BUT EVEN RIKO...

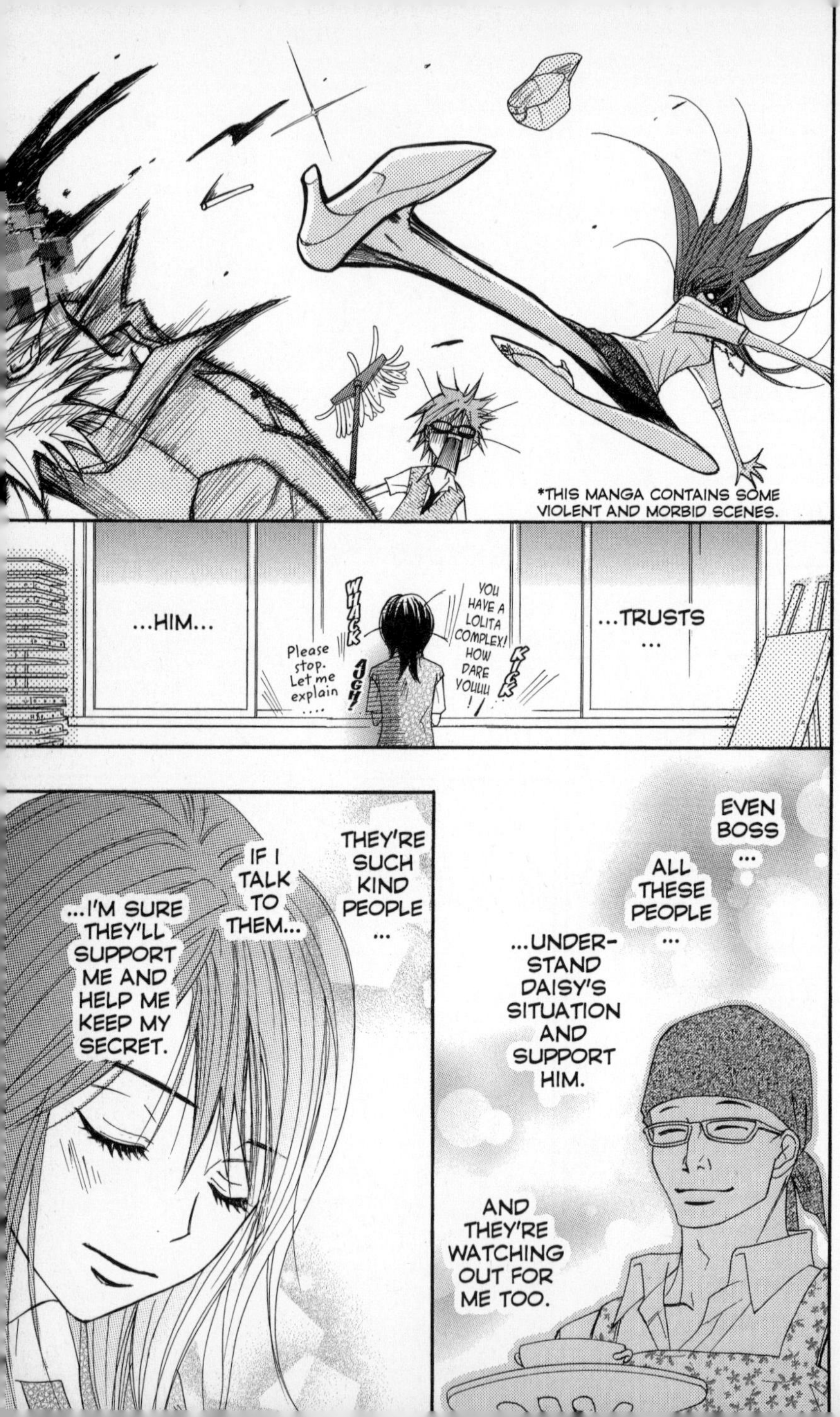
*THIS MANGA CONTAINS SOME VIOLENT AND MORBID SCENES.
...TRUSTS ...
YOU HAVE A LOLITA COMPLEX! HOW DARE YOUUU!
KICK
WHACK
Please stop. Let me explain....
AUGH!
...HIM...
EVEN BOSS ...
ALL THESE PEOPLE ...
...UNDER-STAND DAISY'S SITUATION AND SUPPORT HIM.
AND THEY'RE WATCHING OUT FOR ME TOO.
THEY'RE SUCH KIND PEOPLE ...
IF I TALK TO THEM...
...I'M SURE THEY'LL SUPPORT ME AND HELP ME KEEP MY SECRET.

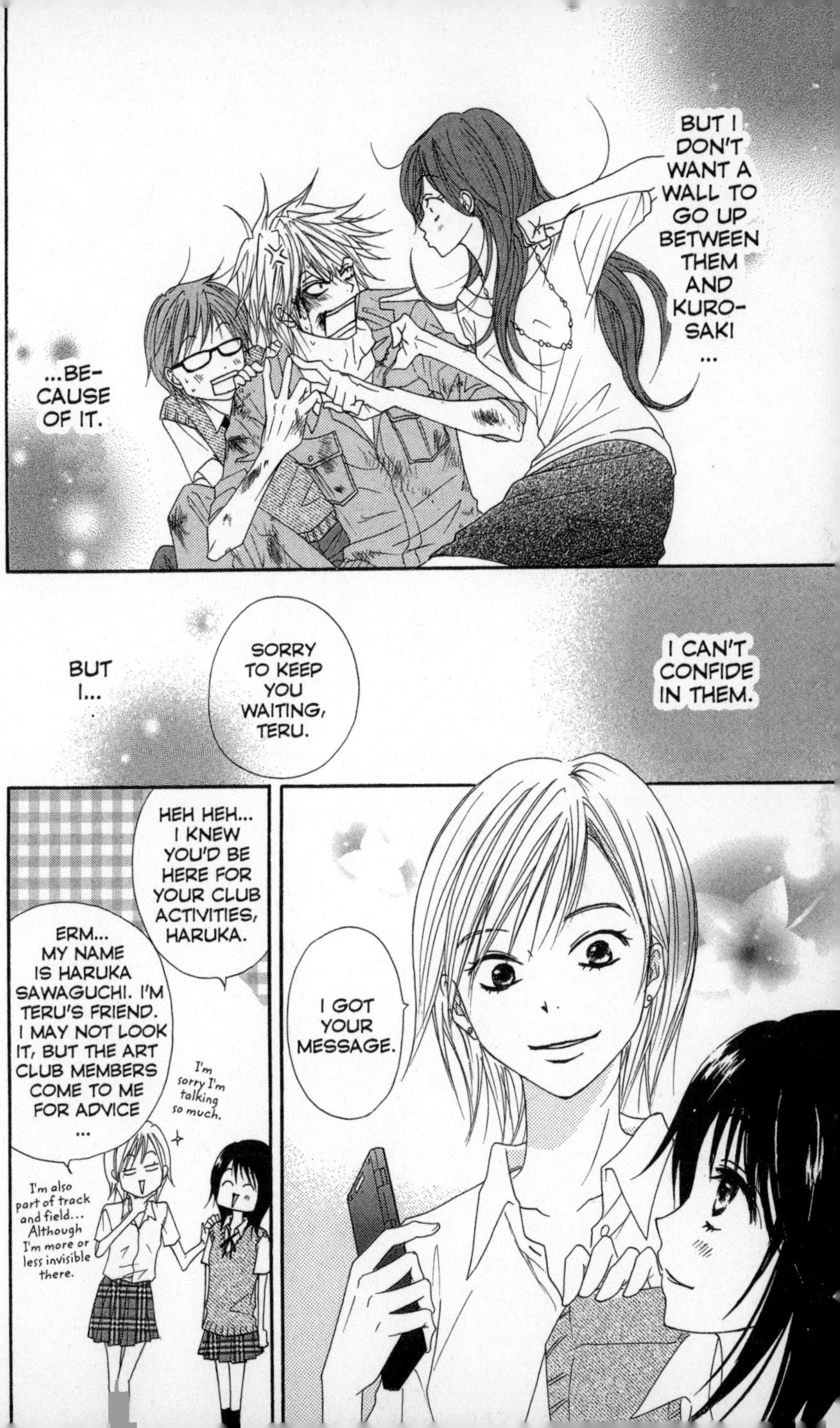
BUT I DON'T WANT A WALL TO GO UP BETWEEN THEM AND KURO-SAKI ...
...BE-CAUSE OF IT.
I CAN'T CONFIDE IN THEM.
SORRY TO KEEP YOU WAITING, TERU.
BUT I...
I GOT YOUR MESSAGE.
HEH HEH... I KNEW YOU'D BE HERE FOR YOUR CLUB ACTIVITIES, HARUKA.
ERM... MY NAME IS HARUKA SAWAGUCHI. I'M TERU'S FRIEND. I MAY NOT LOOK IT, BUT THE ART CLUB MEMBERS COME TO ME FOR ADVICE ...
I'm sorry I'm talking so much.
I'm also part of track and field... Although I'm more or less invisible there.

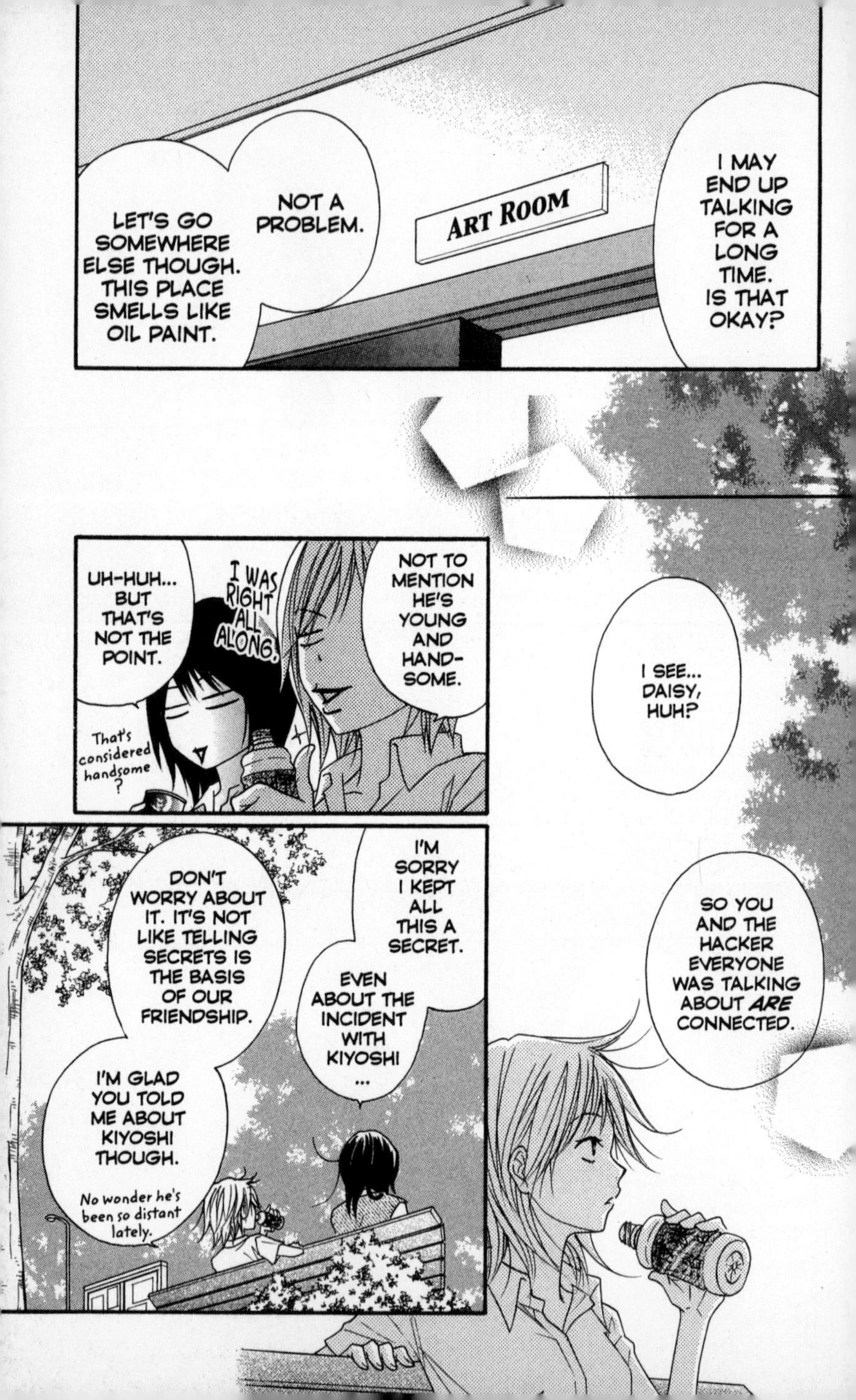
I MAY END UP TALKING FOR A LONG TIME. IS THAT OKAY?
ART ROOM
NOT A PROBLEM.
LET'S GO SOMEWHERE ELSE THOUGH. THIS PLACE SMELLS LIKE OIL PAINT.
I SEE... DAISY, HUH?
SO YOU AND THE HACKER EVERYONE WAS TALKING ABOUT *ARE* CONNECTED.
NOT TO MENTION HE'S YOUNG AND HAND-SOME.
I WAS RIGHT ALL ALONG.
UH-HUH... BUT THAT'S NOT THE POINT.
That's considered handsome?
I'M SORRY I KEPT ALL THIS A SECRET.
EVEN ABOUT THE INCIDENT WITH KIYOSHI...
DON'T WORRY ABOUT IT. IT'S NOT LIKE TELLING SECRETS IS THE BASIS OF OUR FRIENDSHIP.
I'M GLAD YOU TOLD ME ABOUT KIYOSHI THOUGH.
No wonder he's been so distant lately.

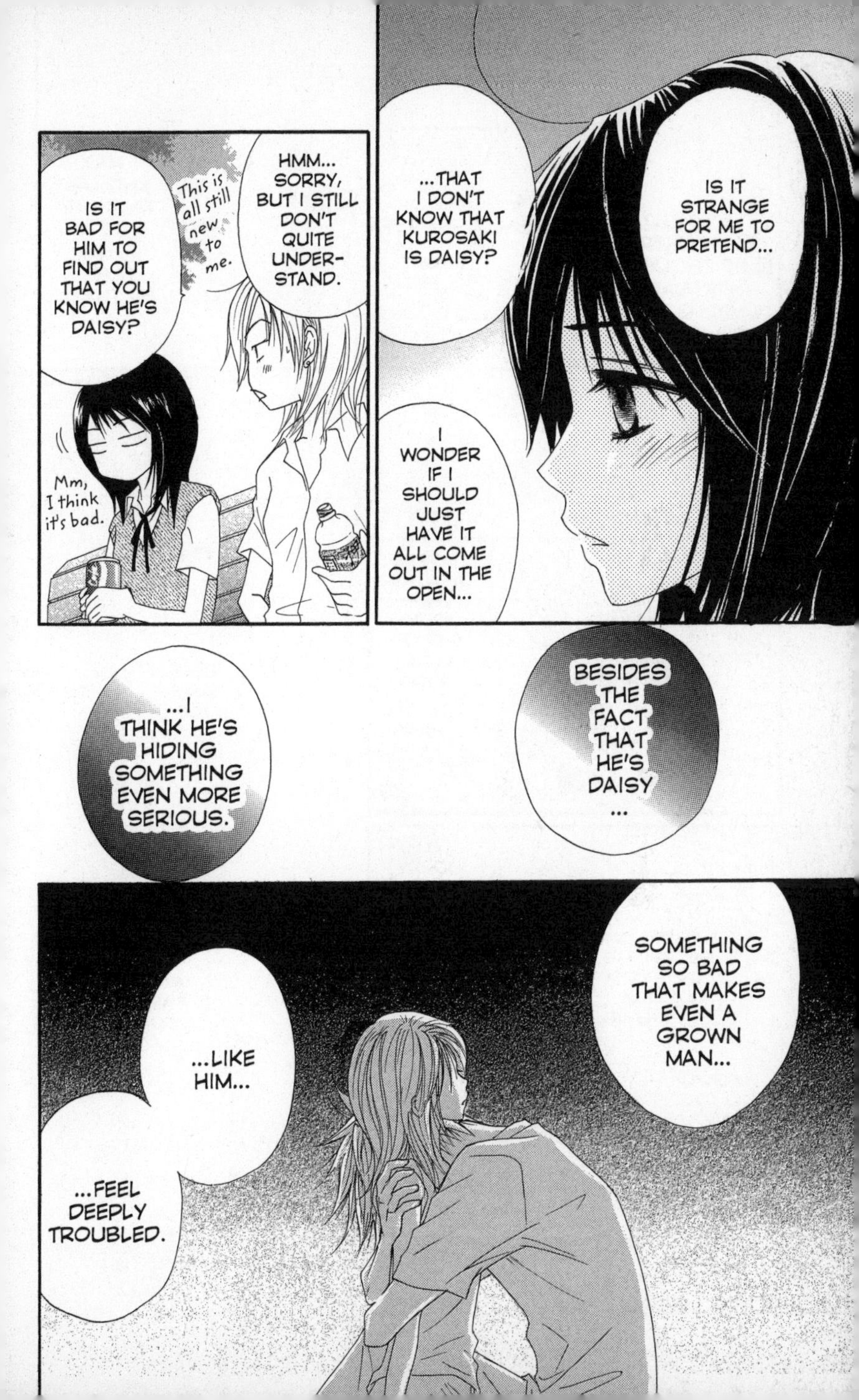
IS IT STRANGE FOR ME TO PRETEND...
...THAT I DON'T KNOW THAT KUROSAKI IS DAISY?
I WONDER IF I SHOULD JUST HAVE IT ALL COME OUT IN THE OPEN...
HMM... SORRY, BUT I STILL DON'T QUITE UNDERSTAND.
This is all still new to me.
IS IT BAD FOR HIM TO FIND OUT THAT YOU KNOW HE'S DAISY?
Mm, I think it's bad.
BESIDES THE FACT THAT HE'S DAISY...
...I THINK HE'S HIDING SOMETHING EVEN MORE SERIOUS.
SOMETHING SO BAD THAT MAKES EVEN A GROWN MAN...
...LIKE HIM...
...FEEL DEEPLY TROUBLED.

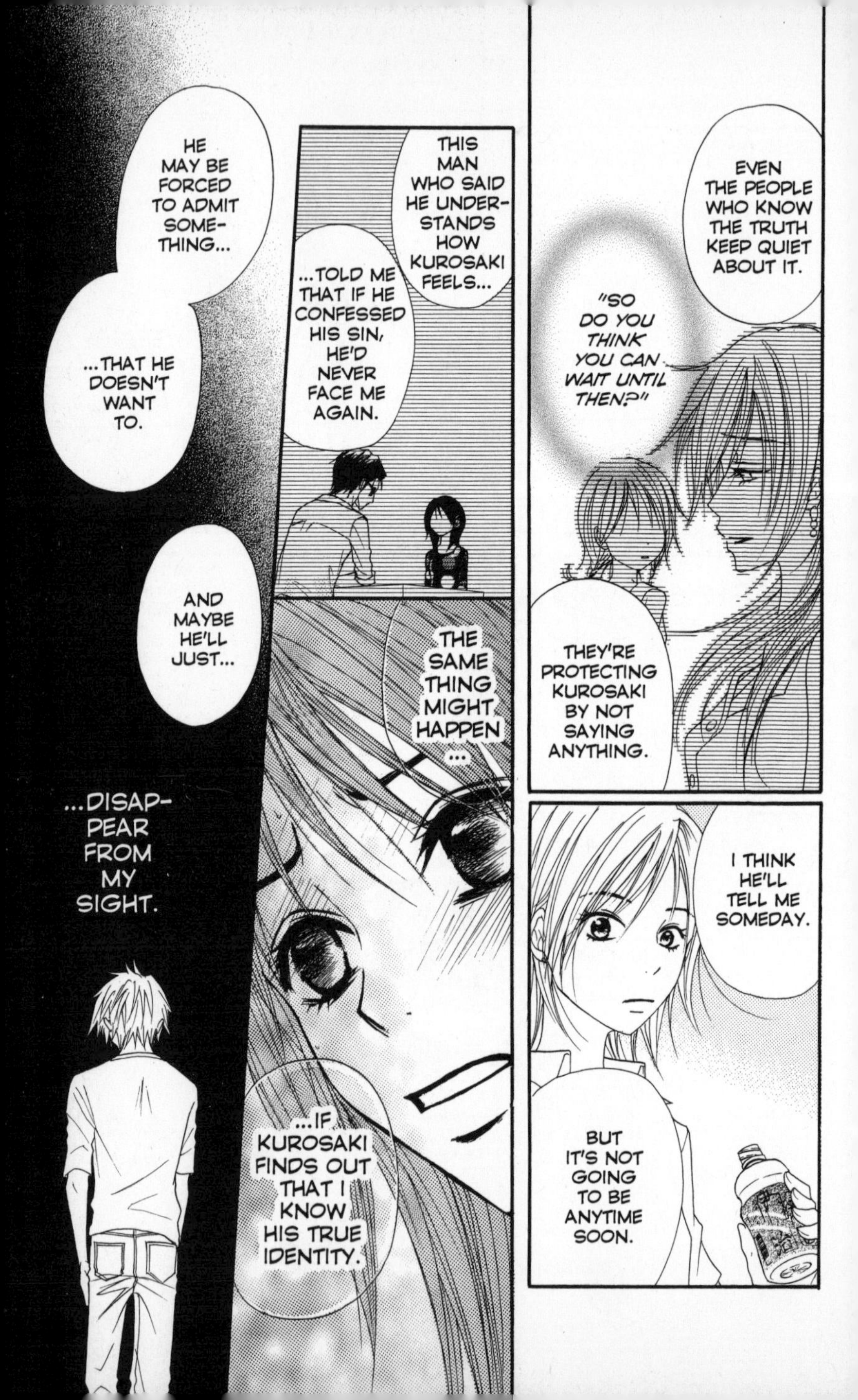
EVEN THE PEOPLE WHO KNOW THE TRUTH KEEP QUIET ABOUT IT.
"SO DO YOU THINK YOU CAN WAIT UNTIL THEN?"
THEY'RE PROTECTING KUROSAKI BY NOT SAYING ANYTHING.
I THINK HE'LL TELL ME SOMEDAY.
BUT IT'S NOT GOING TO BE ANYTIME SOON.
THIS MAN WHO SAID HE UNDERSTANDS HOW KUROSAKI FEELS...
...TOLD ME THAT IF HE CONFESSED HIS SIN, HE'D NEVER FACE ME AGAIN.
THE SAME THING MIGHT HAPPEN ...
...IF KUROSAKI FINDS OUT THAT I KNOW HIS TRUE IDENTITY.
HE MAY BE FORCED TO ADMIT SOMETHING...
...THAT HE DOESN'T WANT TO.
AND MAYBE HE'LL JUST...
...DISAPPEAR FROM MY SIGHT.

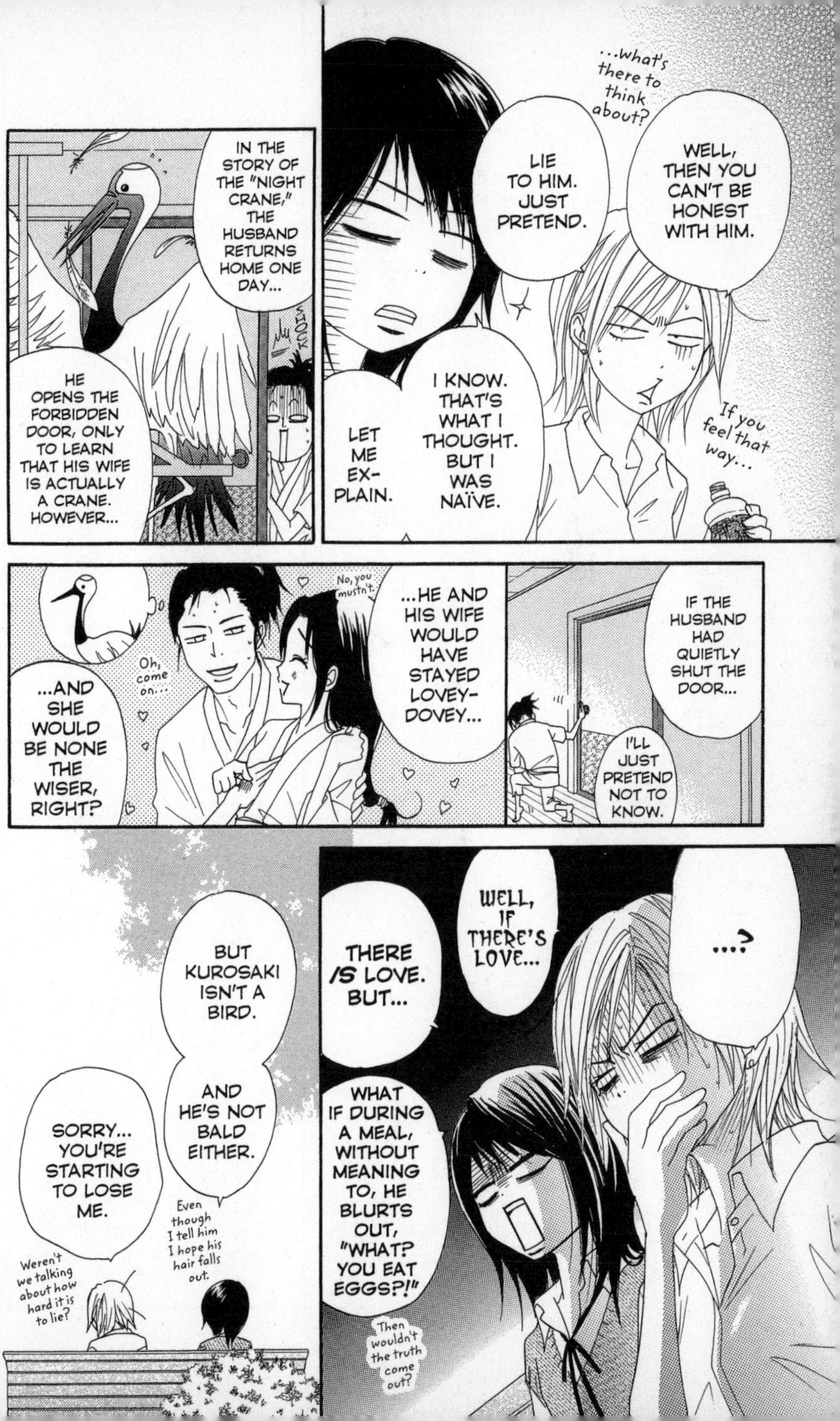
...what's there to think about?
WELL, THEN YOU CAN'T BE HONEST WITH HIM.
LIE TO HIM. JUST PRETEND.
If you feel that way...
I KNOW. THAT'S WHAT I THOUGHT. BUT I WAS NAÏVE.
LET ME EX-PLAIN.
IN THE STORY OF THE "NIGHT CRANE," THE HUSBAND RETURNS HOME ONE DAY...
SHOCK
HE OPENS THE FORBIDDEN DOOR, ONLY TO LEARN THAT HIS WIFE IS ACTUALLY A CRANE. HOWEVER...
IF THE HUSBAND HAD QUIETLY SHUT THE DOOR...
I'LL JUST PRETEND NOT TO KNOW.
...HE AND HIS WIFE WOULD HAVE STAYED LOVEY-DOVEY...
No, you mustn't.
Oh, come on...
...AND SHE WOULD BE NONE THE WISER, RIGHT?
...?
WELL, IF THERE'S LOVE...
THERE *IS* LOVE. BUT...
WHAT IF DURING A MEAL, WITHOUT MEANING TO, HE BLURTS OUT, "WHAT? YOU EAT EGGS?!"
Then wouldn't the truth come out?
BUT KUROSAKI ISN'T A BIRD.
AND HE'S NOT BALD EITHER.
SORRY... YOU'RE STARTING TO LOSE ME.
Even though I tell him I hope his hair falls out.
Weren't we talking about how hard it is to lie?

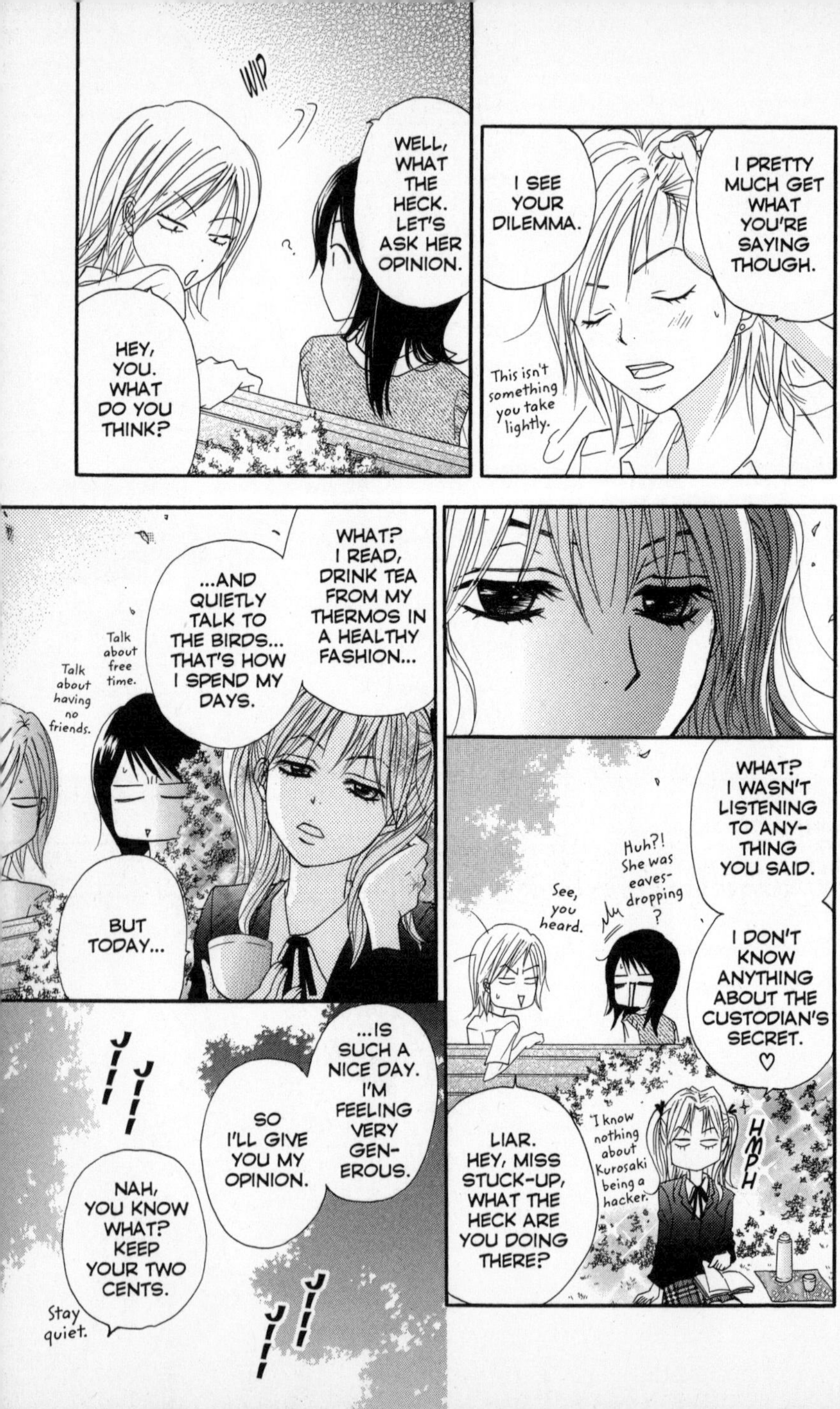
I PRETTY MUCH GET WHAT YOU'RE SAYING THOUGH.
I SEE YOUR DILEMMA.
This isn't something you take lightly.
WIP
WELL, WHAT THE HECK. LET'S ASK HER OPINION.
?
HEY, YOU. WHAT DO YOU THINK?
WHAT? I WASN'T LISTENING TO ANYTHING YOU SAID.
I DON'T KNOW ANYTHING ABOUT THE CUSTODIAN'S SECRET. ♡
Huh?! She was eaves-dropping?
See, you heard.
HMPH
"I know nothing about Kurosaki being a hacker."
LIAR. HEY, MISS STUCK-UP, WHAT THE HECK ARE YOU DOING THERE?
WHAT? I READ, DRINK TEA FROM MY THERMOS IN A HEALTHY FASHION...
...AND QUIETLY TALK TO THE BIRDS... THAT'S HOW I SPEND MY DAYS.
Talk about free time.
Talk about having no friends.
BUT TODAY...
...IS SUCH A NICE DAY. I'M FEELING VERY GEN-EROUS.
SO I'LL GIVE YOU MY OPINION.
JIII JIII
NAH, YOU KNOW WHAT? KEEP YOUR TWO CENTS.
Stay quiet.
JIII JIII

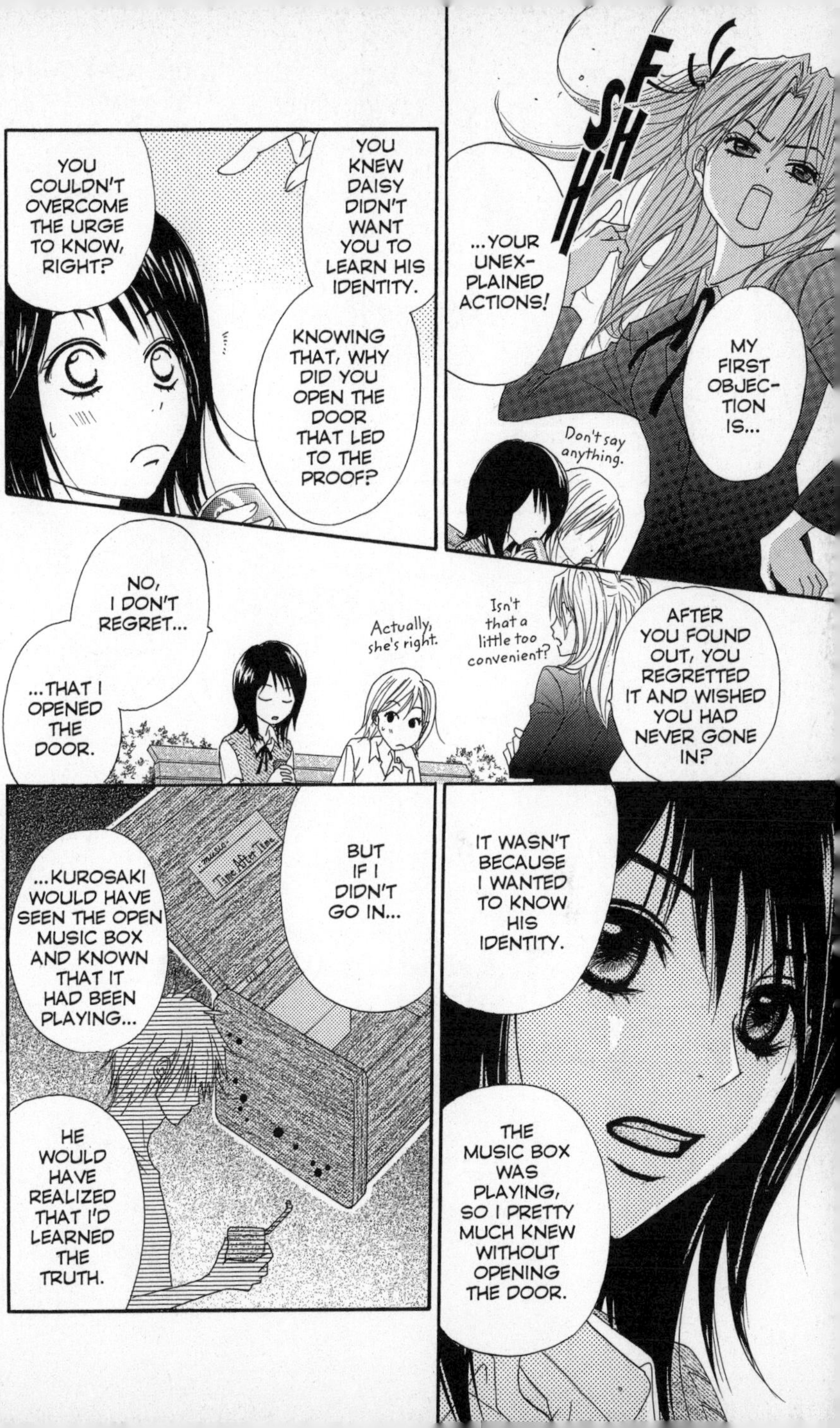
FSHH
MY FIRST OBJECTION IS...
...YOUR UNEXPLAINED ACTIONS!
Don't say anything.
YOU KNEW DAISY DIDN'T WANT YOU TO LEARN HIS IDENTITY.
KNOWING THAT, WHY DID YOU OPEN THE DOOR THAT LED TO THE PROOF?
YOU COULDN'T OVERCOME THE URGE TO KNOW, RIGHT?
AFTER YOU FOUND OUT, YOU REGRETTED IT AND WISHED YOU HAD NEVER GONE IN?
Isn't that a little too convenient?
Actually, she's right.
NO, I DON'T REGRET...
...THAT I OPENED THE DOOR.
IT WASN'T BECAUSE I WANTED TO KNOW HIS IDENTITY.
THE MUSIC BOX WAS PLAYING, SO I PRETTY MUCH KNEW WITHOUT OPENING THE DOOR.
BUT IF I DIDN'T GO IN...
Time After Time
...KUROSAKI WOULD HAVE SEEN THE OPEN MUSIC BOX AND KNOWN THAT IT HAD BEEN PLAYING...
HE WOULD HAVE REALIZED THAT I'D LEARNED THE TRUTH.

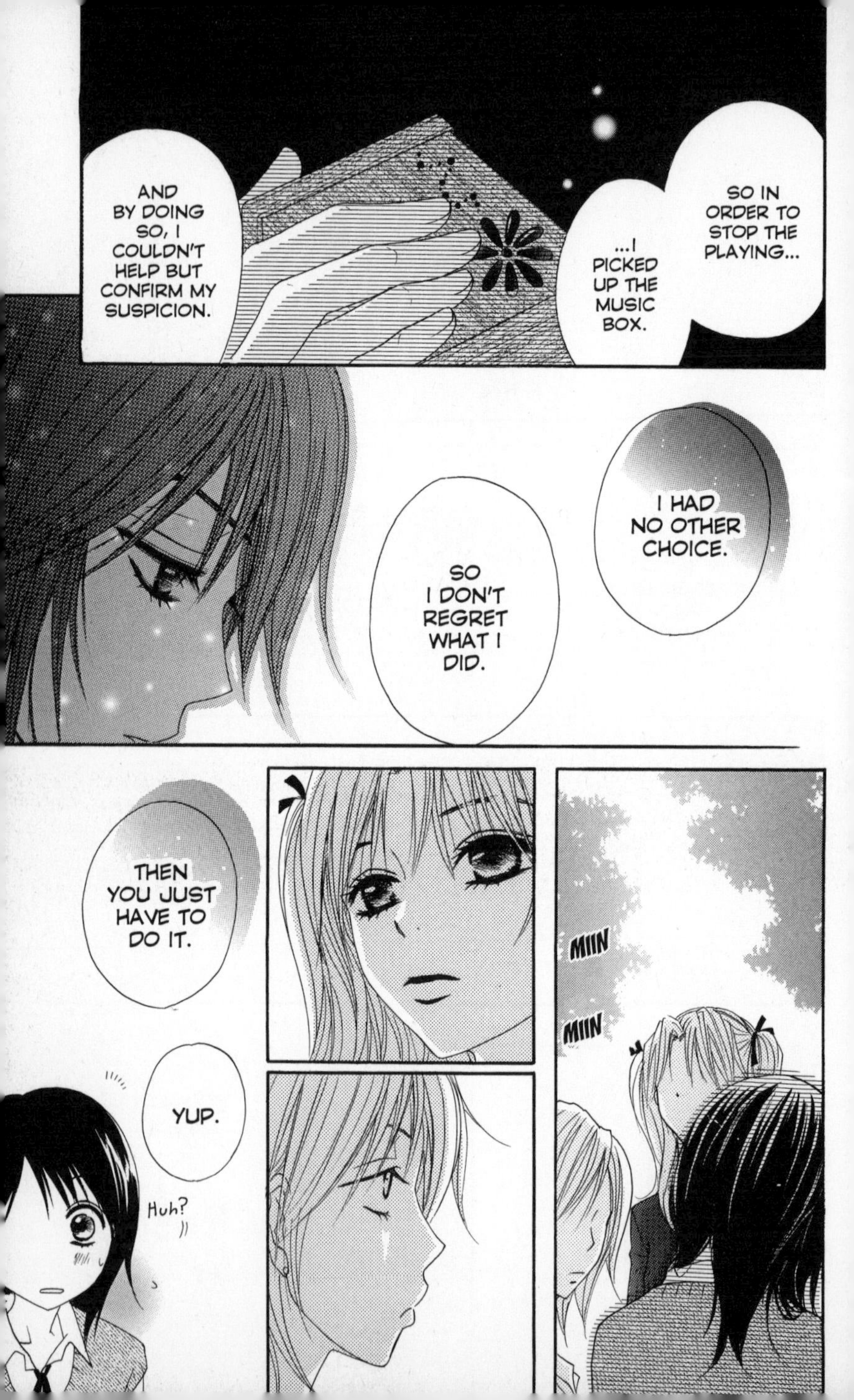
SO IN ORDER TO STOP THE PLAYING...
...I PICKED UP THE MUSIC BOX.
AND BY DOING SO, I COULDN'T HELP BUT CONFIRM MY SUSPICION.
I HAD NO OTHER CHOICE.
SO I DON'T REGRET WHAT I DID.
MIIN
MIIN
THEN YOU JUST HAVE TO DO IT.
YUP.
Huh?

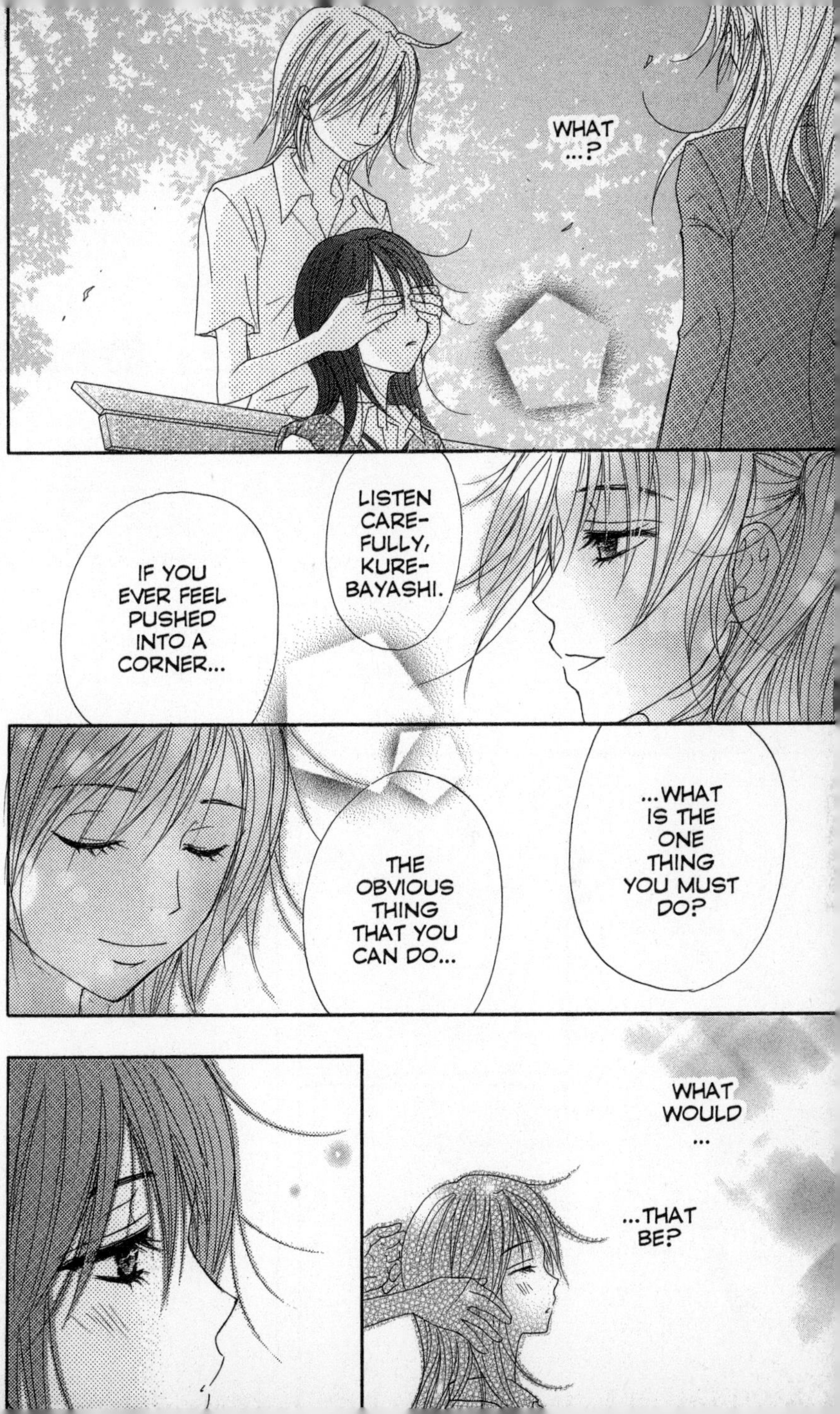
WHAT ...?
LISTEN CAREFULLY, KUREBAYASHI.
IF YOU EVER FEEL PUSHED INTO A CORNER...
...WHAT IS THE ONE THING YOU MUST DO?
THE OBVIOUS THING THAT YOU CAN DO...
WHAT WOULD ...
...THAT BE?

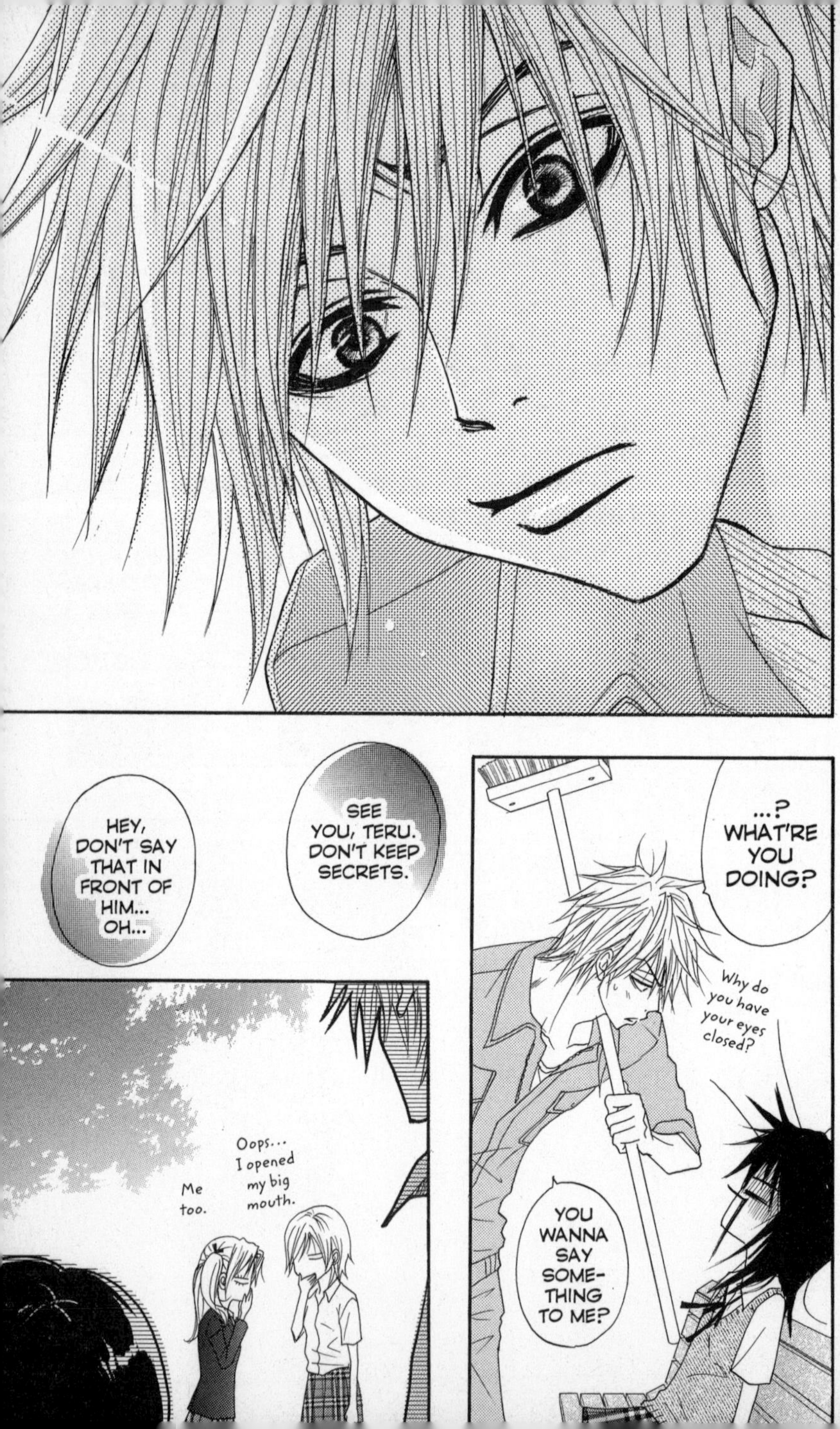
...? WHAT'RE YOU DOING?
Why do you have your eyes closed?
YOU WANNA SAY SOME-THING TO ME?
SEE YOU, TERU. DON'T KEEP SECRETS.
HEY, DON'T SAY THAT IN FRONT OF HIM... OH...
Oops... I opened my big mouth.
Me too.

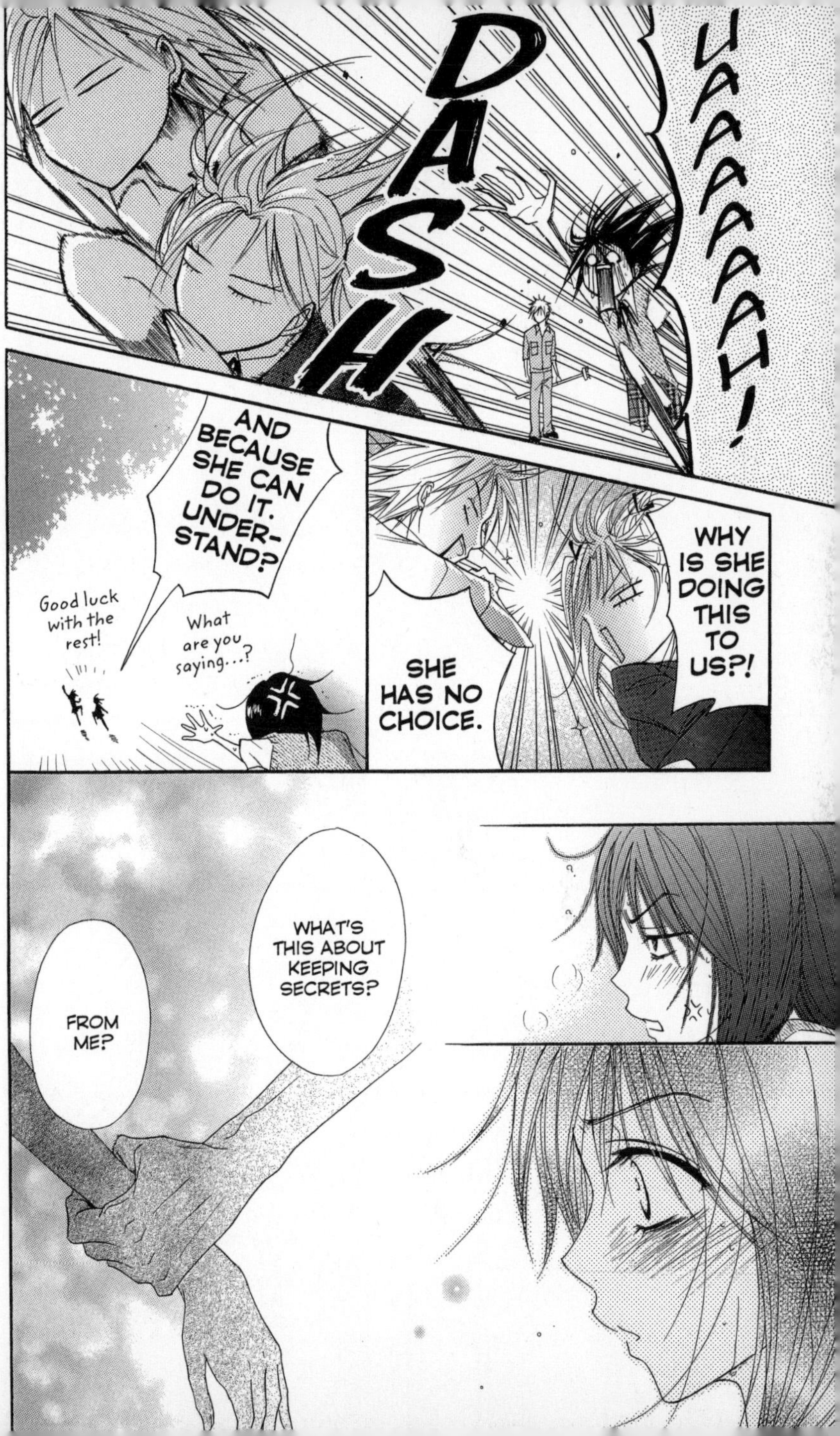

UAAAAAAAH!
DASH
WHY IS SHE DOING THIS TO US?!
SHE HAS NO CHOICE.
AND BECAUSE SHE CAN DO IT. UNDER-STAND?
What are you saying...?
Good luck with the rest!
WHAT'S THIS ABOUT KEEPING SECRETS?
FROM ME?

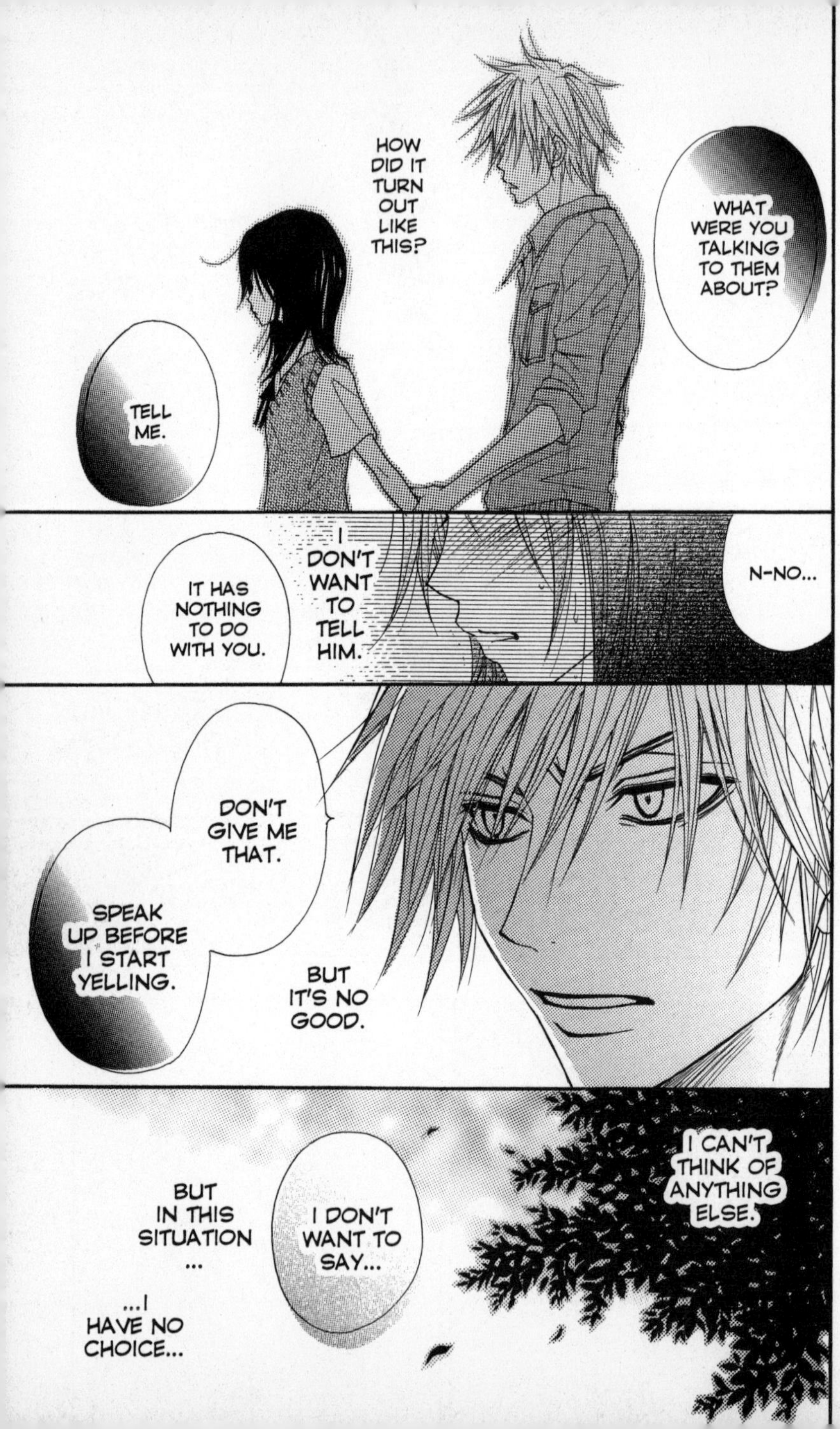
WHAT WERE YOU TALKING TO THEM ABOUT?
HOW DID IT TURN OUT LIKE THIS?
TELL ME.
N-NO...
I DON'T WANT TO TELL HIM.
IT HAS NOTHING TO DO WITH YOU.
DON'T GIVE ME THAT.
SPEAK UP BEFORE I START YELLING.
BUT IT'S NO GOOD.
I CAN'T THINK OF ANYTHING ELSE.
I DON'T WANT TO SAY...
BUT IN THIS SITUATION ...
...I HAVE NO CHOICE...

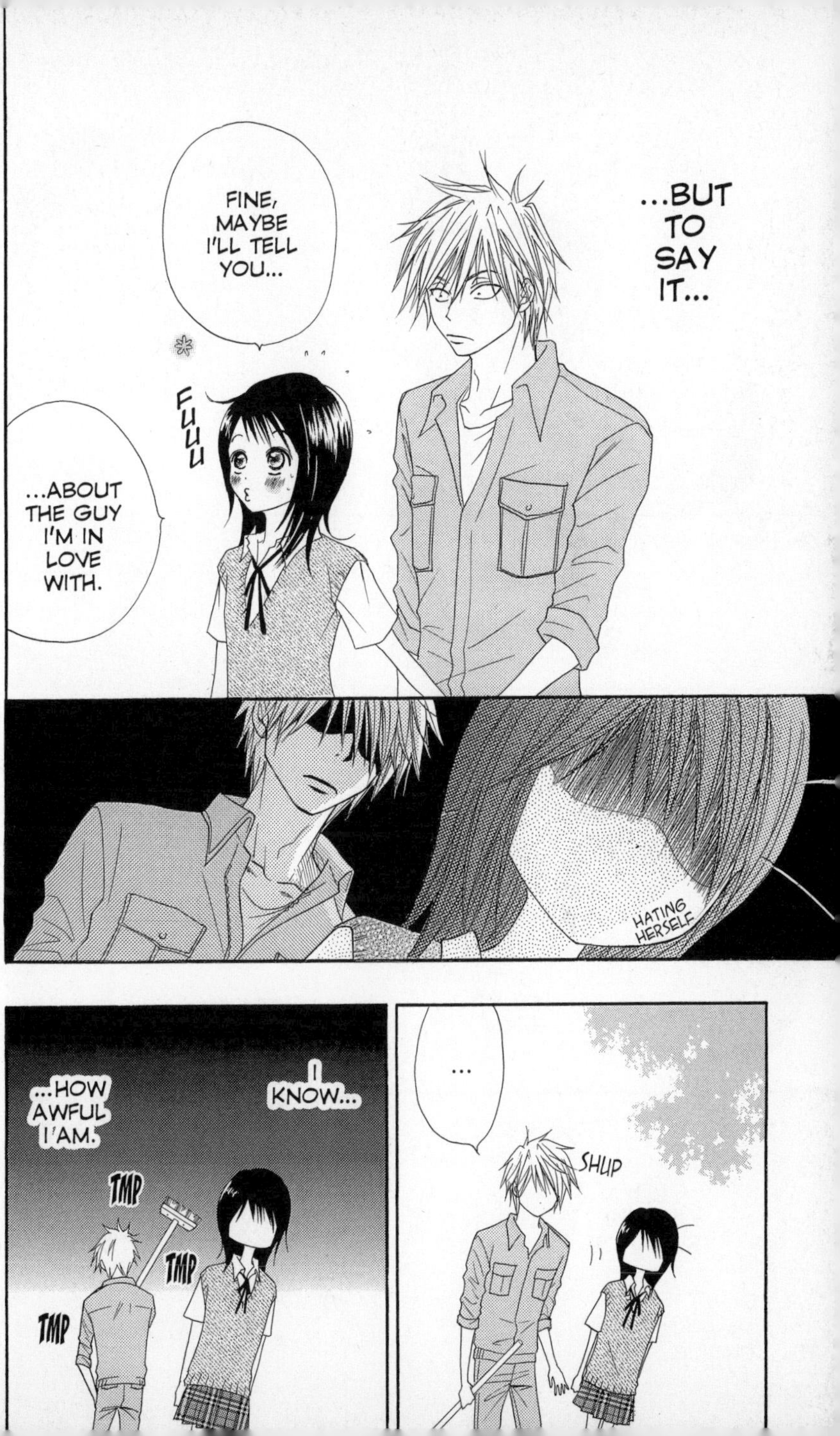
...BUT TO SAY IT...
FINE, MAYBE I'LL TELL YOU...
FUUU
...ABOUT THE GUY I'M IN LOVE WITH.
HATING HERSELF
...
SHUP
I KNOW...
...HOW AWFUL I'AM.
TMP
TMP
TMP

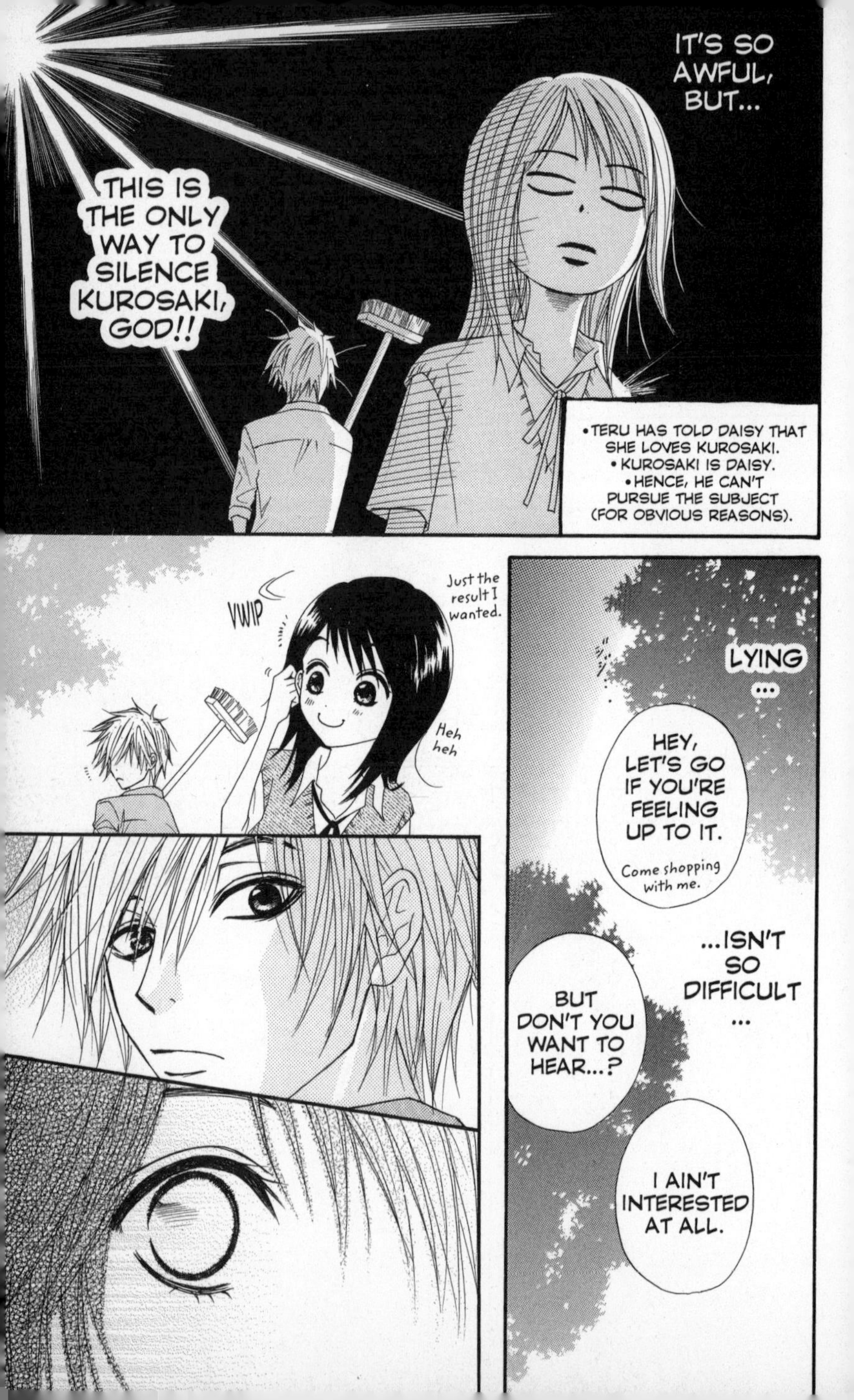
IT'S SO AWFUL, BUT...
THIS IS THE ONLY WAY TO SILENCE KUROSAKI, GOD!!
•TERU HAS TOLD DAISY THAT SHE LOVES KUROSAKI.
• KUROSAKI IS DAISY.
•HENCE, HE CAN'T PURSUE THE SUBJECT (FOR OBVIOUS REASONS).
LYING...
HEY, LET'S GO IF YOU'RE FEELING UP TO IT.
Come shopping with me.
...ISN'T SO DIFFICULT...
BUT DON'T YOU WANT TO HEAR...?
I AIN'T INTERESTED AT ALL.
Just the result I wanted.
VWIP
Heh heh

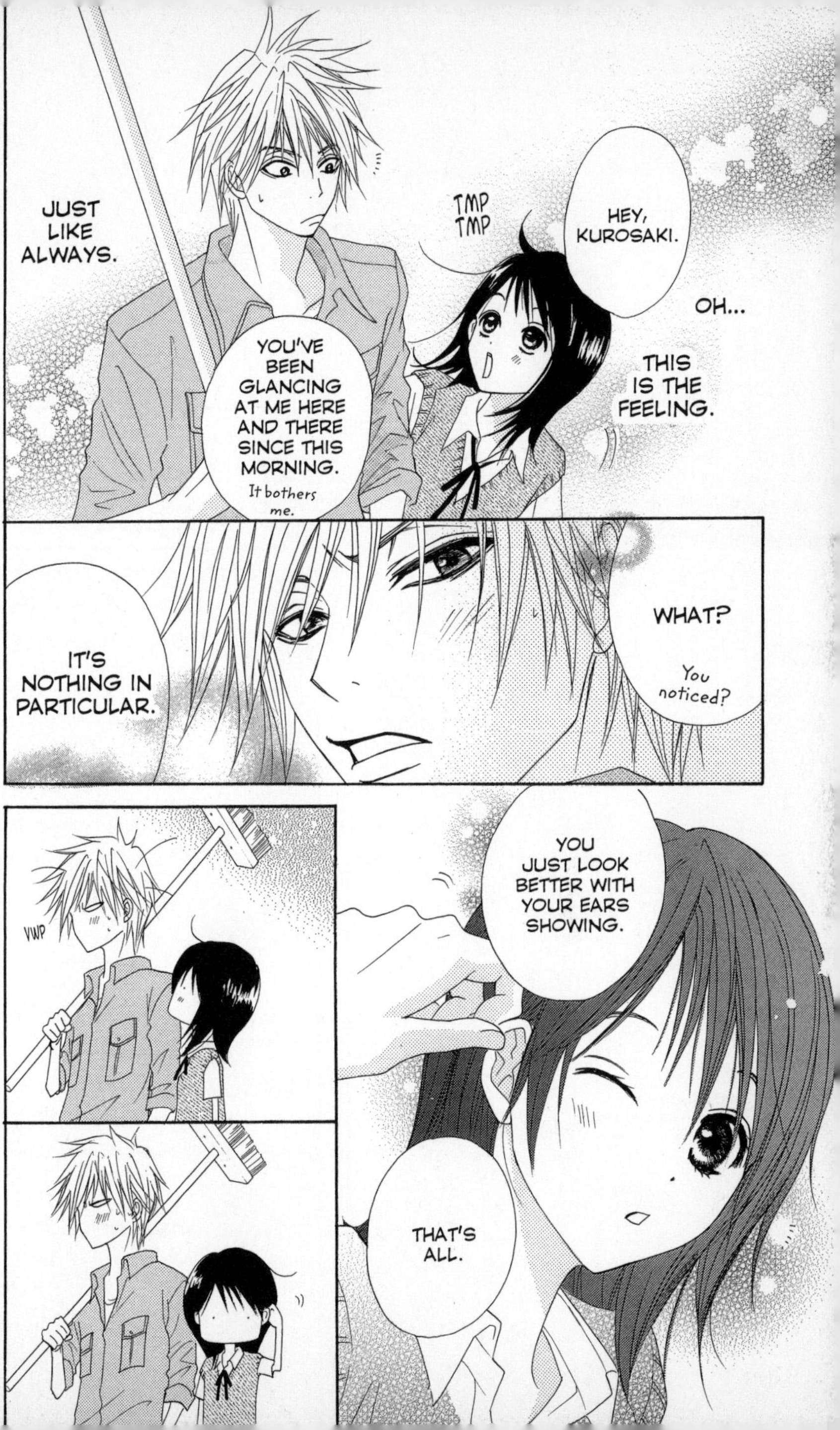
TMP TMP
HEY, KUROSAKI.
YOU'VE BEEN GLANCING AT ME HERE AND THERE SINCE THIS MORNING.
It bothers me.
OH...
THIS IS THE FEELING.
JUST LIKE ALWAYS.
WHAT?
You noticed?
IT'S NOTHING IN PARTICULAR.
YOU JUST LOOK BETTER WITH YOUR EARS SHOWING.
THAT'S ALL.
VWP

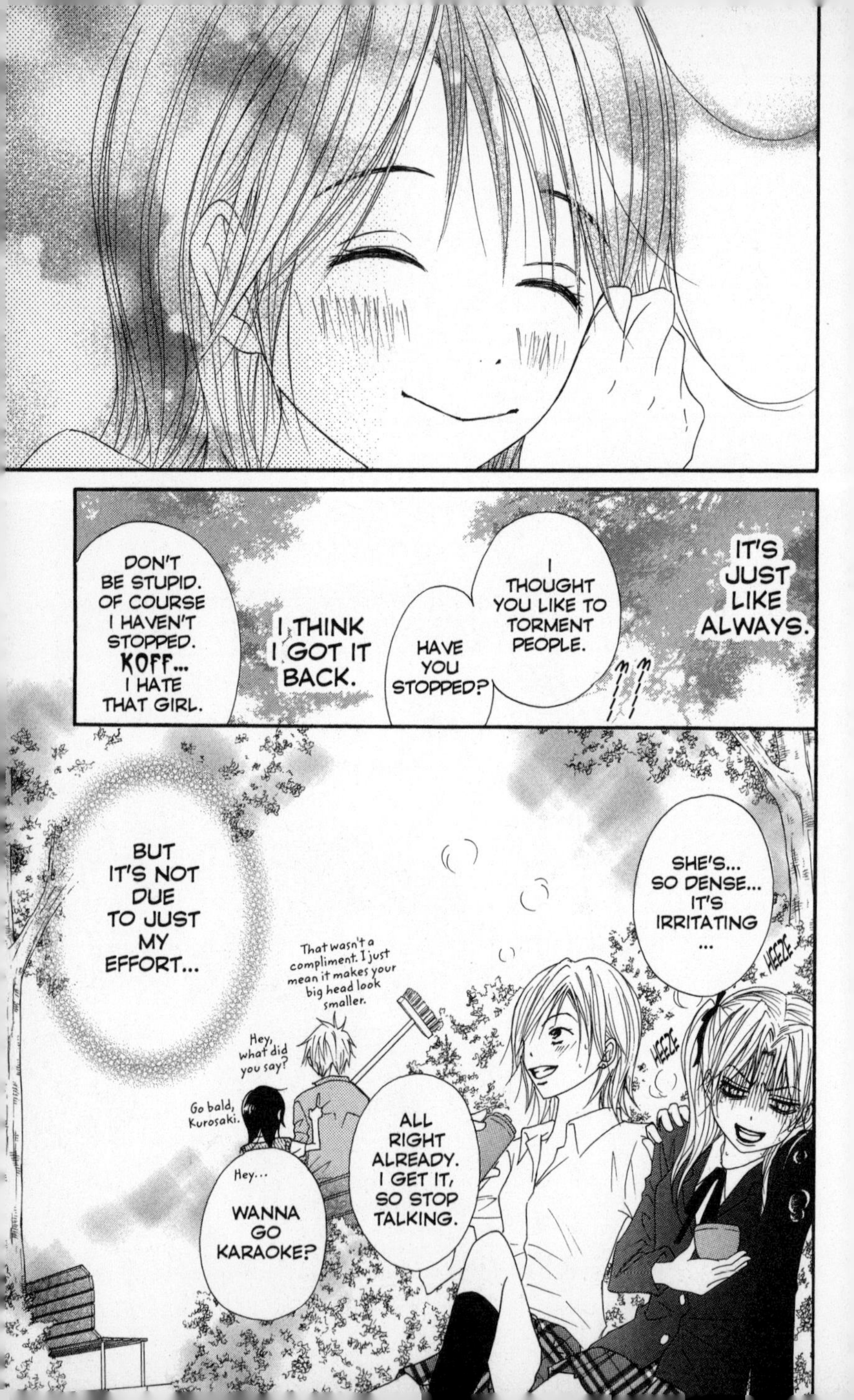
IT'S JUST LIKE ALWAYS.
I THOUGHT YOU LIKE TO TORMENT PEOPLE.
HAVE YOU STOPPED?
I THINK I GOT IT BACK.
DON'T BE STUPID. OF COURSE I HAVEN'T STOPPED. KOFF... I HATE THAT GIRL.
SHE'S... SO DENSE... IT'S IRRITATING ...
HEEZE
HEEZE
ALL RIGHT ALREADY. I GET IT, SO STOP TALKING.
That wasn't a compliment. I just mean it makes your big head look smaller.
Hey, what did you say?
Go bald, Kurosaki.
Hey... WANNA GO KARAOKE?
BUT IT'S NOT DUE TO JUST MY EFFORT...

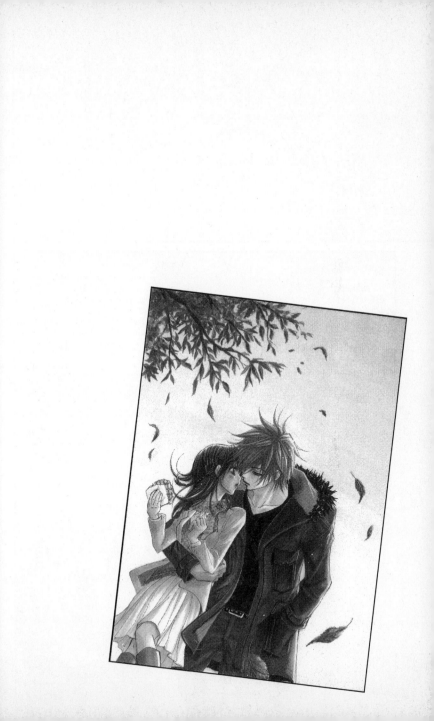

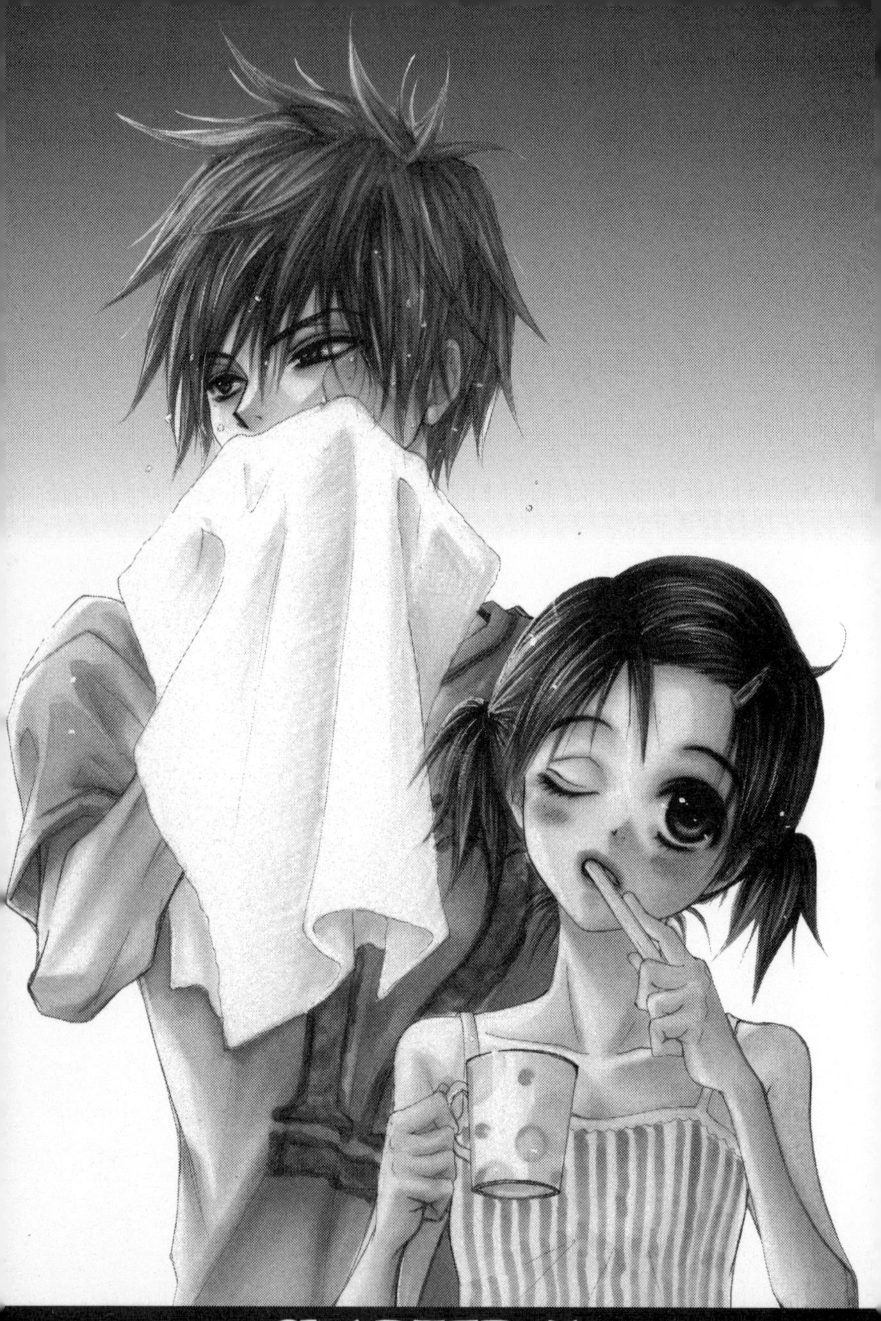

CHAPTER 16: WHICH IS IT YOU FEEL?

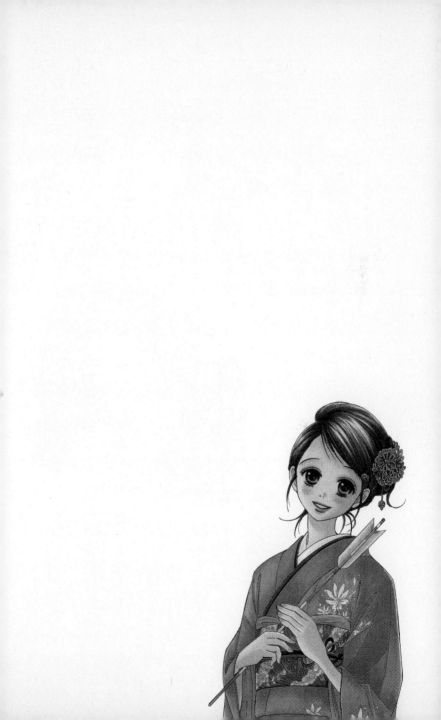

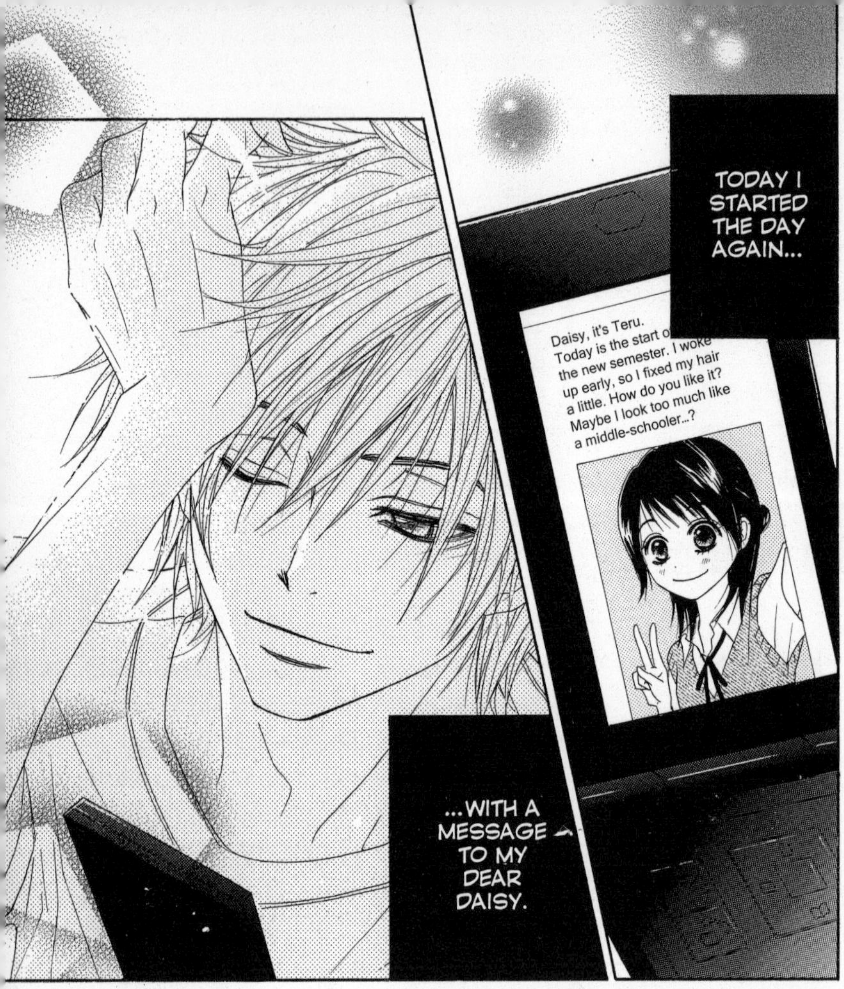
TODAY I STARTED THE DAY AGAIN...
Daisy, it's Teru.
Today is the start o
the new semester. I woke
up early, so I fixed my hair
a little. How do you like it?
Maybe I look too much like
a middle-schooler...?
...WITH A MESSAGE TO MY DEAR DAISY.

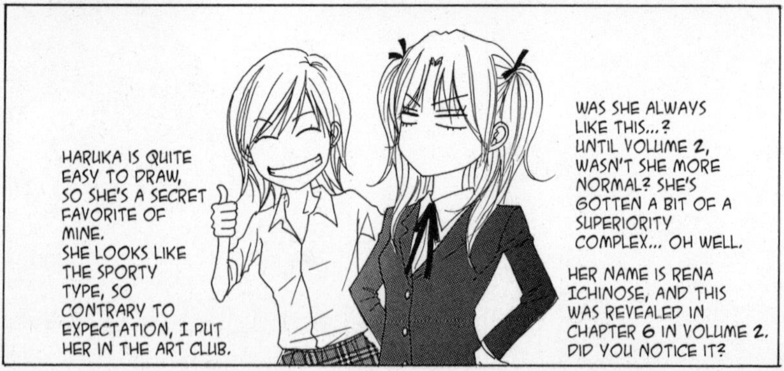
WAS SHE ALWAYS LIKE THIS...? UNTIL VOLUME 2, WASN'T SHE MORE NORMAL? SHE'S GOTTEN A BIT OF A SUPERIORITY COMPLEX... OH WELL.
HER NAME IS RENA ICHINOSE, AND THIS WAS REVEALED IN CHAPTER 6 IN VOLUME 2. DID YOU NOTICE IT?
HARUKA IS QUITE EASY TO DRAW, SO SHE'S A SECRET FAVORITE OF MINE. SHE LOOKS LIKE THE SPORTY TYPE, SO CONTRARY TO EXPECTATION, I PUT HER IN THE ART CLUB.

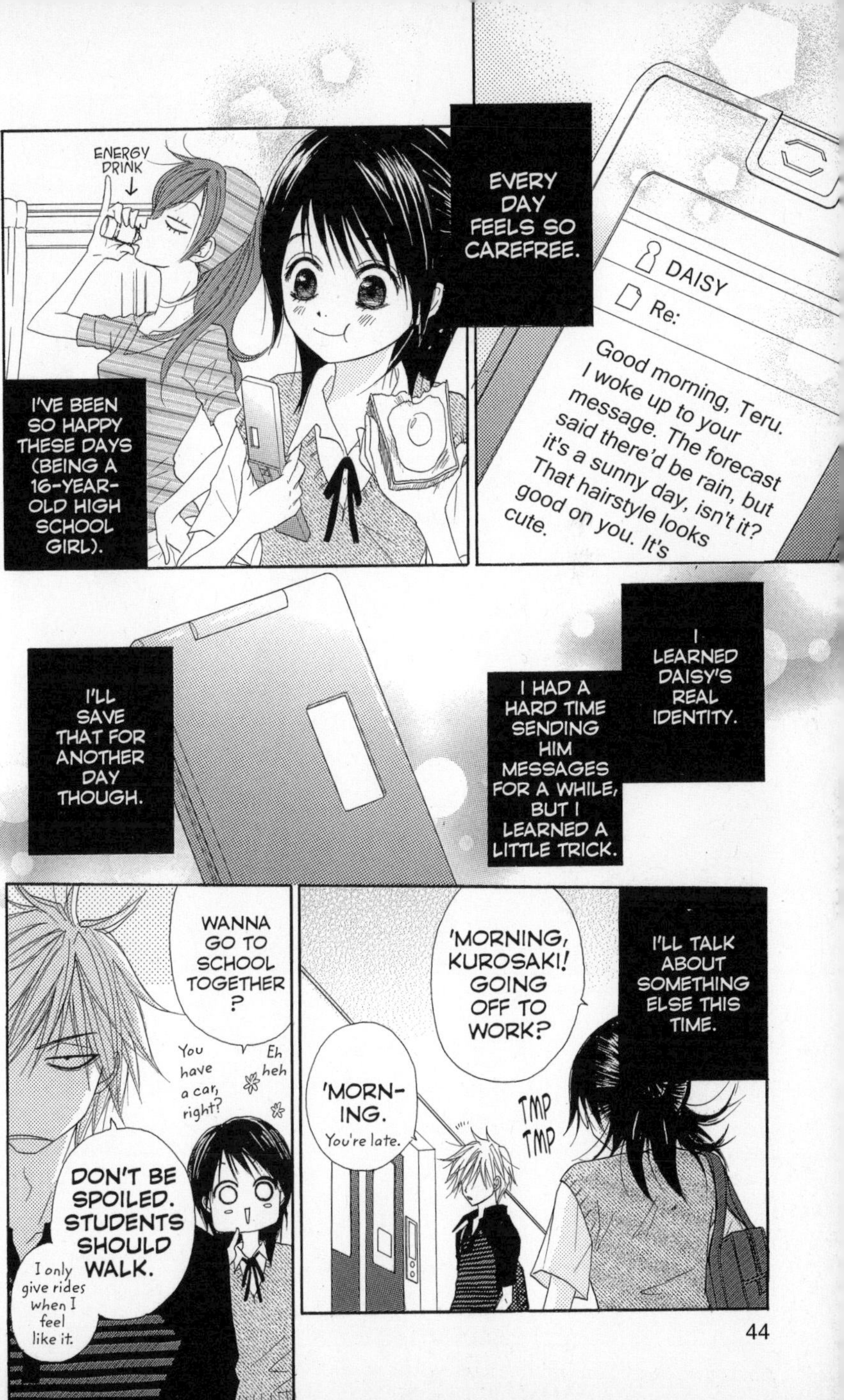
EVERY DAY FEELS SO CAREFREE.
DAISY
Re:
Good morning, Teru. I woke up to your message. The forecast said there'd be rain, but it's a sunny day, isn't it? That hairstyle looks good on you. It's cute.
ENERGY DRINK
I'VE BEEN SO HAPPY THESE DAYS (BEING A 16-YEAR-OLD HIGH SCHOOL GIRL).
I LEARNED DAISY'S REAL IDENTITY.
I HAD A HARD TIME SENDING HIM MESSAGES FOR A WHILE, BUT I LEARNED A LITTLE TRICK.
I'LL SAVE THAT FOR ANOTHER DAY THOUGH.
I'LL TALK ABOUT SOMETHING ELSE THIS TIME.
'MORNING, KUROSAKI! GOING OFF TO WORK?
TMP TMP
'MORN-ING.
You're late.
WANNA GO TO SCHOOL TOGETHER?
Eh heh
You have a car, right?
DON'T BE SPOILED. STUDENTS SHOULD WALK.
I only give rides when I feel like it.

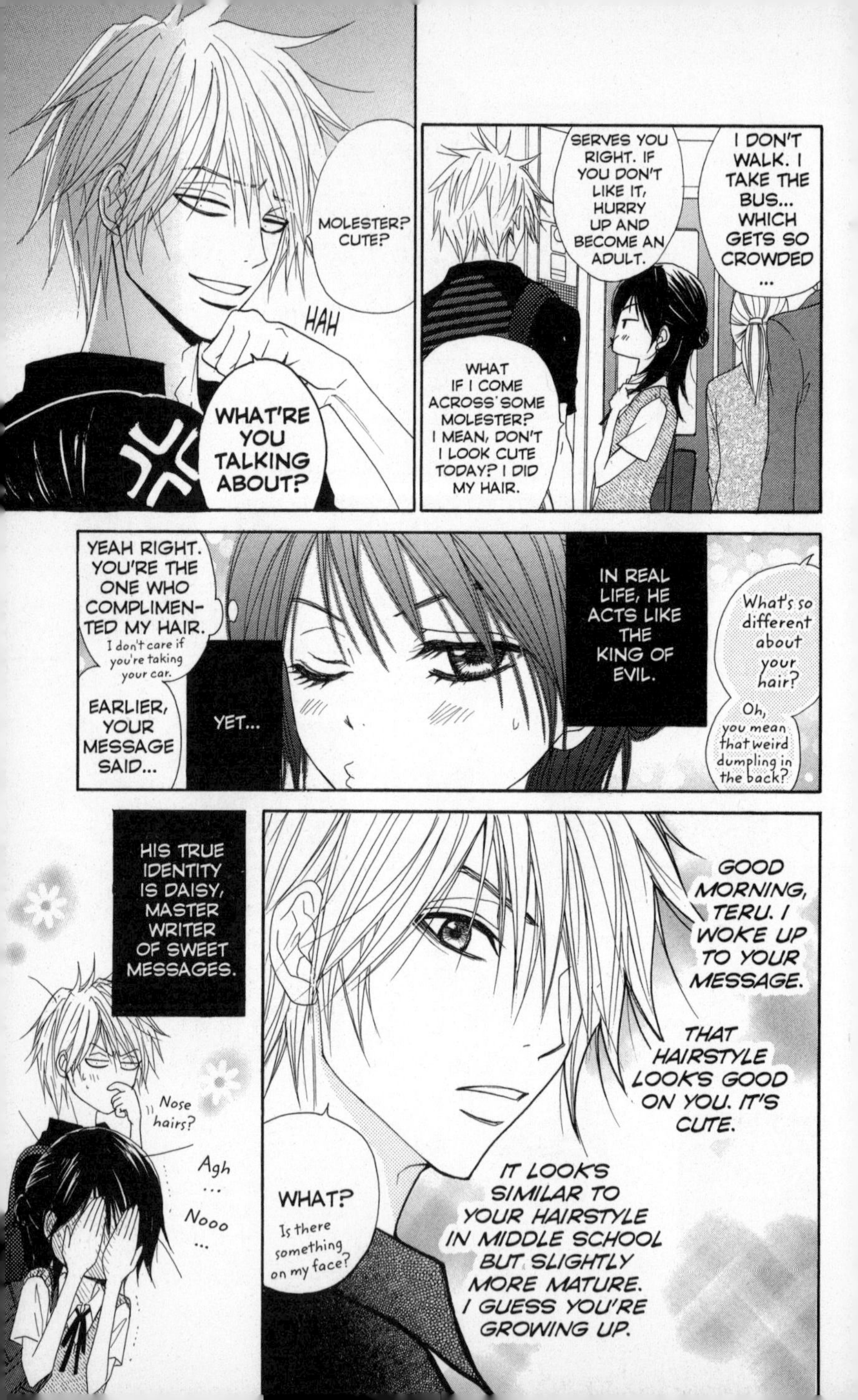
I DON'T WALK. I TAKE THE BUS... WHICH GETS SO CROWDED...
SERVES YOU RIGHT. IF YOU DON'T LIKE IT, HURRY UP AND BECOME AN ADULT.
WHAT IF I COME ACROSS SOME MOLESTER? I MEAN, DON'T I LOOK CUTE TODAY? I DID MY HAIR.
MOLESTER? CUTE?
HAH
WHAT'RE YOU TALKING ABOUT?
What's so different about your hair?
Oh, you mean that weird dumpling in the back?
IN REAL LIFE, HE ACTS LIKE THE KING OF EVIL.
YET...
YEAH RIGHT. YOU'RE THE ONE WHO COMPLIMENTED MY HAIR.
I don't care if you're taking your car.
EARLIER, YOUR MESSAGE SAID...
GOOD MORNING, TERU. I WOKE UP TO YOUR MESSAGE.
THAT HAIRSTYLE LOOKS GOOD ON YOU. IT'S CUTE.
IT LOOKS SIMILAR TO YOUR HAIRSTYLE IN MIDDLE SCHOOL BUT SLIGHTLY MORE MATURE. I GUESS YOU'RE GROWING UP.
WHAT?
Is there something on my face?
HIS TRUE IDENTITY IS DAISY, MASTER WRITER OF SWEET MESSAGES.
Nose hairs?
Agh...
Nooo...

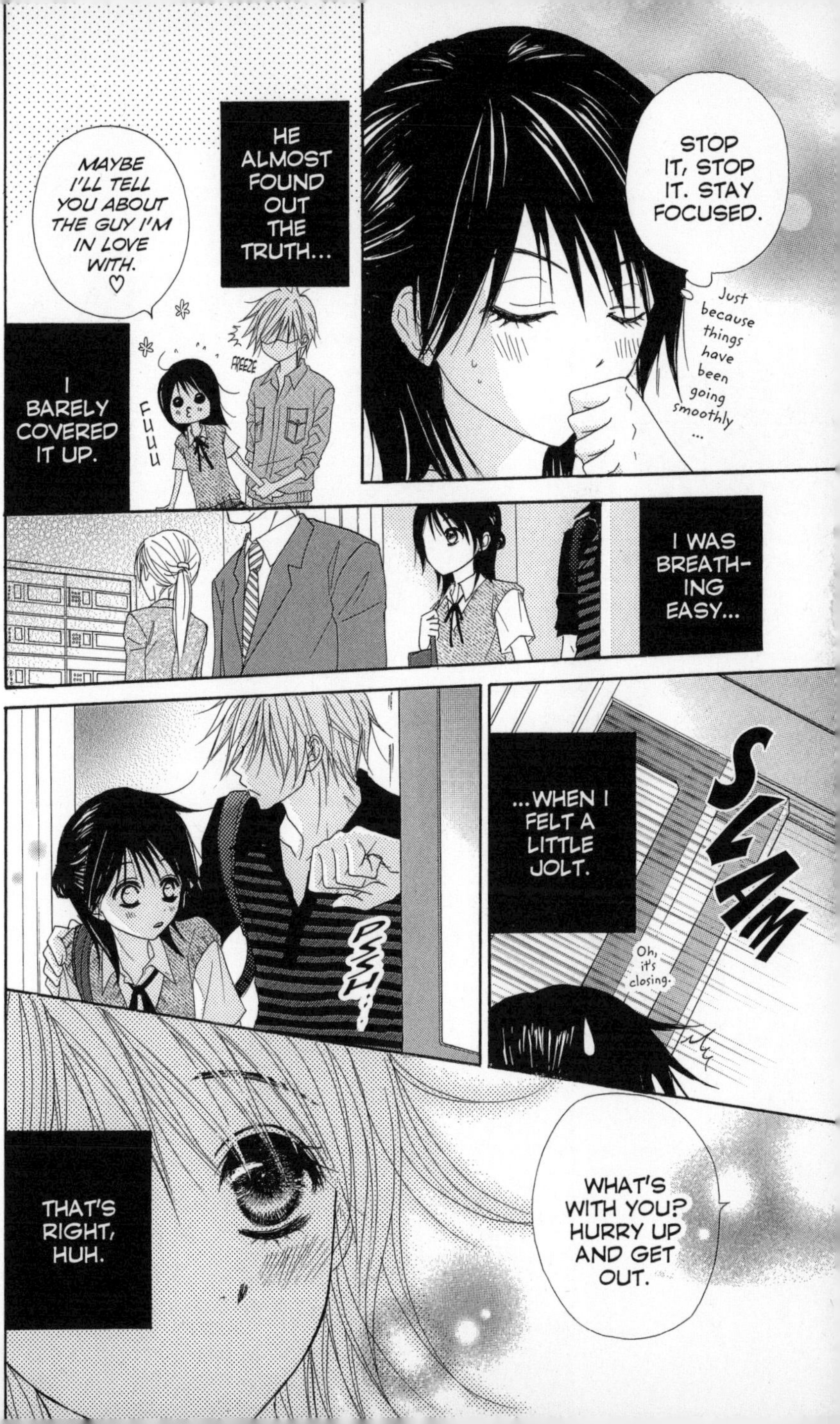
STOP IT, STOP IT. STAY FOCUSED.
Just because things have been going smoothly...
HE ALMOST FOUND OUT THE TRUTH...
MAYBE I'LL TELL YOU ABOUT THE GUY I'M IN LOVE WITH. ♡
FREEZE
I BARELY COVERED IT UP.
FUUU
I WAS BREATHING-ING EASY...
...WHEN I FELT A LITTLE JOLT.
SLAM
Oh, it's closing.
WHAT'S WITH YOU? HURRY UP AND GET OUT.
THAT'S RIGHT, HUH.

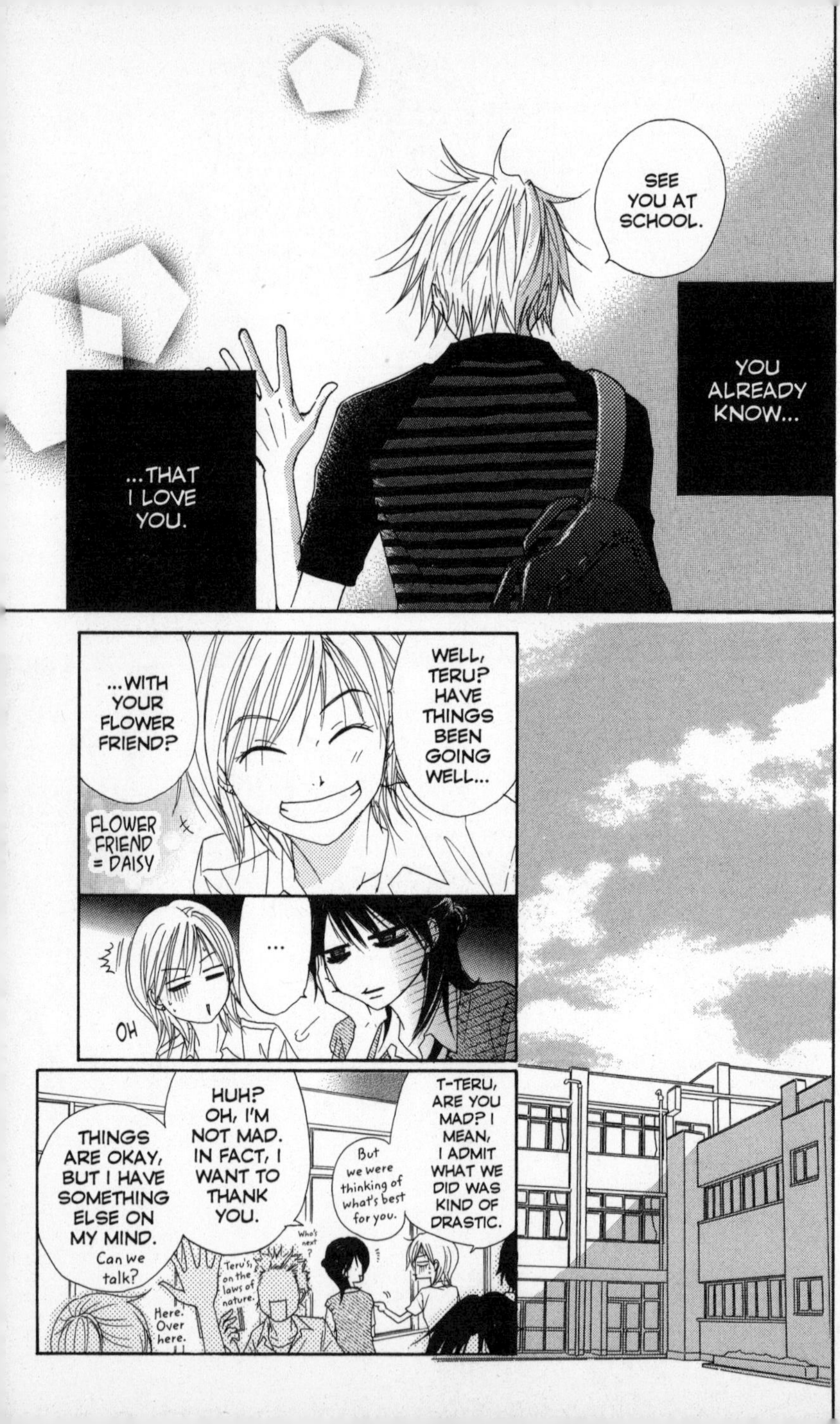
SEE YOU AT SCHOOL.
YOU ALREADY KNOW...
...THAT I LOVE YOU.
WELL, TERU? HAVE THINGS BEEN GOING WELL...
...WITH YOUR FLOWER FRIEND?
FLOWER FRIEND = DAISY
...
OH
T-TERU, ARE YOU MAD? I MEAN, I ADMIT WHAT WE DID WAS KIND OF DRASTIC.
But we were thinking of what's best for you.
HUH? OH, I'M NOT MAD. IN FACT, I WANT TO THANK YOU.
THINGS ARE OKAY, BUT I HAVE SOMETHING ELSE ON MY MIND. Can we talk?
Who's next?
Teru's on the laws of nature.
Here. Over here.

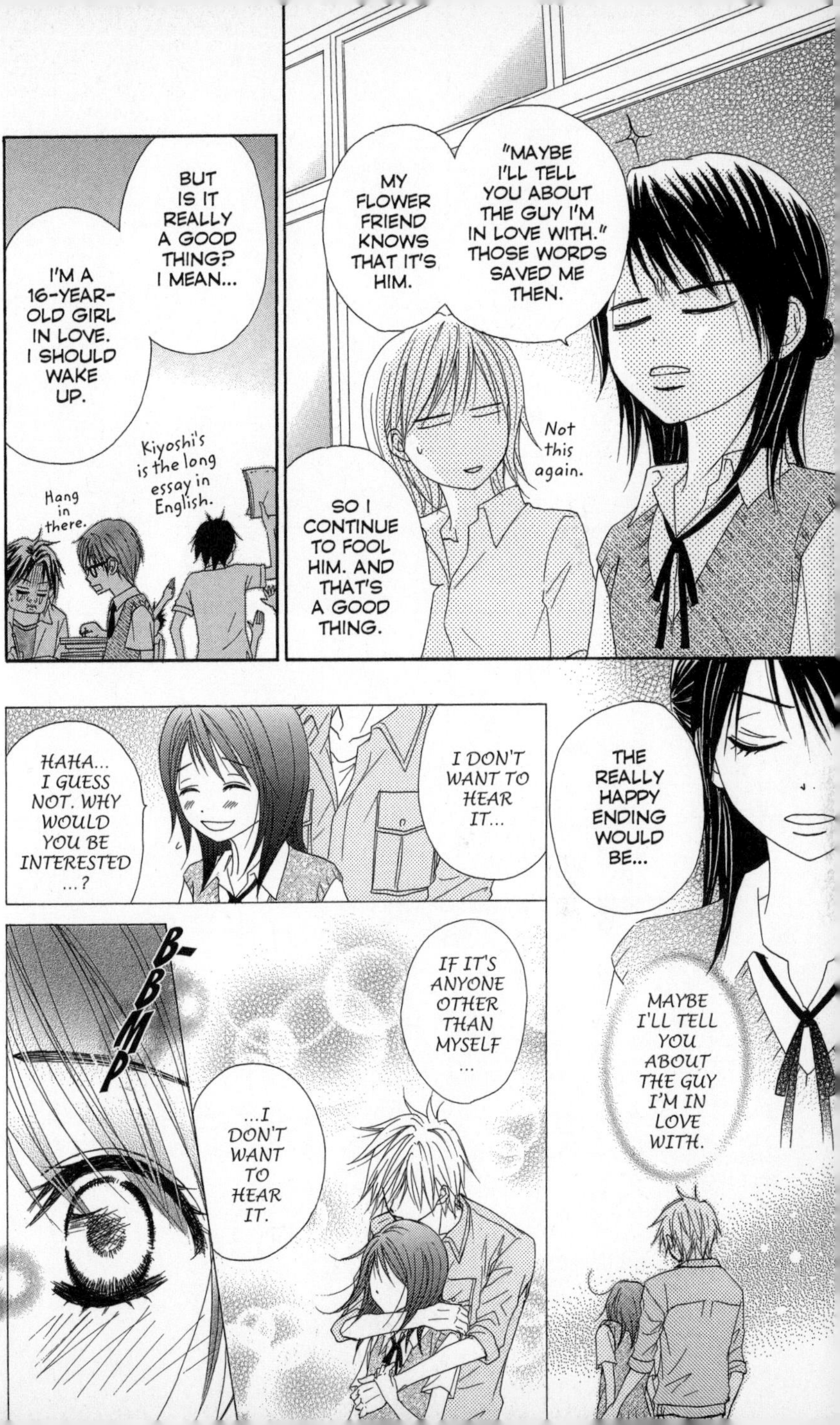
"MAYBE I'LL TELL YOU ABOUT THE GUY I'M IN LOVE WITH." THOSE WORDS SAVED ME THEN.
MY FLOWER FRIEND KNOWS THAT IT'S HIM.
Not this again.
SO I CONTINUE TO FOOL HIM. AND THAT'S A GOOD THING.
BUT IS IT REALLY A GOOD THING? I MEAN...
I'M A 16-YEAR-OLD GIRL IN LOVE. I SHOULD WAKE UP.
Kiyoshi's is the long essay in English.
Hang in there.
THE REALLY HAPPY ENDING WOULD BE...
MAYBE I'LL TELL YOU ABOUT THE GUY I'M IN LOVE WITH.
I DON'T WANT TO HEAR IT...
HAHA... I GUESS NOT. WHY WOULD YOU BE INTERESTED ...?
IF IT'S ANYONE OTHER THAN MYSELF ...
...I DON'T WANT TO HEAR IT.
B-BMP

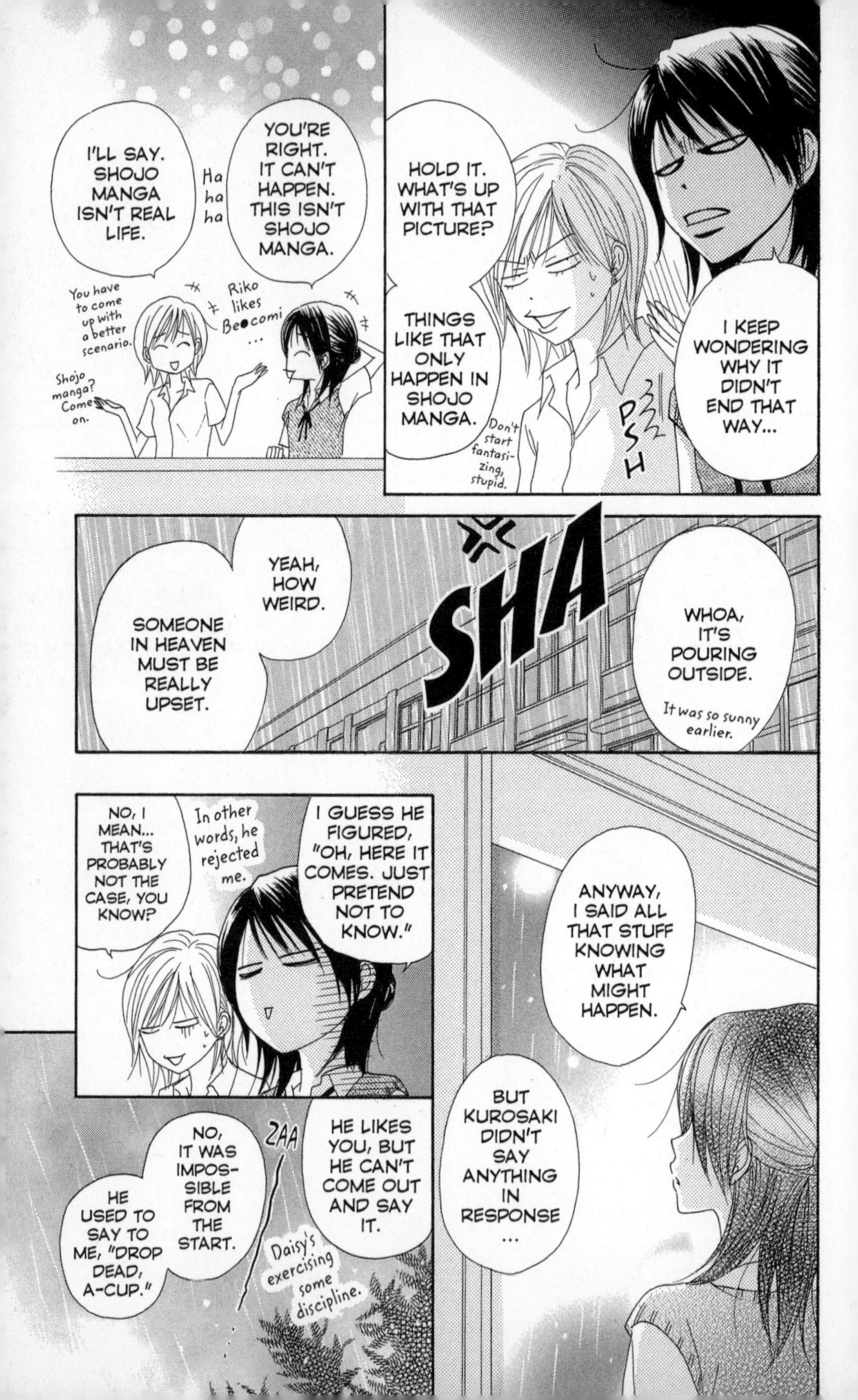
I KEEP WONDERING WHY IT DIDN'T END THAT WAY...
HOLD IT. WHAT'S UP WITH THAT PICTURE?
PSH
THINGS LIKE THAT ONLY HAPPEN IN SHOJO MANGA.
Don't start fantasi-zing, stupid.
YOU'RE RIGHT. IT CAN'T HAPPEN. THIS ISN'T SHOJO MANGA.
Ha ha ha
I'LL SAY. SHOJO MANGA ISN'T REAL LIFE.
Riko likes Be●comi...
You have to come up with a better scenario.
Shojo manga? Come on.
SHA
WHOA, IT'S POURING OUTSIDE.
It was so sunny earlier.
YEAH, HOW WEIRD.
SOMEONE IN HEAVEN MUST BE REALLY UPSET.
ANYWAY, I SAID ALL THAT STUFF KNOWING WHAT MIGHT HAPPEN.
BUT KUROSAKI DIDN'T SAY ANYTHING IN RESPONSE...
I GUESS HE FIGURED, "OH, HERE IT COMES. JUST PRETEND NOT TO KNOW."
In other words, he rejected me.
NO, I MEAN... THAT'S PROBABLY NOT THE CASE, YOU KNOW?
HE LIKES YOU, BUT HE CAN'T COME OUT AND SAY IT.
ZAA
NO, IT WAS IMPOS-SIBLE FROM THE START.
HE USED TO SAY TO ME, "DROP DEAD, A-CUP."
Daisy's exercising some discipline.

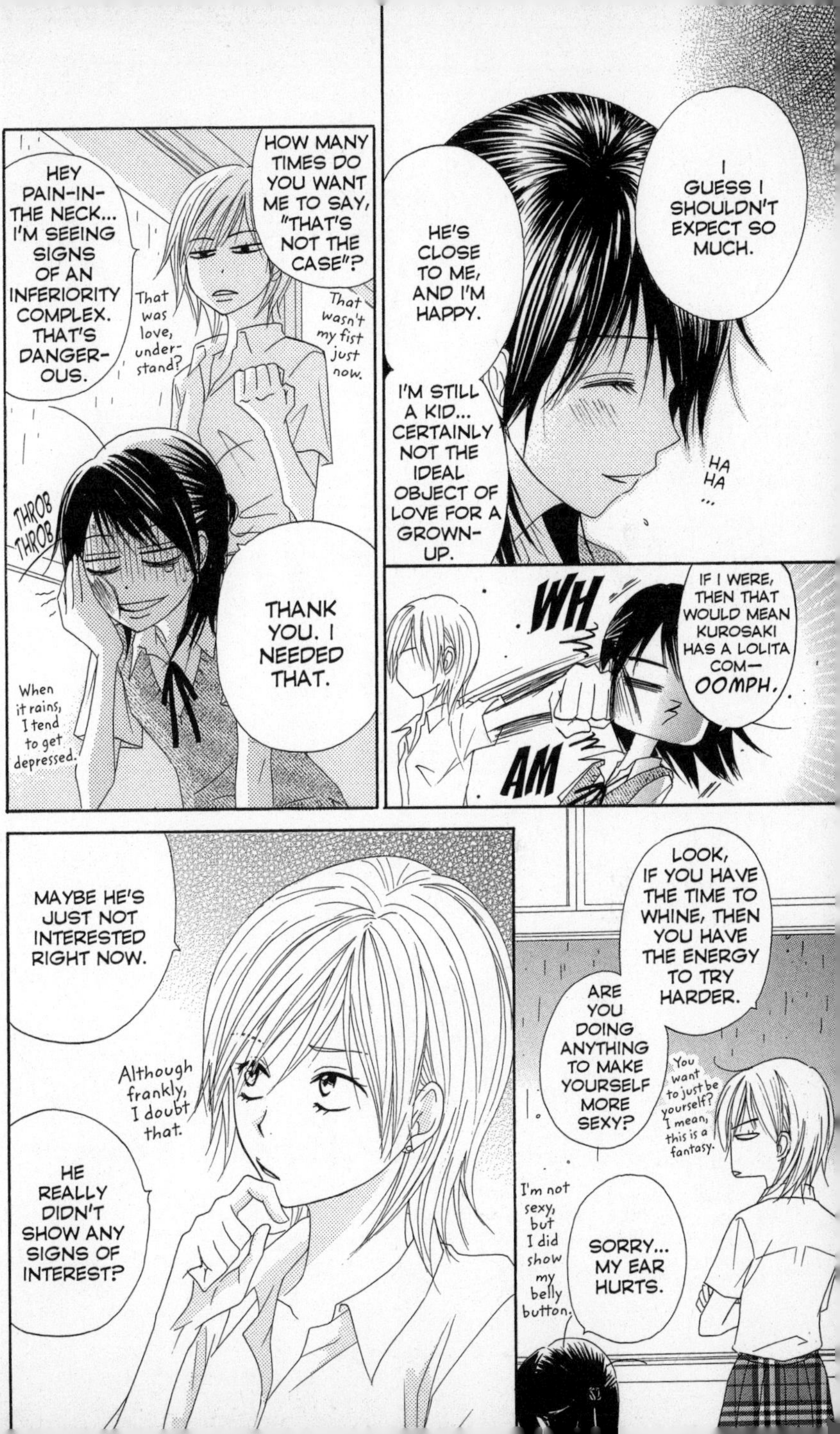
I GUESS I SHOULDN'T EXPECT SO MUCH.
HE'S CLOSE TO ME, AND I'M HAPPY.
I'M STILL A KID... CERTAINLY NOT THE IDEAL OBJECT OF LOVE FOR A GROWN-UP.
HA HA ...
IF I WERE, THEN THAT WOULD MEAN KUROSAKI HAS A LOLITA COM— OOMPH.
WH
AM
HOW MANY TIMES DO YOU WANT ME TO SAY, "THAT'S NOT THE CASE"?
That wasn't my fist just now.
HEY PAIN-IN-THE NECK... I'M SEEING SIGNS OF AN INFERIORITY COMPLEX. THAT'S DANGER-OUS.
That was love, understand?
THROB THROB
THANK YOU. I NEEDED THAT.
When it rains, I tend to get depressed.
LOOK, IF YOU HAVE THE TIME TO WHINE, THEN YOU HAVE THE ENERGY TO TRY HARDER.
ARE YOU DOING ANYTHING TO MAKE YOURSELF MORE SEXY?
You want to just be yourself? I mean, this is a fantasy.
SORRY... MY EAR HURTS.
I'm not sexy, but I did show my belly button.
MAYBE HE'S JUST NOT INTERESTED RIGHT NOW.
Although frankly, I doubt that.
HE REALLY DIDN'T SHOW ANY SIGNS OF INTEREST?

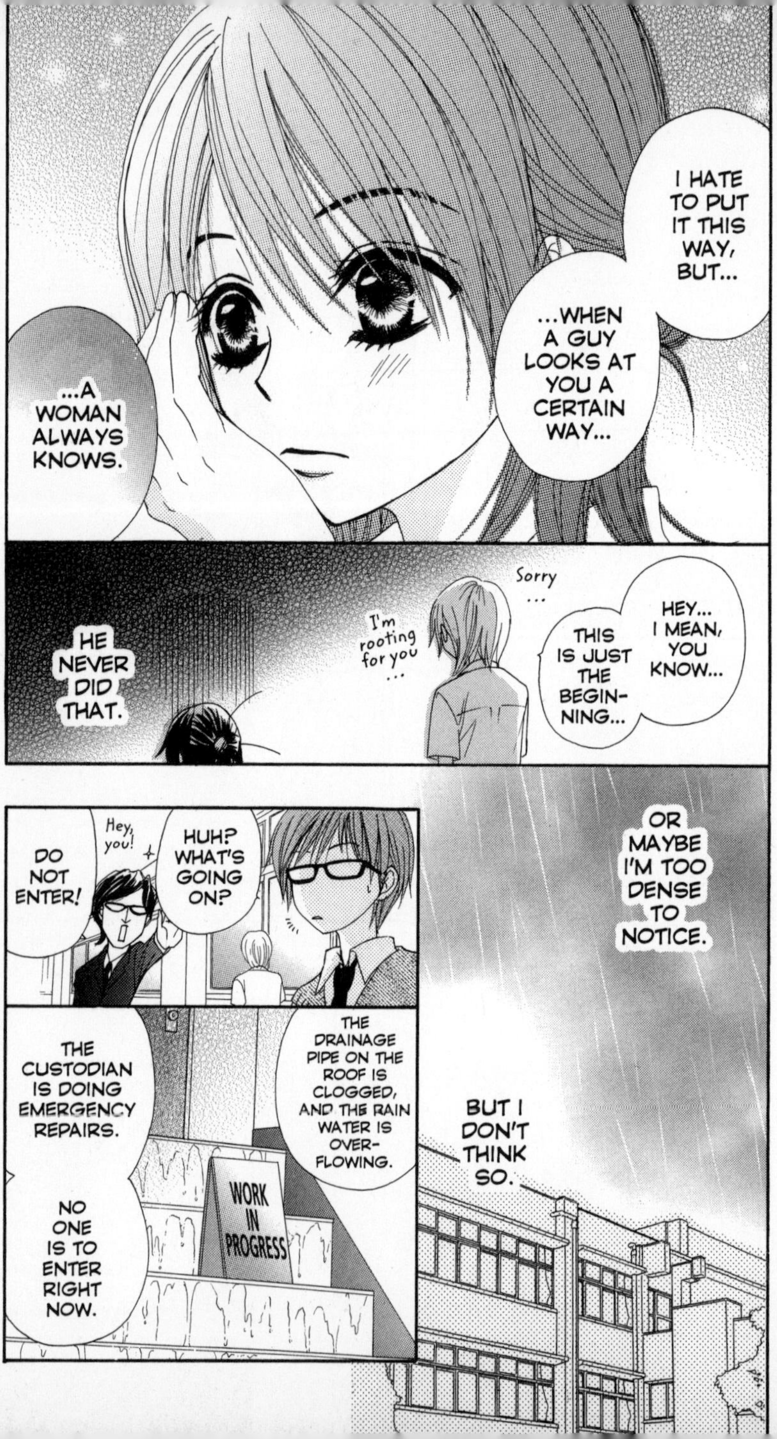
I HATE TO PUT IT THIS WAY, BUT...
...WHEN A GUY LOOKS AT YOU A CERTAIN WAY...
...A WOMAN ALWAYS KNOWS.
HEY... I MEAN, YOU KNOW...
Sorry ...
THIS IS JUST THE BEGINNING...
I'm rooting for you ...
HE NEVER DID THAT.
OR MAYBE I'M TOO DENSE TO NOTICE.
BUT I DON'T THINK SO.
HUH? WHAT'S GOING ON?
Hey, you!
DO NOT ENTER!
THE DRAINAGE PIPE ON THE ROOF IS CLOGGED, AND THE RAIN WATER IS OVERFLOWING.
THE CUSTODIAN IS DOING EMERGENCY REPAIRS.
WORK IN PROGRESS
NO ONE IS TO ENTER RIGHT NOW.

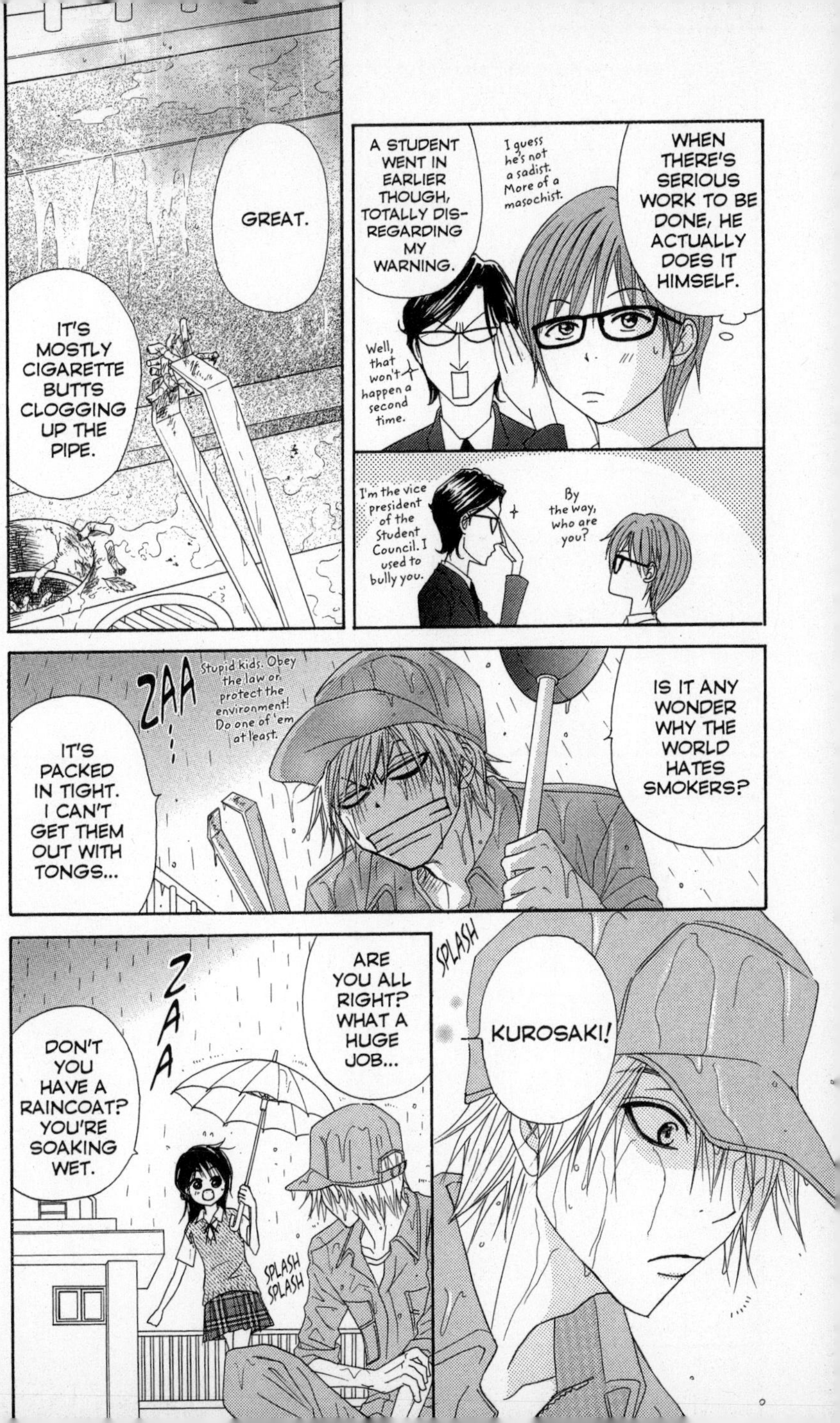
WHEN THERE'S SERIOUS WORK TO BE DONE, HE ACTUALLY DOES IT HIMSELF.
I guess he's not a sadist. More of a masochist.
A STUDENT WENT IN EARLIER THOUGH, TOTALLY DISREGARDING MY WARNING.
Well, that won't happen a second time.
By the way, who are you?
I'm the vice president of the Student Council. I used to bully you.
GREAT.
IT'S MOSTLY CIGARETTE BUTTS CLOGGING UP THE PIPE.
IS IT ANY WONDER WHY THE WORLD HATES SMOKERS?
Stupid kids. Obey the law or protect the environment! Do one of 'em at least.
ZAA
IT'S PACKED IN TIGHT. I CAN'T GET THEM OUT WITH TONGS...
SPLASH
KUROSAKI!
ARE YOU ALL RIGHT? WHAT A HUGE JOB...
ZAA
DON'T YOU HAVE A RAINCOAT? YOU'RE SOAKING WET.
SPLASH SPLASH

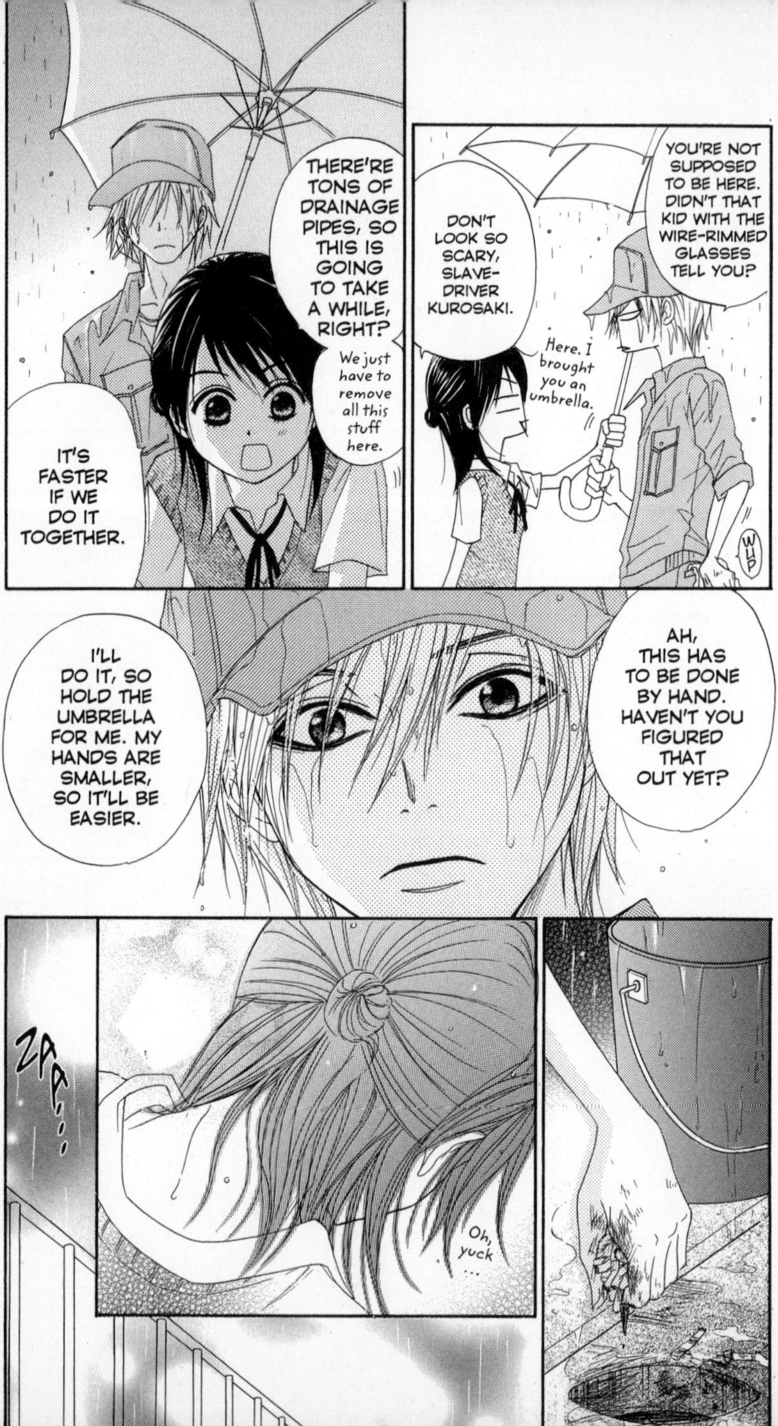
YOU'RE NOT SUPPOSED TO BE HERE. DIDN'T THAT KID WITH THE WIRE-RIMMED GLASSES TELL YOU?
DON'T LOOK SO SCARY, SLAVE-DRIVER KUROSAKI.
Here. I brought you an umbrella.
WUP
THERE'RE TONS OF DRAINAGE PIPES, SO THIS IS GOING TO TAKE A WHILE, RIGHT?
We just have to remove all this stuff here.
IT'S FASTER IF WE DO IT TOGETHER.
AH, THIS HAS TO BE DONE BY HAND. HAVEN'T YOU FIGURED THAT OUT YET?
I'LL DO IT, SO HOLD THE UMBRELLA FOR ME. MY HANDS ARE SMALLER, SO IT'LL BE EASIER.
Oh, yuck...
ZAA...

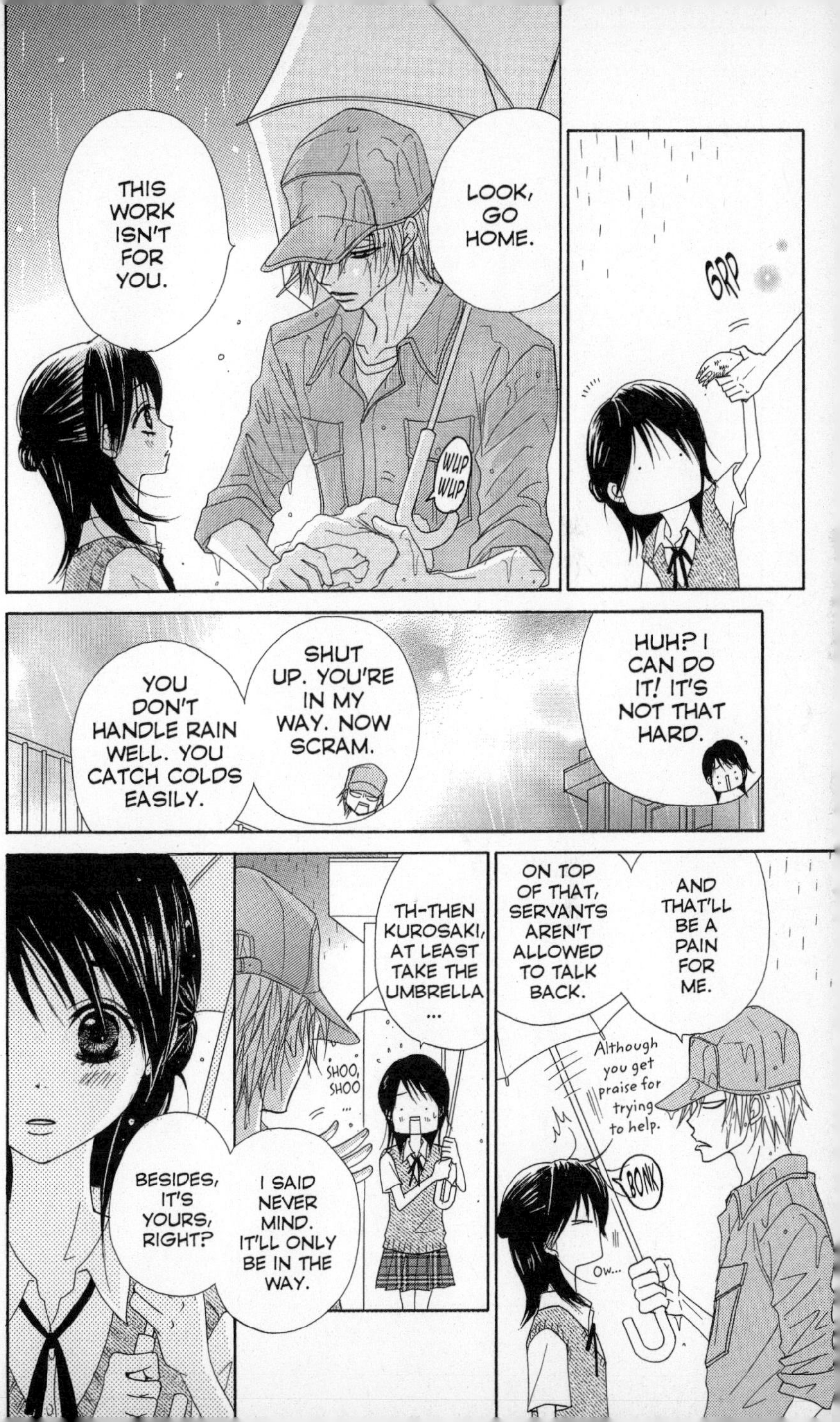
GRP
LOOK, GO HOME.
THIS WORK ISN'T FOR YOU.
WUP WUP
HUH? I CAN DO IT! IT'S NOT THAT HARD.
SHUT UP. YOU'RE IN MY WAY. NOW SCRAM.
YOU DON'T HANDLE RAIN WELL. YOU CATCH COLDS EASILY.
AND THAT'LL BE A PAIN FOR ME.
ON TOP OF THAT, SERVANTS AREN'T ALLOWED TO TALK BACK.
Although you get praise for trying to help.
BONK
Ow...
TH-THEN KUROSAKI, AT LEAST TAKE THE UMBRELLA ...
SHOO, SHOO ...
I SAID NEVER MIND. IT'LL ONLY BE IN THE WAY.
BESIDES, IT'S YOURS, RIGHT?

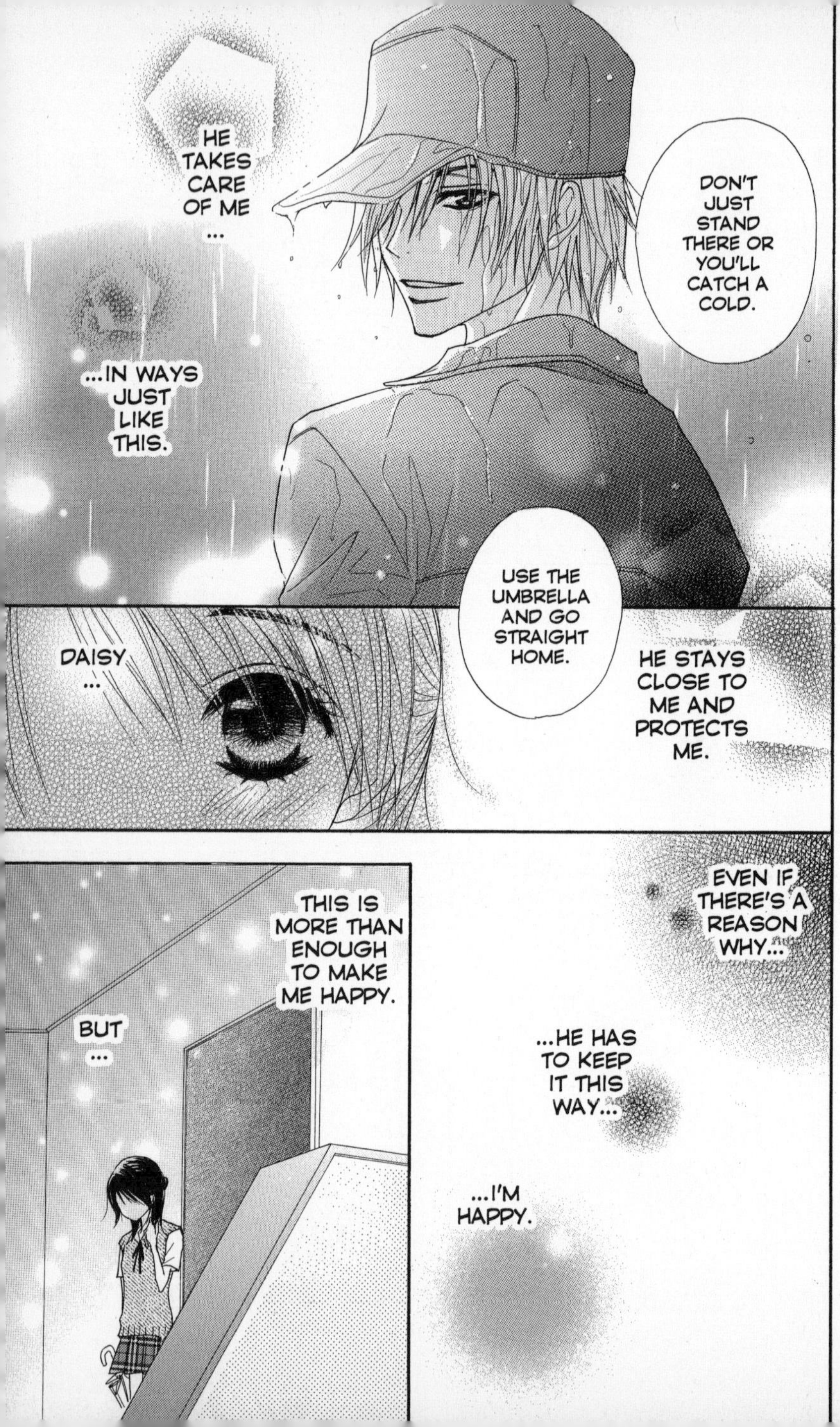
DON'T JUST STAND THERE OR YOU'LL CATCH A COLD.
HE TAKES CARE OF ME...
...IN WAYS JUST LIKE THIS.
USE THE UMBRELLA AND GO STRAIGHT HOME.
HE STAYS CLOSE TO ME AND PROTECTS ME.
DAISY...
EVEN IF THERE'S A REASON WHY...
...HE HAS TO KEEP IT THIS WAY...
...I'M HAPPY.
THIS IS MORE THAN ENOUGH TO MAKE ME HAPPY.
BUT...

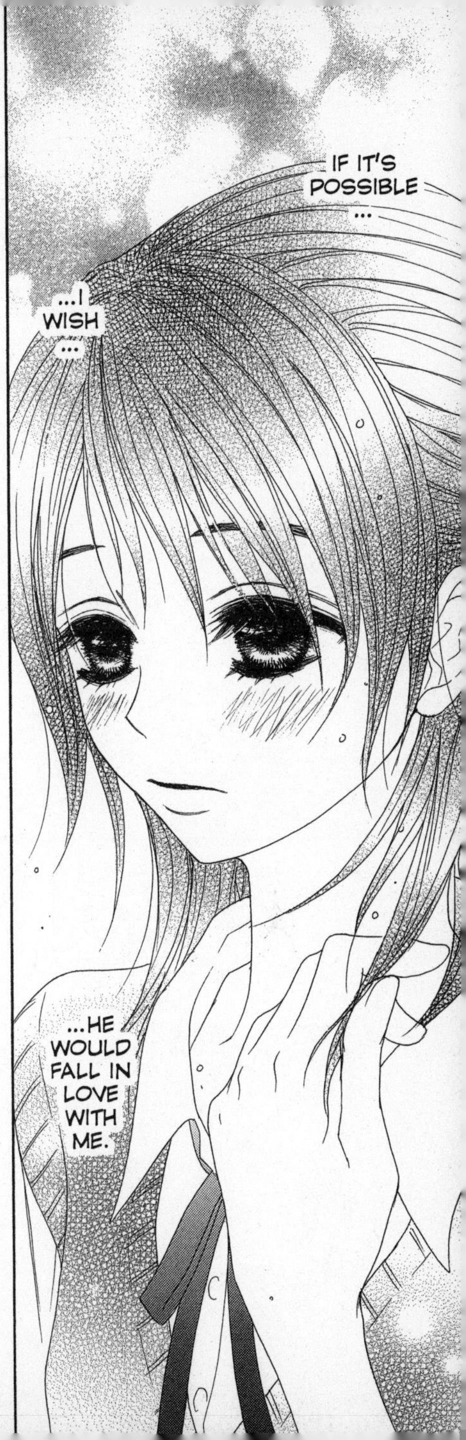
IF IT'S POSSIBLE ...
...I WISH ...
...HE WOULD FALL IN LOVE WITH ME.

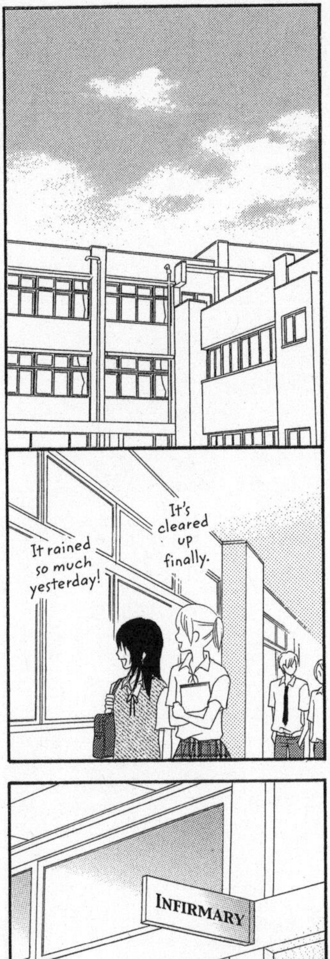
It's cleared up finally.
It rained so much yesterday!
INFIRMARY

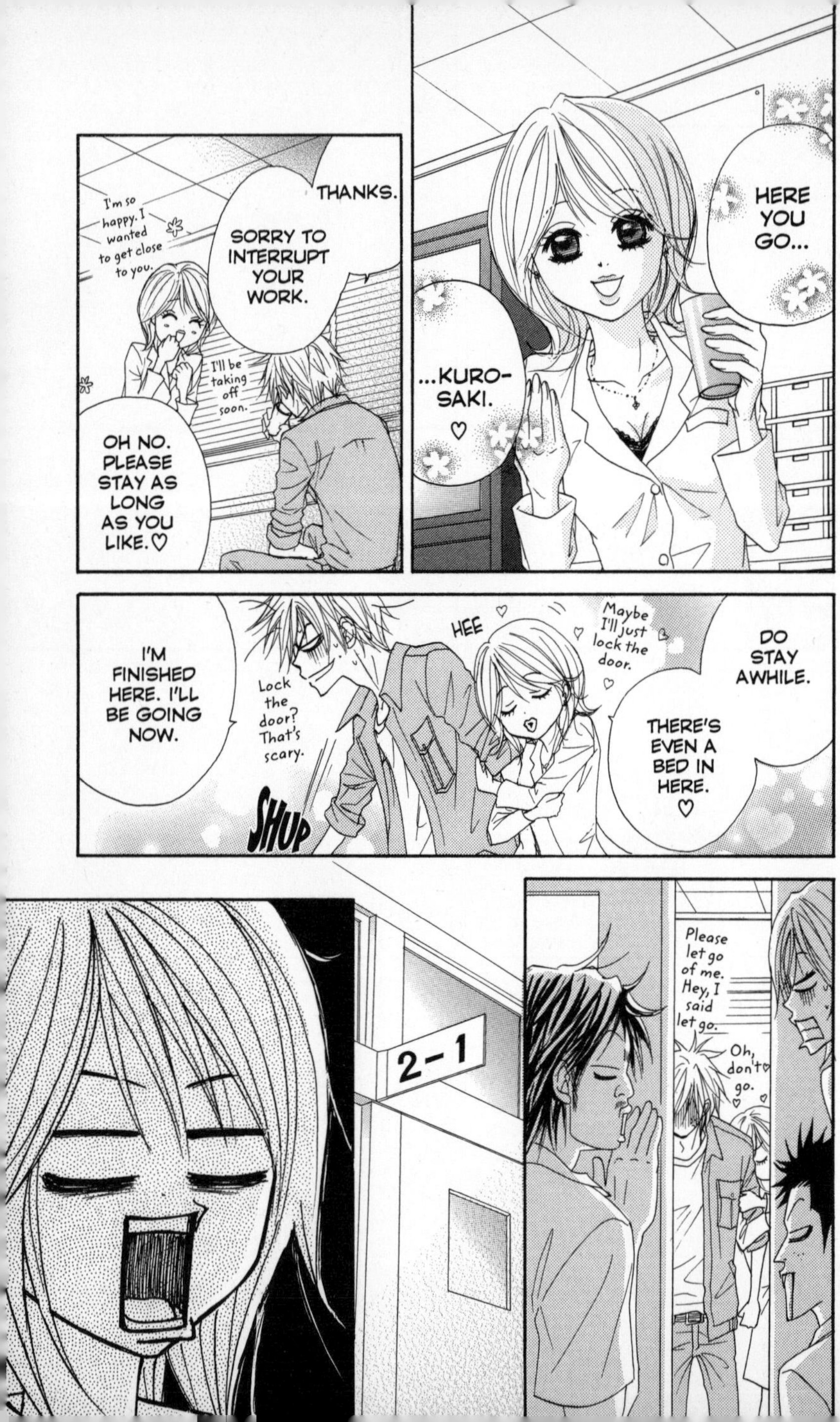
HERE YOU GO...
...KURO-SAKI. ♡
THANKS.
SORRY TO INTERRUPT YOUR WORK.
I'm so happy. I wanted to get close to you.
I'll be taking off soon.
OH NO. PLEASE STAY AS LONG AS YOU LIKE. ♡
DO STAY AWHILE.
THERE'S EVEN A BED IN HERE. ♡
Maybe I'll just lock the door.
HEE
Lock the door? That's scary.
I'M FINISHED HERE. I'LL BE GOING NOW.
SHUP
Please let go of me. Hey, I said let go.
Oh, don't ♡ go.
2-1

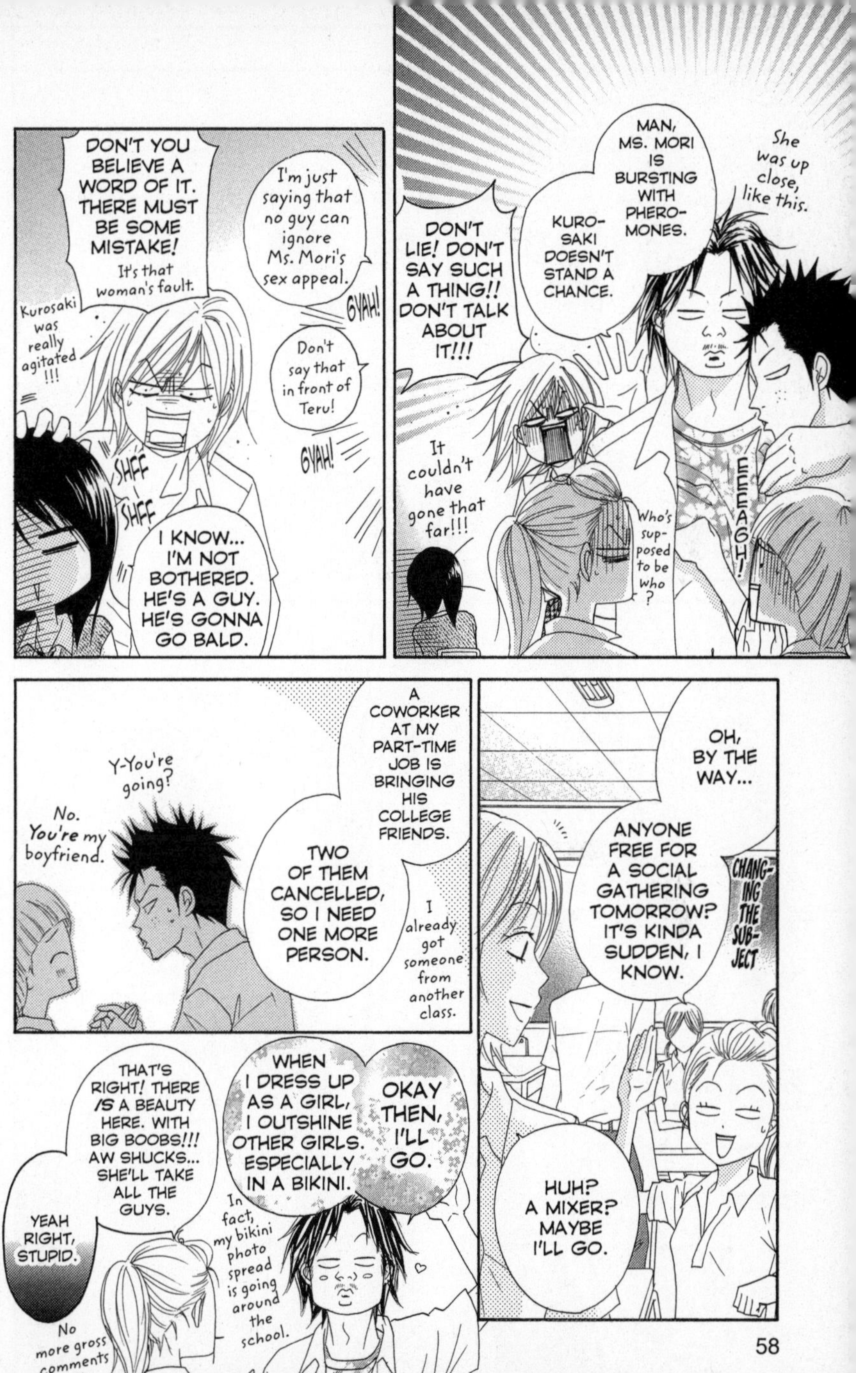
She was up close, like this.
MAN, MS. MORI IS BURSTING WITH PHERO-MONES.
KURO-SAKI DOESN'T STAND A CHANCE.
DON'T LIE! DON'T SAY SUCH A THING!! DON'T TALK ABOUT IT!!!
EEEAGH!
Who's sup-posed to be who?
It couldn't have gone that far!!!
I'm just saying that no guy can ignore Ms. Mori's sex appeal.
DON'T YOU BELIEVE A WORD OF IT. THERE MUST BE SOME MISTAKE!
It's that woman's fault.
GYAH!
Don't say that in front of Teru!
GYAH!
Kurosaki was really agitated!!!
SHFF
SHFF
I KNOW... I'M NOT BOTHERED. HE'S A GUY. HE'S GONNA GO BALD.
OH, BY THE WAY...
ANYONE FREE FOR A SOCIAL GATHERING TOMORROW? IT'S KINDA SUDDEN, I KNOW.
CHANGING THE SUBJECT
HUH? A MIXER? MAYBE I'LL GO.
A COWORKER AT MY PART-TIME JOB IS BRINGING HIS COLLEGE FRIENDS.
TWO OF THEM CANCELLED, SO I NEED ONE MORE PERSON.
I already got someone from another class.
Y-You're going?
No. You're my boyfriend.
OKAY THEN, I'LL GO.
WHEN I DRESS UP AS A GIRL, I OUTSHINE OTHER GIRLS. ESPECIALLY IN A BIKINI.
In fact, my bikini photo spread is going around the school.
THAT'S RIGHT! THERE IS A BEAUTY HERE. WITH BIG BOOBS!!! AW SHUCKS... SHE'LL TAKE ALL THE GUYS.
YEAH RIGHT, STUPID.
No more gross comments outta you.

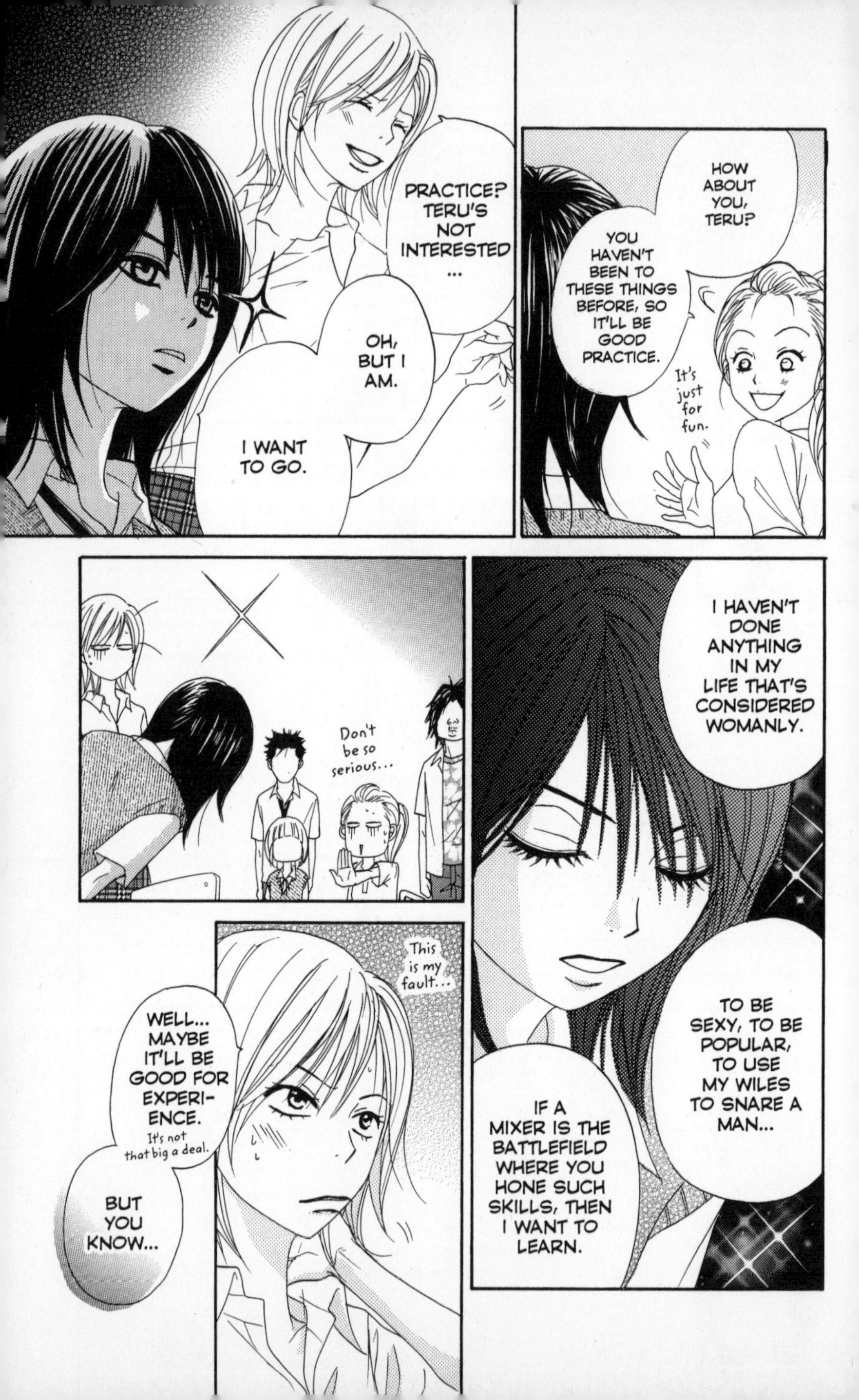
HOW ABOUT YOU, TERU?
YOU HAVEN'T BEEN TO THESE THINGS BEFORE, SO IT'LL BE GOOD PRACTICE.
It's just for fun.
PRACTICE? TERU'S NOT INTERESTED...
OH, BUT I AM.
I WANT TO GO.
I HAVEN'T DONE ANYTHING IN MY LIFE THAT'S CONSIDERED WOMANLY.
TO BE SEXY, TO BE POPULAR, TO USE MY WILES TO SNARE A MAN...
IF A MIXER IS THE BATTLEFIELD WHERE YOU HONE SUCH SKILLS, THEN I WANT TO LEARN.
Don't be so serious...
This is my fault...
WELL... MAYBE IT'LL BE GOOD FOR EXPERIENCE.
It's not that big a deal.
BUT YOU KNOW...

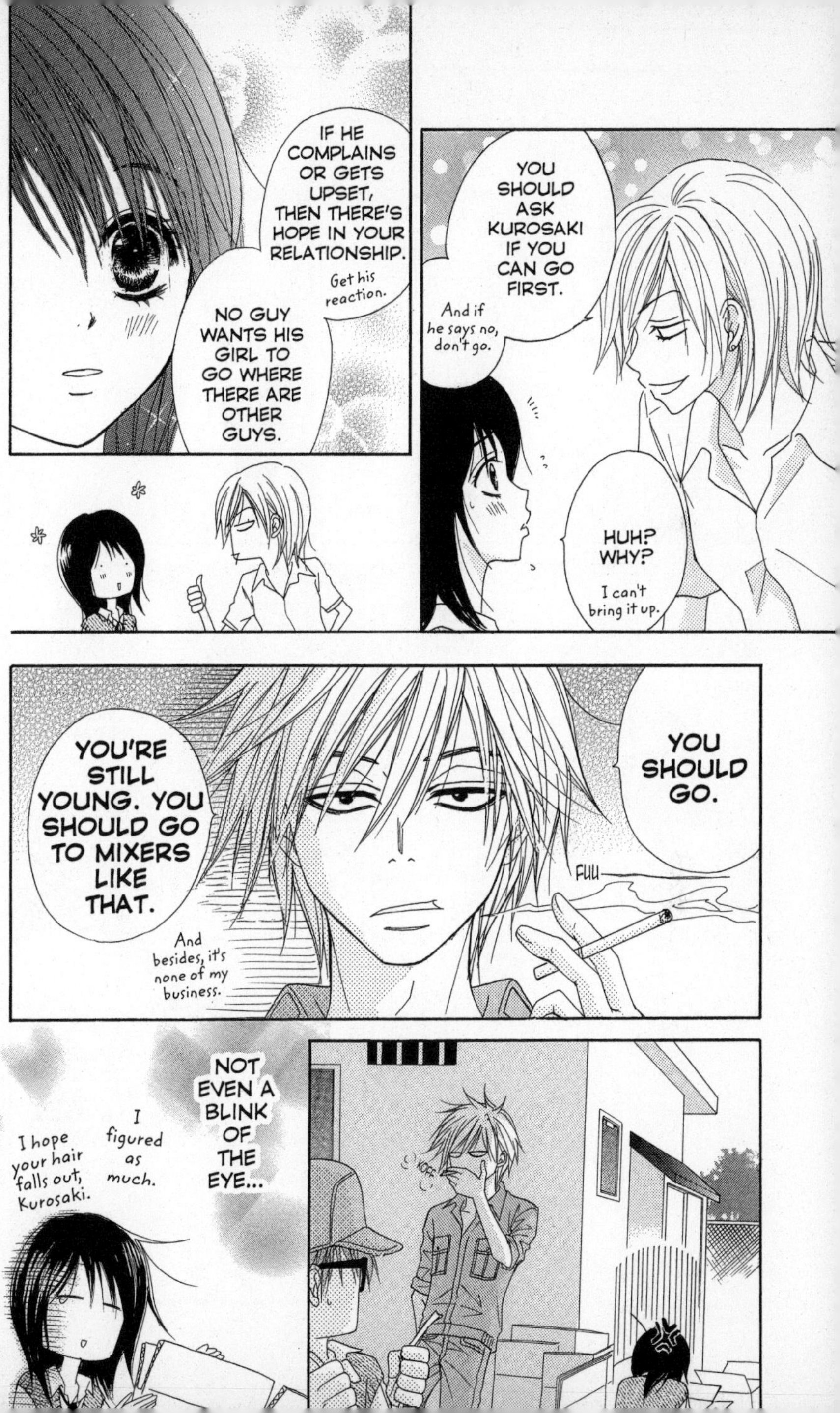
YOU SHOULD ASK KUROSAKI IF YOU CAN GO FIRST.
And if he says no, don't go.
HUH? WHY?
I can't bring it up.
IF HE COMPLAINS OR GETS UPSET, THEN THERE'S HOPE IN YOUR RELATIONSHIP.
Get his reaction.
NO GUY WANTS HIS GIRL TO GO WHERE THERE ARE OTHER GUYS.
YOU SHOULD GO.
FUU
YOU'RE STILL YOUNG. YOU SHOULD GO TO MIXERS LIKE THAT.
And besides, it's none of my business.
KOFF
NOT EVEN A BLINK OF THE EYE...
I figured as much.
I hope your hair falls out, Kurosaki.

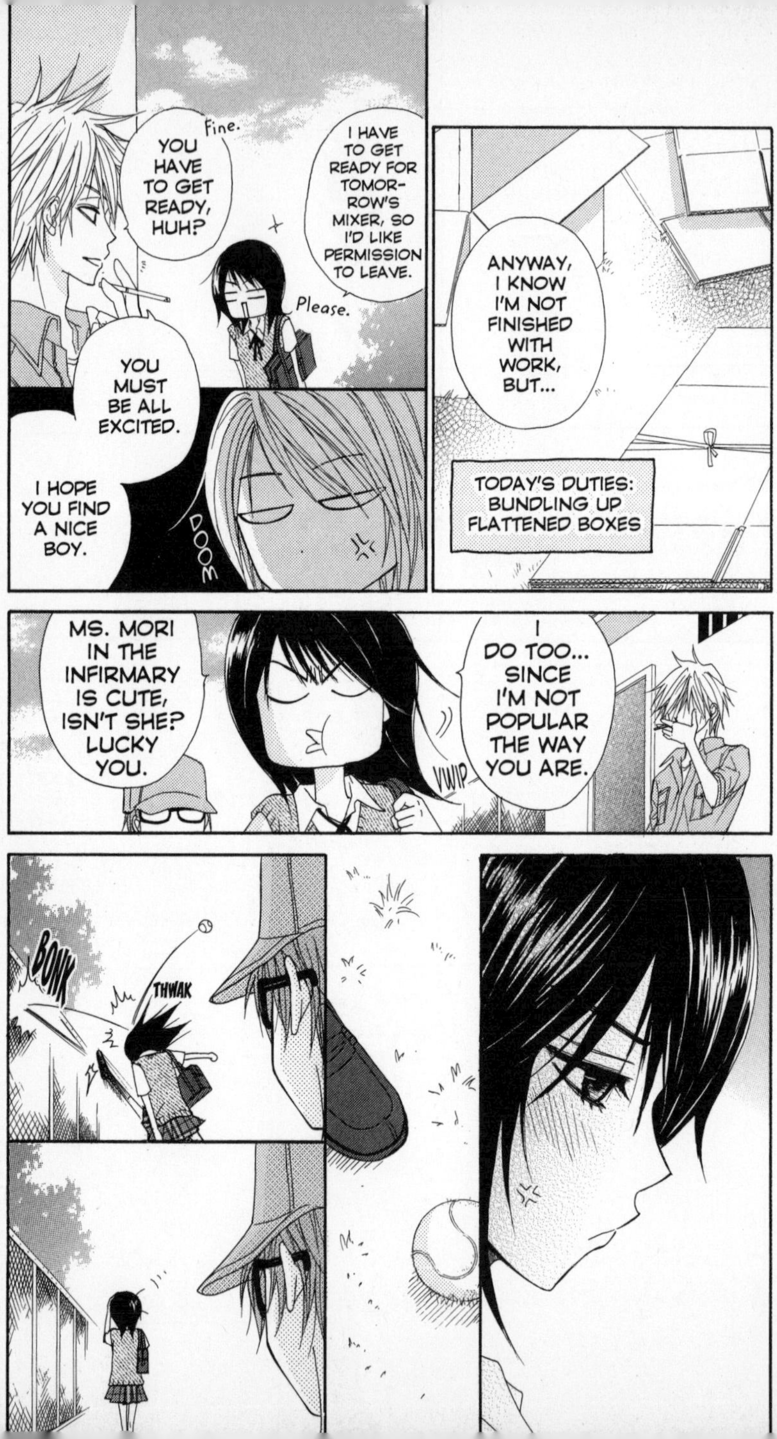
ANYWAY, I KNOW I'M NOT FINISHED WITH WORK, BUT...
TODAY'S DUTIES: BUNDLING UP FLATTENED BOXES
I HAVE TO GET READY FOR TOMOR-ROW'S MIXER, SO I'D LIKE PERMISSION TO LEAVE.
Please.
Fine.
YOU HAVE TO GET READY, HUH?
YOU MUST BE ALL EXCITED.
I HOPE YOU FIND A NICE BOY.
DOOM
I DO TOO... SINCE I'M NOT POPULAR THE WAY YOU ARE.
VWIP
MS. MORI IN THE INFIRMARY IS CUTE, ISN'T SHE? LUCKY YOU.
THWAK
BONK

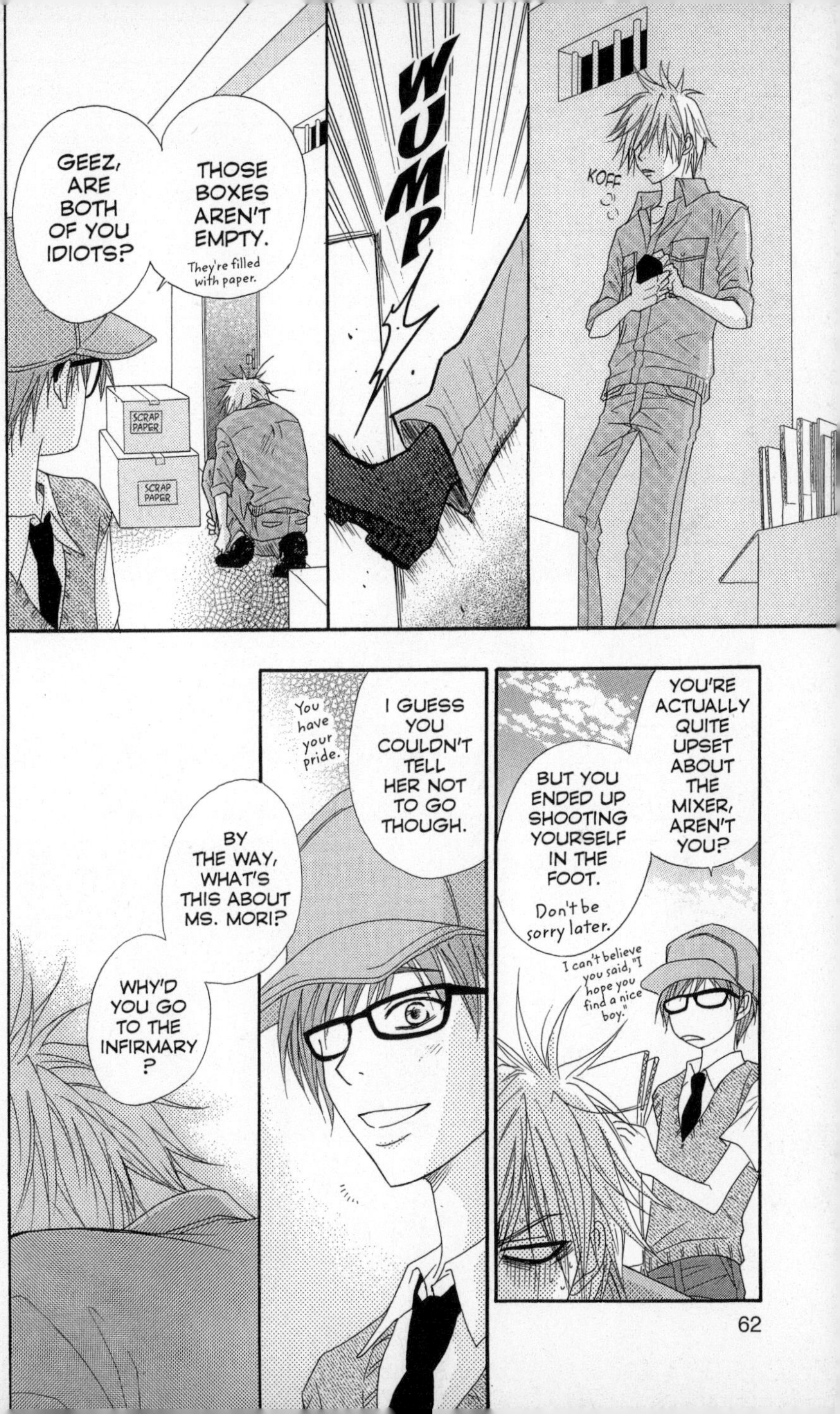
KOFF
WUMP
THOSE BOXES AREN'T EMPTY.
They're filled with paper.
GEEZ, ARE BOTH OF YOU IDIOTS?
SCRAP PAPER
SCRAP PAPER
YOU'RE ACTUALLY QUITE UPSET ABOUT THE MIXER, AREN'T YOU?
BUT YOU ENDED UP SHOOTING YOURSELF IN THE FOOT.
Don't be sorry later.
I can't believe you said, "I hope you find a nice boy."
I GUESS YOU COULDN'T TELL HER NOT TO GO THOUGH.
You have your pride.
BY THE WAY, WHAT'S THIS ABOUT MS. MORI?
WHY'D YOU GO TO THE INFIRMARY?

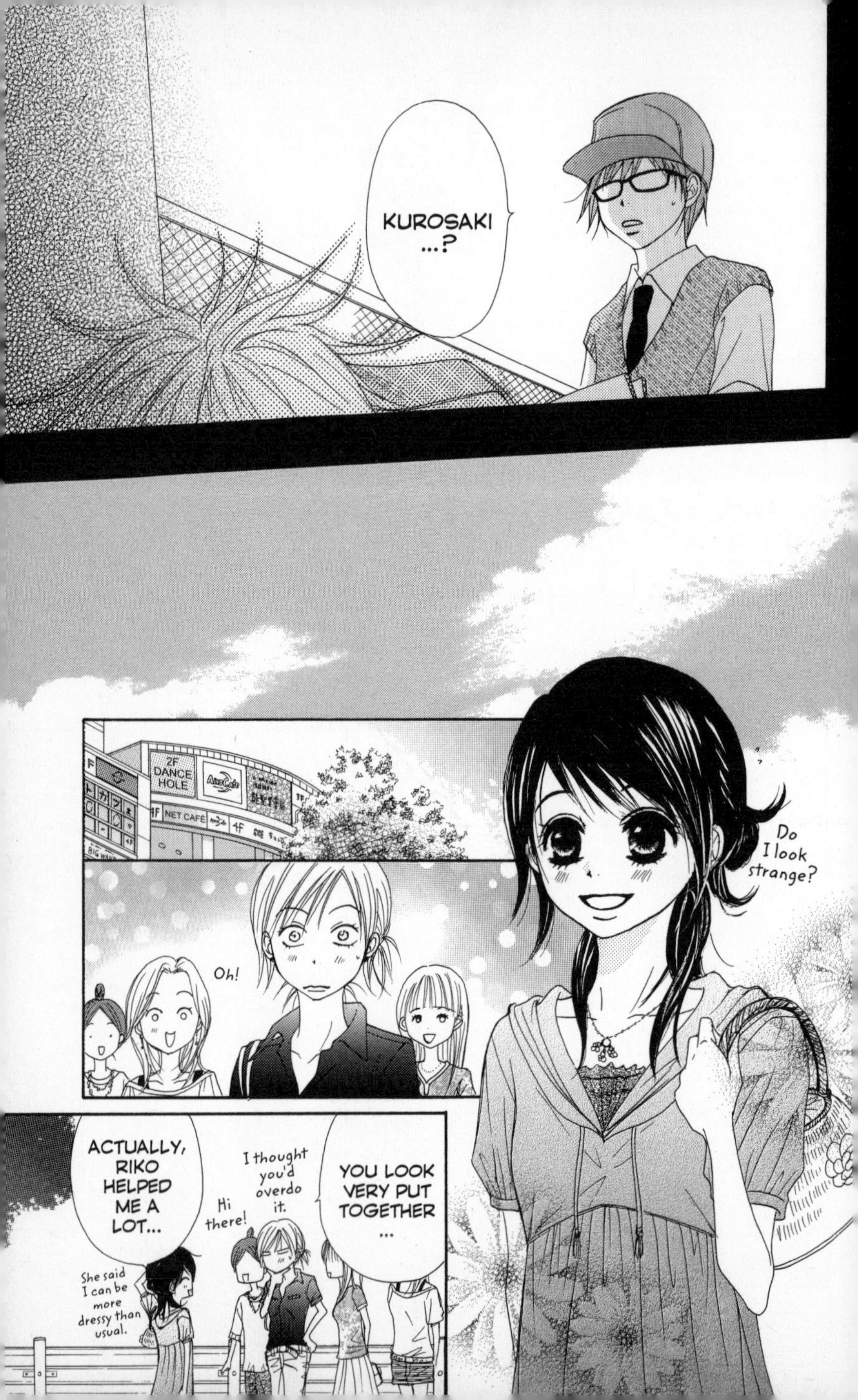
KUROSAKI ...?
Do I look strange?
Oh!
YOU LOOK VERY PUT TOGETHER ...
I thought you'd overdo it.
Hi there!
ACTUALLY, RIKO HELPED ME A LOT...
She said I can be more dressy than usual.

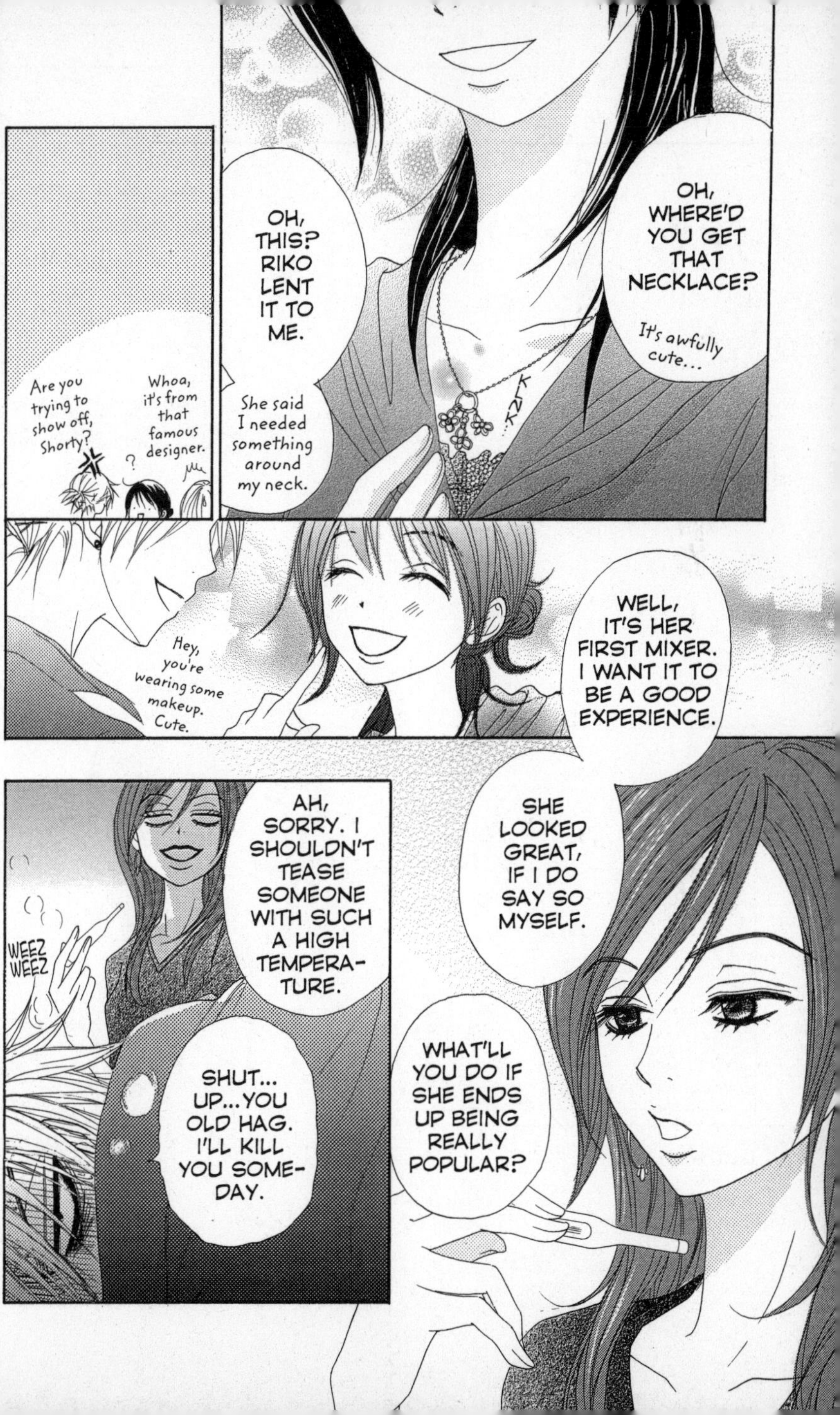
OH, WHERE'D YOU GET THAT NECKLACE?
It's awfully cute...
OH, THIS? RIKO LENT IT TO ME.
She said I needed something around my neck.
Whoa, it's from that famous designer.
Are you trying to show off, Shorty?
?
WELL, IT'S HER FIRST MIXER. I WANT IT TO BE A GOOD EXPERIENCE.
Hey, you're wearing some makeup. Cute.
SHE LOOKED GREAT, IF I DO SAY SO MYSELF.
WHAT'LL YOU DO IF SHE ENDS UP BEING REALLY POPULAR?
AH, SORRY. I SHOULDN'T TEASE SOMEONE WITH SUCH A HIGH TEMPERA-TURE.
WEEZ WEEZ
SHUT... UP...YOU OLD HAG. I'LL KILL YOU SOME-DAY.

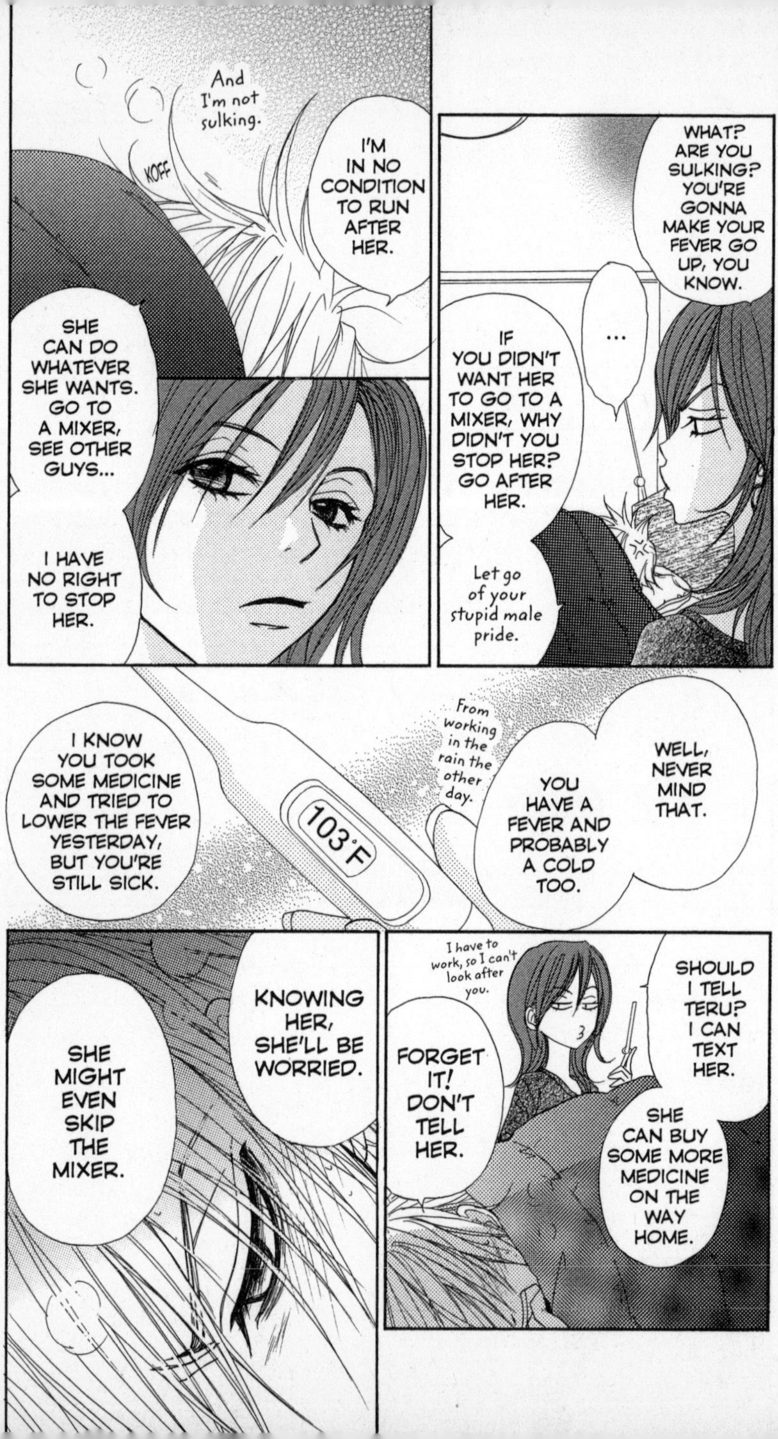
WHAT? ARE YOU SULKING? YOU'RE GONNA MAKE YOUR FEVER GO UP, YOU KNOW.
...
IF YOU DIDN'T WANT HER TO GO TO A MIXER, WHY DIDN'T YOU STOP HER? GO AFTER HER.
Let go of your stupid male pride.
And I'm not sulking.
I'M IN NO CONDITION TO RUN AFTER HER.
KOFF
SHE CAN DO WHATEVER SHE WANTS. GO TO A MIXER, SEE OTHER GUYS...
I HAVE NO RIGHT TO STOP HER.
WELL, NEVER MIND THAT.
YOU HAVE A FEVER AND PROBABLY A COLD TOO.
From working in the rain the other day.
103°F
I KNOW YOU TOOK SOME MEDICINE AND TRIED TO LOWER THE FEVER YESTERDAY, BUT YOU'RE STILL SICK.
SHOULD I TELL TERU? I CAN TEXT HER.
I have to work, so I can't look after you.
SHE CAN BUY SOME MORE MEDICINE ON THE WAY HOME.
FORGET IT! DON'T TELL HER.
KNOWING HER, SHE'LL BE WORRIED.
SHE MIGHT EVEN SKIP THE MIXER.

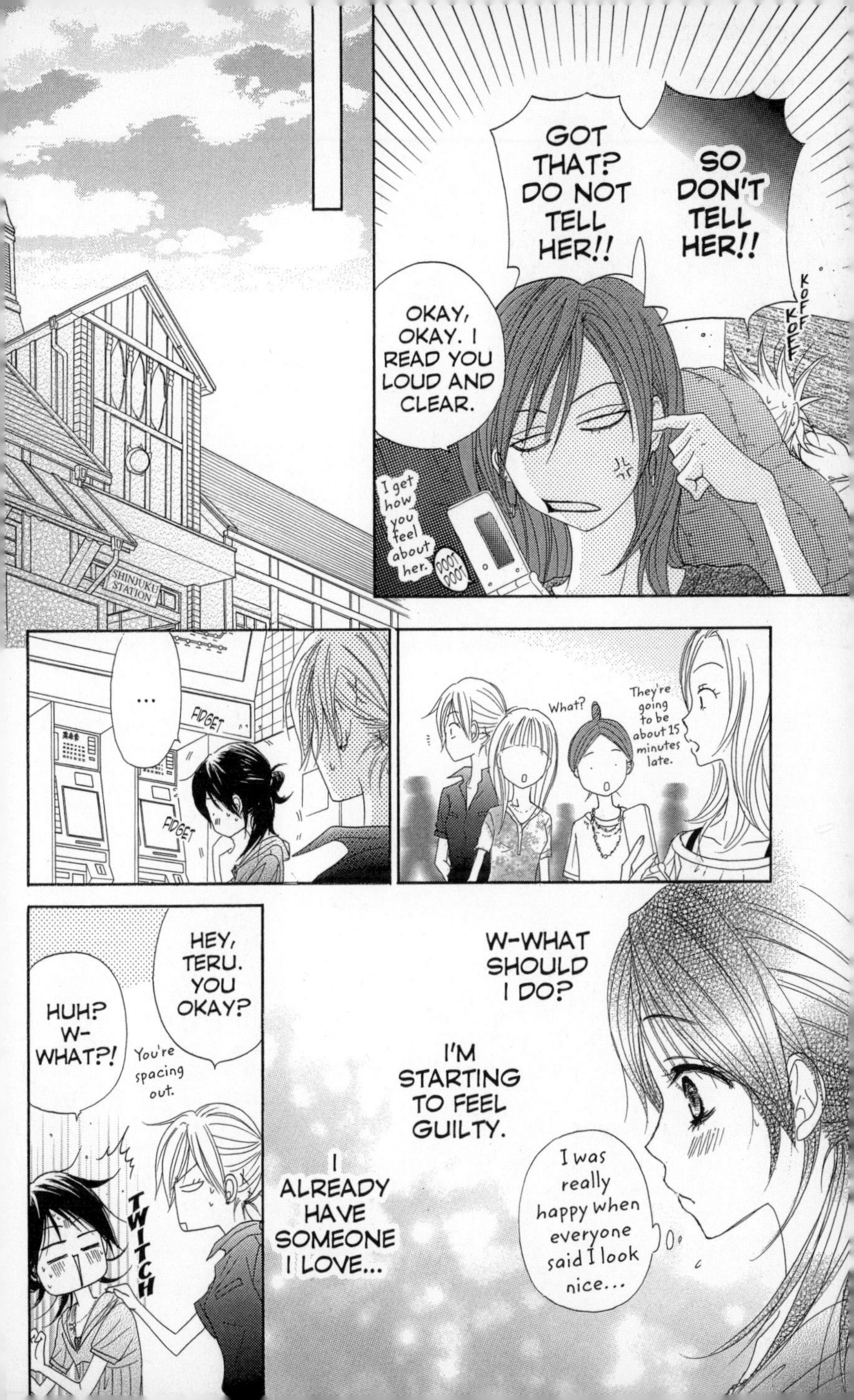
SO DON'T TELL HER!!
GOT THAT? DO NOT TELL HER!!
KOFF KOFF
OKAY, OKAY. I READ YOU LOUD AND CLEAR.
I get how you feel about her.
DOOT DOOT
SHINJUKU STATION
They're going to be about 15 minutes late.
What?
...
FIDGET
FIDGET
W-WHAT SHOULD I DO?
I'M STARTING TO FEEL GUILTY.
I ALREADY HAVE SOMEONE I LOVE...
I was really happy when everyone said I look nice...
HEY, TERU. YOU OKAY?
You're spacing out.
HUH? W-WHAT?!
TWITCH

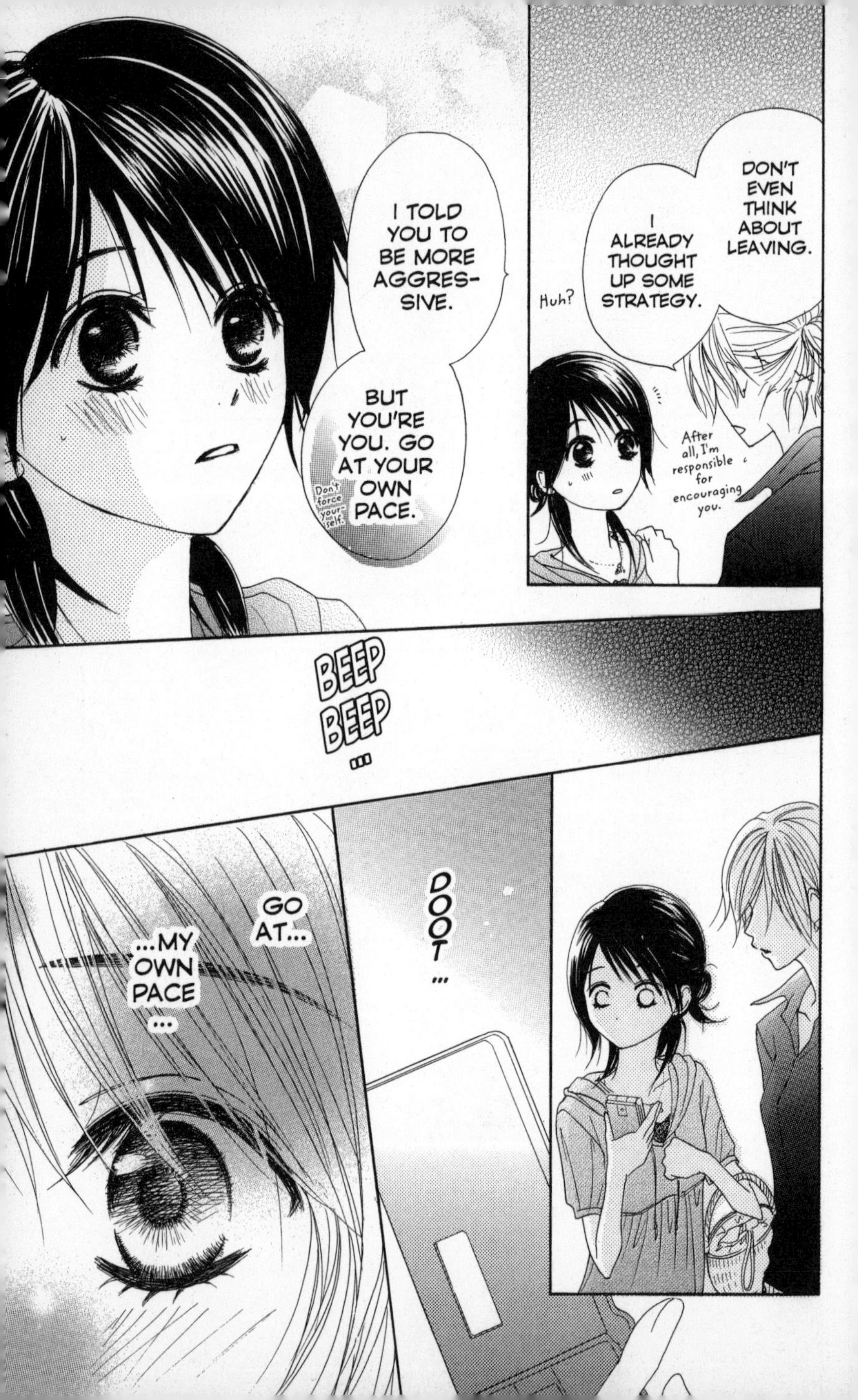
DON'T EVEN THINK ABOUT LEAVING.
I ALREADY THOUGHT UP SOME STRATEGY.
Huh?
After all, I'm responsible for encouraging you.
I TOLD YOU TO BE MORE AGGRES-SIVE.
BUT YOU'RE YOU. GO AT YOUR OWN PACE.
Don't force your-self.
BEEP BEEP...
DOOT...
GO AT...
...MY OWN PACE...

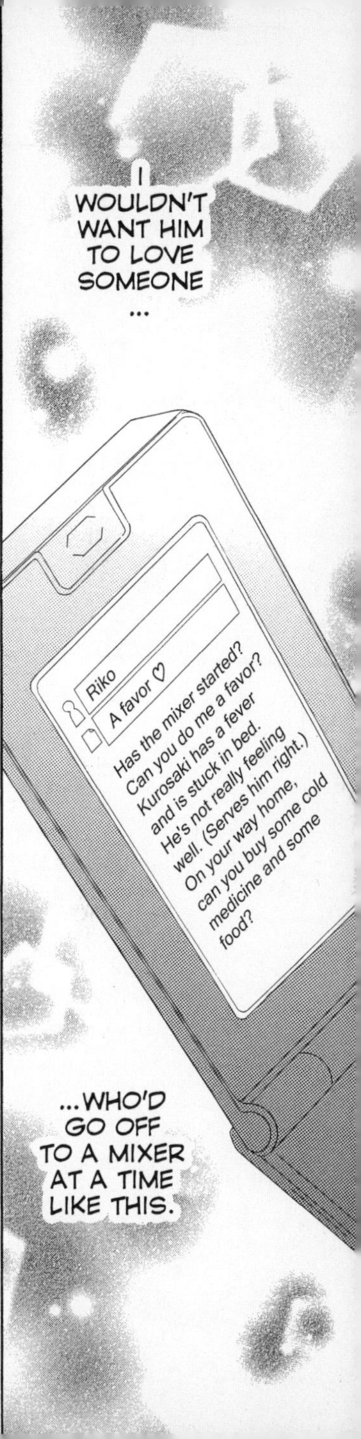
I WOULDN'T WANT HIM TO LOVE SOMEONE ...
Riko
A favor ♡
Has the mixer started? Can you do me a favor? Kurosaki has a fever and is stuck in bed. He's not really feeling well. (Serves him right.) On your way home, can you buy some cold medicine and some food?
...WHO'D GO OFF TO A MIXER AT A TIME LIKE THIS.

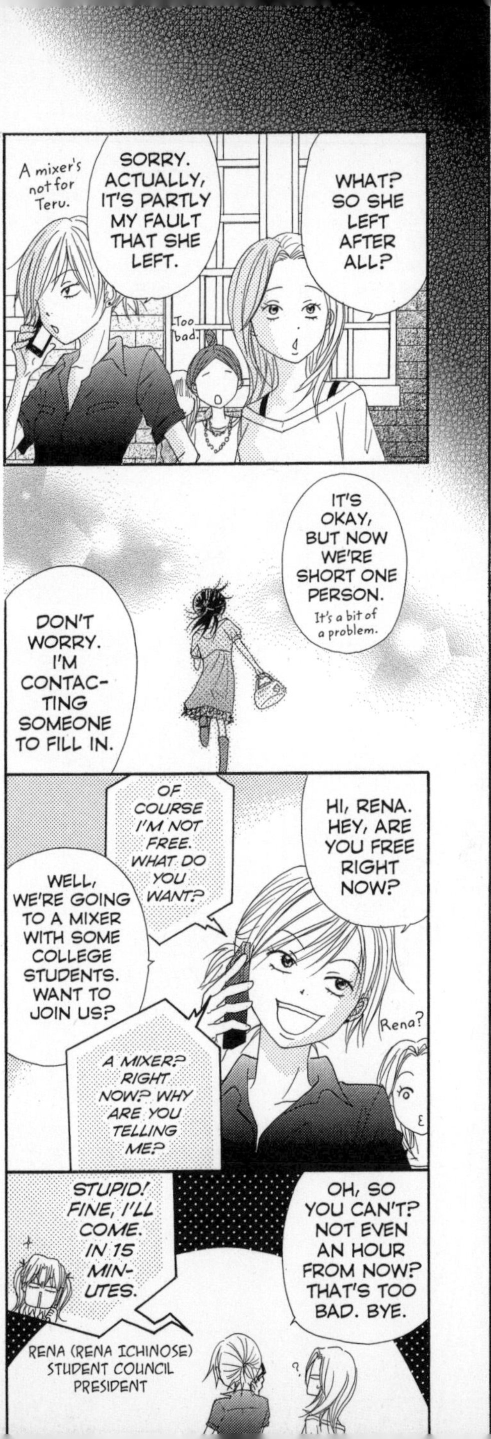
WHAT? SO SHE LEFT AFTER ALL?
SORRY. ACTUALLY, IT'S PARTLY MY FAULT THAT SHE LEFT.
Too bad.
A mixer's not for Teru.
IT'S OKAY, BUT NOW WE'RE SHORT ONE PERSON.
It's a bit of a problem.
DON'T WORRY. I'M CONTAC-TING SOMEONE TO FILL IN.
HI, RENA. HEY, ARE YOU FREE RIGHT NOW?
OF COURSE I'M NOT FREE. WHAT DO YOU WANT?
WELL, WE'RE GOING TO A MIXER WITH SOME COLLEGE STUDENTS. WANT TO JOIN US?
Rena?
A MIXER? RIGHT NOW? WHY ARE YOU TELLING ME?
OH, SO YOU CAN'T? NOT EVEN AN HOUR FROM NOW? THAT'S TOO BAD. BYE.
STUPID! FINE, I'LL COME. IN 15 MIN-UTES.
RENA (RENA ICHINOSE) STUDENT COUNCIL PRESIDENT

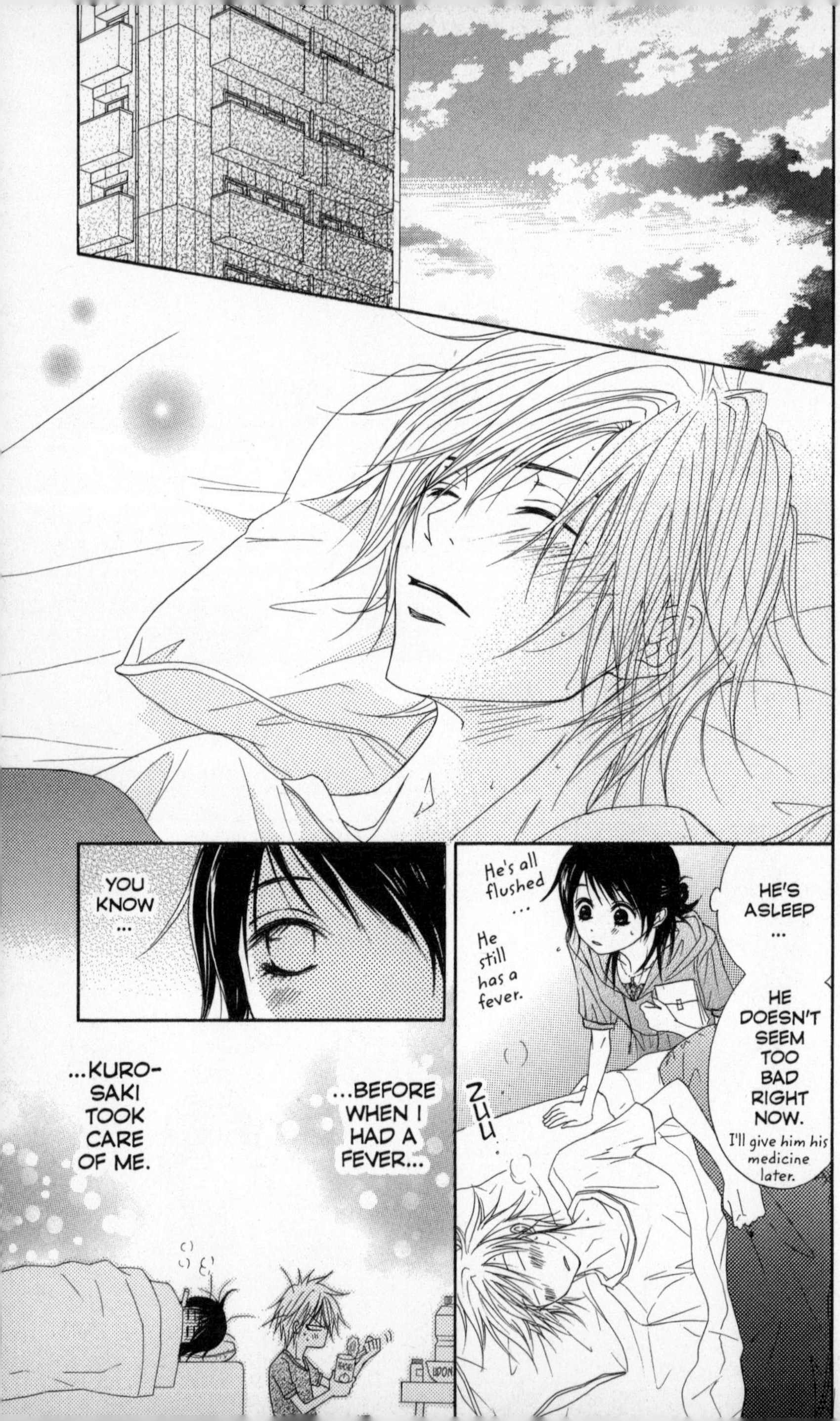
HE'S ASLEEP...
HE DOESN'T SEEM TOO BAD RIGHT NOW.
I'll give him his medicine later.
He's all flushed...
He still has a fever.
ZUU
YOU KNOW...
...BEFORE WHEN I HAD A FEVER...
...KURO-SAKI TOOK CARE OF ME.

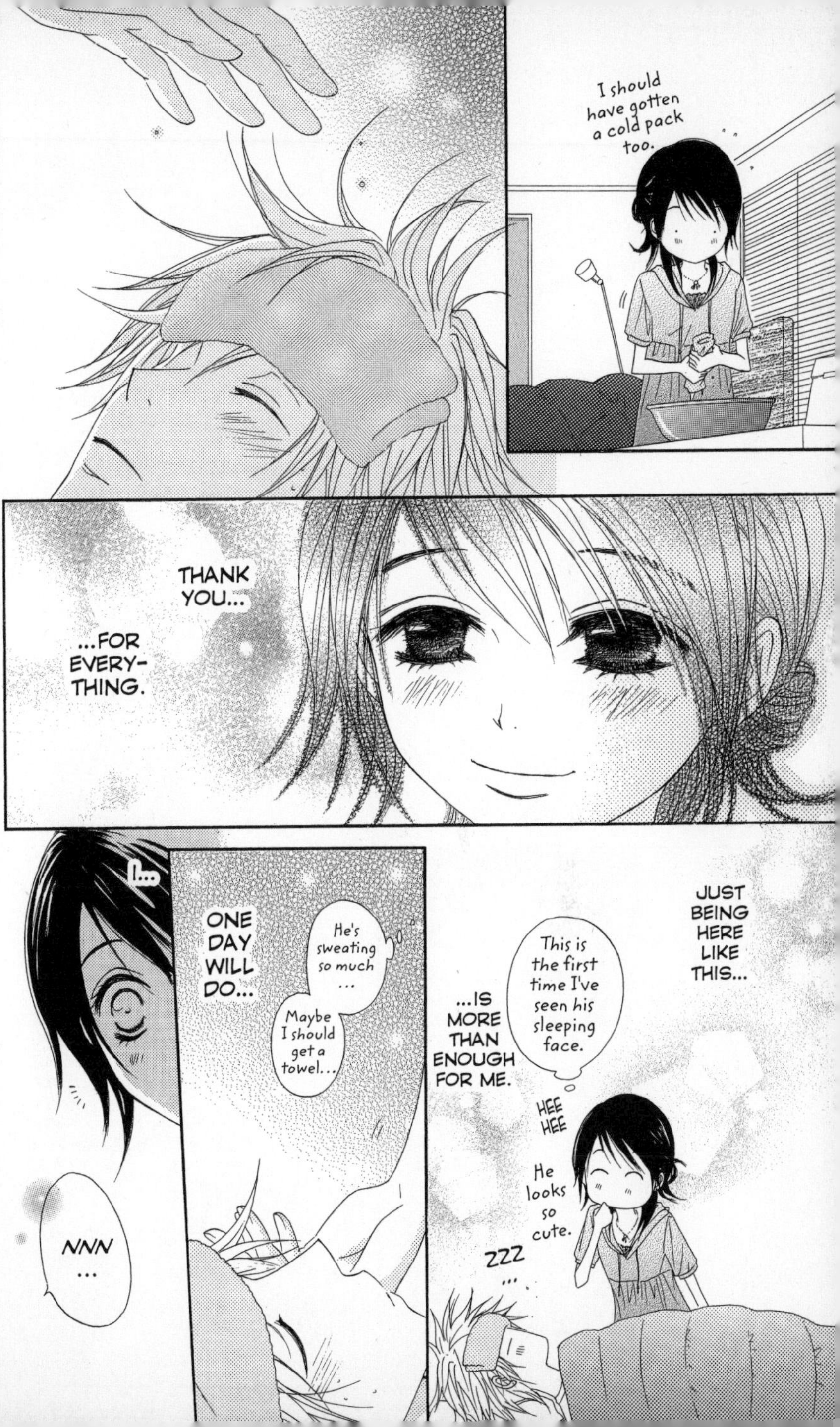
I should have gotten a cold pack too.
THANK YOU...
...FOR EVERYTHING.
JUST BEING HERE LIKE THIS...
This is the first time I've seen his sleeping face.
...IS MORE THAN ENOUGH FOR ME.
HEE HEE
He looks so cute.
ZZZ...
ONE DAY WILL DO...
He's sweating so much ...
Maybe I should get a towel...
!...
NNN ...

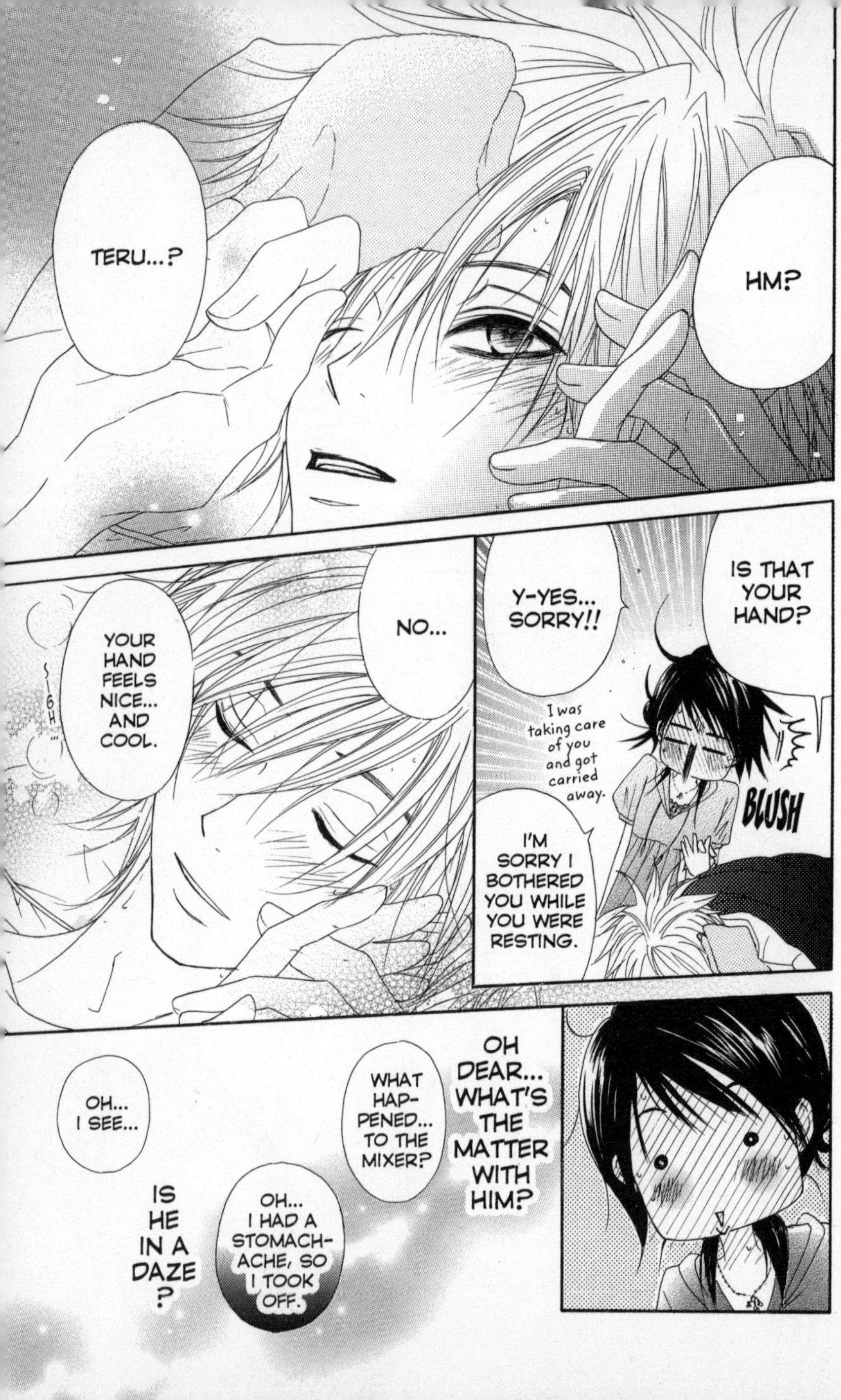
HM?
TERU...?
IS THAT YOUR HAND?
Y-YES... SORRY!!
I was taking care of you and got carried away.
BLUSH
I'M SORRY I BOTHERED YOU WHILE YOU WERE RESTING.
NO...
YOUR HAND FEELS NICE... AND COOL.
SIGH...
OH DEAR... WHAT'S THE MATTER WITH HIM?
WHAT HAPPENED... TO THE MIXER?
OH... I SEE...
OH... I HAD A STOMACHACHE, SO I TOOK OFF.
IS HE IN A DAZE?

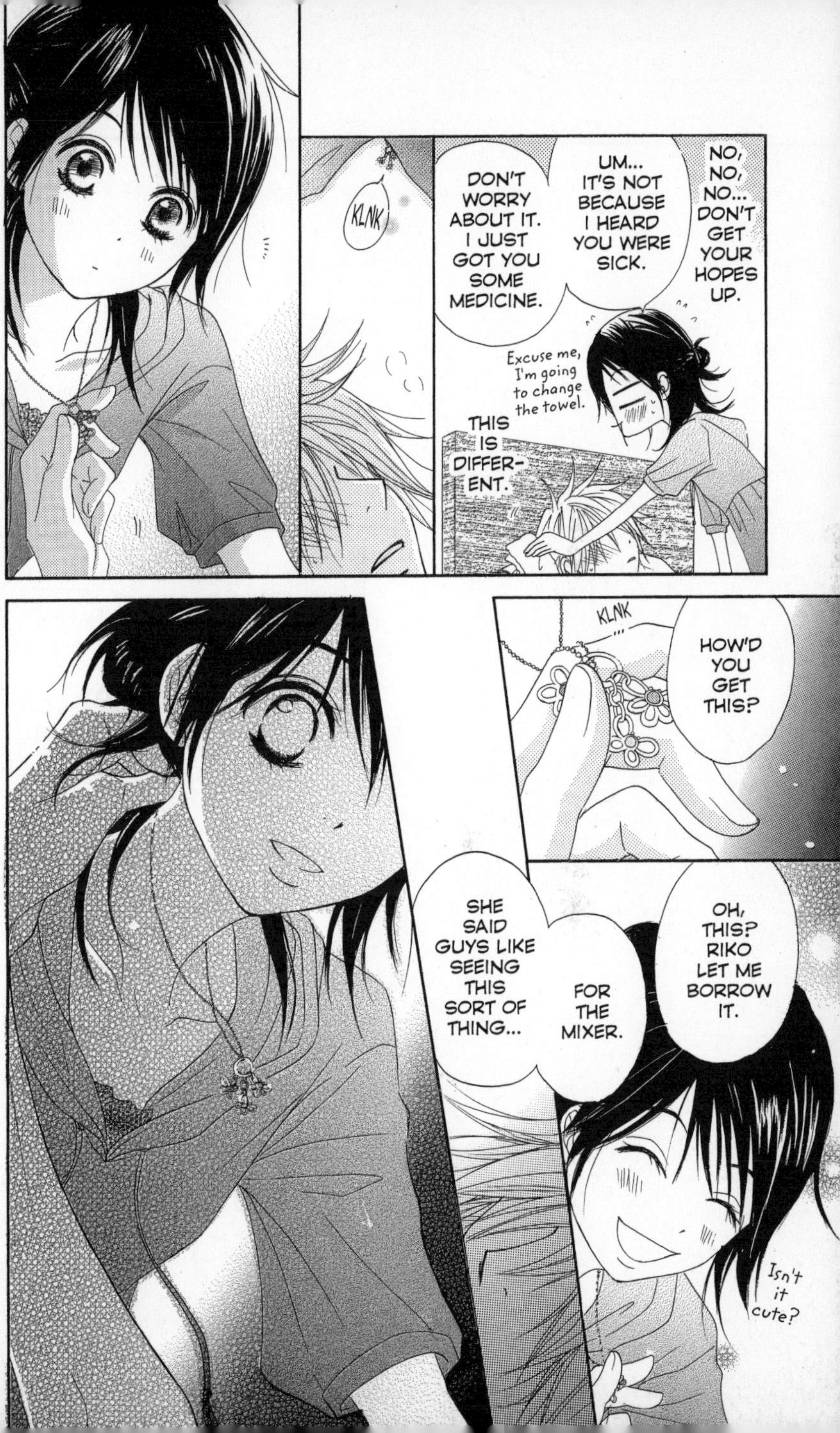

NO, NO, NO... DON'T GET YOUR HOPES UP.
UM... IT'S NOT BECAUSE I HEARD YOU WERE SICK.
DON'T WORRY ABOUT IT. I JUST GOT YOU SOME MEDICINE.
Excuse me, I'm going to change the towel.
THIS IS DIFFERENT.
KLNK
KLNK
HOW'D YOU GET THIS?
OH, THIS? RIKO LET ME BORROW IT.
FOR THE MIXER.
SHE SAID GUYS LIKE SEEING THIS SORT OF THING...
Isn't it cute?

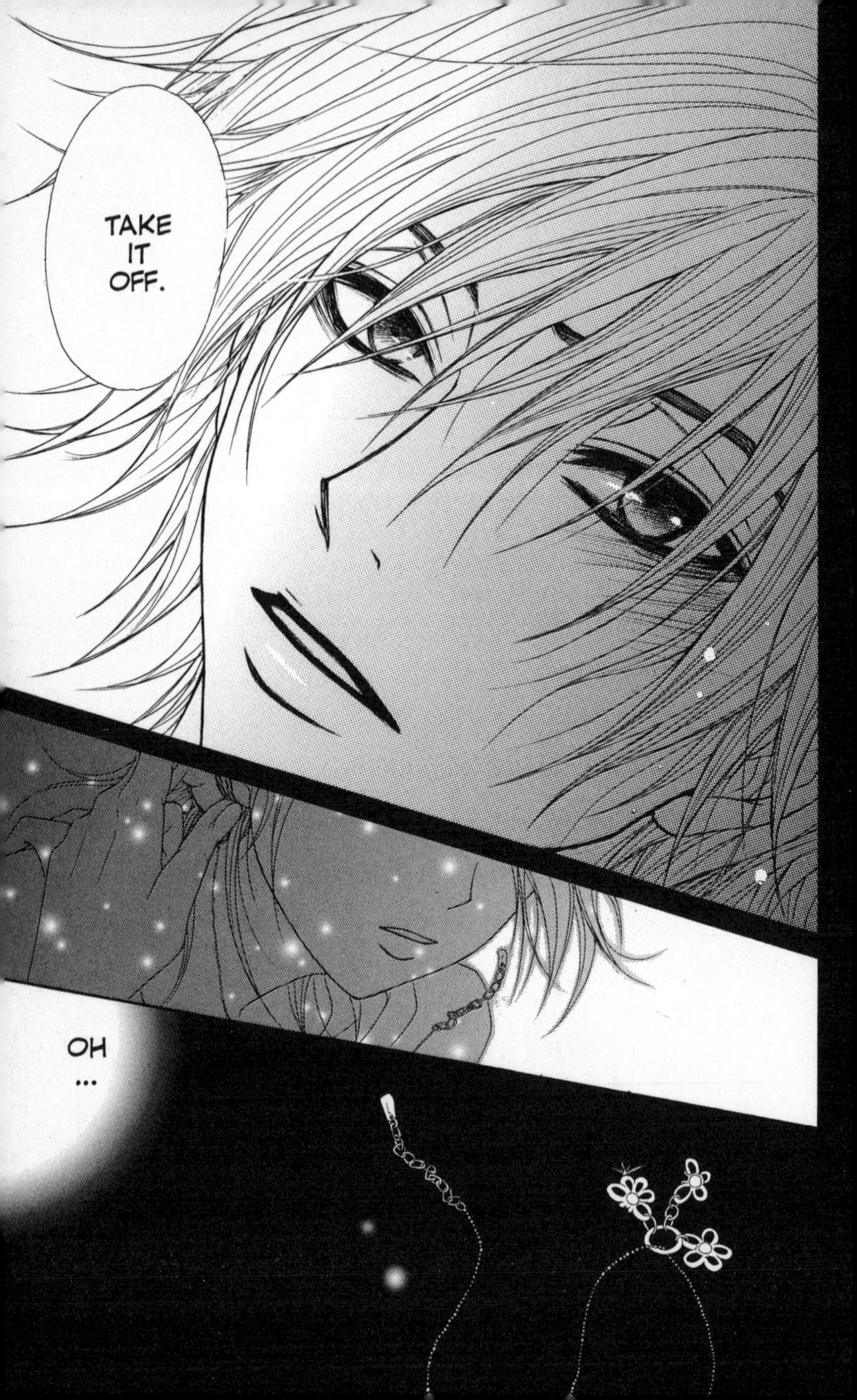
TAKE IT OFF.
OH ...

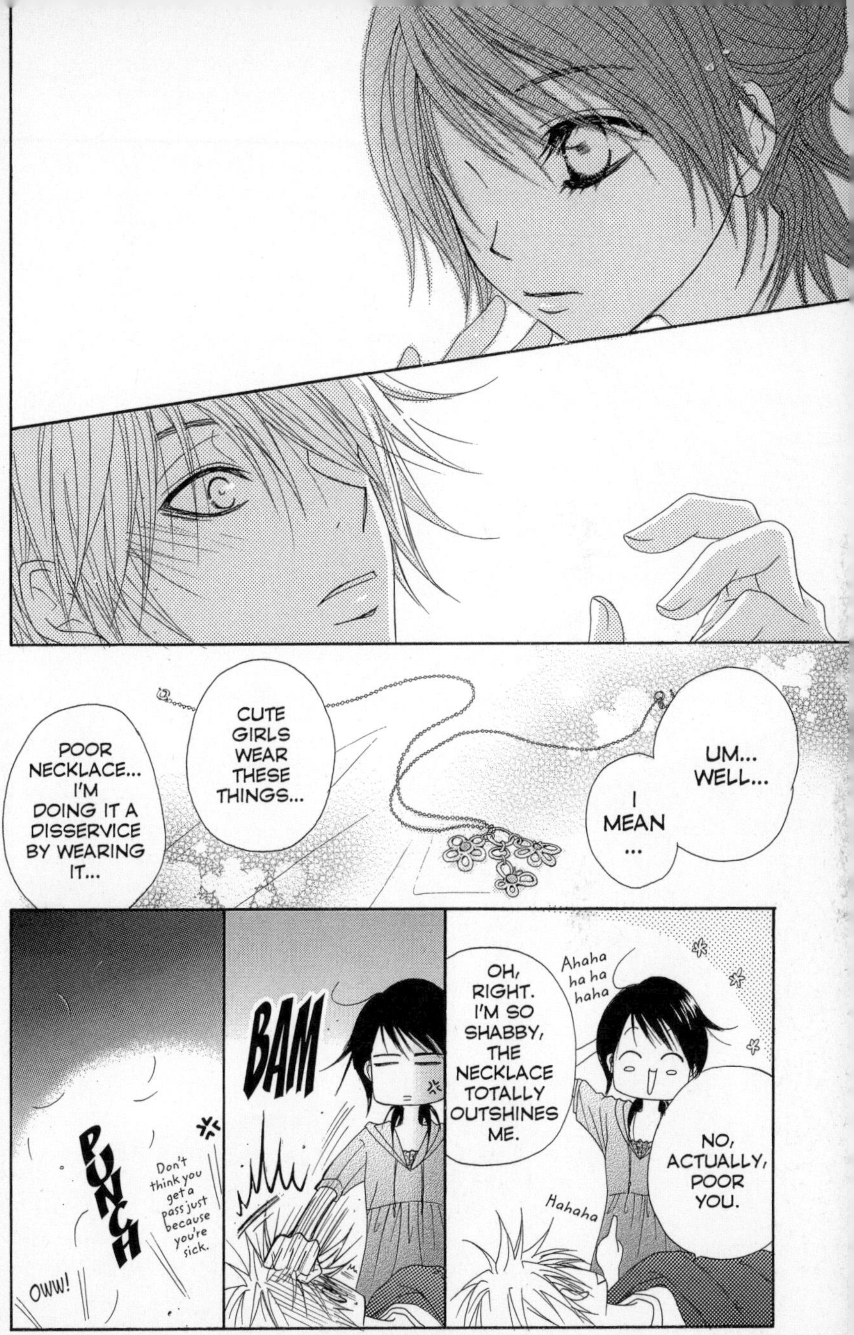
UM... WELL...
I MEAN ...
CUTE GIRLS WEAR THESE THINGS...
POOR NECKLACE... I'M DOING IT A DISSERVICE BY WEARING IT...
Ahaha ha ha haha
OH, RIGHT. I'M SO SHABBY, THE NECKLACE TOTALLY OUTSHINES ME.
NO, ACTUALLY, POOR YOU.
Hahaha
BAM
PUNCH
Don't think you get a pass just because you're sick.
OWW!

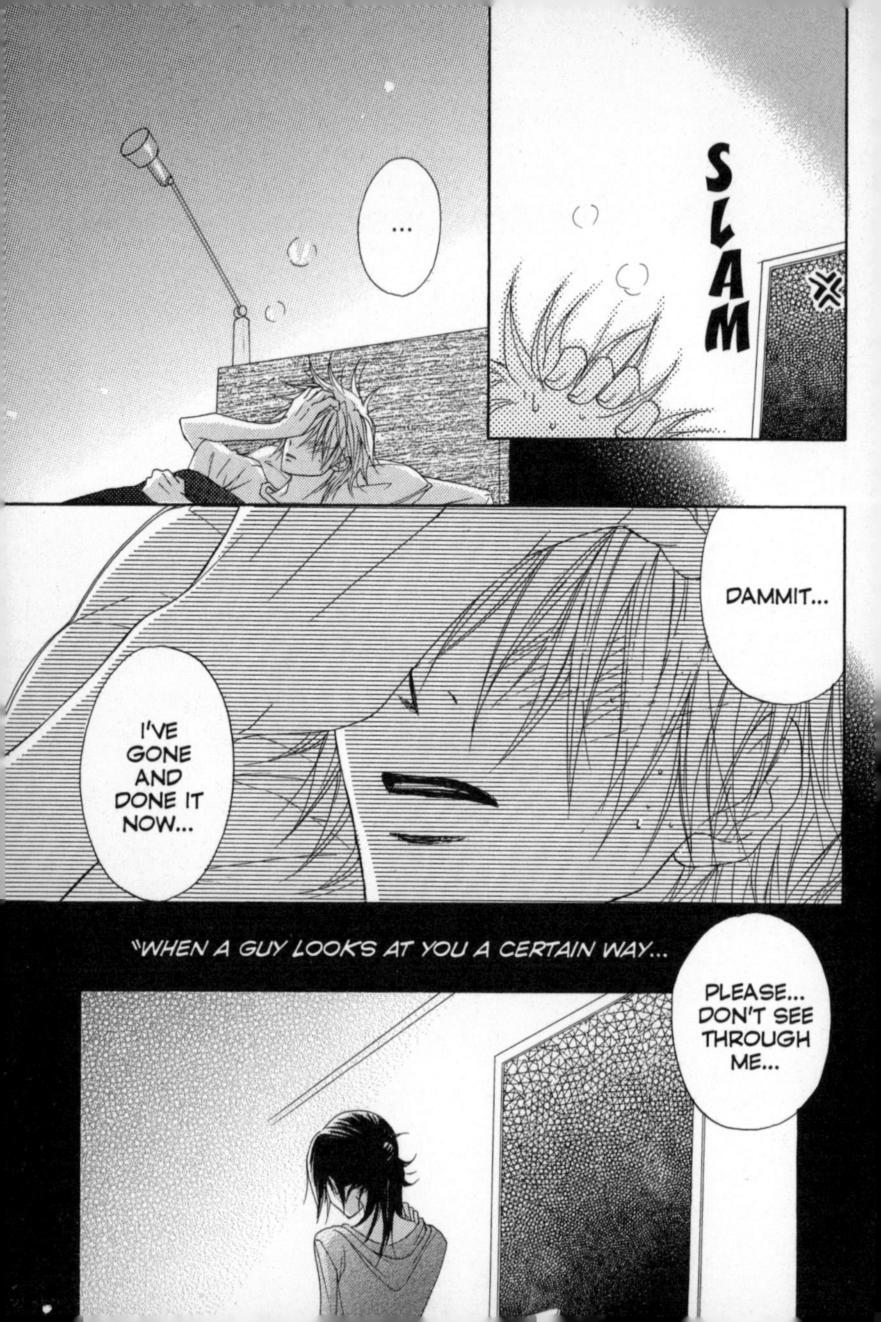
SLAM
...
DAMMIT...
I'VE GONE AND DONE IT NOW...
"WHEN A GUY LOOKS AT YOU A CERTAIN WAY...
PLEASE... DON'T SEE THROUGH ME...

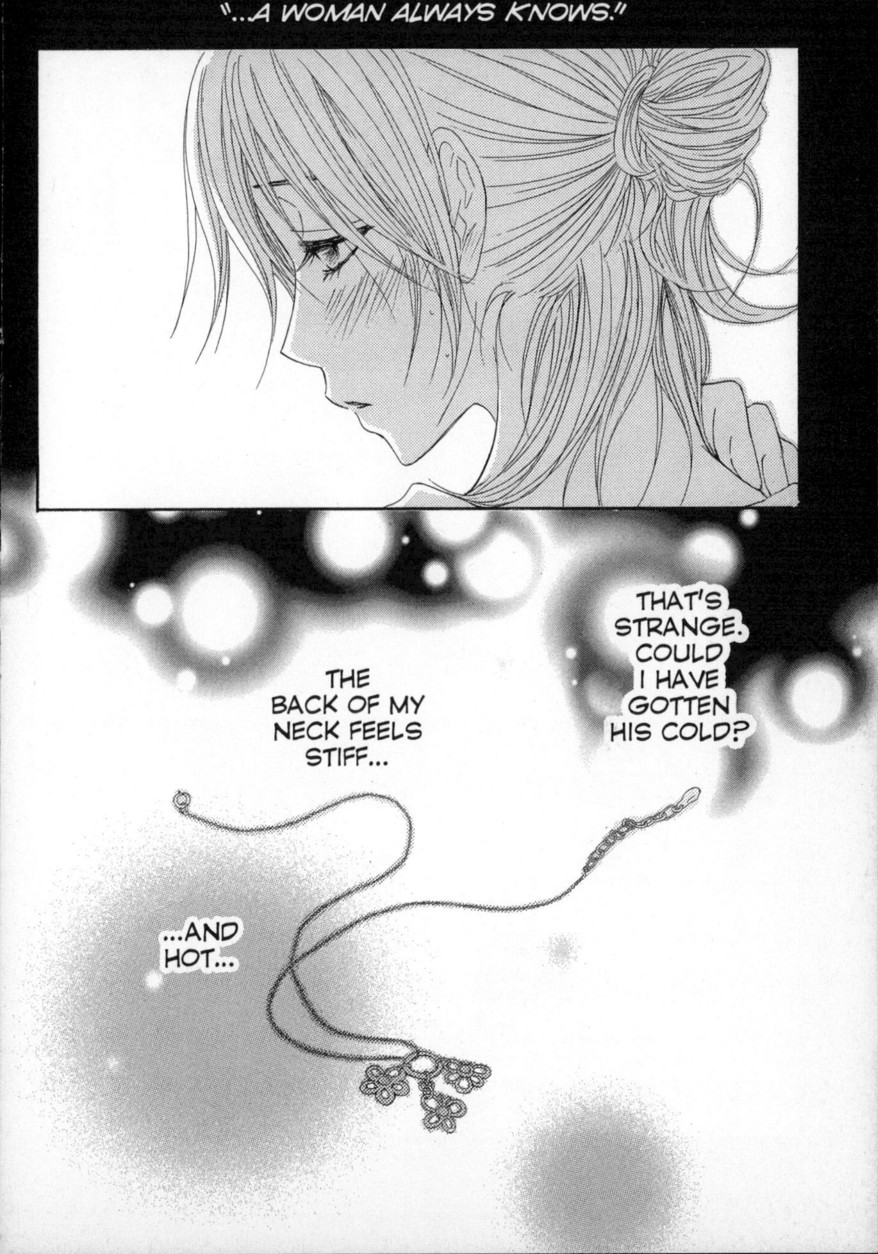
"...A WOMAN ALWAYS KNOWS."
THAT'S STRANGE. COULD I HAVE GOTTEN HIS COLD?
THE BACK OF MY NECK FEELS STIFF...
...AND HOT...

CHAPTER 17: THE NAME OF THAT FLOWER

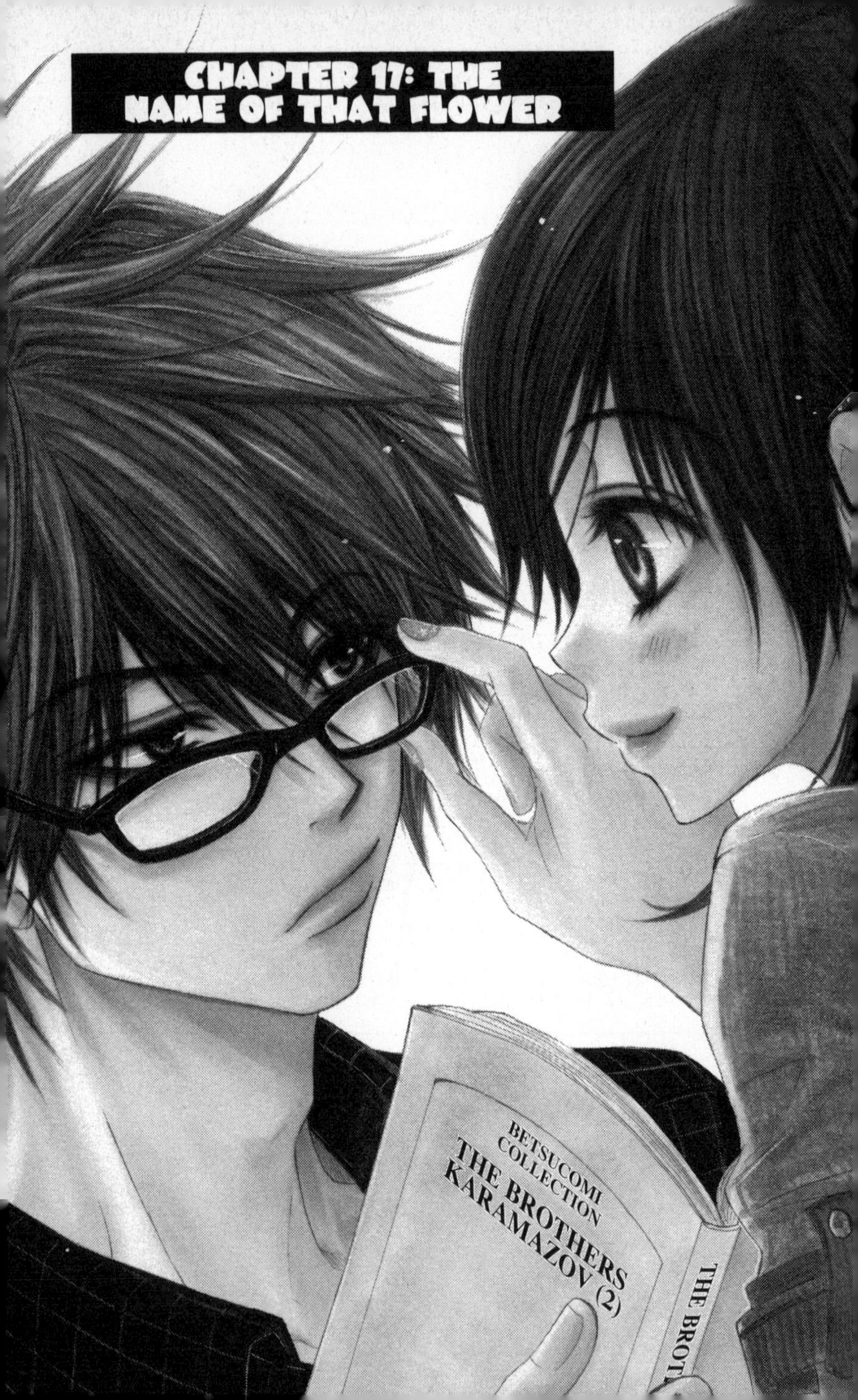
BETSUCOMI COLLECTION
THE BROTHERS KARAMAZOV (2)
THE BROT

CREATED BY: YASUKO (EVERYTHING IS HANDWRITTEN)

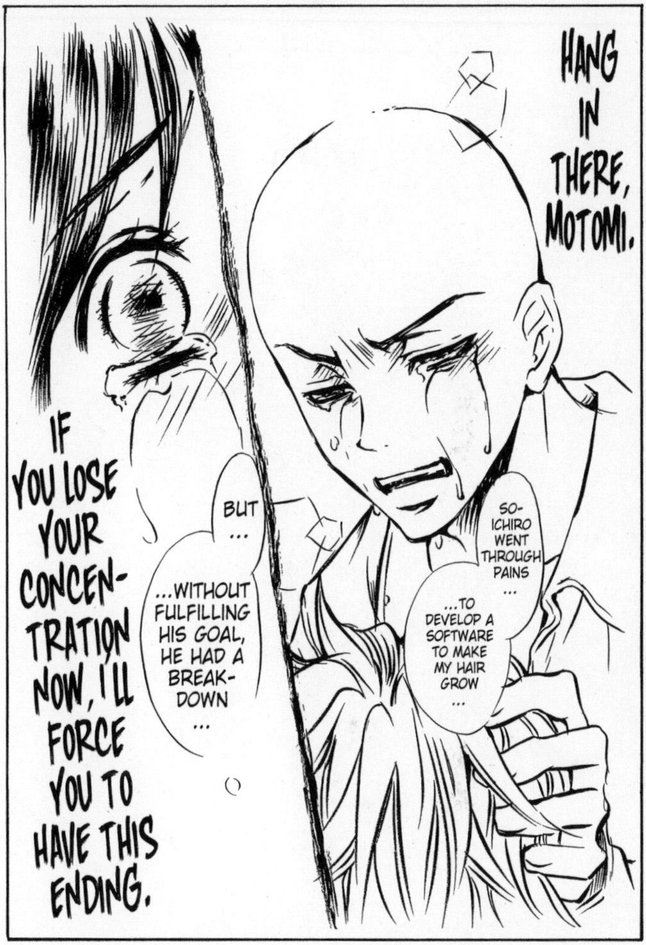
HANG IN THERE, MOTOMI.
SO-ICHIRO WENT THROUGH PAINS ...
...TO DEVELOP A SOFTWARE TO MAKE MY HAIR GROW ...
BUT ...
...WITHOUT FULFILLING HIS GOAL, HE HAD A BREAK-DOWN ...
IF YOU LOSE YOUR CONCEN-TRATION NOW, I'LL FORCE YOU TO HAVE THIS ENDING.

MY WORK WASN'T GOING WELL, AND I THOUGHT I'D HAVE TO COMMIT RITUAL SUICIDE... DURING THAT HELLISH TIME, I RECEIVED THIS FROM YASUKO-SAMA WHO IS A MANGA ARTIST FOR *BETSUCOMI*.
THIS ONE-PAGE MANGA (OR RATHER, DRAWING) GAVE ME THE STRENGTH TO KEEP ON LIVING.
IT IS WITH SINCERE GRATITUDE THAT I PUBLISH THIS HERE.

Anyway, what kind of software makes hair grow?

✿ YASUKO-SAN HAS HAD MANY WORKS PUBLISHED, INCLUDING HER LATEST WORK *HOLIDAY*. THEY ARE VERY POPULAR RIGHT NOW.
HER STORIES FLOW WITH CREATIVITY AND WARMTH. SHE IS AN AUTHOR WHOM I LIKE AND RESPECT DEEPLY. I'VE NEVER ONCE THOUGHT OF HER AS BEING A FOOL LIKE ME. NOT ONCE.

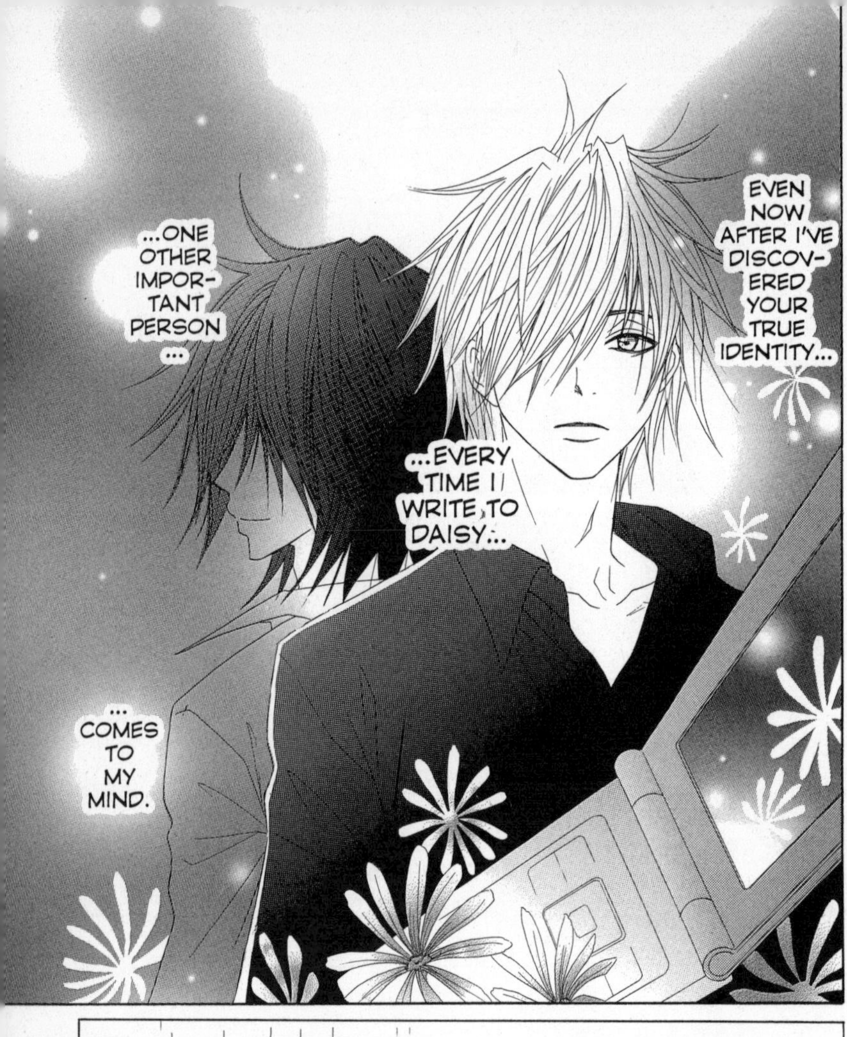
EVEN NOW AFTER I'VE DISCOV-ERED YOUR TRUE IDENTITY...
...EVERY TIME I WRITE TO DAISY...
...ONE OTHER IMPOR-TANT PERSON ...
... COMES TO MY MIND.

THIS IS NEITHER HERE NOR THERE, BUT DURING MOMENTS WHEN BALDY (KUROSAKI) SEEMS LOVE STRUCK BY TERU OR APPEARS TO BE EXPLODING INSIDE, MY EDITOR AND I USE THE TERM "TERU-TERU" TO DESCRIBE HIM. FOR EXAMPLE, BALDY TELLS TERU SHE SHOULD SHOW HER EARS IN CHAPTER 15, AND HE TAKES HER HAND AND WIPES IT IN CHAPTER 16... THESE MOMENTS ARE WHEN HE SEEMS "TERU-TERU."

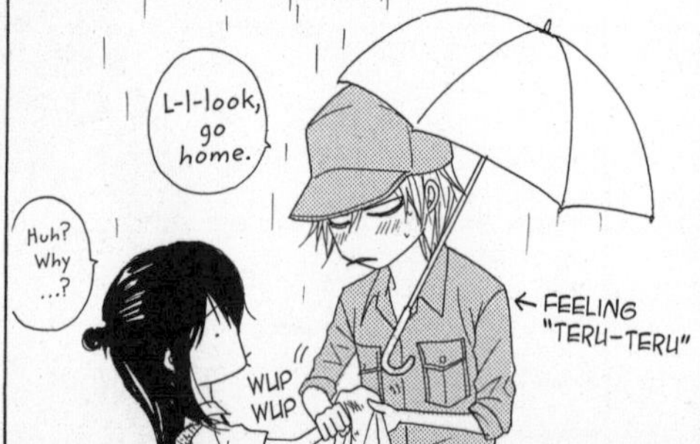
L-l-look, go home.
Huh? Why ...?
WUP WUP
← FEELING "TERU-TERU"

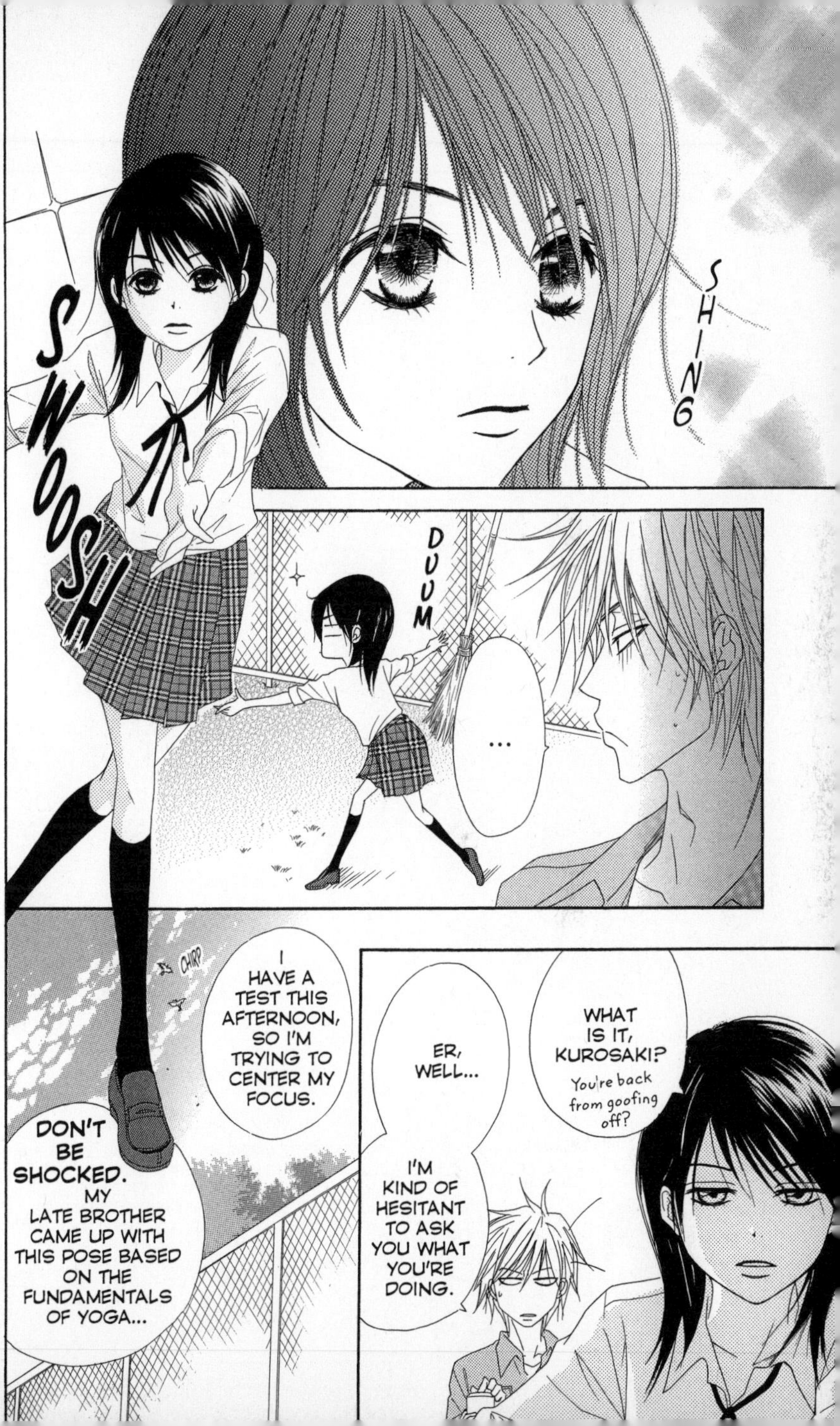
SHING
SWOOSH
DUUM
...
WHAT IS IT, KUROSAKI?
You're back from goofing off?
ER, WELL...
I'M KIND OF HESITANT TO ASK YOU WHAT YOU'RE DOING.
CHIRP
I HAVE A TEST THIS AFTERNOON, SO I'M TRYING TO CENTER MY FOCUS.
DON'T BE SHOCKED. MY LATE BROTHER CAME UP WITH THIS POSE BASED ON THE FUNDAMENTALS OF YOGA...

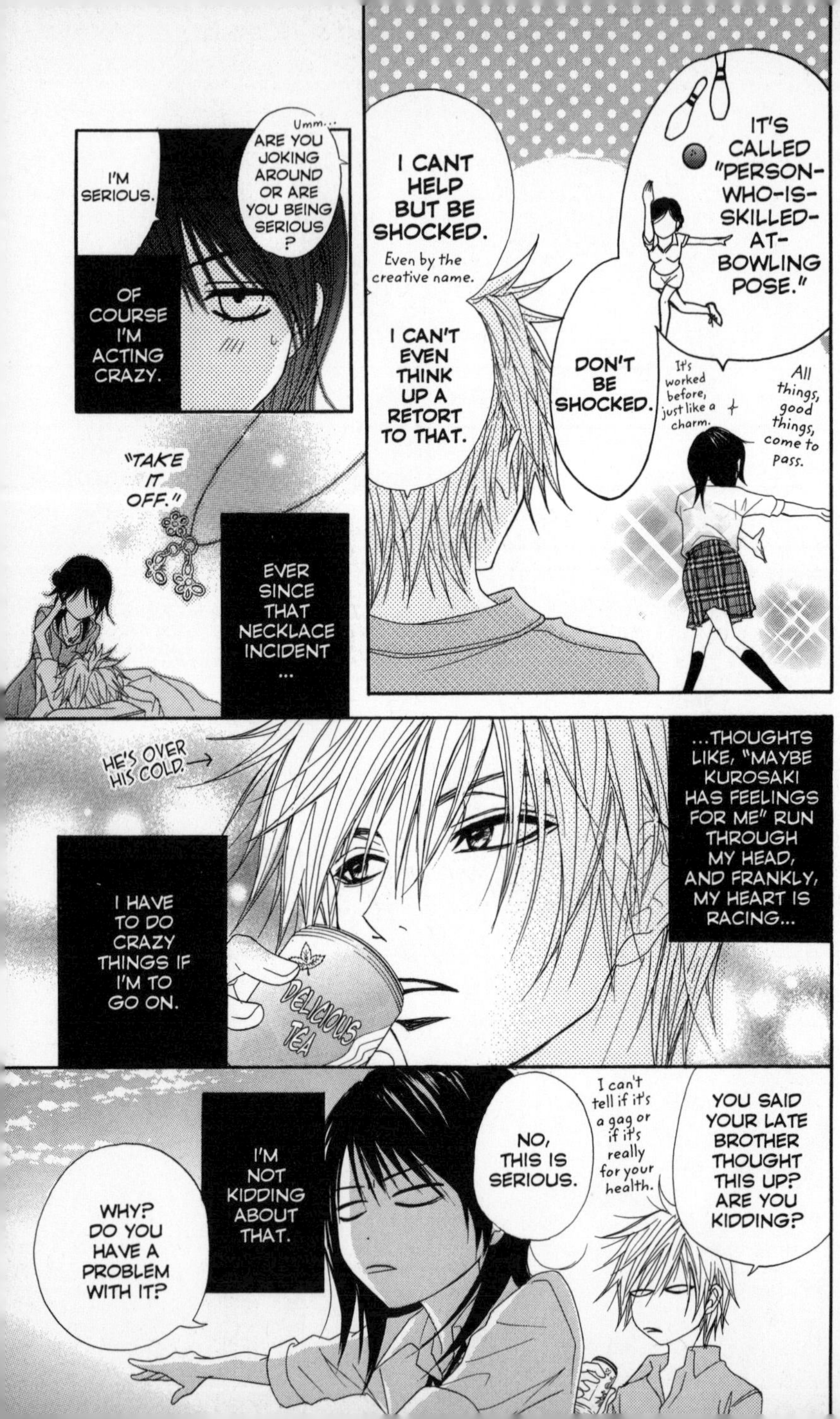
IT'S CALLED "PERSON-WHO-IS-SKILLED-AT-BOWLING POSE."
I CANT HELP BUT BE SHOCKED.
Even by the creative name.
DON'T BE SHOCKED.
It's worked before, just like a charm.
All things, good things, come to pass.
I CAN'T EVEN THINK UP A RETORT TO THAT.
Umm... ARE YOU JOKING AROUND OR ARE YOU BEING SERIOUS?
I'M SERIOUS.
OF COURSE I'M ACTING CRAZY.
"TAKE IT OFF."
EVER SINCE THAT NECKLACE INCIDENT...
...THOUGHTS LIKE, "MAYBE KUROSAKI HAS FEELINGS FOR ME" RUN THROUGH MY HEAD, AND FRANKLY, MY HEART IS RACING...
HE'S OVER HIS COLD.
DELICIOUS TEA
I HAVE TO DO CRAZY THINGS IF I'M TO GO ON.
YOU SAID YOUR LATE BROTHER THOUGHT THIS UP? ARE YOU KIDDING?
I can't tell if it's a gag or if it's really for your health.
NO, THIS IS SERIOUS.
I'M NOT KIDDING ABOUT THAT.
WHY? DO YOU HAVE A PROBLEM WITH IT?

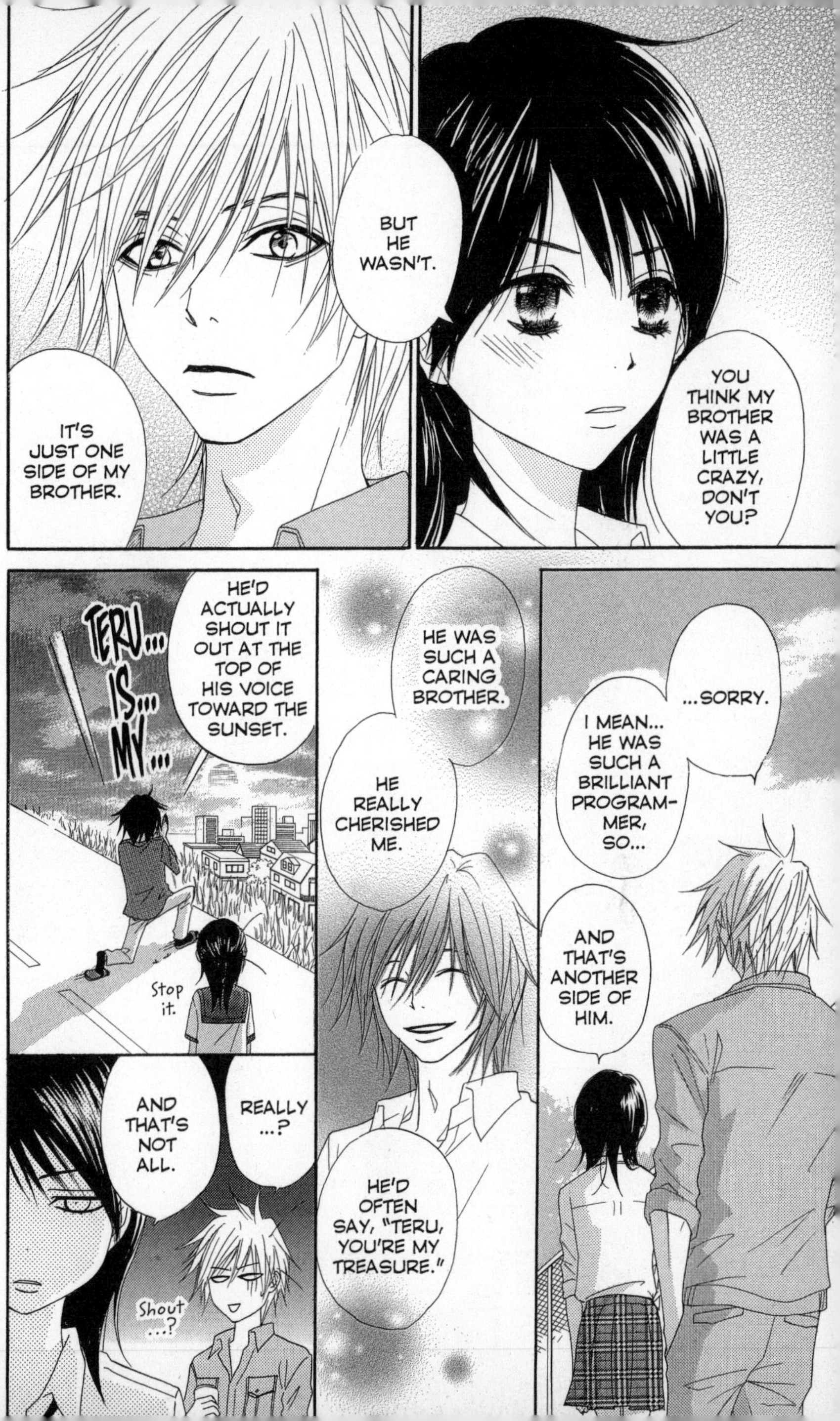
YOU THINK MY BROTHER WAS A LITTLE CRAZY, DON'T YOU?
BUT HE WASN'T.
IT'S JUST ONE SIDE OF MY BROTHER.
...SORRY.
I MEAN... HE WAS SUCH A BRILLIANT PROGRAM-MER, SO...
AND THAT'S ANOTHER SIDE OF HIM.
HE WAS SUCH A CARING BROTHER.
HE REALLY CHERISHED ME.
HE'D OFTEN SAY, "TERU, YOU'RE MY TREASURE."
HE'D ACTUALLY SHOUT IT OUT AT THE TOP OF HIS VOICE TOWARD THE SUNSET.
TERU... IS... MY...
Stop it.
REALLY ...?
AND THAT'S NOT ALL.
Shout ...?

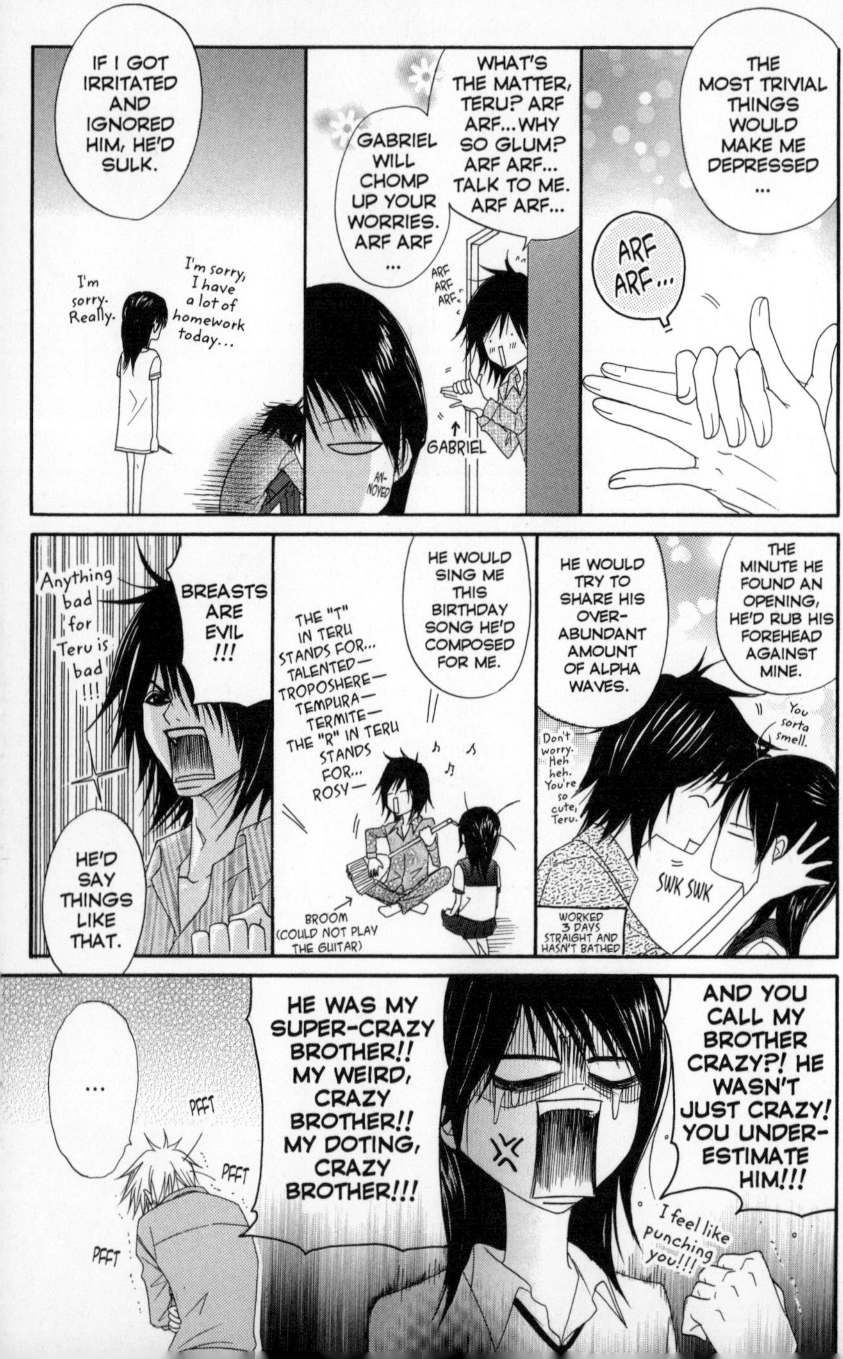
THE MOST TRIVIAL THINGS WOULD MAKE ME DEPRESSED ...
ARF ARF...
WHAT'S THE MATTER, TERU? ARF ARF... WHY SO GLUM? ARF ARF... TALK TO ME. ARF ARF...
GABRIEL WILL CHOMP UP YOUR WORRIES. ARF ARF ...
ARF ARF ARF...
GABRIEL
ANNOYED
IF I GOT IRRITATED AND IGNORED HIM, HE'D SULK.
I'm sorry, I have a lot of homework today...
I'm sorry. Really.
THE MINUTE HE FOUND AN OPENING, HE'D RUB HIS FOREHEAD AGAINST MINE.
HE WOULD TRY TO SHARE HIS OVER-ABUNDANT AMOUNT OF ALPHA WAVES.
You sorta smell.
Don't worry. Heh heh. You're so cute, Teru.
SWK SWK
WORKED 3 DAYS STRAIGHT AND HASN'T BATHED
HE WOULD SING ME THIS BIRTHDAY SONG HE'D COMPOSED FOR ME.
THE "T" IN TERU STANDS FOR... TALENTED— TROPOSHERE— TEMPURA— TERMITE— THE "R" IN TERU STANDS FOR... ROSY—
BROOM (COULD NOT PLAY THE GUITAR)
BREASTS ARE EVIL!!!
Anything bad for Teru is bad!!!
HE'D SAY THINGS LIKE THAT.
AND YOU CALL MY BROTHER CRAZY?! HE WASN'T JUST CRAZY! YOU UNDER-ESTIMATE HIM!!!
I feel like punching you!!!
HE WAS MY SUPER-CRAZY BROTHER!! MY WEIRD, CRAZY BROTHER!! MY DOTING, CRAZY BROTHER!!!
...
PFFT
PFFT
PFFT

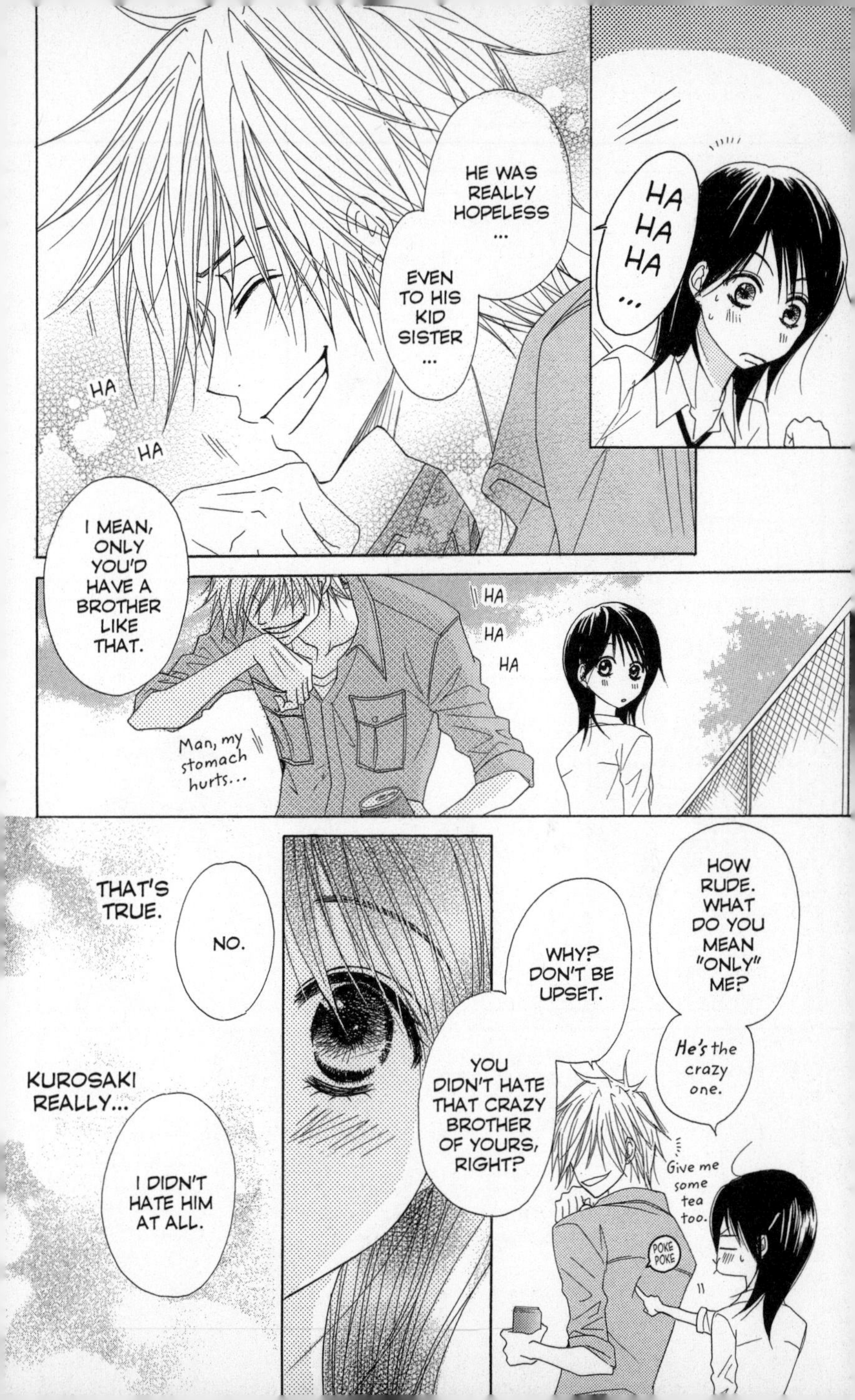
HA HA HA ...
HE WAS REALLY HOPELESS ...
EVEN TO HIS KID SISTER ...
HA
HA
I MEAN, ONLY YOU'D HAVE A BROTHER LIKE THAT.
HA
HA
HA
Man, my stomach hurts...
HOW RUDE. WHAT DO YOU MEAN "ONLY" ME?
He's the crazy one.
WHY? DON'T BE UPSET.
YOU DIDN'T HATE THAT CRAZY BROTHER OF YOURS, RIGHT?
Give me some tea too.
POKE POKE
NO.
I DIDN'T HATE HIM AT ALL.
THAT'S TRUE.
KUROSAKI REALLY...

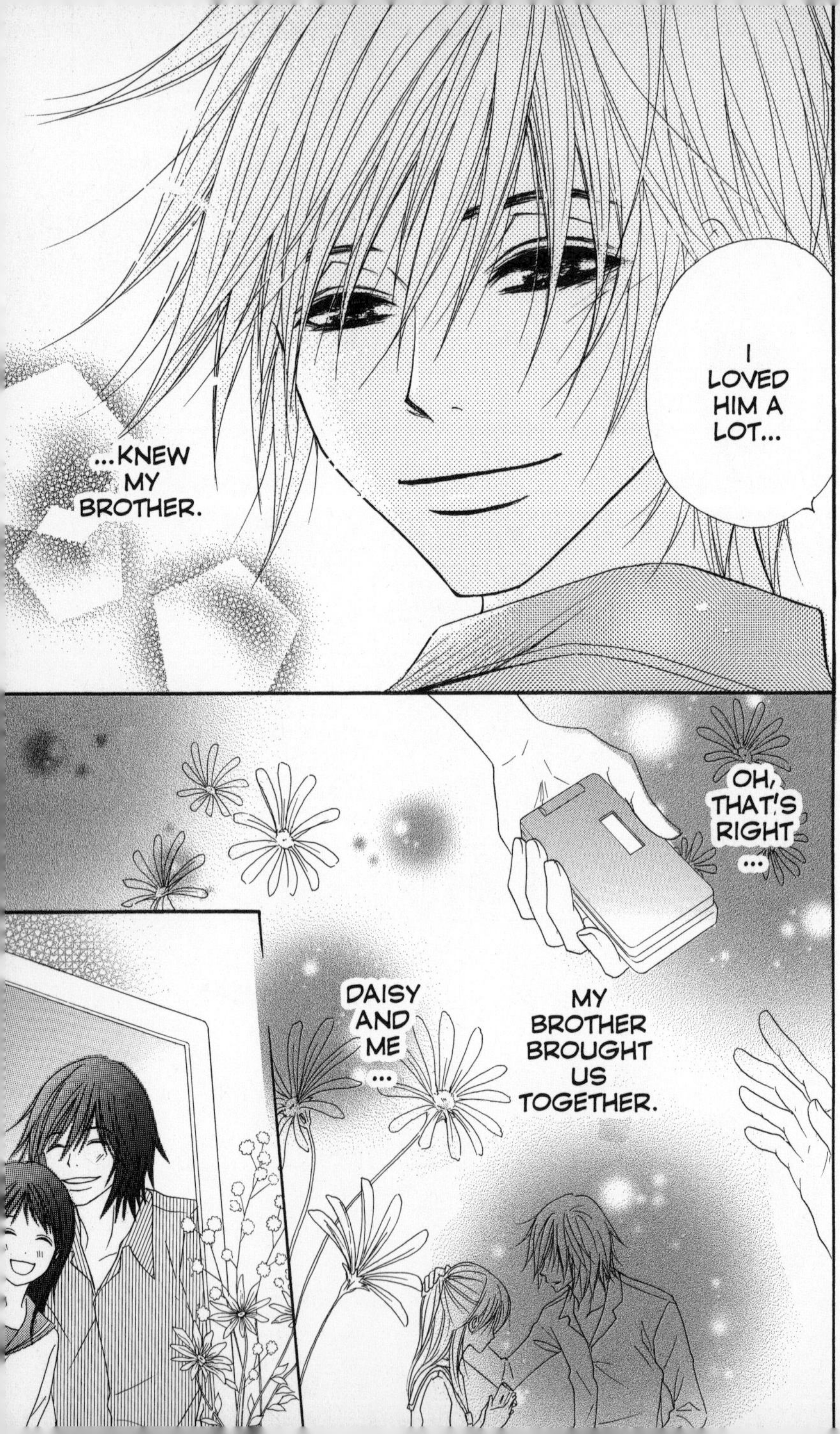
I LOVED HIM A LOT...
...KNEW MY BROTHER.
OH, THAT'S RIGHT...
MY BROTHER BROUGHT US TOGETHER.
DAISY AND ME...

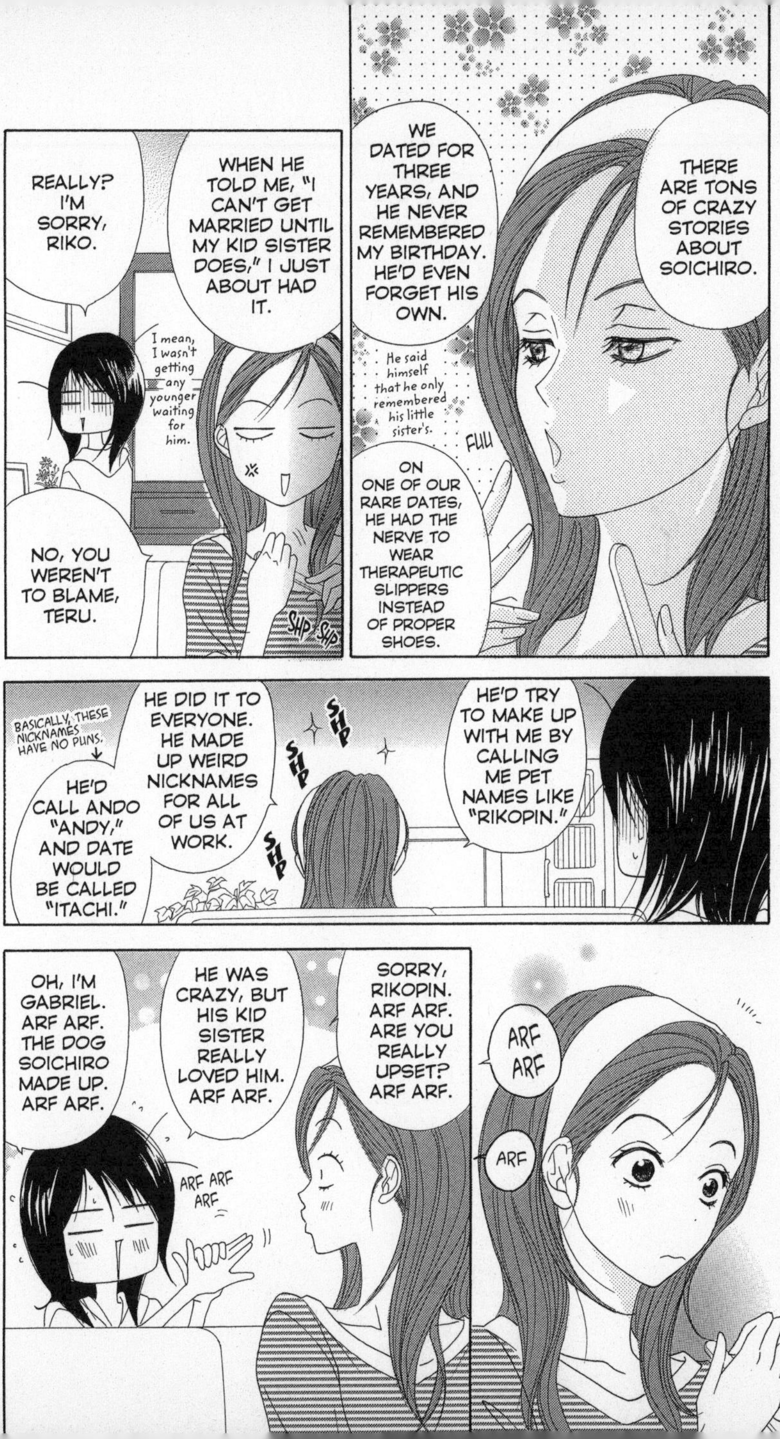
THERE ARE TONS OF CRAZY STORIES ABOUT SOICHIRO.
WE DATED FOR THREE YEARS, AND HE NEVER REMEMBERED MY BIRTHDAY. HE'D EVEN FORGET HIS OWN.
He said himself that he only remembered his little sister's.
FUU
ON ONE OF OUR RARE DATES, HE HAD THE NERVE TO WEAR THERAPEUTIC SLIPPERS INSTEAD OF PROPER SHOES.
WHEN HE TOLD ME, "I CAN'T GET MARRIED UNTIL MY KID SISTER DOES," I JUST ABOUT HAD IT.
REALLY? I'M SORRY, RIKO.
I mean, I wasn't getting any younger waiting for him.
NO, YOU WEREN'T TO BLAME, TERU.
SHP SHP
HE'D TRY TO MAKE UP WITH ME BY CALLING ME PET NAMES LIKE "RIKOPIN."
SHP
SHP
SHP
HE DID IT TO EVERYONE. HE MADE UP WEIRD NICKNAMES FOR ALL OF US AT WORK.
BASICALLY, THESE NICKNAMES HAVE NO PUNS.
HE'D CALL ANDO "ANDY," AND DATE WOULD BE CALLED "ITACHI."
ARF ARF
ARF
SORRY, RIKOPIN. ARF ARF. ARE YOU REALLY UPSET? ARF ARF.
HE WAS CRAZY, BUT HIS KID SISTER REALLY LOVED HIM. ARF ARF.
OH, I'M GABRIEL. ARF ARF. THE DOG SOICHIRO MADE UP. ARF ARF.
ARF ARF ARF

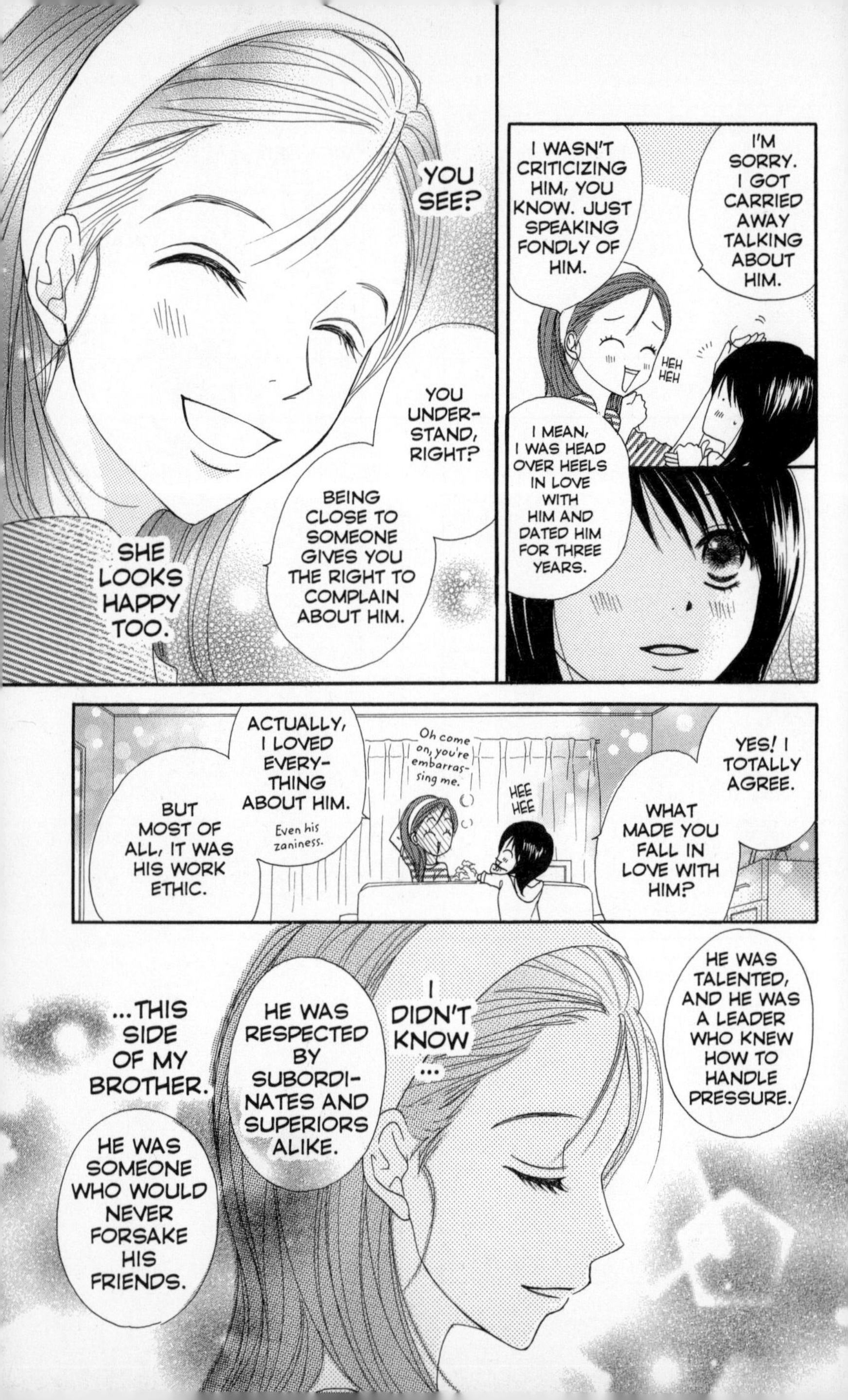
I'M SORRY. I GOT CARRIED AWAY TALKING ABOUT HIM.
I WASN'T CRITICIZING HIM, YOU KNOW. JUST SPEAKING FONDLY OF HIM.
HEH HEH
I MEAN, I WAS HEAD OVER HEELS IN LOVE WITH HIM AND DATED HIM FOR THREE YEARS.
YOU SEE?
YOU UNDERSTAND, RIGHT?
BEING CLOSE TO SOMEONE GIVES YOU THE RIGHT TO COMPLAIN ABOUT HIM.
SHE LOOKS HAPPY TOO.
YES! I TOTALLY AGREE.
WHAT MADE YOU FALL IN LOVE WITH HIM?
HEE HEE
Oh come on, you're embarrassing me.
ACTUALLY, I LOVED EVERYTHING ABOUT HIM.
Even his zaniness.
BUT MOST OF ALL, IT WAS HIS WORK ETHIC.
HE WAS TALENTED, AND HE WAS A LEADER WHO KNEW HOW TO HANDLE PRESSURE.
I DIDN'T KNOW...
HE WAS RESPECTED BY SUBORDINATES AND SUPERIORS ALIKE.
...THIS SIDE OF MY BROTHER.
HE WAS SOMEONE WHO WOULD NEVER FORSAKE HIS FRIENDS.

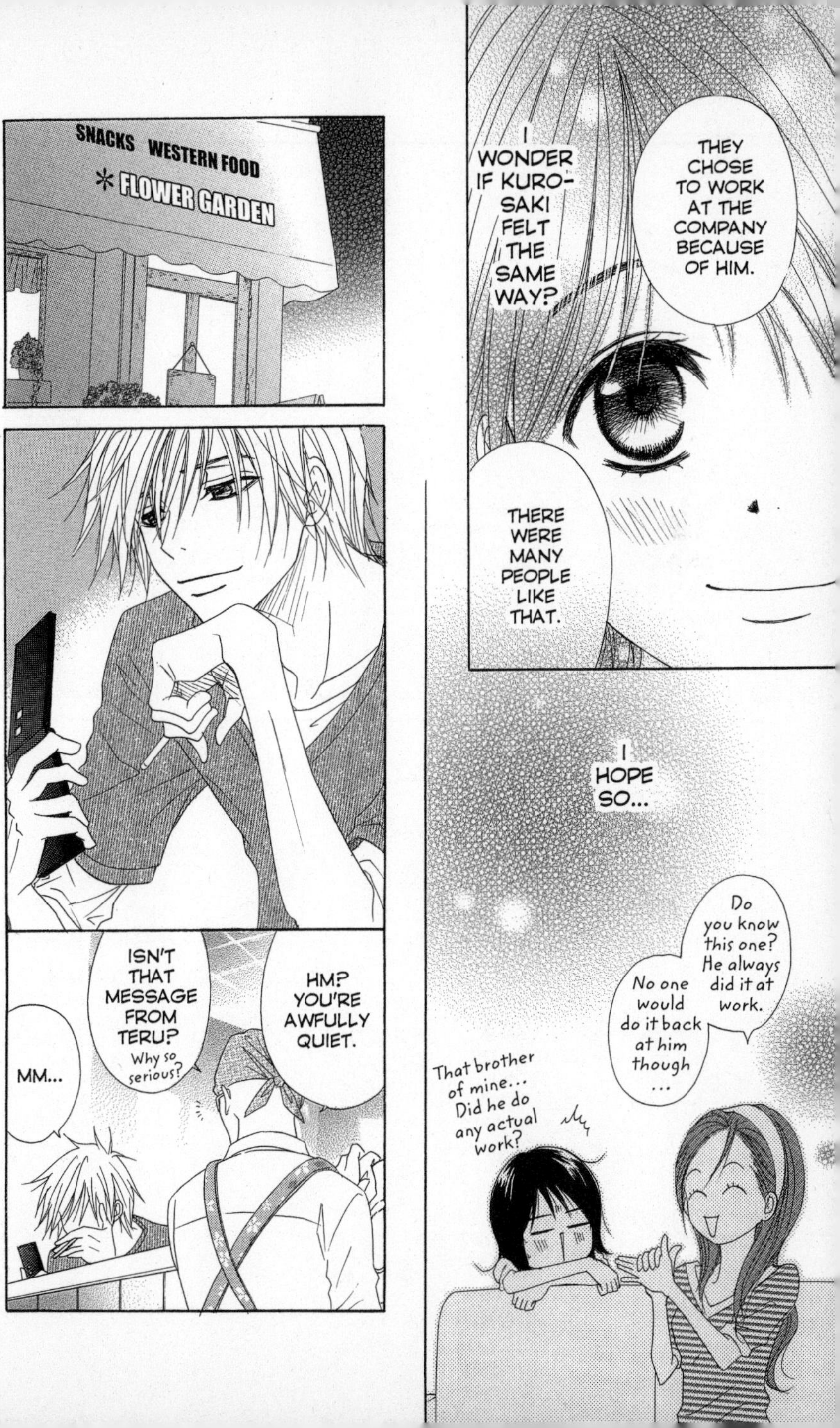
THEY CHOSE TO WORK AT THE COMPANY BECAUSE OF HIM.
I WONDER IF KURO-SAKI FELT THE SAME WAY?
THERE WERE MANY PEOPLE LIKE THAT.
I HOPE SO...
Do you know this one? He always did it at work.
No one would do it back at him though...
That brother of mine... Did he do any actual work?
SNACKS WESTERN FOOD
FLOWER GARDEN
HM? YOU'RE AWFULLY QUIET.
ISN'T THAT MESSAGE FROM TERU? Why so serious?
MM...

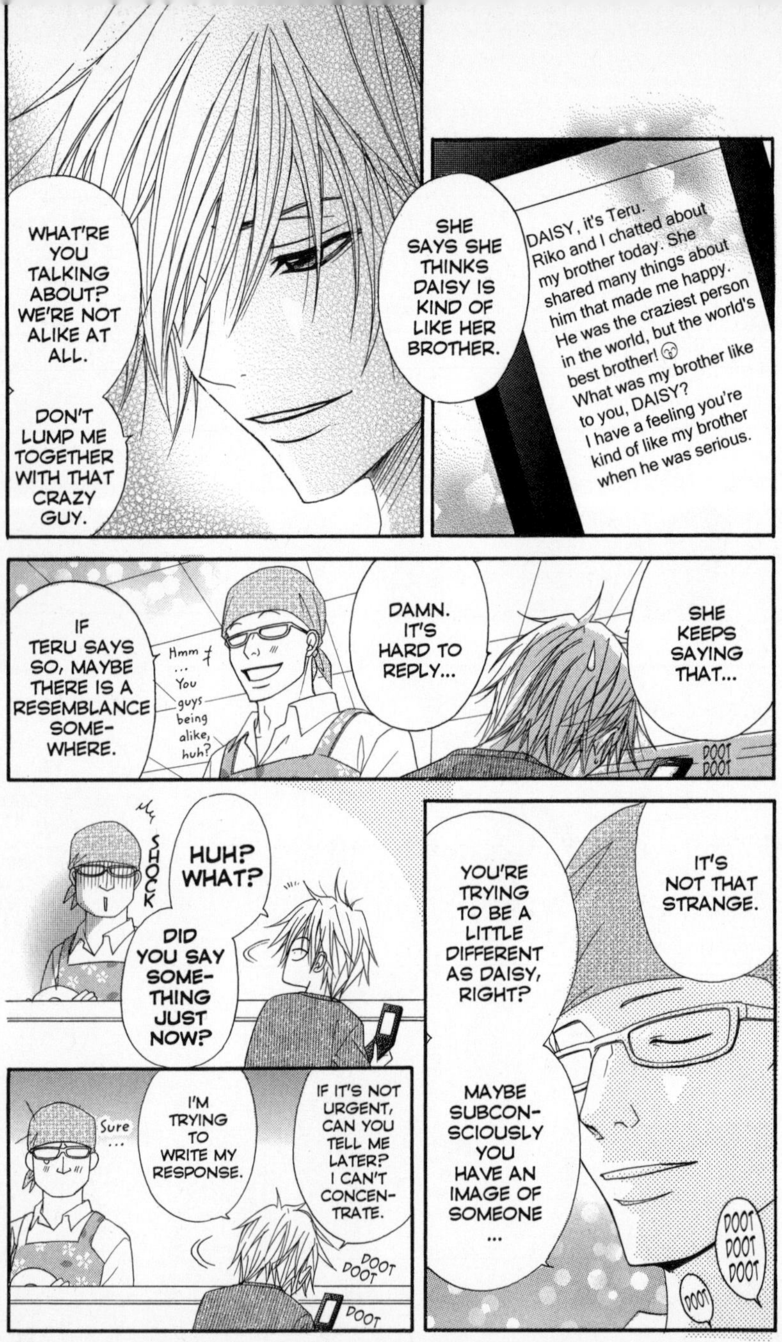
DAISY, it's Teru.
Riko and I chatted about my brother today. She shared many things about him that made me happy. He was the craziest person in the world, but the world's best brother!
What was my brother like to you, DAISY?
I have a feeling you're kind of like my brother when he was serious.
SHE SAYS SHE THINKS DAISY IS KIND OF LIKE HER BROTHER.
WHAT'RE YOU TALKING ABOUT? WE'RE NOT ALIKE AT ALL.
DON'T LUMP ME TOGETHER WITH THAT CRAZY GUY.
SHE KEEPS SAYING THAT...
DOOT DOOT
DAMN. IT'S HARD TO REPLY...
Hmm ... You guys being alike, huh?
IF TERU SAYS SO, MAYBE THERE IS A RESEMBLANCE SOME-WHERE.
IT'S NOT THAT STRANGE.
YOU'RE TRYING TO BE A LITTLE DIFFERENT AS DAISY, RIGHT?
MAYBE SUBCON-SCIOUSLY YOU HAVE AN IMAGE OF SOMEONE ...
DOOT DOOT DOOT
DOOT
SHOCK
HUH? WHAT?
DID YOU SAY SOME-THING JUST NOW?
IF IT'S NOT URGENT, CAN YOU TELL ME LATER? I CAN'T CONCEN-TRATE.
I'M TRYING TO WRITE MY RESPONSE.
Sure ...
DOOT DOOT
DOOT

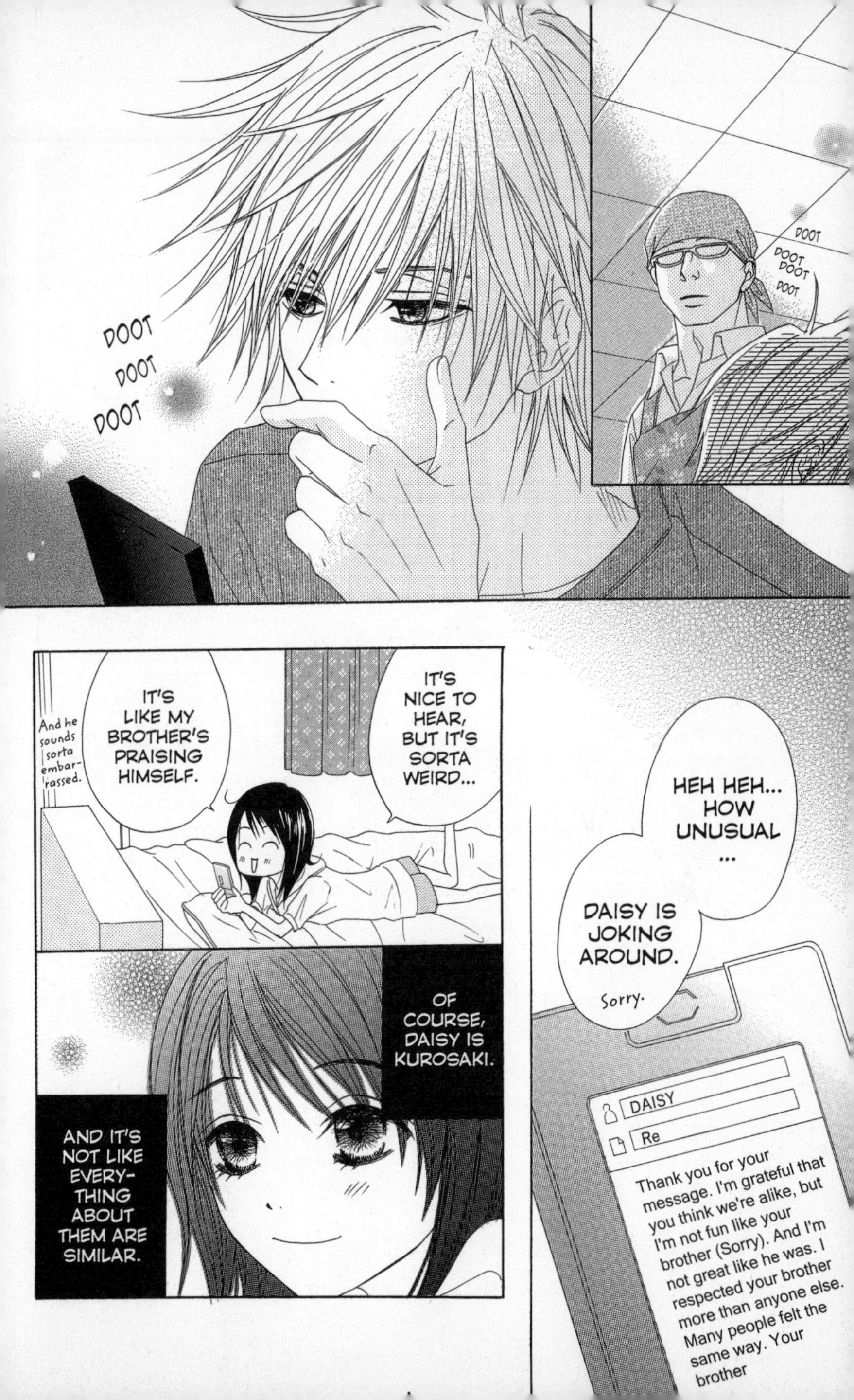
DOOT
DOOT
DOOT
DOOT
DOOT
DOOT
DOOT
HEH HEH... HOW UNUSUAL ...
DAISY IS JOKING AROUND.
Sorry.
DAISY
Re
Thank you for your message. I'm grateful that you think we're alike, but I'm not fun like your brother (Sorry). And I'm not great like he was. I respected your brother more than anyone else. Many people felt the same way. Your brother
IT'S NICE TO HEAR, BUT IT'S SORTA WEIRD...
IT'S LIKE MY BROTHER'S PRAISING HIMSELF.
And he sounds sorta embar-rassed.
OF COURSE, DAISY IS KUROSAKI.
AND IT'S NOT LIKE EVERY-THING ABOUT THEM ARE SIMILAR.

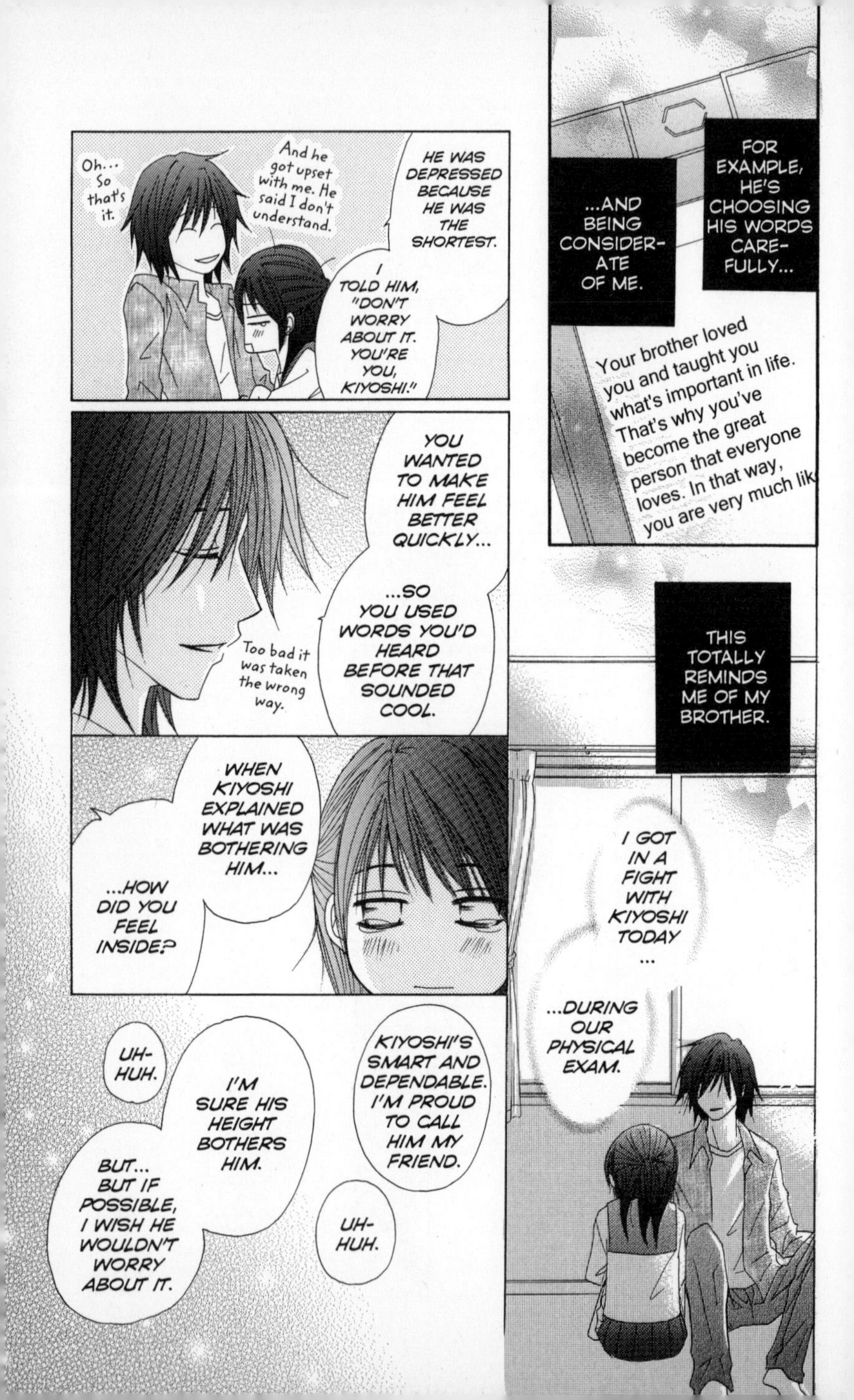
FOR EXAMPLE, HE'S CHOOSING HIS WORDS CARE-FULLY...
...AND BEING CONSIDER-ATE OF ME.
Your brother loved you and taught you what's important in life. That's why you've become the great person that everyone loves. In that way, you are very much lik
THIS TOTALLY REMINDS ME OF MY BROTHER.
I GOT IN A FIGHT WITH KIYOSHI TODAY...
...DURING OUR PHYSICAL EXAM.
KIYOSHI'S SMART AND DEPENDABLE. I'M PROUD TO CALL HIM MY FRIEND.
UH-HUH.
I'M SURE HIS HEIGHT BOTHERS HIM.
UH-HUH.
BUT... BUT IF POSSIBLE, I WISH HE WOULDN'T WORRY ABOUT IT.
HE WAS DEPRESSED BECAUSE HE WAS THE SHORTEST.
I TOLD HIM, "DON'T WORRY ABOUT IT. YOU'RE YOU, KIYOSHI."
And he got upset with me. He said I don't understand.
Oh... So that's it.
YOU WANTED TO MAKE HIM FEEL BETTER QUICKLY...
...SO YOU USED WORDS YOU'D HEARD BEFORE THAT SOUNDED COOL.
Too bad it was taken the wrong way.
WHEN KIYOSHI EXPLAINED WHAT WAS BOTHERING HIM...
...HOW DID YOU FEEL INSIDE?

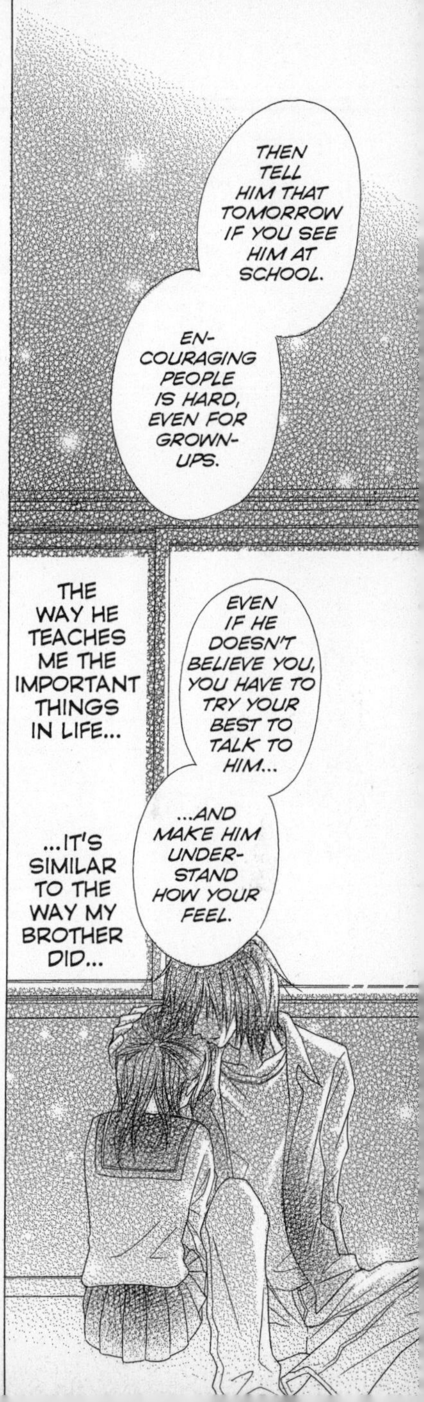
THEN TELL HIM THAT TOMORROW IF YOU SEE HIM AT SCHOOL.
EN-COURAGING PEOPLE IS HARD, EVEN FOR GROWN-UPS.
EVEN IF HE DOESN'T BELIEVE YOU, YOU HAVE TO TRY YOUR BEST TO TALK TO HIM...
...AND MAKE HIM UNDER-STAND HOW YOUR FEEL.
THE WAY HE TEACHES ME THE IMPORTANT THINGS IN LIFE...
...IT'S SIMILAR TO THE WAY MY BROTHER DID...

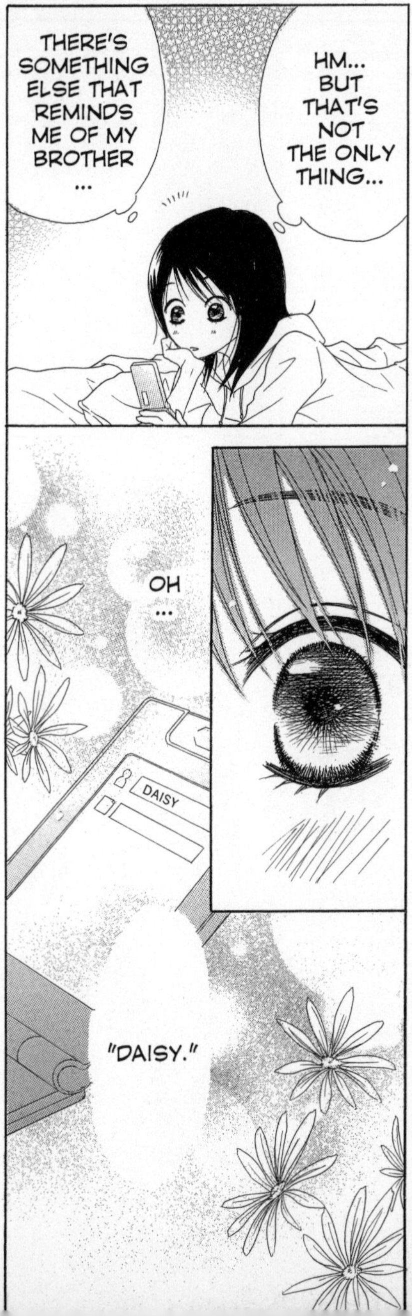
HM... BUT THAT'S NOT THE ONLY THING...
THERE'S SOMETHING ELSE THAT REMINDS ME OF MY BROTHER ...
OH ...
DAISY
"DAISY."

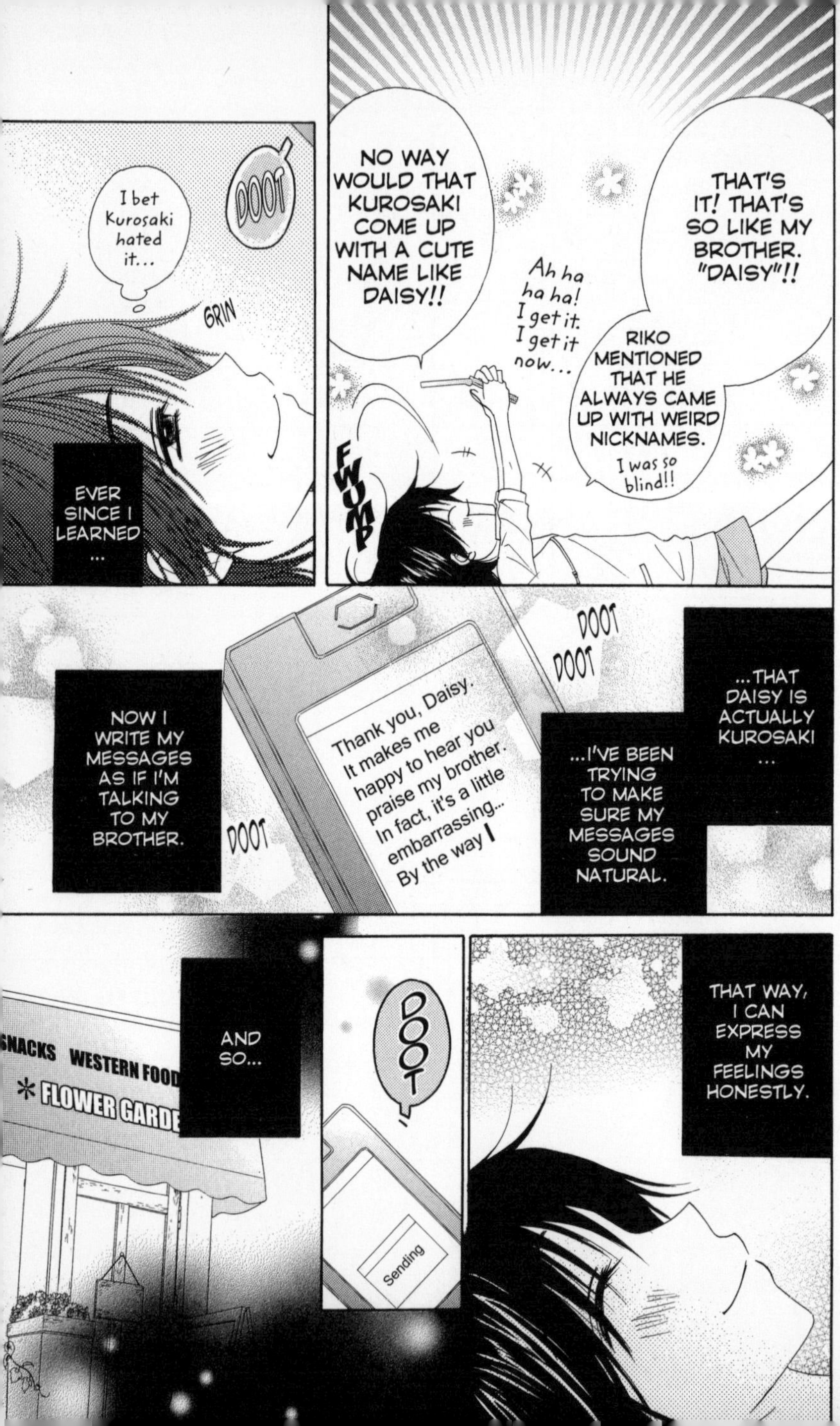
THAT'S IT! THAT'S SO LIKE MY BROTHER. "DAISY"!!
RIKO MENTIONED THAT HE ALWAYS CAME UP WITH WEIRD NICKNAMES.
I was so blind!!
Ah ha ha ha! I get it. I get it now...
NO WAY WOULD THAT KUROSAKI COME UP WITH A CUTE NAME LIKE DAISY!!
FWUMP
DOOT
I bet Kurosaki hated it...
GRIN
EVER SINCE I LEARNED...
...THAT DAISY IS ACTUALLY KUROSAKI...
...I'VE BEEN TRYING TO MAKE SURE MY MESSAGES SOUND NATURAL.
DOOT DOOT
Thank you, Daisy. It makes me happy to hear you praise my brother. In fact, it's a little embarrassing... By the way
DOOT
NOW I WRITE MY MESSAGES AS IF I'M TALKING TO MY BROTHER.
THAT WAY, I CAN EXPRESS MY FEELINGS HONESTLY.
DOOT
Sending
AND SO...
SNACKS WESTERN FOOD
* FLOWER GARDE

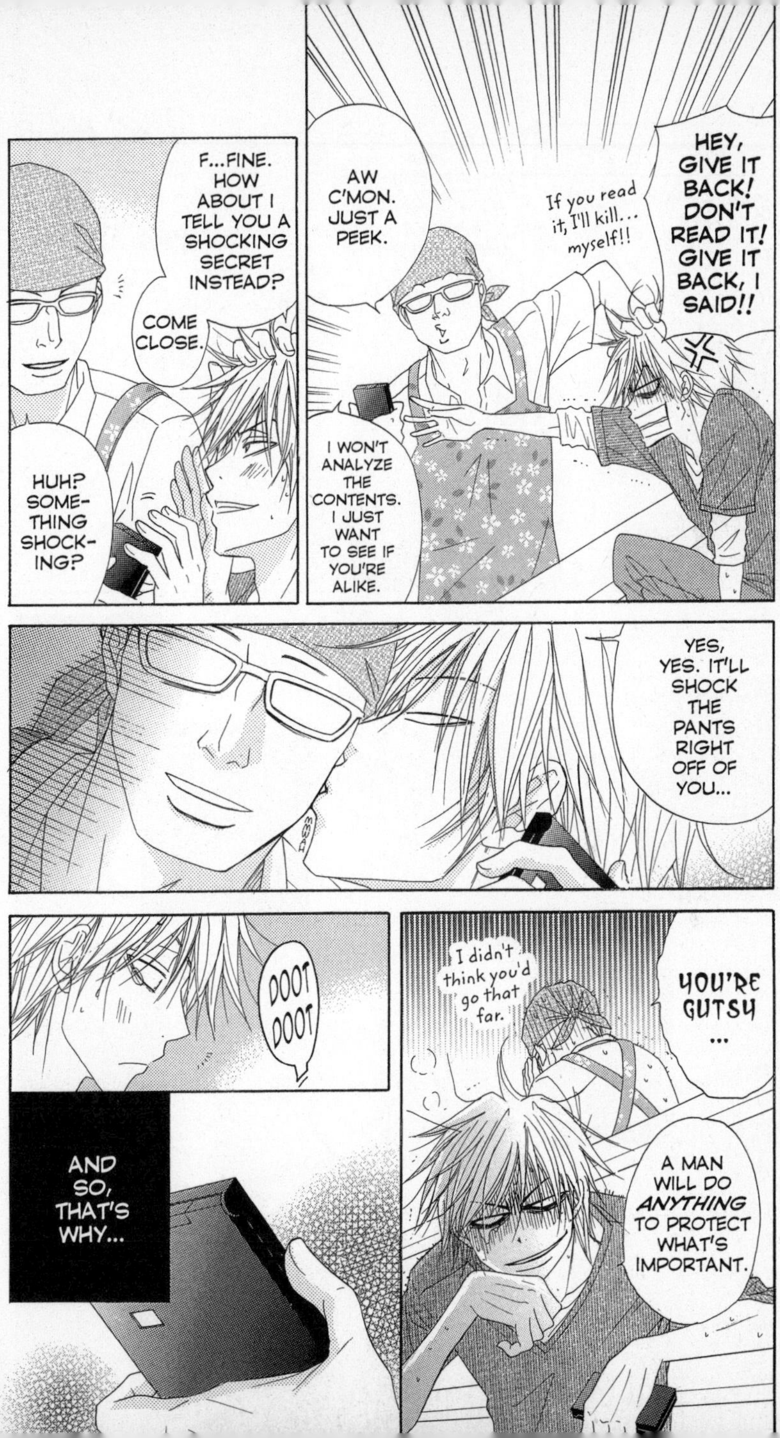
HEY, GIVE IT BACK! DON'T READ IT! GIVE IT BACK, I SAID!!
If you read it, I'll kill... myself!!
AW C'MON. JUST A PEEK.
I WON'T ANALYZE THE CONTENTS. I JUST WANT TO SEE IF YOU'RE ALIKE.
F...FINE. HOW ABOUT I TELL YOU A SHOCKING SECRET INSTEAD?
COME CLOSE.
HUH? SOME-THING SHOCK-ING?
YES, YES. IT'LL SHOCK THE PANTS RIGHT OFF OF YOU...
YOU'RE GUTSY...
I didn't think you'd go that far.
A MAN WILL DO *ANYTHING* TO PROTECT WHAT'S IMPORTANT.
DOOT DOOT
AND SO, THAT'S WHY...

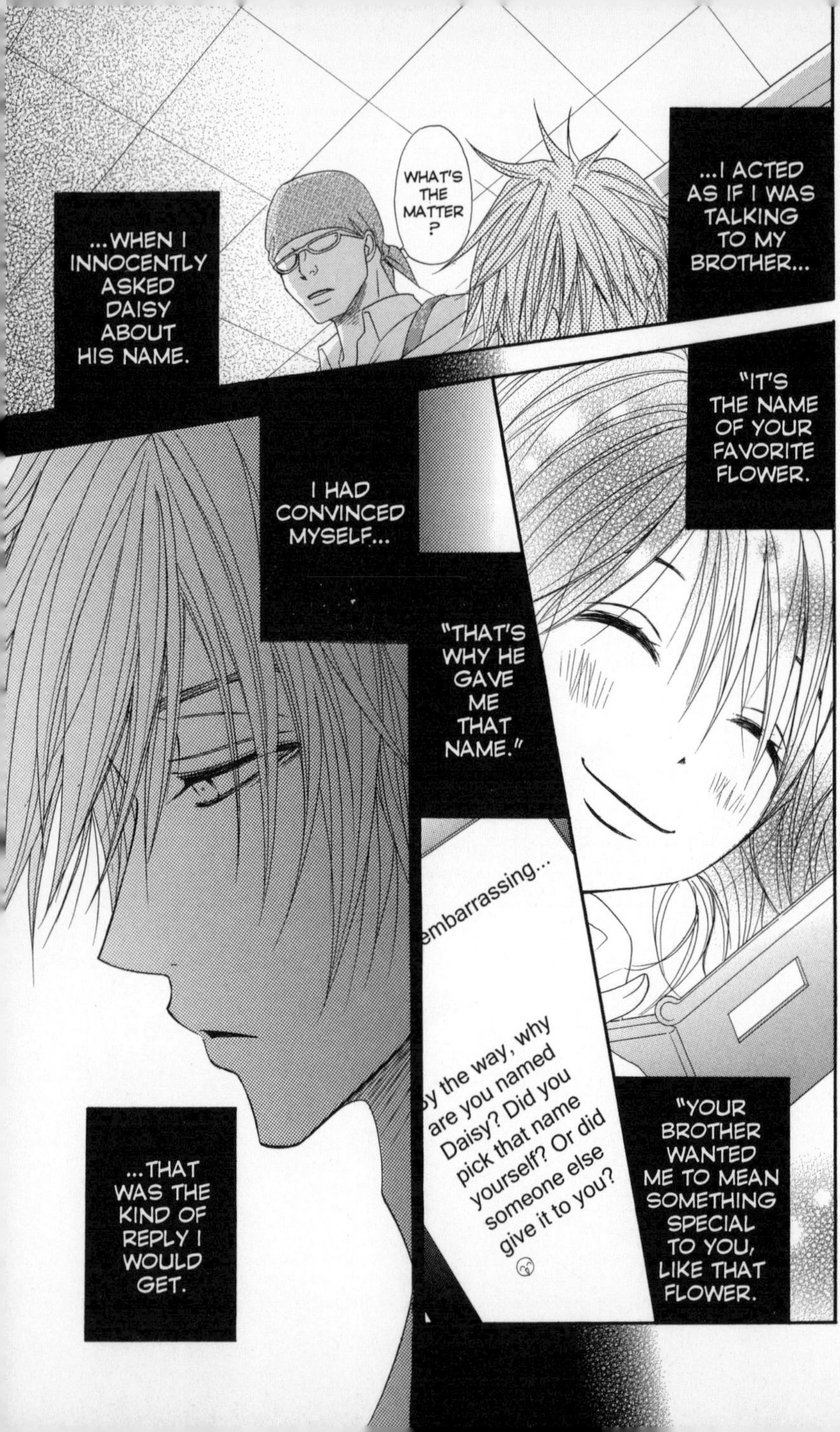
...I ACTED AS IF I WAS TALKING TO MY BROTHER...
WHAT'S THE MATTER?
...WHEN I INNOCENTLY ASKED DAISY ABOUT HIS NAME.
"IT'S THE NAME OF YOUR FAVORITE FLOWER.
"THAT'S WHY HE GAVE ME THAT NAME."
embarrassing...
y the way, why are you named Daisy? Did you pick that name yourself? Or did someone else give it to you?
"YOUR BROTHER WANTED ME TO MEAN SOMETHING SPECIAL TO YOU, LIKE THAT FLOWER.
I HAD CONVINCED MYSELF...
...THAT WAS THE KIND OF REPLY I WOULD GET.

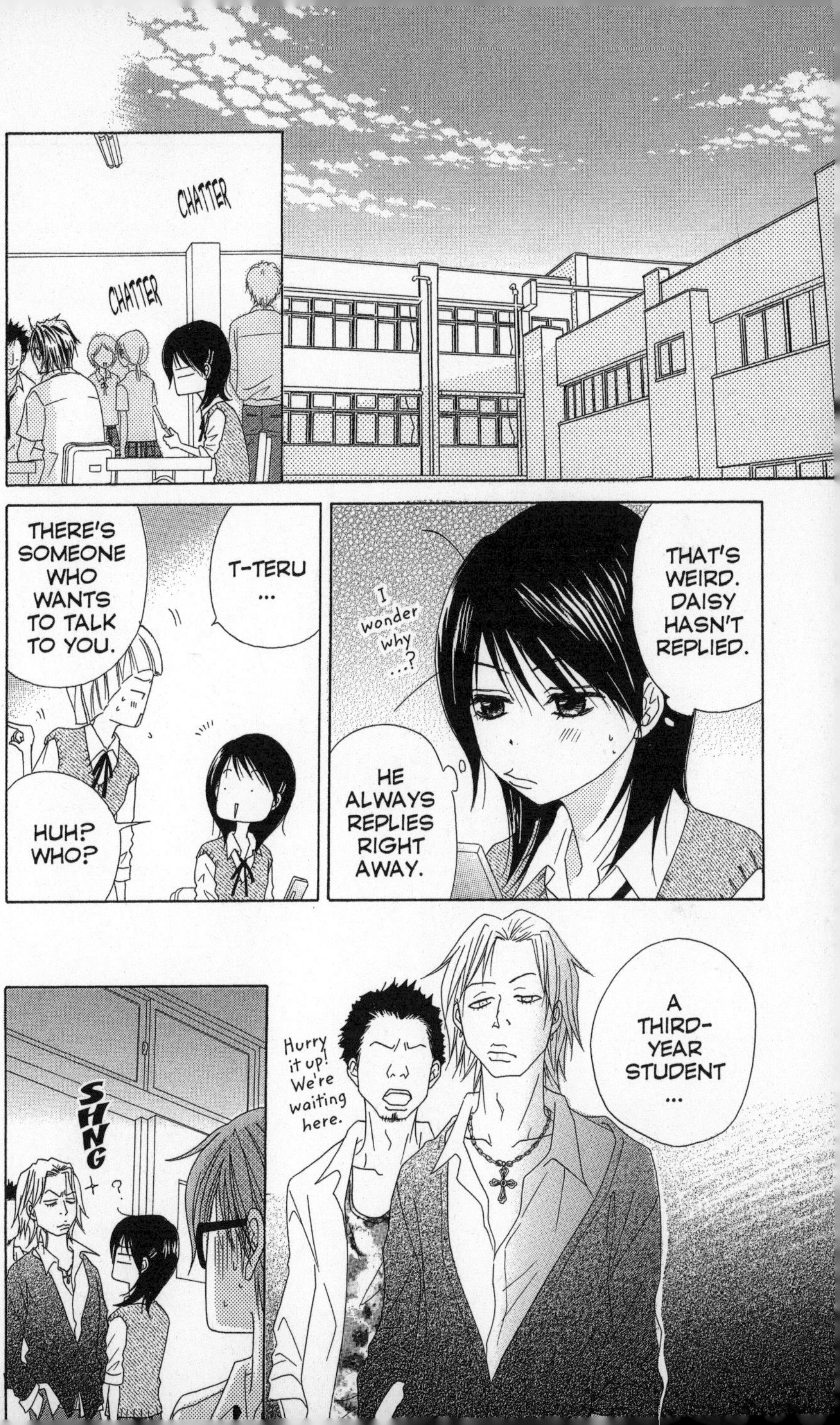
CHATTER
CHATTER
THAT'S WEIRD. DAISY HASN'T REPLIED.
I wonder why ...?
HE ALWAYS REPLIES RIGHT AWAY.
T-TERU ...
THERE'S SOMEONE WHO WANTS TO TALK TO YOU.
HUH? WHO?
A THIRD-YEAR STUDENT ...
Hurry it up! We're waiting here.
SHNG

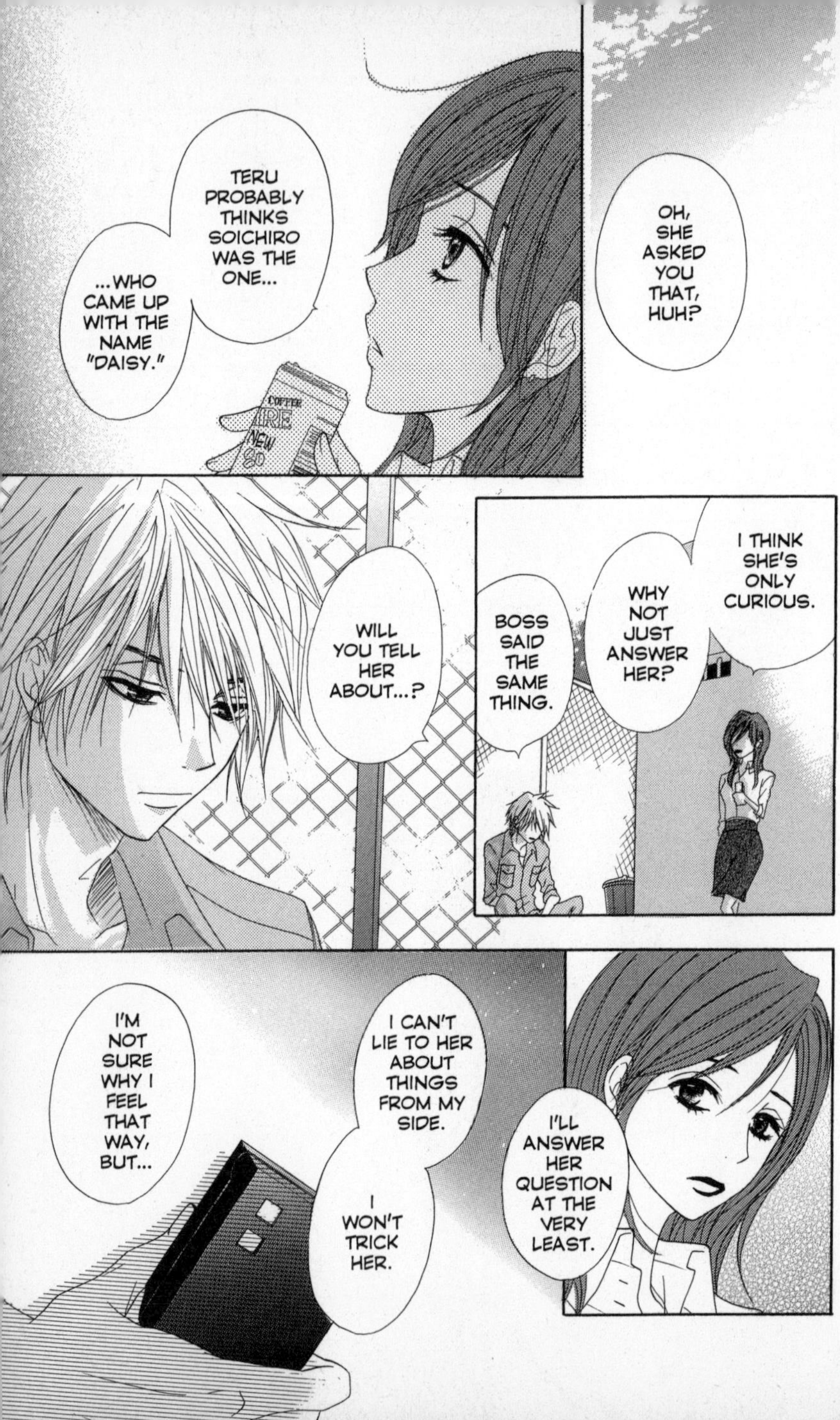
OH, SHE ASKED YOU THAT, HUH?
TERU PROBABLY THINKS SOICHIRO WAS THE ONE...
...WHO CAME UP WITH THE NAME "DAISY."
COFFEE
I THINK SHE'S ONLY CURIOUS.
WHY NOT JUST ANSWER HER?
BOSS SAID THE SAME THING.
WILL YOU TELL HER ABOUT...?
I'LL ANSWER HER QUESTION AT THE VERY LEAST.
I CAN'T LIE TO HER ABOUT THINGS FROM MY SIDE.
I WON'T TRICK HER.
I'M NOT SURE WHY I FEEL THAT WAY, BUT...

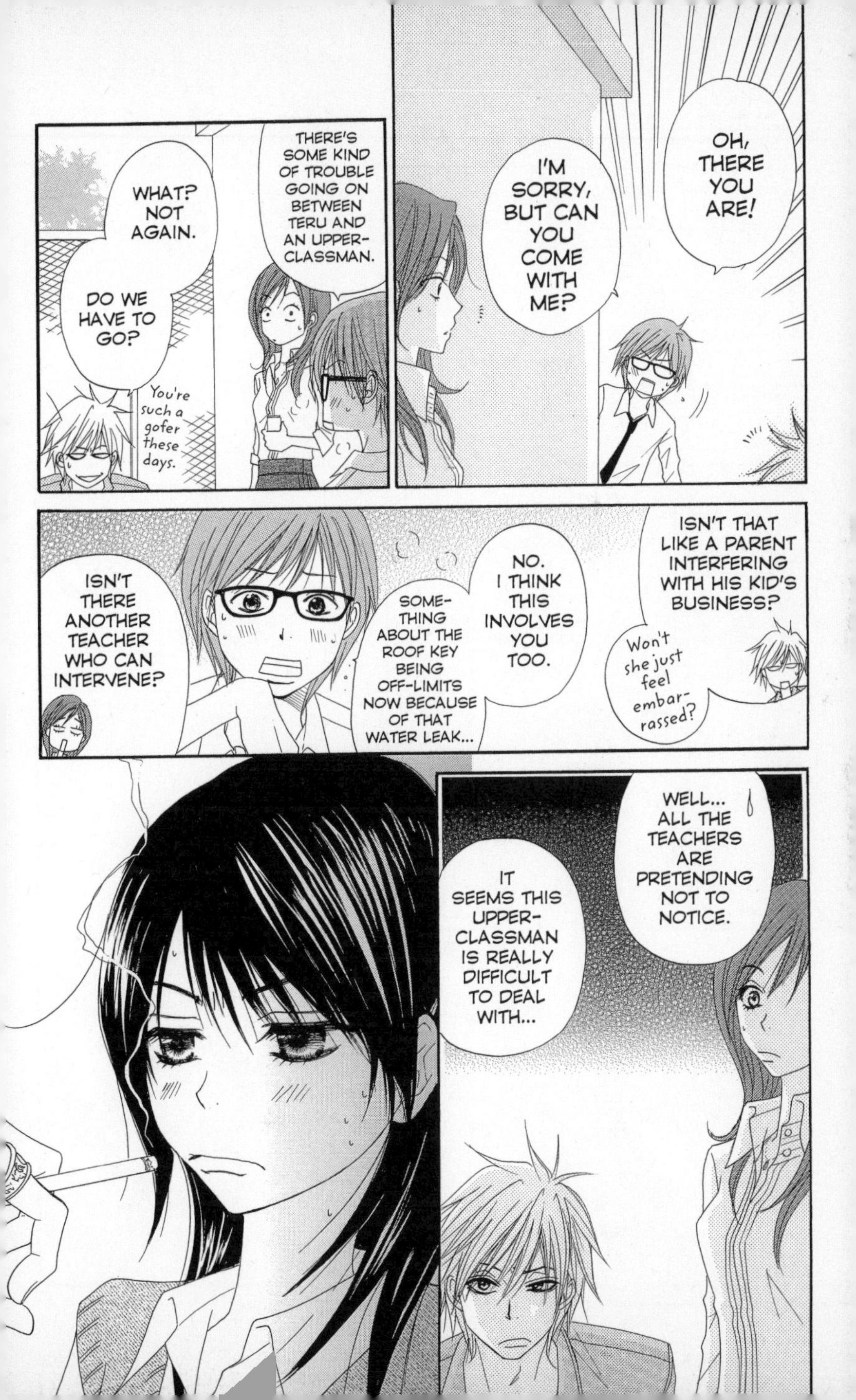
OH, THERE YOU ARE!
I'M SORRY, BUT CAN YOU COME WITH ME?
THERE'S SOME KIND OF TROUBLE GOING ON BETWEEN TERU AND AN UPPER-CLASSMAN.
WHAT? NOT AGAIN.
DO WE HAVE TO GO?
You're such a gofer these days.
ISN'T THAT LIKE A PARENT INTERFERING WITH HIS KID'S BUSINESS?
Won't she just feel embar-rassed?
NO. I THINK THIS INVOLVES YOU TOO.
SOME-THING ABOUT THE ROOF KEY BEING OFF-LIMITS NOW BECAUSE OF THAT WATER LEAK...
ISN'T THERE ANOTHER TEACHER WHO CAN INTERVENE?
WELL... ALL THE TEACHERS ARE PRETENDING NOT TO NOTICE.
IT SEEMS THIS UPPER-CLASSMAN IS REALLY DIFFICULT TO DEAL WITH...

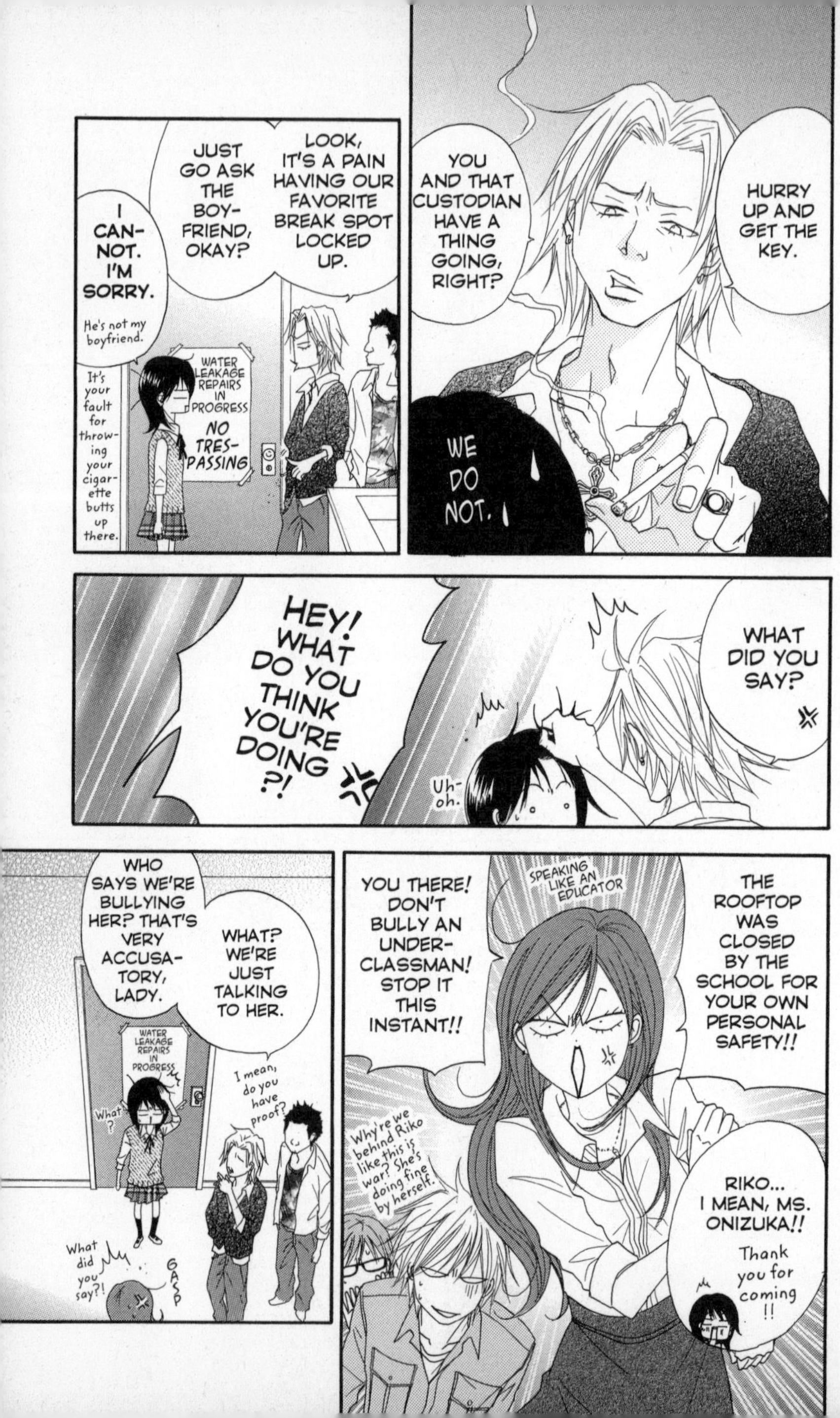
HURRY UP AND GET THE KEY.
YOU AND THAT CUSTODIAN HAVE A THING GOING, RIGHT?
WE DO NOT.
LOOK, IT'S A PAIN HAVING OUR FAVORITE BREAK SPOT LOCKED UP.
JUST GO ASK THE BOY-FRIEND, OKAY?
I CAN-NOT. I'M SORRY.
He's not my boyfriend.
It's your fault for throwing your cigarette butts up there.
WATER LEAKAGE REPAIRS IN PROGRESS
NO TRES-PASSING
WHAT DID YOU SAY?
Uh-oh.
HEY! WHAT DO YOU THINK YOU'RE DOING?!
THE ROOFTOP WAS CLOSED BY THE SCHOOL FOR YOUR OWN PERSONAL SAFETY!!
SPEAKING LIKE AN EDUCATOR
YOU THERE! DON'T BULLY AN UNDER-CLASSMAN! STOP IT THIS INSTANT!!
Why're we behind Riko like this is war? She's doing fine by herself.
RIKO... I MEAN, MS. ONIZUKA!!
Thank you for coming!!
WHAT? WE'RE JUST TALKING TO HER.
WHO SAYS WE'RE BULLYING HER? THAT'S VERY ACCUSA-TORY, LADY.
WATER LEAKAGE REPAIRS IN PROGRESS
I mean, do you have proof?
What?
What did you say?!
GASP

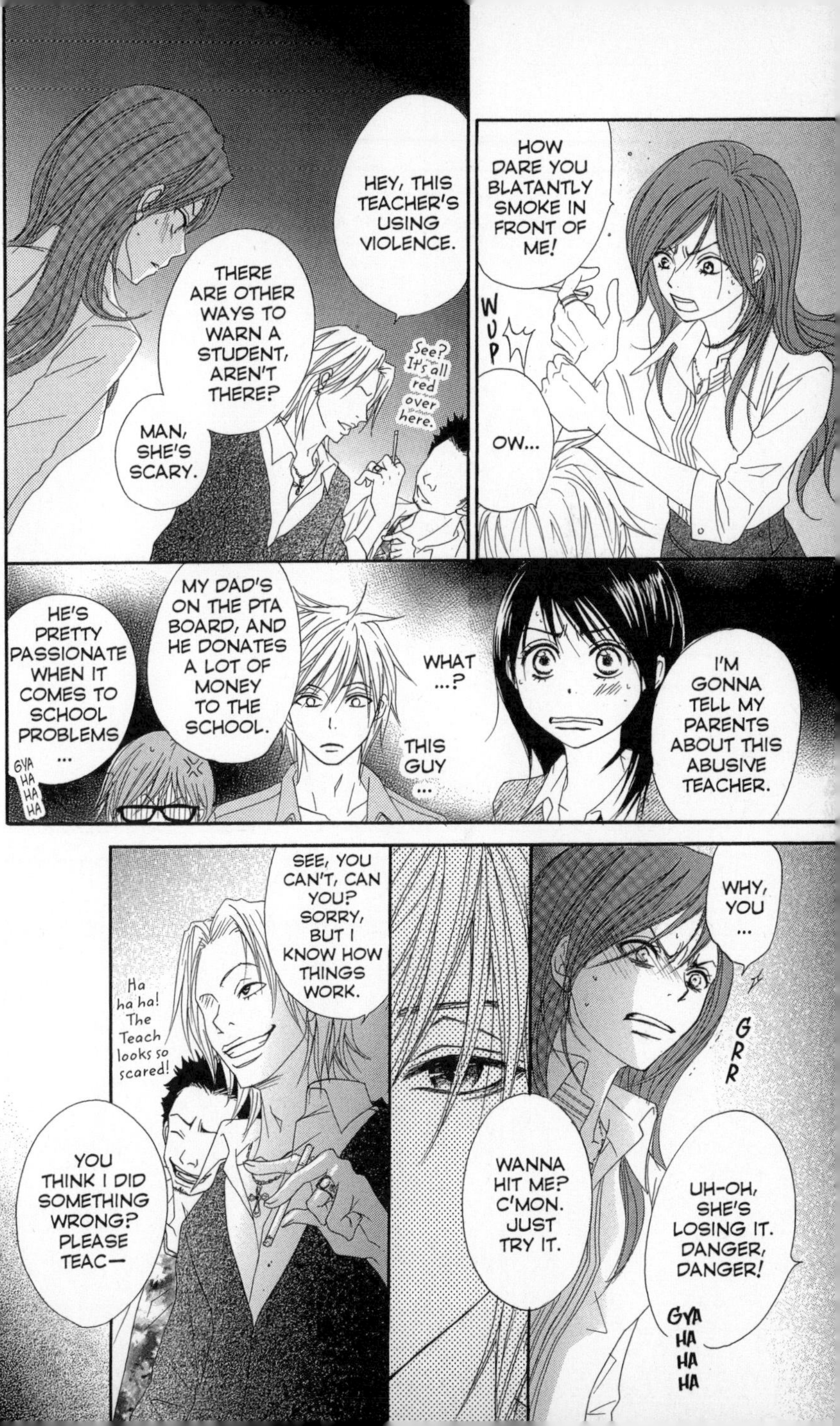
HOW DARE YOU BLATANTLY SMOKE IN FRONT OF ME!
WUP
OW...
HEY, THIS TEACHER'S USING VIOLENCE.
See? It's all red over here.
THERE ARE OTHER WAYS TO WARN A STUDENT, AREN'T THERE?
MAN, SHE'S SCARY.
I'M GONNA TELL MY PARENTS ABOUT THIS ABUSIVE TEACHER.
WHAT ...?
THIS GUY ...
MY DAD'S ON THE PTA BOARD, AND HE DONATES A LOT OF MONEY TO THE SCHOOL.
HE'S PRETTY PASSIONATE WHEN IT COMES TO SCHOOL PROBLEMS ...
GYA HA HA HA
WHY, YOU ...
GRR
UH-OH, SHE'S LOSING IT. DANGER, DANGER!
GYA HA HA HA
WANNA HIT ME? C'MON. JUST TRY IT.
SEE, YOU CAN'T, CAN YOU? SORRY, BUT I KNOW HOW THINGS WORK.
Ha ha ha! The Teach looks so scared!
YOU THINK I DID SOMETHING WRONG? PLEASE TEAC—

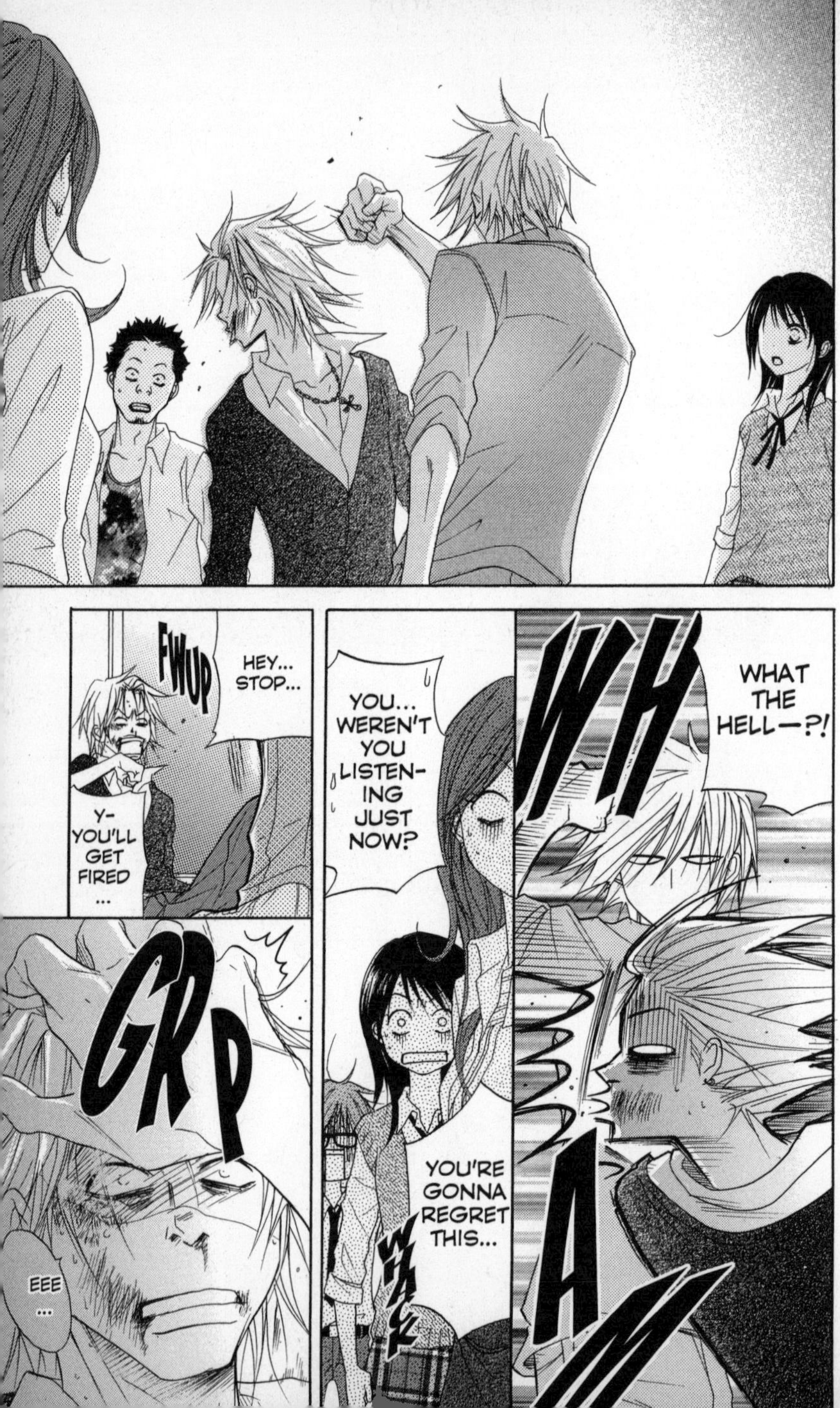
WH
AM
WHAT THE HELL—?!
YOU... WEREN'T YOU LISTEN-ING JUST NOW?
YOU'RE GONNA REGRET THIS...
WHACK
FWUP
HEY... STOP...
Y- YOU'LL GET FIRED ...
GRP
EEE ...

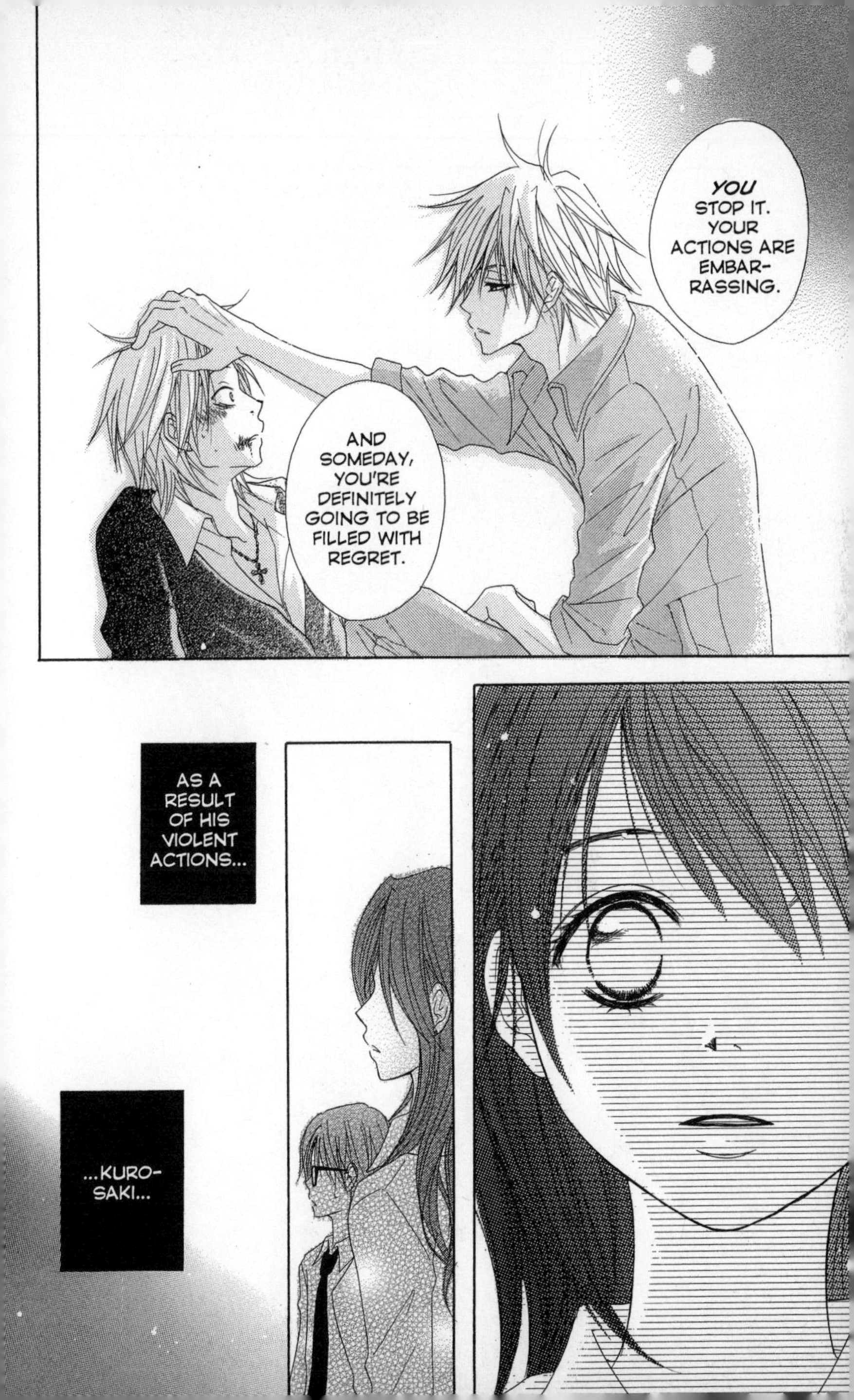
YOU STOP IT. YOUR ACTIONS ARE EMBAR-RASSING.
AND SOMEDAY, YOU'RE DEFINITELY GOING TO BE FILLED WITH REGRET.
AS A RESULT OF HIS VIOLENT ACTIONS...
...KURO-SAKI...

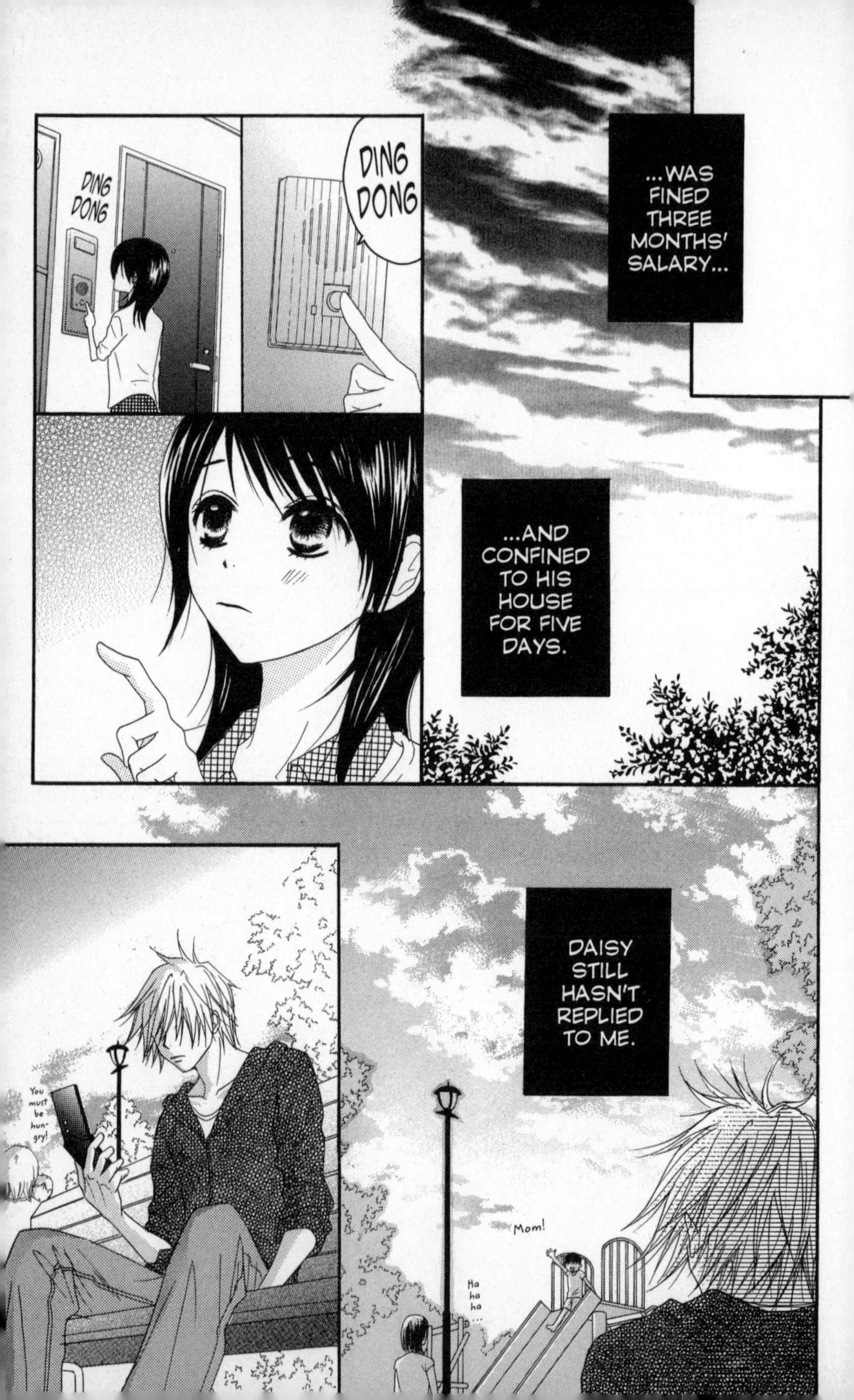
...WAS FINED THREE MONTHS' SALARY...
...AND CONFINED TO HIS HOUSE FOR FIVE DAYS.
DING DONG
DING DONG
DAISY STILL HASN'T REPLIED TO ME.
Mom!
Ha ha ha...
You must be hun-gry!

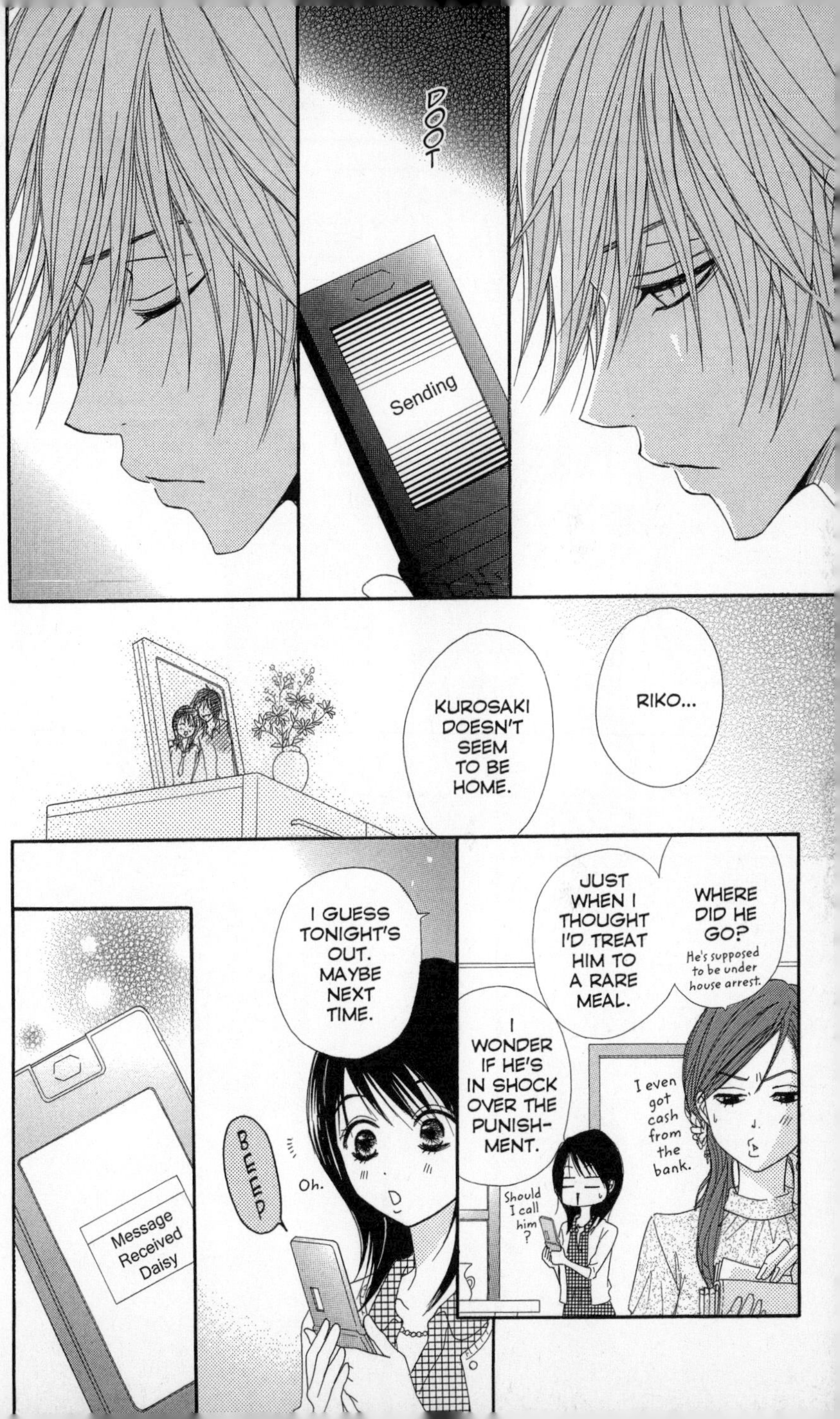
DOOOT
Sending
RIKO...
KUROSAKI DOESN'T SEEM TO BE HOME.
WHERE DID HE GO?
He's supposed to be under house arrest.
JUST WHEN I THOUGHT I'D TREAT HIM TO A RARE MEAL.
I even got cash from the bank.
I WONDER IF HE'S IN SHOCK OVER THE PUNISHMENT.
Should I call him?
I GUESS TONIGHT'S OUT. MAYBE NEXT TIME.
BEEP
Oh.
Message Received Daisy

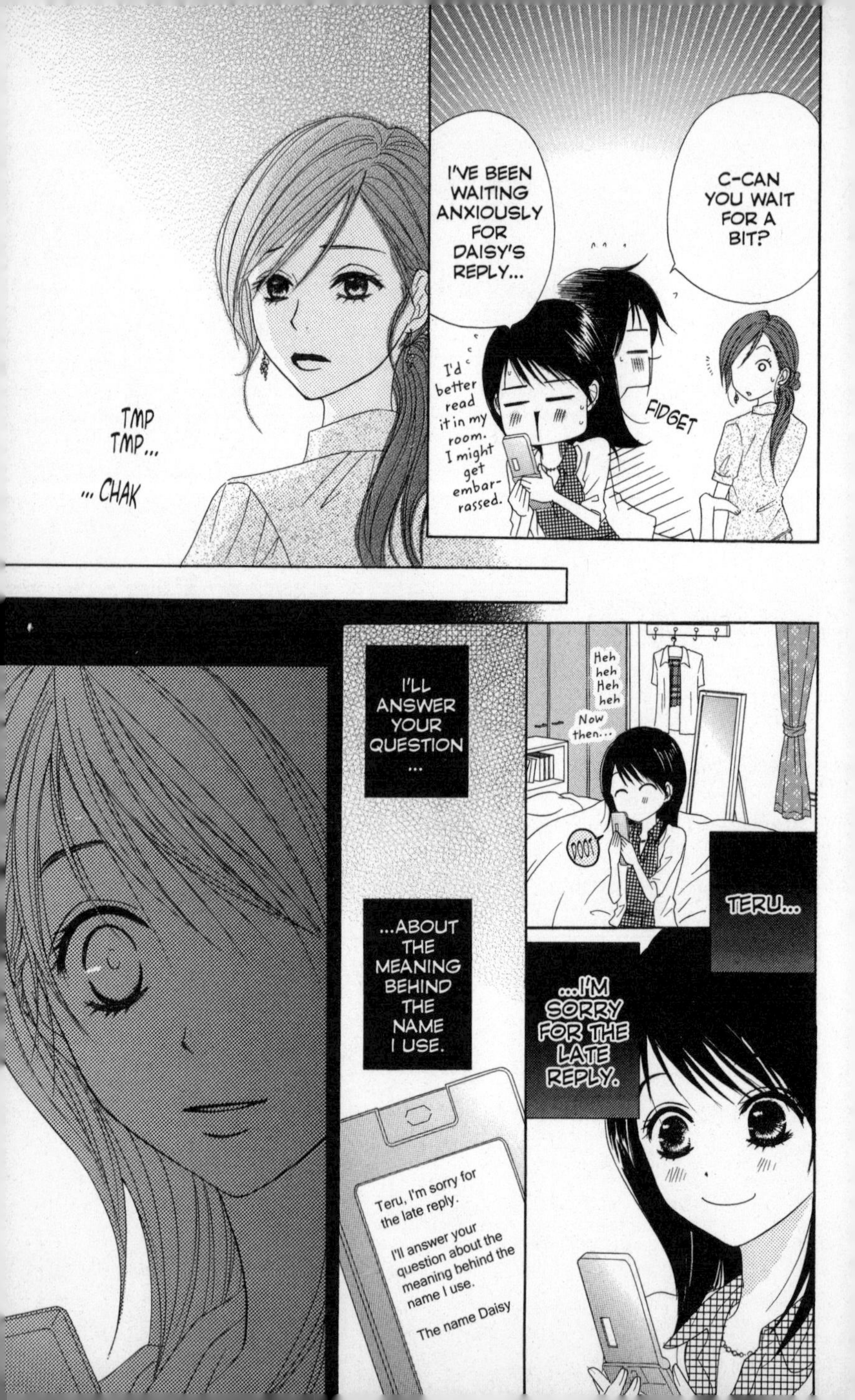
C-CAN YOU WAIT FOR A BIT?
I'VE BEEN WAITING ANXIOUSLY FOR DAISY'S REPLY...
FIDGET
I'd better read it in my room. I might get embarrassed.
TMP TMP...
...CHAK
Heh heh Heh heh
Now then...
DOOT
TERU...
...I'M SORRY FOR THE LATE REPLY.
I'LL ANSWER YOUR QUESTION...
...ABOUT THE MEANING BEHIND THE NAME I USE.
Teru, I'm sorry for the late reply.
I'll answer your question about the meaning behind the name I use.
The name Daisy

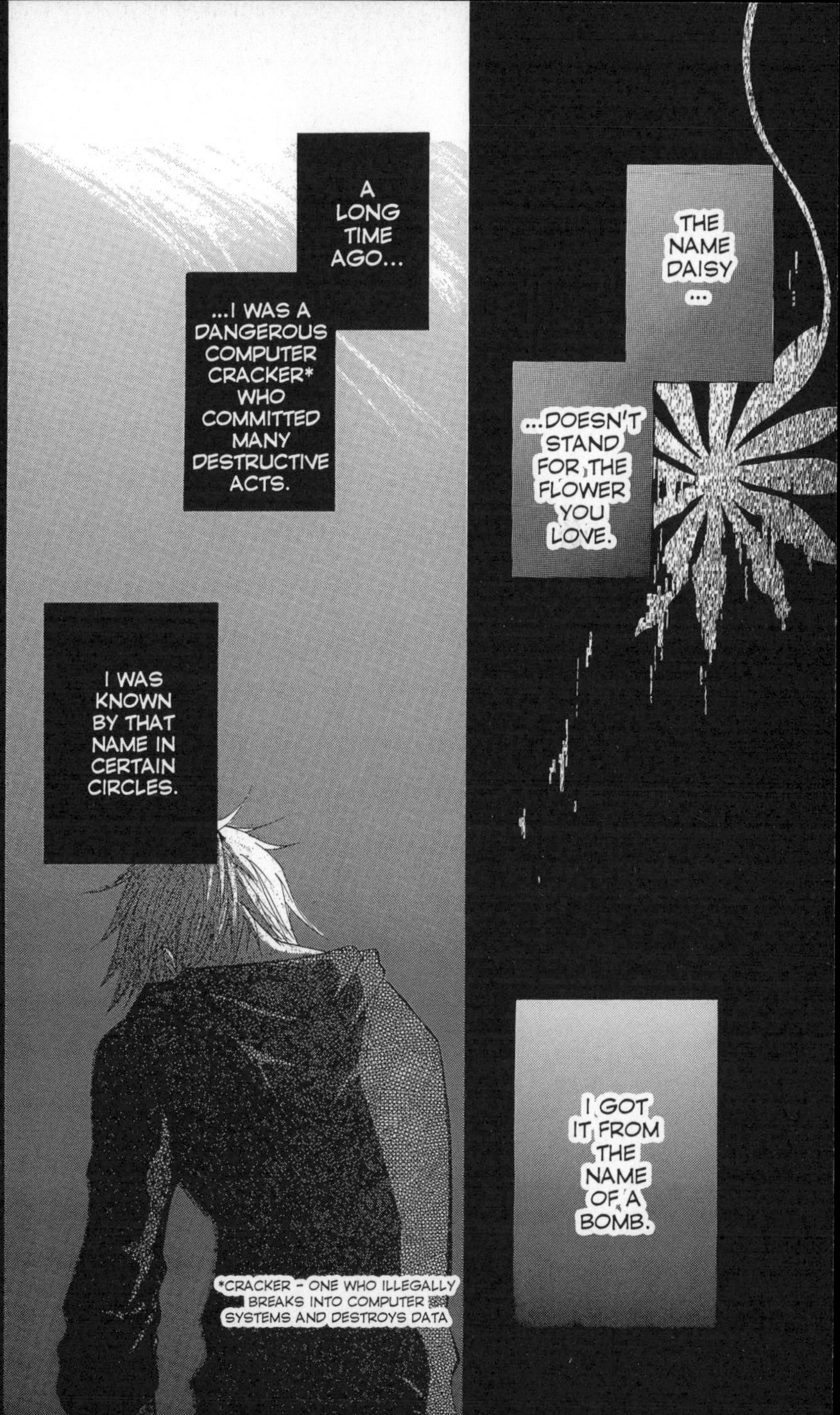
THE NAME DAISY ...
...DOESN'T STAND FOR THE FLOWER YOU LOVE.
I GOT IT FROM THE NAME OF A BOMB.
A LONG TIME AGO...
...I WAS A DANGEROUS COMPUTER CRACKER* WHO COMMITTED MANY DESTRUCTIVE ACTS.
I WAS KNOWN BY THAT NAME IN CERTAIN CIRCLES.
*CRACKER - ONE WHO ILLEGALLY BREAKS INTO COMPUTER SYSTEMS AND DESTROYS DATA

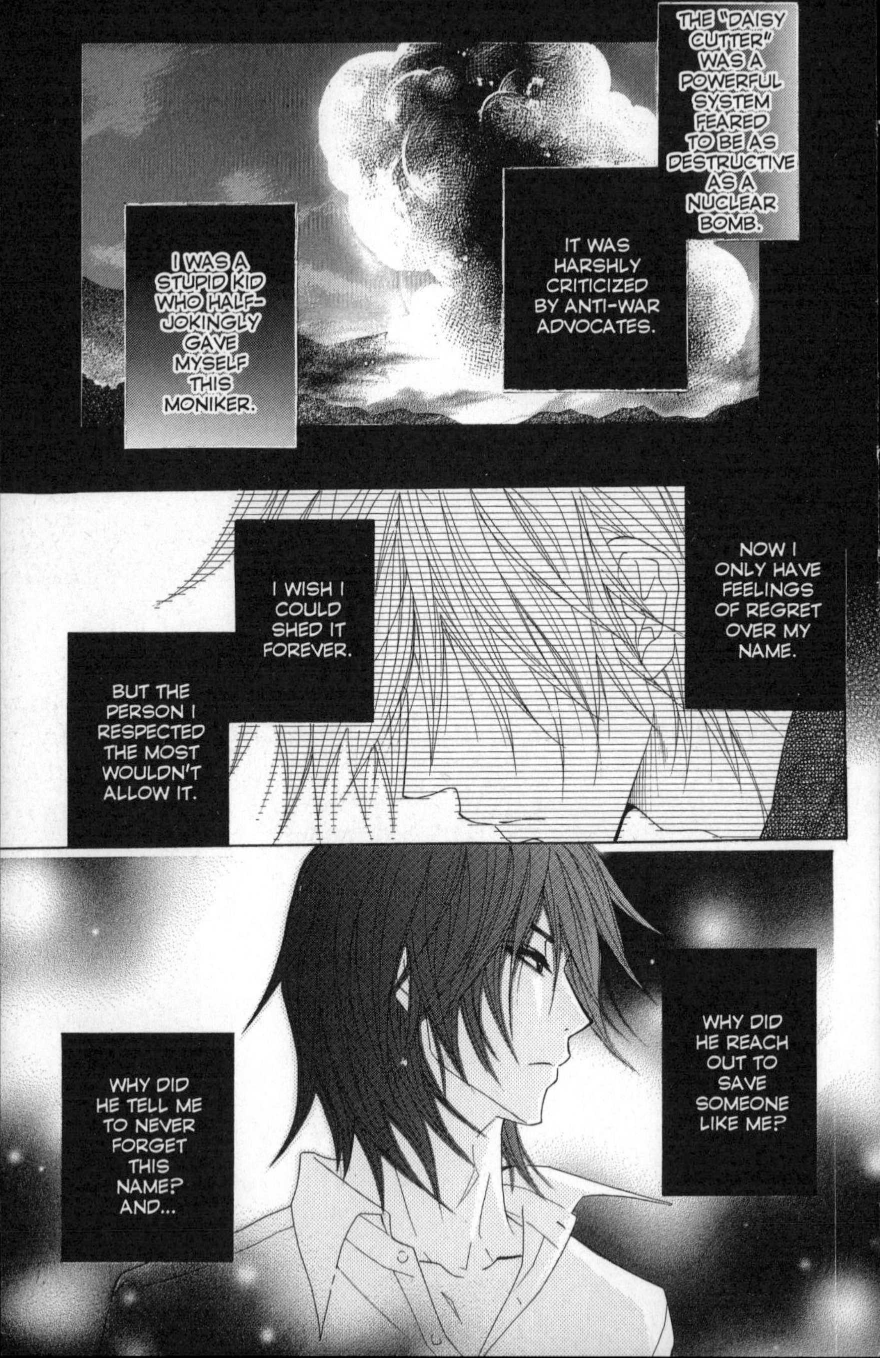
THE "DAISY CUTTER" WAS A POWERFUL SYSTEM FEARED TO BE AS DESTRUCTIVE AS A NUCLEAR BOMB.
IT WAS HARSHLY CRITICIZED BY ANTI-WAR ADVOCATES.
I WAS A STUPID KID WHO HALF-JOKINGLY GAVE MYSELF THIS MONIKER.
NOW I ONLY HAVE FEELINGS OF REGRET OVER MY NAME.
I WISH I COULD SHED IT FOREVER.
BUT THE PERSON I RESPECTED THE MOST WOULDN'T ALLOW IT.
WHY DID HE REACH OUT TO SAVE SOMEONE LIKE ME?
WHY DID HE TELL ME TO NEVER FORGET THIS NAME? AND...

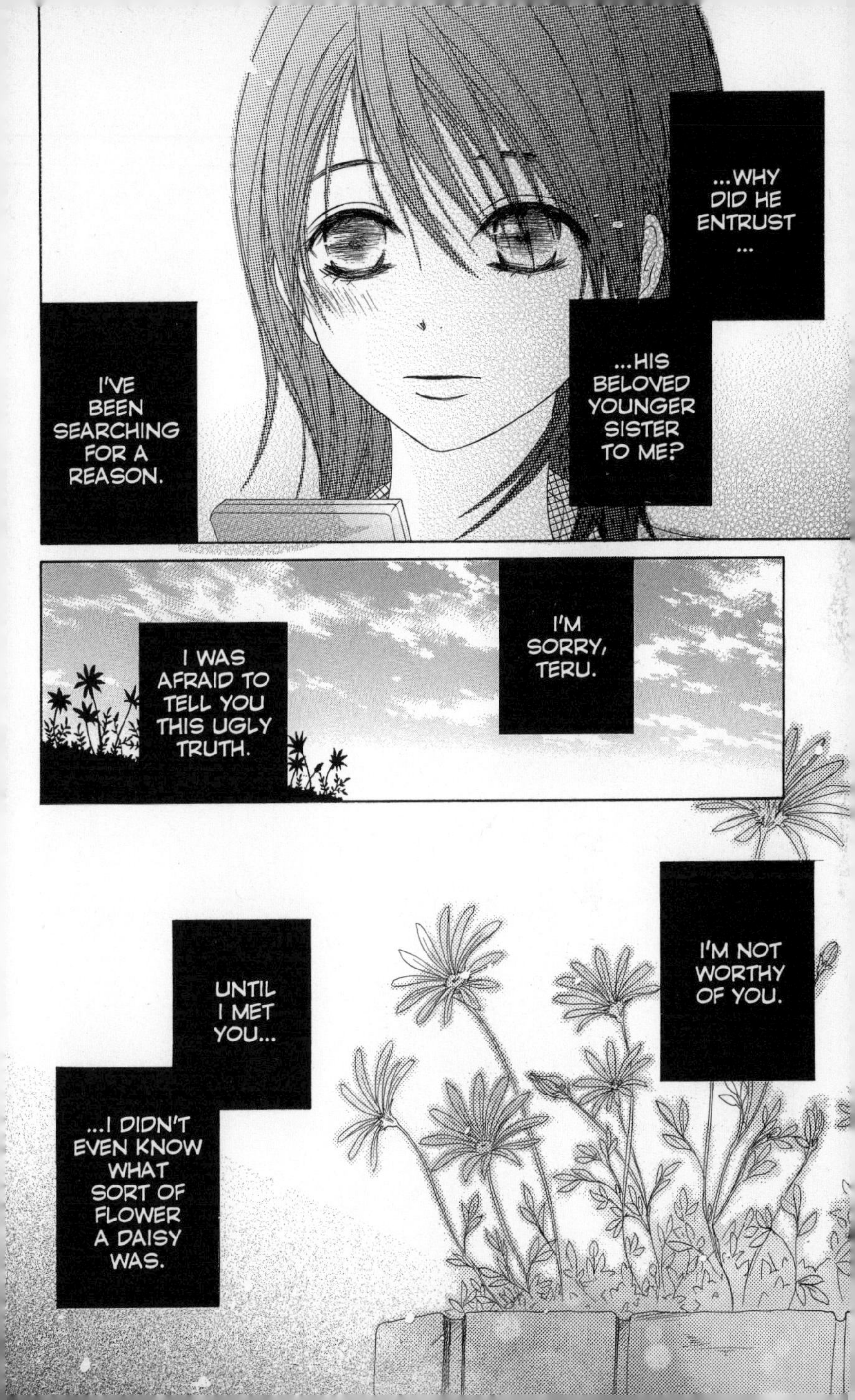
...WHY DID HE ENTRUST ...
...HIS BELOVED YOUNGER SISTER TO ME?
I'VE BEEN SEARCHING FOR A REASON.
I'M SORRY, TERU.
I WAS AFRAID TO TELL YOU THIS UGLY TRUTH.
I'M NOT WORTHY OF YOU.
UNTIL I MET YOU...
...I DIDN'T EVEN KNOW WHAT SORT OF FLOWER A DAISY WAS.

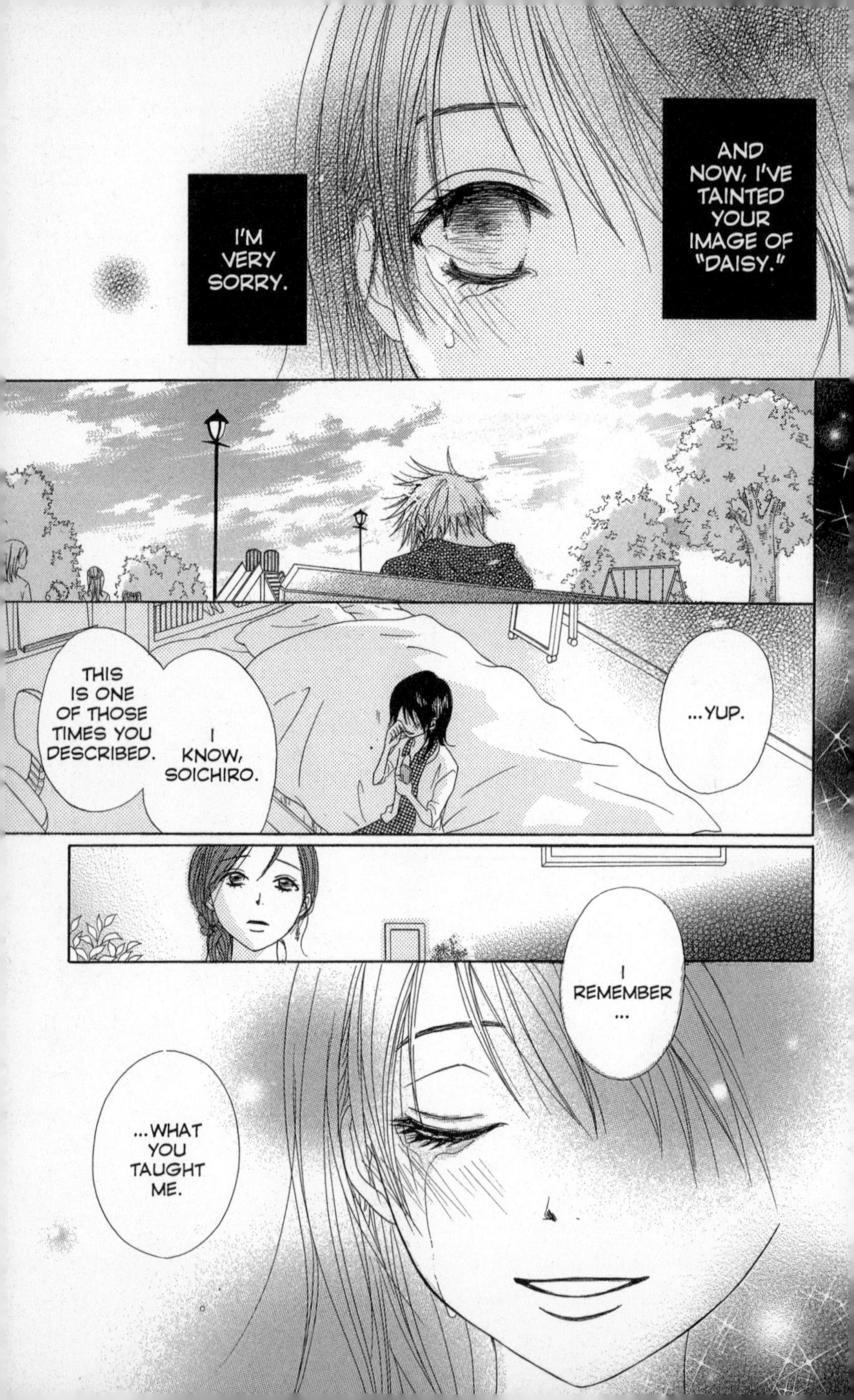
AND NOW, I'VE TAINTED YOUR IMAGE OF "DAISY."
I'M VERY SORRY.
...YUP.
I KNOW, SOICHIRO.
THIS IS ONE OF THOSE TIMES YOU DESCRIBED.
I REMEMBER...
...WHAT YOU TAUGHT ME.

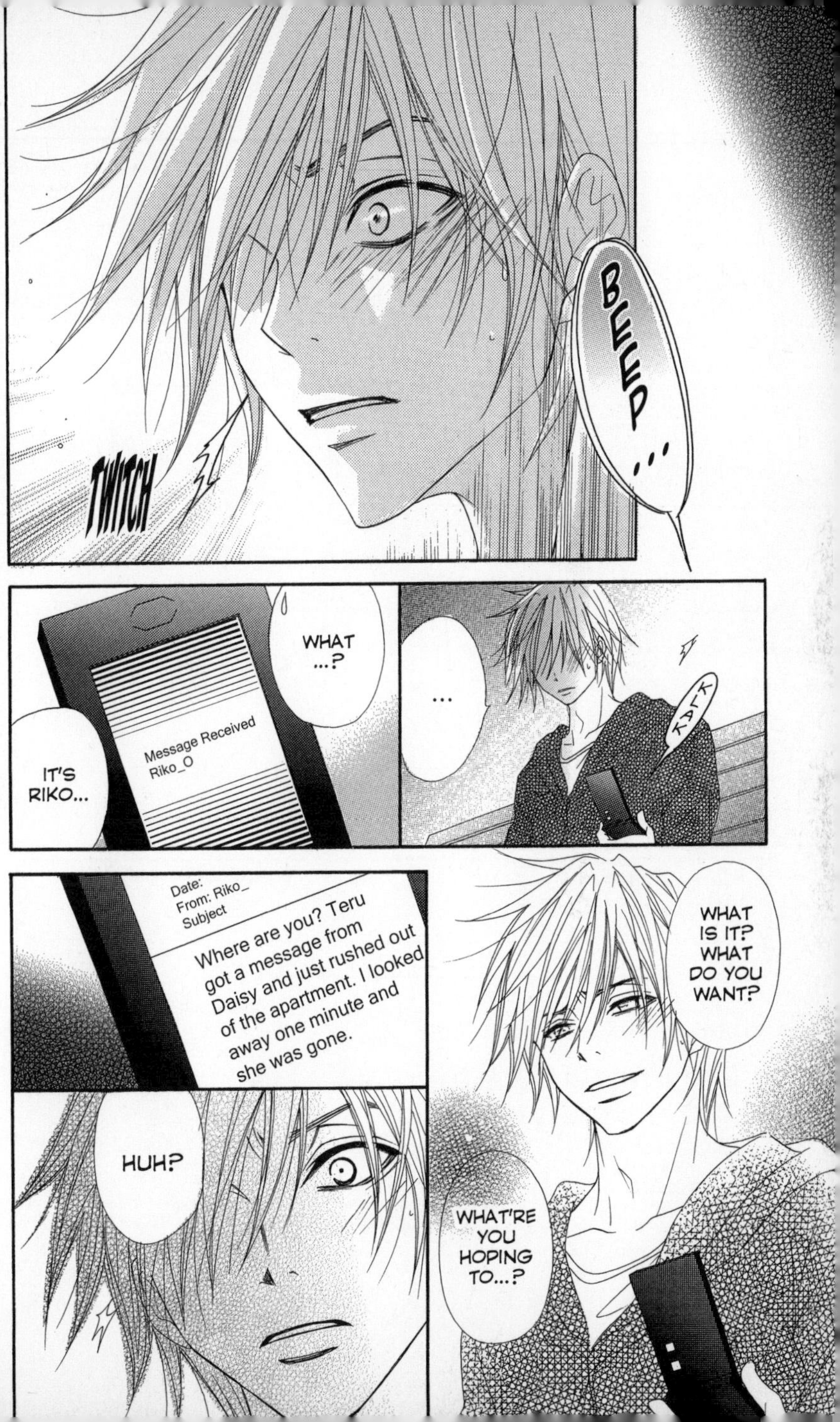
BEEP...
TWITCH
KLAK
...
WHAT ...?
Message Received
Riko_O
IT'S RIKO...
WHAT IS IT? WHAT DO YOU WANT?
WHAT'RE YOU HOPING TO...?
Date:
From: Riko_
Subject
Where are you? Teru got a message from Daisy and just rushed out of the apartment. I looked away one minute and she was gone.
HUH?

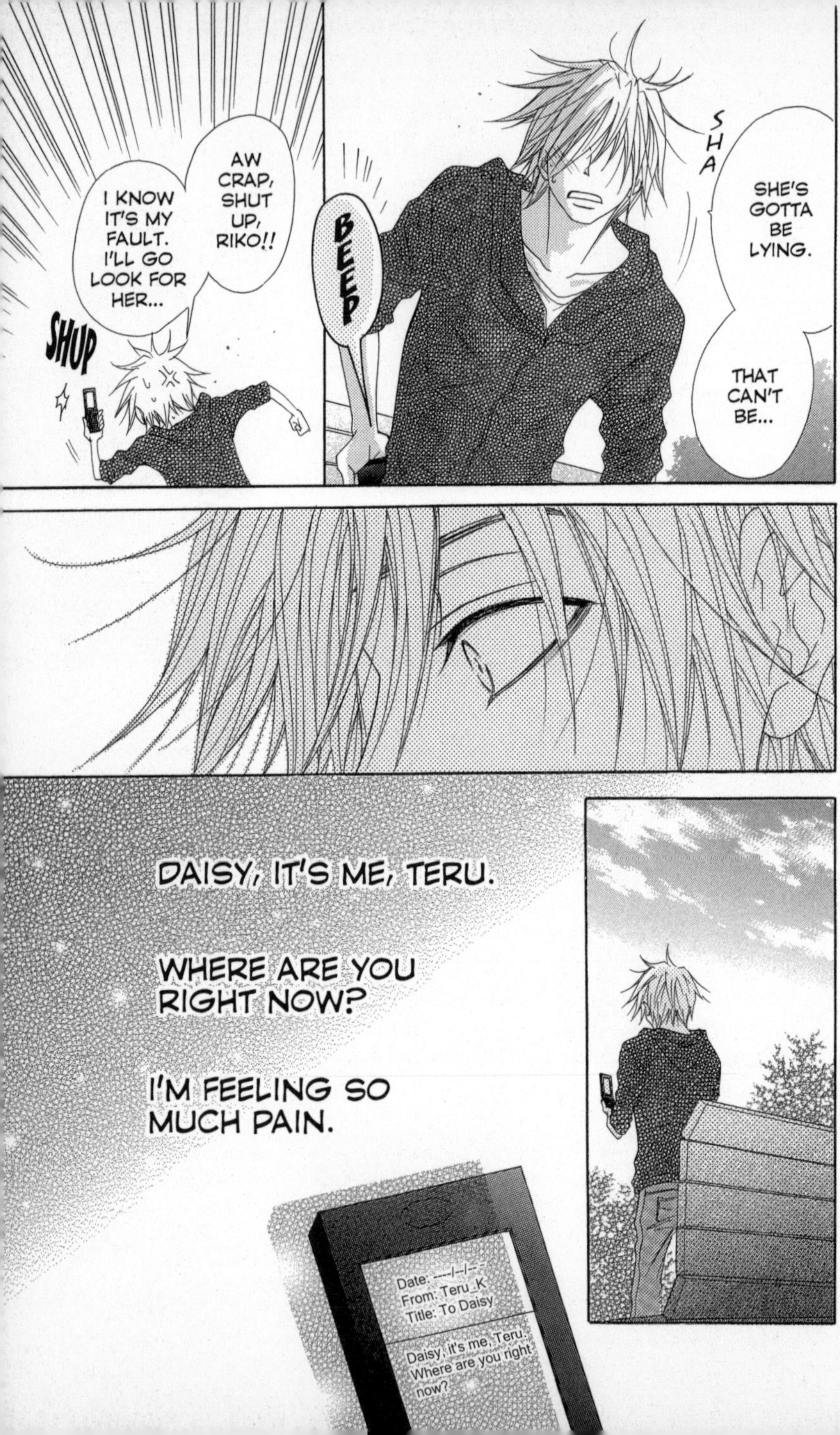
SHA
SHE'S GOTTA BE LYING.
THAT CAN'T BE...
BEEP
AW CRAP, SHUT UP, RIKO!!
I KNOW IT'S MY FAULT. I'LL GO LOOK FOR HER...
SHUP
DAISY, IT'S ME, TERU.
WHERE ARE YOU RIGHT NOW?
I'M FEELING SO MUCH PAIN.
Date: ----/--/-- --
From: Teru_K
Title: To Daisy
Daisy, it's me, Teru. Where are you right now?

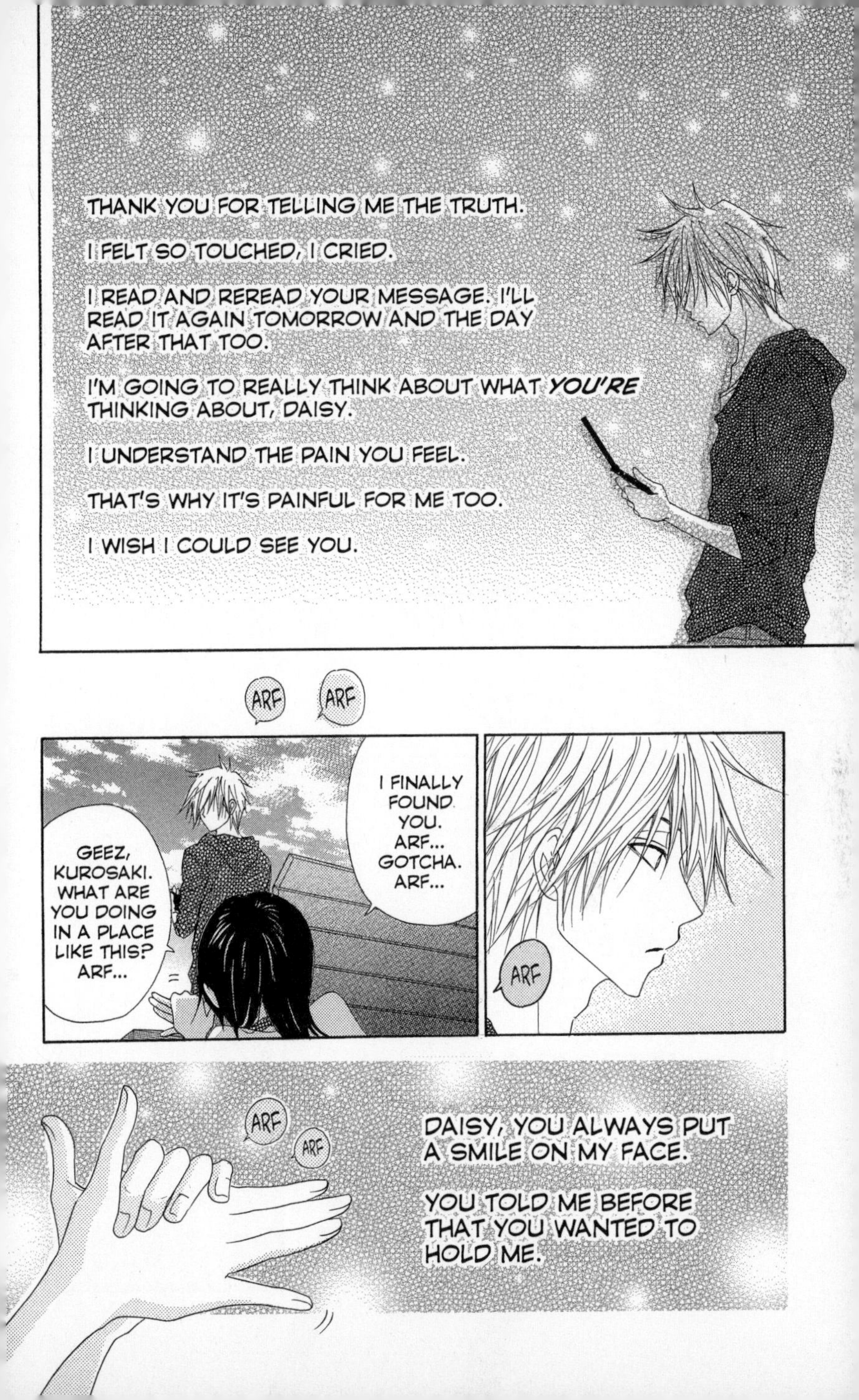
THANK YOU FOR TELLING ME THE TRUTH.
I FELT SO TOUCHED, I CRIED.
I READ AND REREAD YOUR MESSAGE. I'LL READ IT AGAIN TOMORROW AND THE DAY AFTER THAT TOO.
I'M GOING TO REALLY THINK ABOUT WHAT *YOU'RE* THINKING ABOUT, DAISY.
I UNDERSTAND THE PAIN YOU FEEL.
THAT'S WHY IT'S PAINFUL FOR ME TOO.
I WISH I COULD SEE YOU.
ARF
ARF
ARF
I FINALLY FOUND YOU. ARF... GOTCHA. ARF...
GEEZ, KUROSAKI. WHAT ARE YOU DOING IN A PLACE LIKE THIS? ARF...
DAISY, YOU ALWAYS PUT A SMILE ON MY FACE.
YOU TOLD ME BEFORE THAT YOU WANTED TO HOLD ME.
ARF
ARF

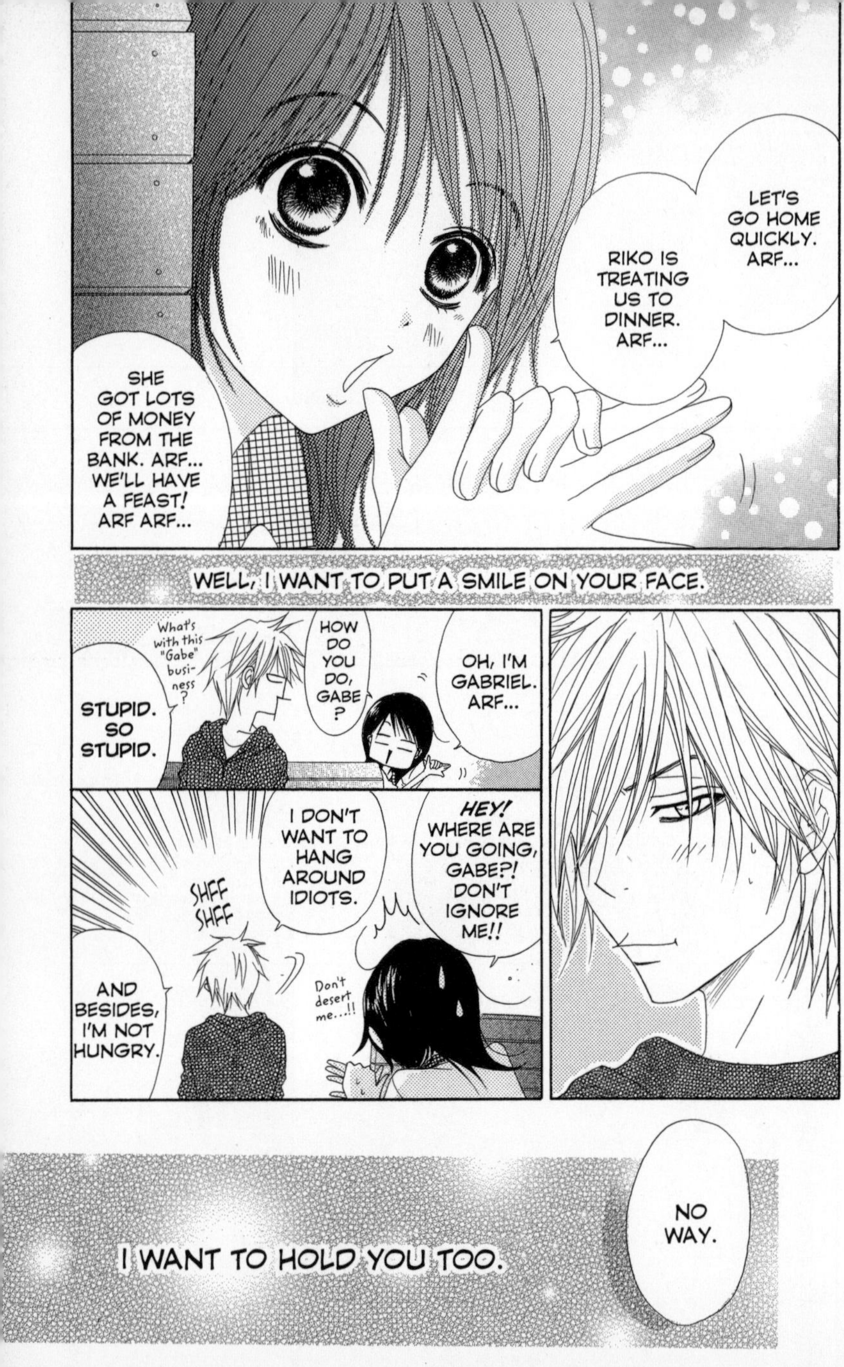
LET'S GO HOME QUICKLY. ARF...
RIKO IS TREATING US TO DINNER. ARF...
SHE GOT LOTS OF MONEY FROM THE BANK. ARF... WE'LL HAVE A FEAST! ARF ARF...
WELL, I WANT TO PUT A SMILE ON YOUR FACE.
OH, I'M GABRIEL. ARF...
HOW DO YOU DO, GABE?
What's with this "Gabe" business?
STUPID. SO STUPID.
HEY! WHERE ARE YOU GOING, GABE?! DON'T IGNORE ME!!
I DON'T WANT TO HANG AROUND IDIOTS.
SHFF SHFF
Don't desert me...!!
AND BESIDES, I'M NOT HUNGRY.
NO WAY.
I WANT TO HOLD YOU TOO.

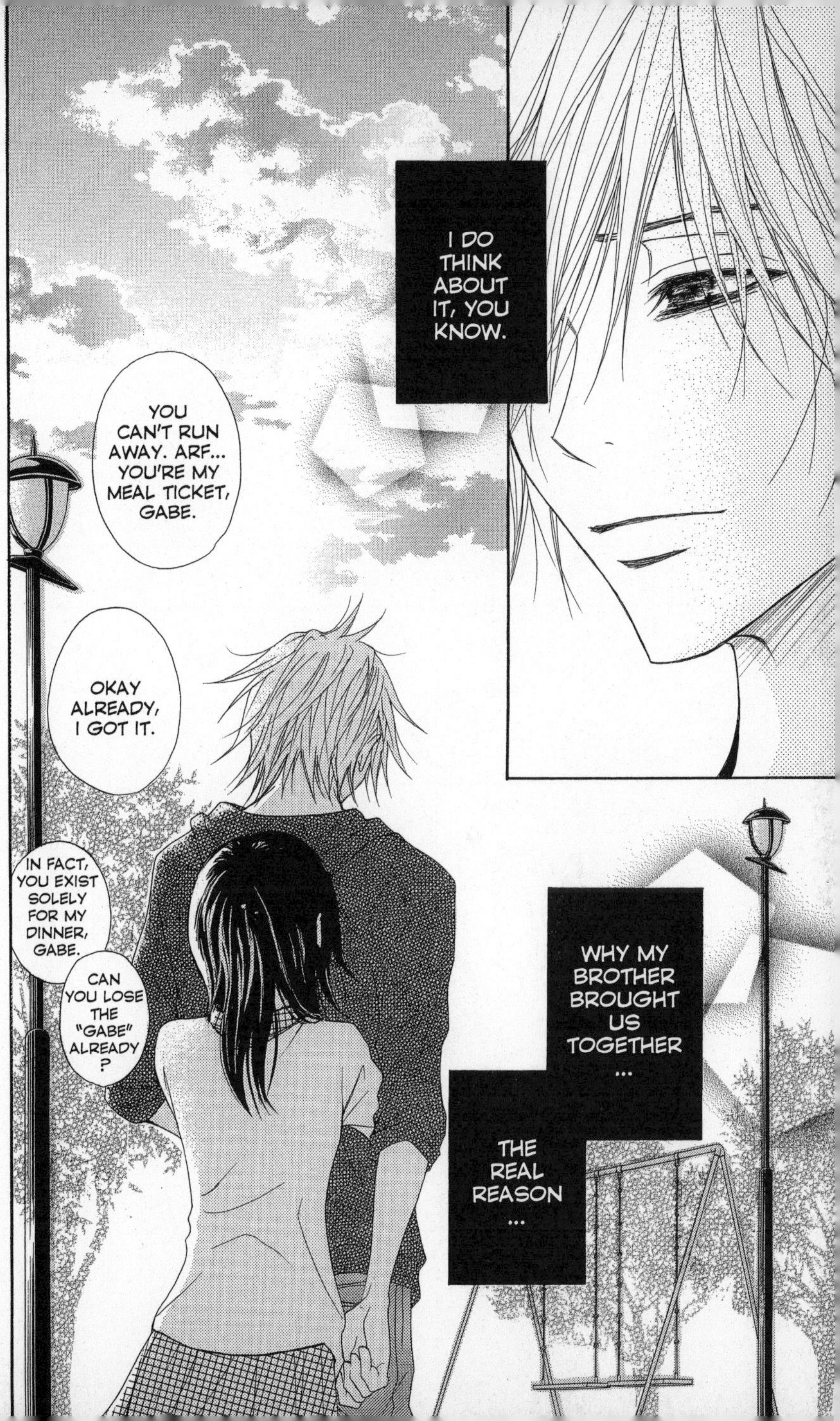
I DO THINK ABOUT IT, YOU KNOW.
YOU CAN'T RUN AWAY. ARF... YOU'RE MY MEAL TICKET, GABE.
OKAY ALREADY, I GOT IT.
IN FACT, YOU EXIST SOLELY FOR MY DINNER, GABE.
CAN YOU LOSE THE "GABE" ALREADY?
WHY MY BROTHER BROUGHT US TOGETHER...
THE REAL REASON...

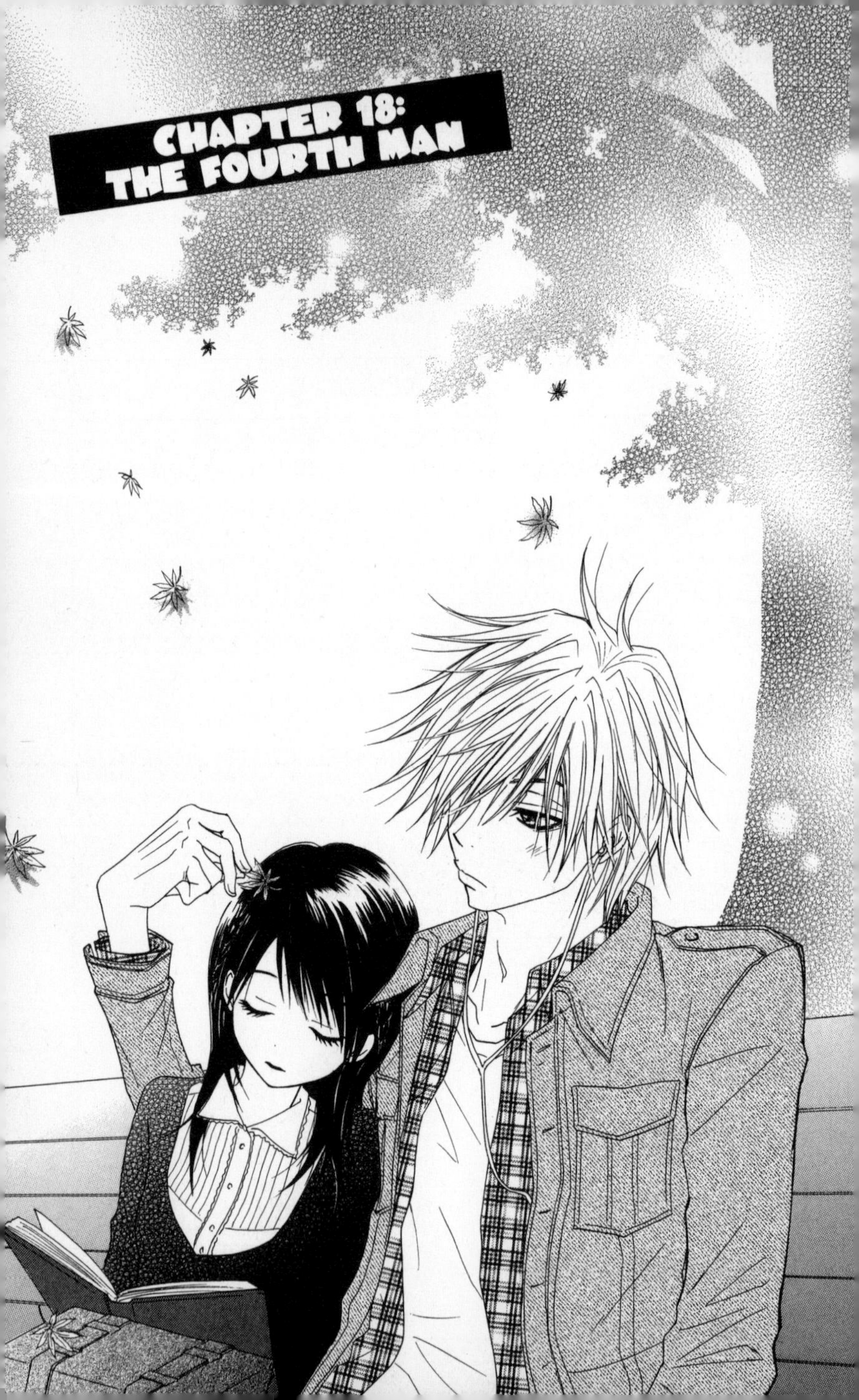
CHAPTER 18:
THE FOURTH MAN

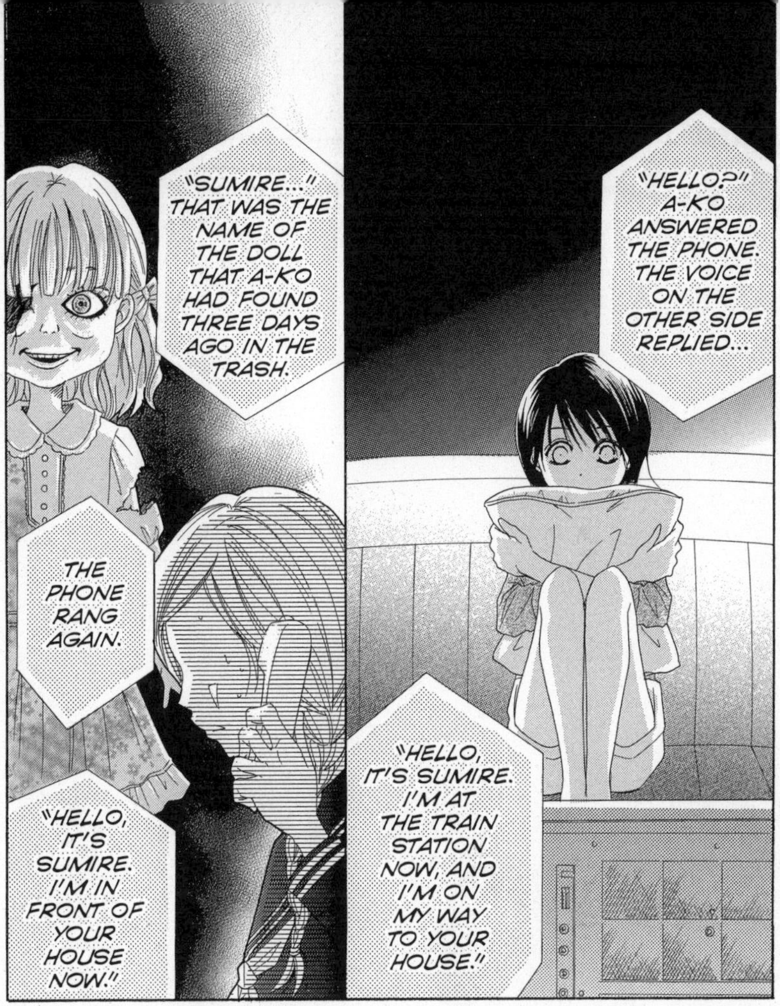
"HELLO?" A-KO ANSWERED THE PHONE. THE VOICE ON THE OTHER SIDE REPLIED...
"HELLO, IT'S SUMIRE. I'M AT THE TRAIN STATION NOW, AND I'M ON MY WAY TO YOUR HOUSE."
"SUMIRE..." THAT WAS THE NAME OF THE DOLL THAT A-KO HAD FOUND THREE DAYS AGO IN THE TRASH.
THE PHONE RANG AGAIN.
"HELLO, IT'S SUMIRE. I'M IN FRONT OF YOUR HOUSE NOW."

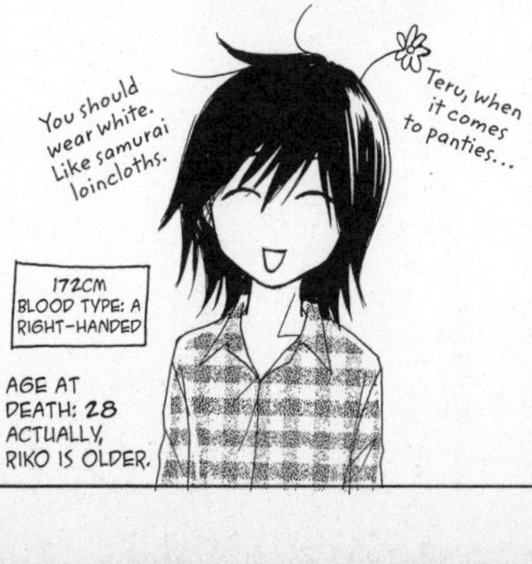
Teru, when it comes to panties...
You should wear white. Like samurai loincloths.
172CM
BLOOD TYPE: A
RIGHT-HANDED
AGE AT DEATH: 28
ACTUALLY, RIKO IS OLDER.

IT WAS REVEALED IN CHAPTER 17 THAT TERU'S BROTHER, SOICHIRO, IS ACTUALLY VERY ZANY. EVER SINCE, HIS POPULARITY HAS SKYROCKETED. IT'S HELPFUL THAT *DAISY* READERS ARE QUITE UNDERSTANDING WHEN IT COMES TO CRAZINESS. THANK YOU FOR CONTINUING TO SUPPORT *DENGEKI DAISY*, WHERE 90 PERCENT OF THE CHARACTERS THAT APPEAR HEREAFTER ARE PRETTY CRAZY.

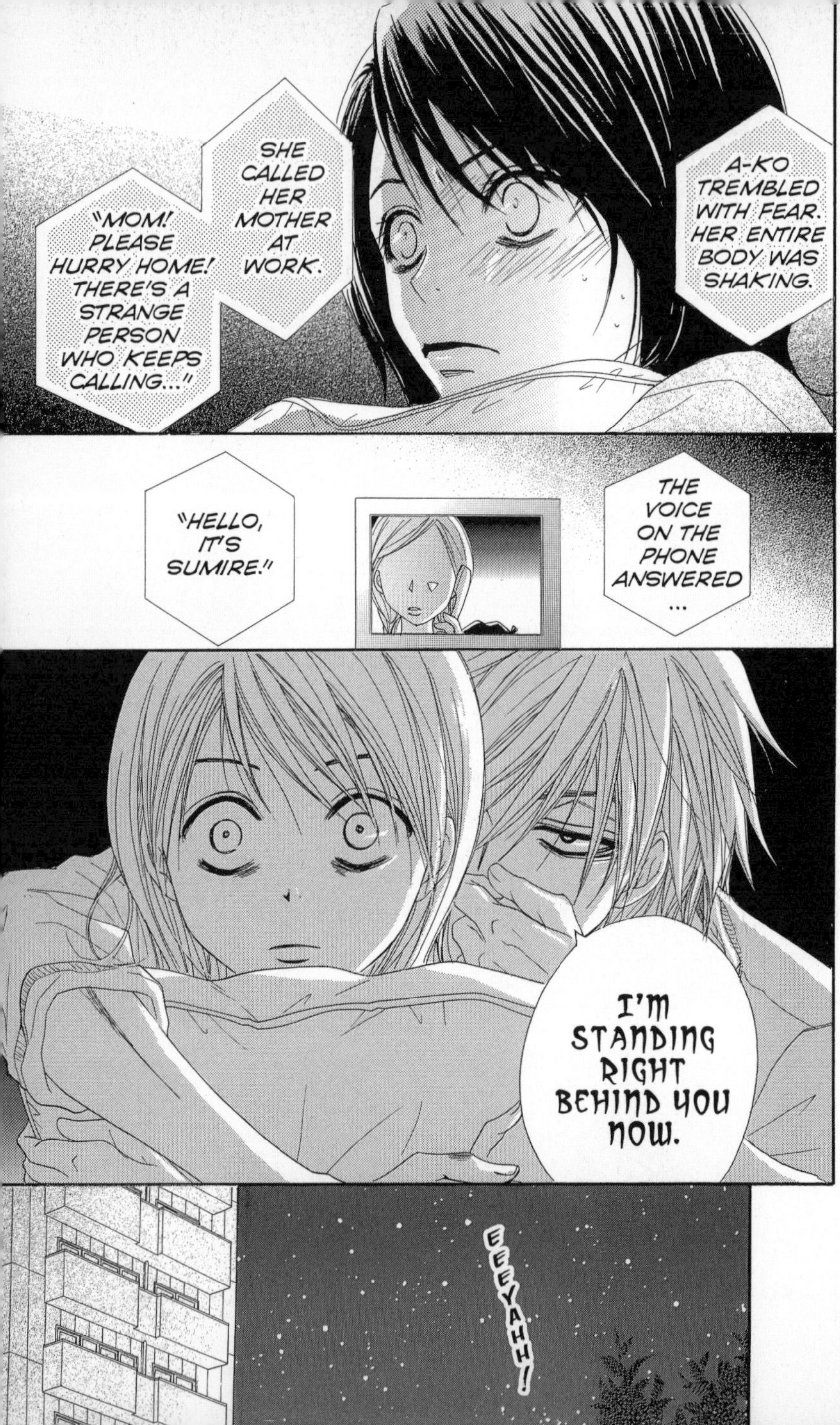
A-KO TREMBLED WITH FEAR. HER ENTIRE BODY WAS SHAKING.
SHE CALLED HER MOTHER AT WORK.
"MOM! PLEASE HURRY HOME! THERE'S A STRANGE PERSON WHO KEEPS CALLING..."
THE VOICE ON THE PHONE ANSWERED ...
"HELLO, IT'S SUMIRE."
I'M STANDING RIGHT BEHIND YOU NOW.
EEEYAHH!

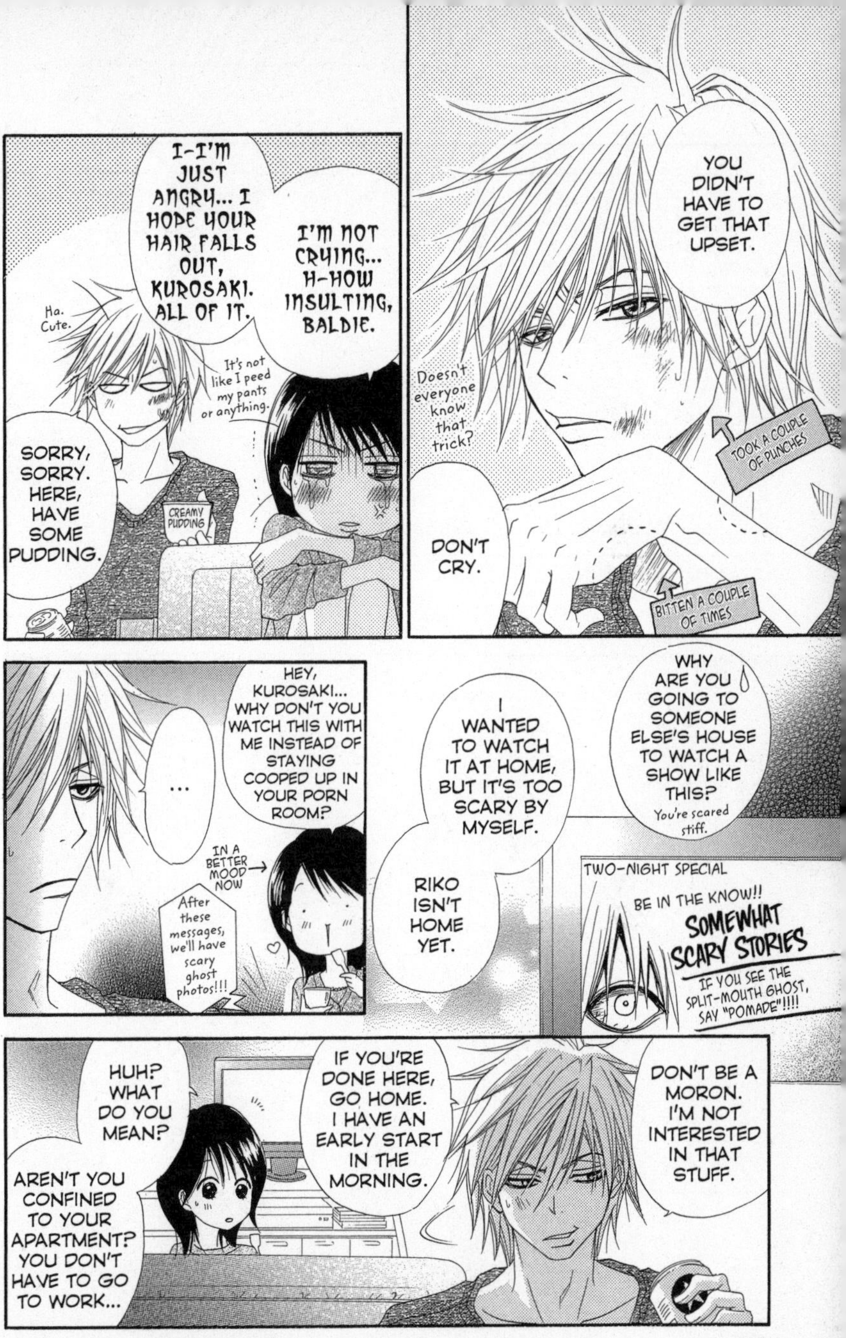
YOU DIDN'T HAVE TO GET THAT UPSET.
Doesn't everyone know that trick?
TOOK A COUPLE OF PUNCHES
DON'T CRY.
BITTEN A COUPLE OF TIMES
I'M NOT CRYING... H-HOW INSULTING, BALDIE.
I-I'M JUST ANGRY... I HOPE YOUR HAIR FALLS OUT, KUROSAKI. ALL OF IT.
Ha. Cute.
It's not like I peed my pants or anything.
SORRY, SORRY. HERE, HAVE SOME PUDDING.
CREAMY PUDDING
WHY ARE YOU GOING TO SOMEONE ELSE'S HOUSE TO WATCH A SHOW LIKE THIS?
You're scared stiff.
I WANTED TO WATCH IT AT HOME, BUT IT'S TOO SCARY BY MYSELF.
RIKO ISN'T HOME YET.
TWO-NIGHT SPECIAL
BE IN THE KNOW!!
SOMEWHAT SCARY STORIES
IF YOU SEE THE SPLIT-MOUTH GHOST, SAY "POMADE"!!!!
HEY, KUROSAKI... WHY DON'T YOU WATCH THIS WITH ME INSTEAD OF STAYING COOPED UP IN YOUR PORN ROOM?
...
IN A BETTER MOOD NOW
After these messages, we'll have scary ghost photos!!!
DON'T BE A MORON. I'M NOT INTERESTED IN THAT STUFF.
IF YOU'RE DONE HERE, GO HOME. I HAVE AN EARLY START IN THE MORNING.
HUH? WHAT DO YOU MEAN?
AREN'T YOU CONFINED TO YOUR APARTMENT? YOU DON'T HAVE TO GO TO WORK...

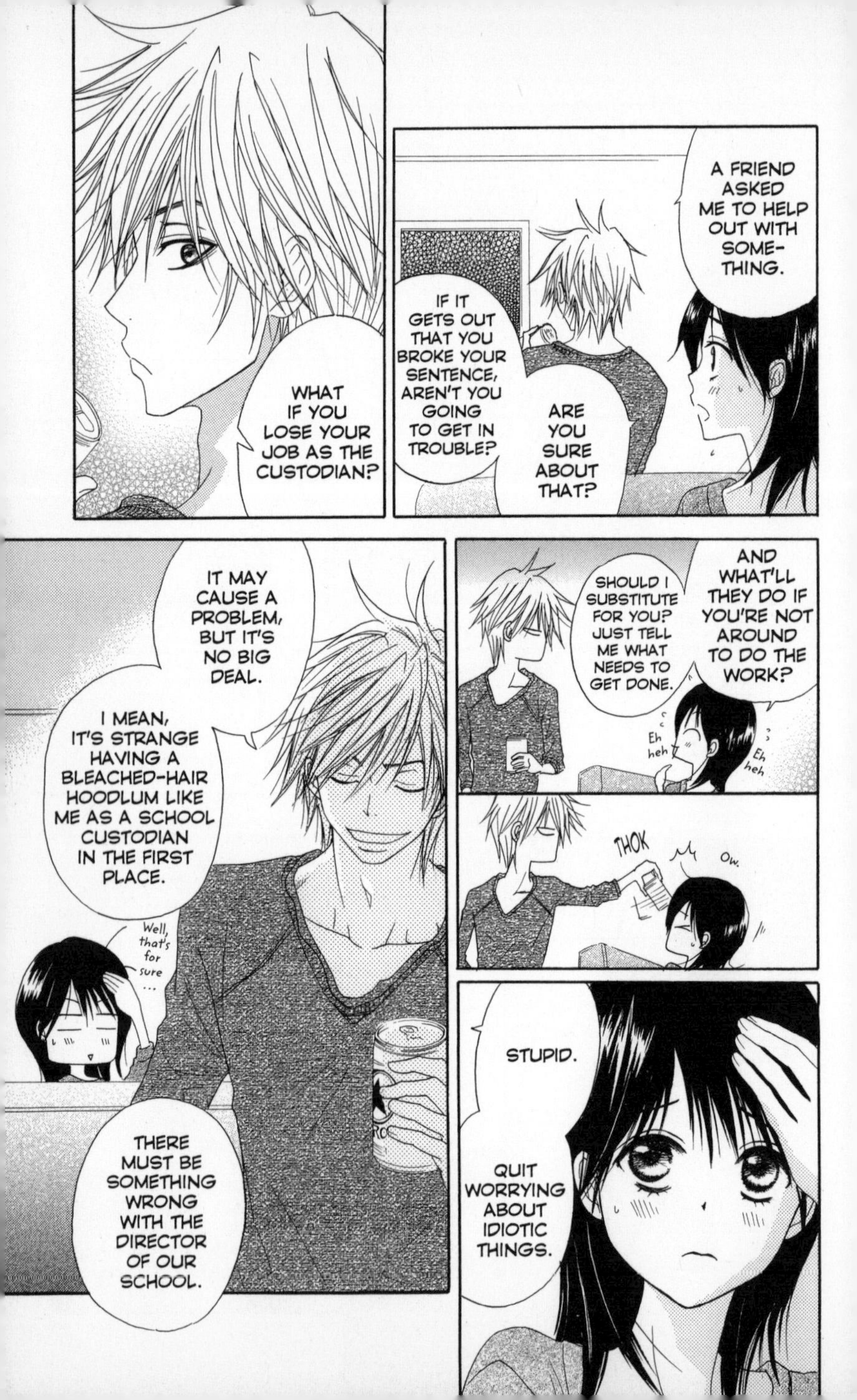
A FRIEND ASKED ME TO HELP OUT WITH SOME-THING.
ARE YOU SURE ABOUT THAT?
IF IT GETS OUT THAT YOU BROKE YOUR SENTENCE, AREN'T YOU GOING TO GET IN TROUBLE?
WHAT IF YOU LOSE YOUR JOB AS THE CUSTODIAN?
AND WHAT'LL THEY DO IF YOU'RE NOT AROUND TO DO THE WORK?
SHOULD I SUBSTITUTE FOR YOU? JUST TELL ME WHAT NEEDS TO GET DONE.
Eh heh
Eh heh
Ow.
THOK
STUPID.
QUIT WORRYING ABOUT IDIOTIC THINGS.
IT MAY CAUSE A PROBLEM, BUT IT'S NO BIG DEAL.
I MEAN, IT'S STRANGE HAVING A BLEACHED-HAIR HOODLUM LIKE ME AS A SCHOOL CUSTODIAN IN THE FIRST PLACE.
Well, that's for sure...
THERE MUST BE SOMETHING WRONG WITH THE DIRECTOR OF OUR SCHOOL.

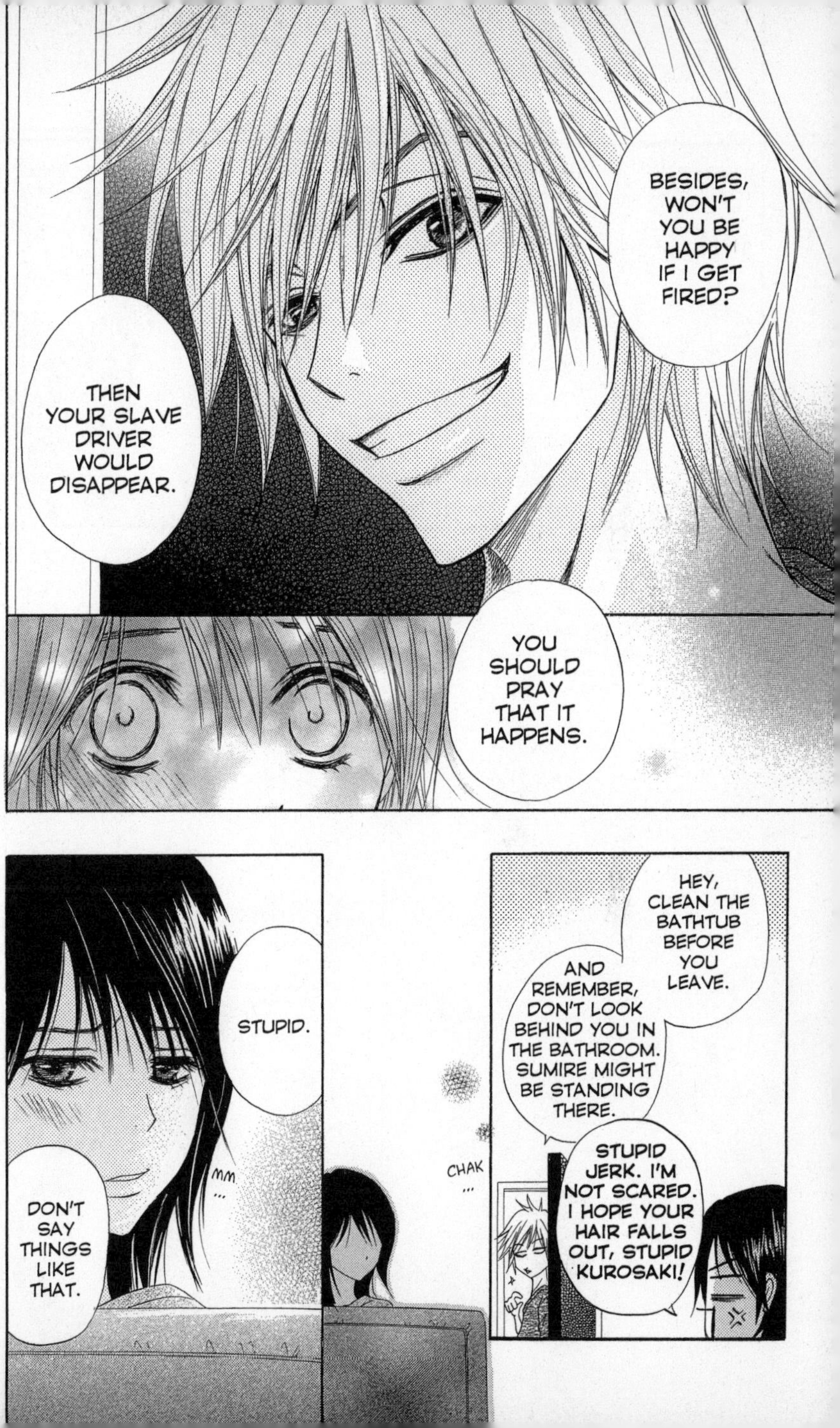
BESIDES, WON'T YOU BE HAPPY IF I GET FIRED?
THEN YOUR SLAVE DRIVER WOULD DISAPPEAR.
YOU SHOULD PRAY THAT IT HAPPENS.
HEY, CLEAN THE BATHTUB BEFORE YOU LEAVE.
AND REMEMBER, DON'T LOOK BEHIND YOU IN THE BATHROOM. SUMIRE MIGHT BE STANDING THERE.
STUPID JERK. I'M NOT SCARED. I HOPE YOUR HAIR FALLS OUT, STUPID KUROSAKI!
CHAK...
STUPID.
MM...
DON'T SAY THINGS LIKE THAT.

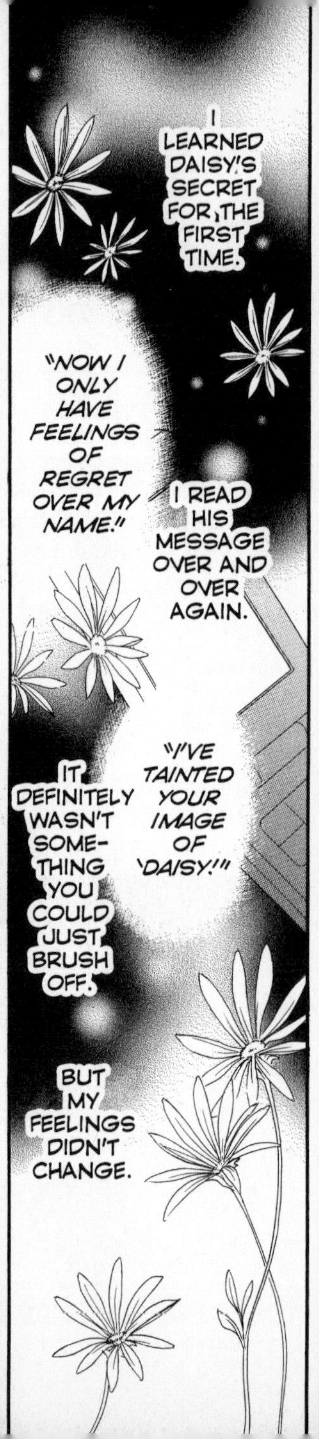
I LEARNED DAISY'S SECRET FOR THE FIRST TIME.
"NOW I ONLY HAVE FEELINGS OF REGRET OVER MY NAME."
I READ HIS MESSAGE OVER AND OVER AGAIN.
"I'VE TAINTED YOUR IMAGE OF 'DAISY!'"
IT DEFINITELY WASN'T SOME-THING YOU COULD JUST BRUSH OFF.
BUT MY FEELINGS DIDN'T CHANGE.

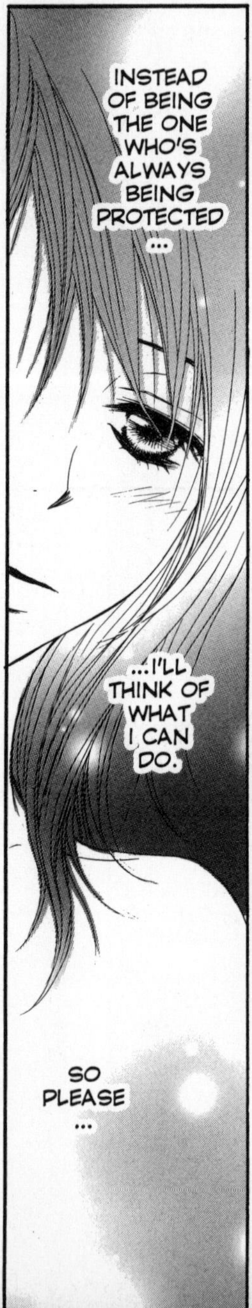
INSTEAD OF BEING THE ONE WHO'S ALWAYS BEING PROTECTED...
...I'LL THINK OF WHAT I CAN DO.
SO PLEASE...

WELL... ABOUT THIS SPACE HERE... WHEN THE COMIC WAS SERIALIZED IN THE MONTHLY MAGAZINE, THIS SPACE WAS SUPPOSED TO BE USED FOR ITS ADS. NOT MUCH EFFORT WAS MADE, HOWEVER, SO I FILLED THE SPACE WITH MANGA INSTEAD. THEN I WAS TOLD THAT WITH A LITTLE MORE ADVERTISING, I COULD MAYBE SELL TWO TO THREE MORE BOOKS. SO RECENTLY, THERE HAVE BEEN PROMOTIONAL ADS HERE.

ANYWAY, THERE'S GOING TO BE A FEW OF THESE SPACES FROM NOW ON. OTHER THAN WORKING ON MANGA, THIS AUTHOR GENERALLY SPENDS TIME SLEEPING. (THE STONE SAUNAS I MENTIONED NEAR THE BACK OF THE BOOK ARE ACTUALLY QUITE RARE FOR ME.) THAT'S WHY I DON'T HAVE MUCH TO WRITE ABOUT. I'M SORRY TO BE SO BLUNT.

SO ANYWAY, WE'RE GOING TO USE THIS SPACE AS A CORNER TO RESPOND TO READERS' QUESTIONS AND COMMENTS.

SO EVERYONE, PLEASE HELP KYOUSUKE MOTOMI OUT.

(CONTINUES IN THE NEXT SPACE)

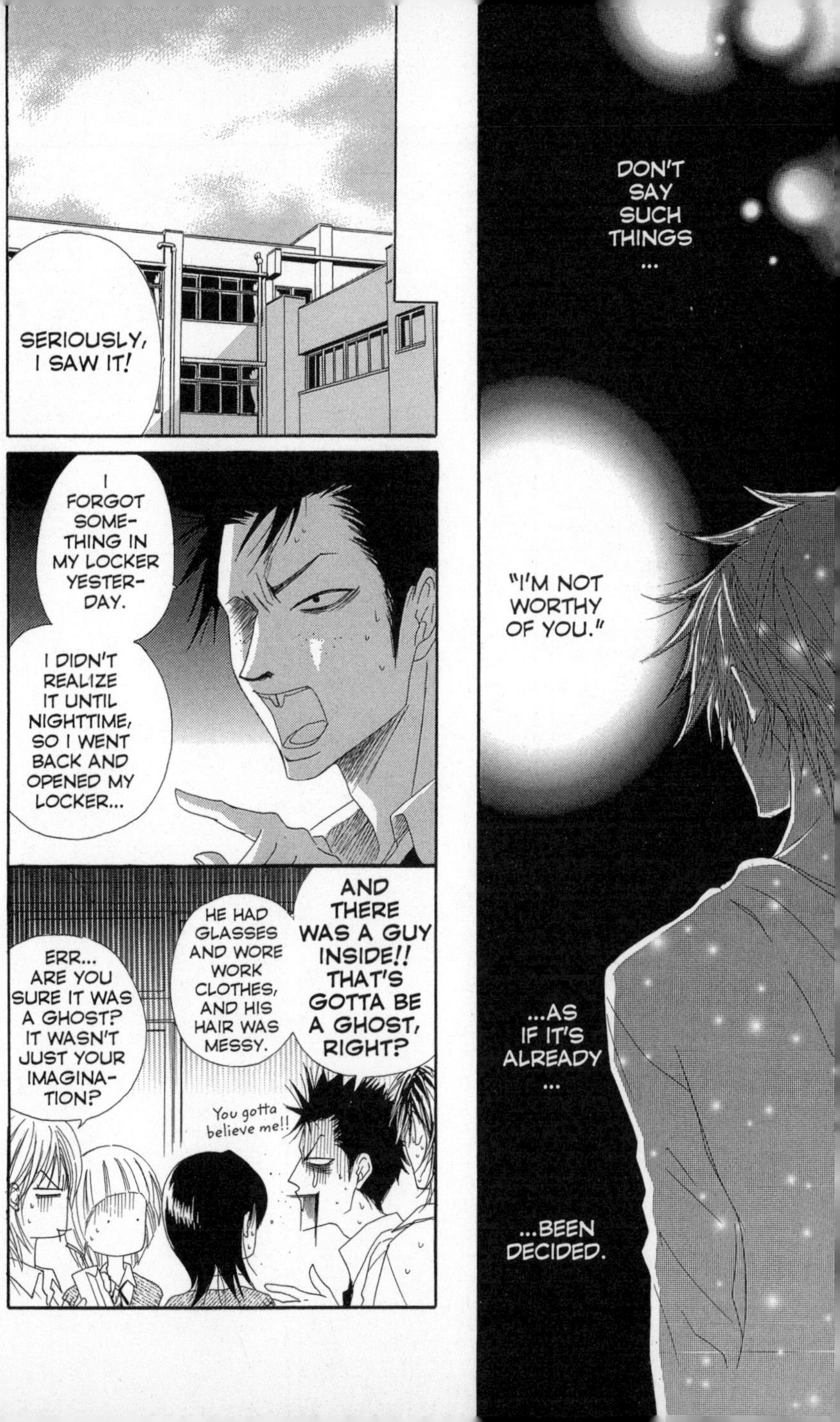
DON'T SAY SUCH THINGS ...
"I'M NOT WORTHY OF YOU."
...AS IF IT'S ALREADY ...
...BEEN DECIDED.
SERIOUSLY, I SAW IT!
I FORGOT SOME-THING IN MY LOCKER YESTER-DAY.
I DIDN'T REALIZE IT UNTIL NIGHTTIME, SO I WENT BACK AND OPENED MY LOCKER...
AND THERE WAS A GUY INSIDE!! THAT'S GOTTA BE A GHOST, RIGHT?
HE HAD GLASSES AND WORE WORK CLOTHES, AND HIS HAIR WAS MESSY.
ERR... ARE YOU SURE IT WAS A GHOST? IT WASN'T JUST YOUR IMAGINA-TION?
You gotta believe me!!

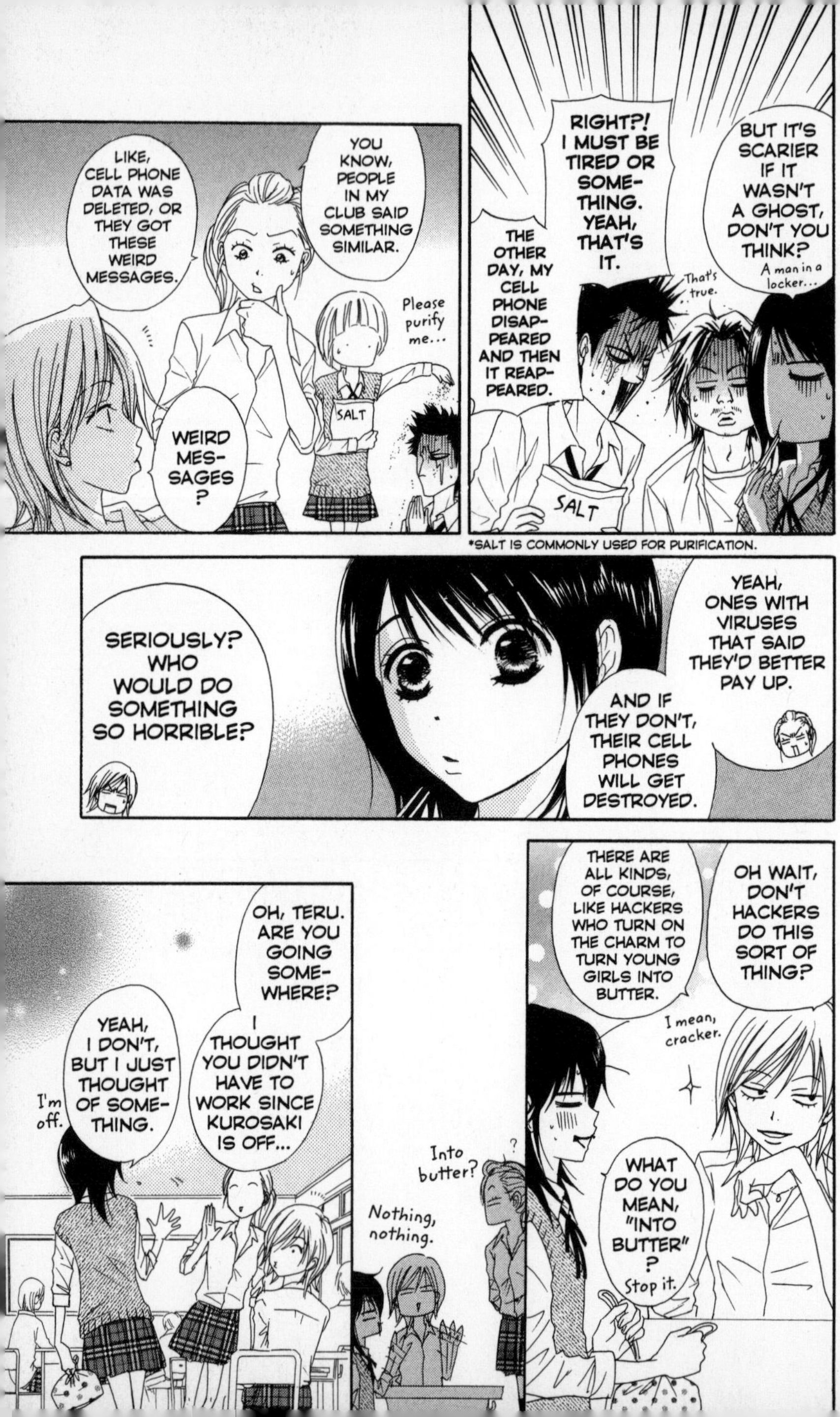
BUT IT'S SCARIER IF IT WASN'T A GHOST, DON'T YOU THINK?
A man in a locker...
RIGHT?! I MUST BE TIRED OR SOMETHING. YEAH, THAT'S IT.
That's true.
THE OTHER DAY, MY CELL PHONE DISAPPEARED AND THEN IT REAPPEARED.
SALT
YOU KNOW, PEOPLE IN MY CLUB SAID SOMETHING SIMILAR.
Please purify me...
LIKE, CELL PHONE DATA WAS DELETED, OR THEY GOT THESE WEIRD MESSAGES.
SALT
WEIRD MESSAGES?
*SALT IS COMMONLY USED FOR PURIFICATION.
YEAH, ONES WITH VIRUSES THAT SAID THEY'D BETTER PAY UP.
AND IF THEY DON'T, THEIR CELL PHONES WILL GET DESTROYED.
SERIOUSLY? WHO WOULD DO SOMETHING SO HORRIBLE?
OH WAIT, DON'T HACKERS DO THIS SORT OF THING?
THERE ARE ALL KINDS, OF COURSE, LIKE HACKERS WHO TURN ON THE CHARM TO TURN YOUNG GIRLS INTO BUTTER.
I mean, cracker.
WHAT DO YOU MEAN, "INTO BUTTER"?
Stop it.
Into butter?
Nothing, nothing.
OH, TERU. ARE YOU GOING SOMEWHERE?
I THOUGHT YOU DIDN'T HAVE TO WORK SINCE KUROSAKI IS OFF...
YEAH, I DON'T, BUT I JUST THOUGHT OF SOMETHING.
I'm off.

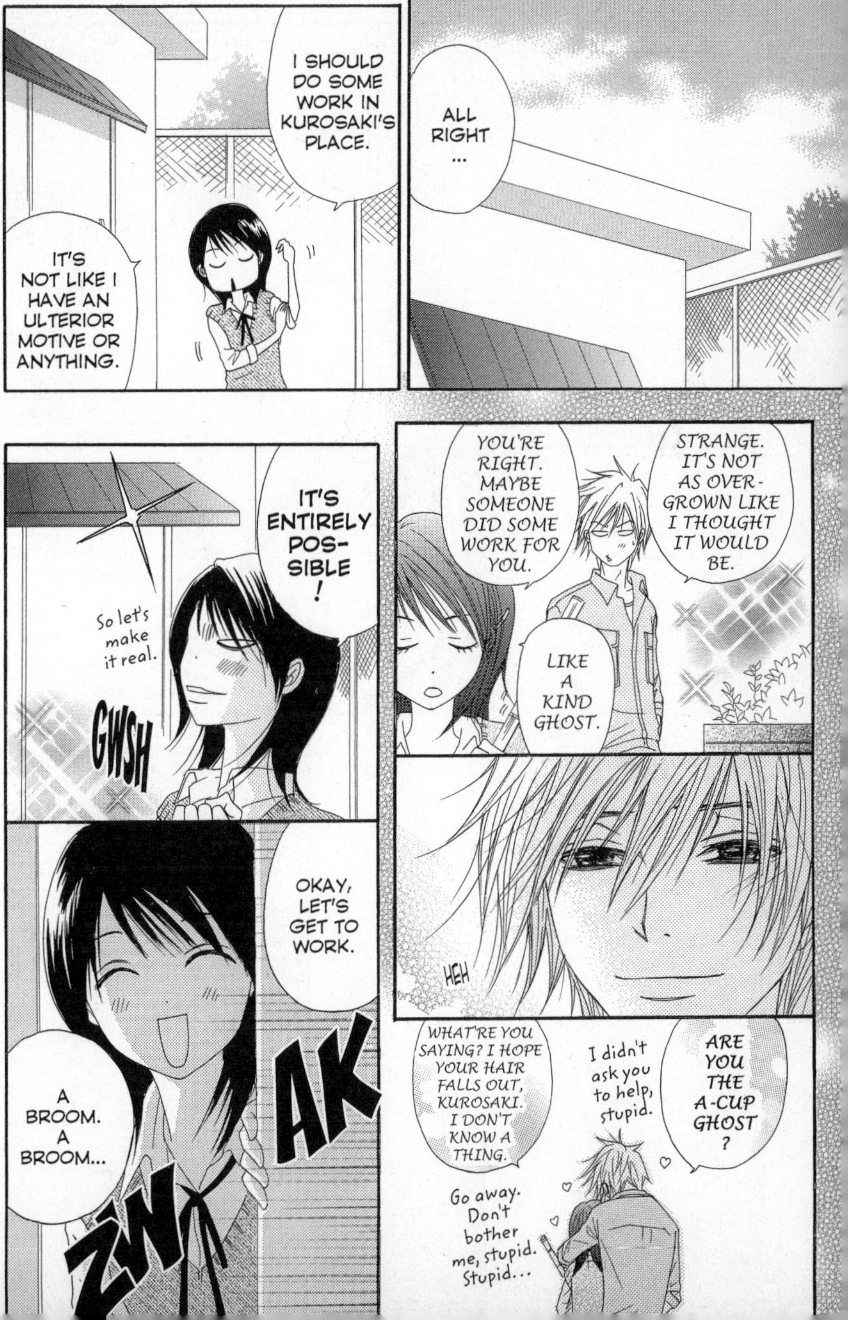
ALL RIGHT ...
I SHOULD DO SOME WORK IN KUROSAKI'S PLACE.
IT'S NOT LIKE I HAVE AN ULTERIOR MOTIVE OR ANYTHING.
STRANGE. IT'S NOT AS OVER-GROWN LIKE I THOUGHT IT WOULD BE.
YOU'RE RIGHT. MAYBE SOMEONE DID SOME WORK FOR YOU.
LIKE A KIND GHOST.
HEH
ARE YOU THE A-CUP GHOST?
I didn't ask you to help, stupid.
WHAT'RE YOU SAYING? I HOPE YOUR HAIR FALLS OUT, KUROSAKI. I DON'T KNOW A THING.
Go away. Don't bother me, stupid. Stupid...
IT'S ENTIRELY POS-SIBLE!
So let's make it real.
GWSH
OKAY, LET'S GET TO WORK.
AK
ZN
A BROOM. A BROOM...

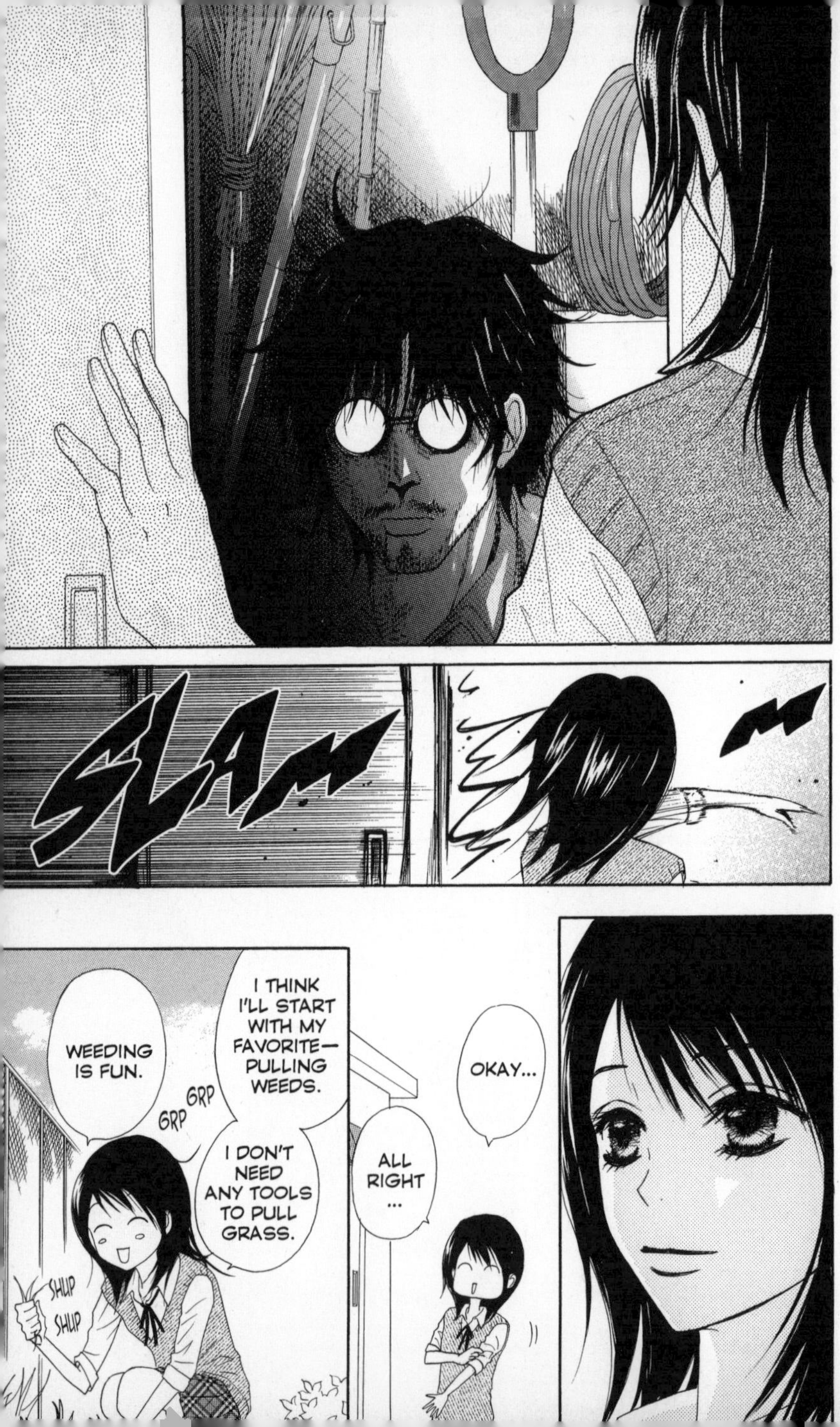
SLAM
OKAY...
ALL RIGHT ...
I THINK I'LL START WITH MY FAVORITE—PULLING WEEDS.
WEEDING IS FUN.
GRP GRP
I DON'T NEED ANY TOOLS TO PULL GRASS.
SHUP SHUP

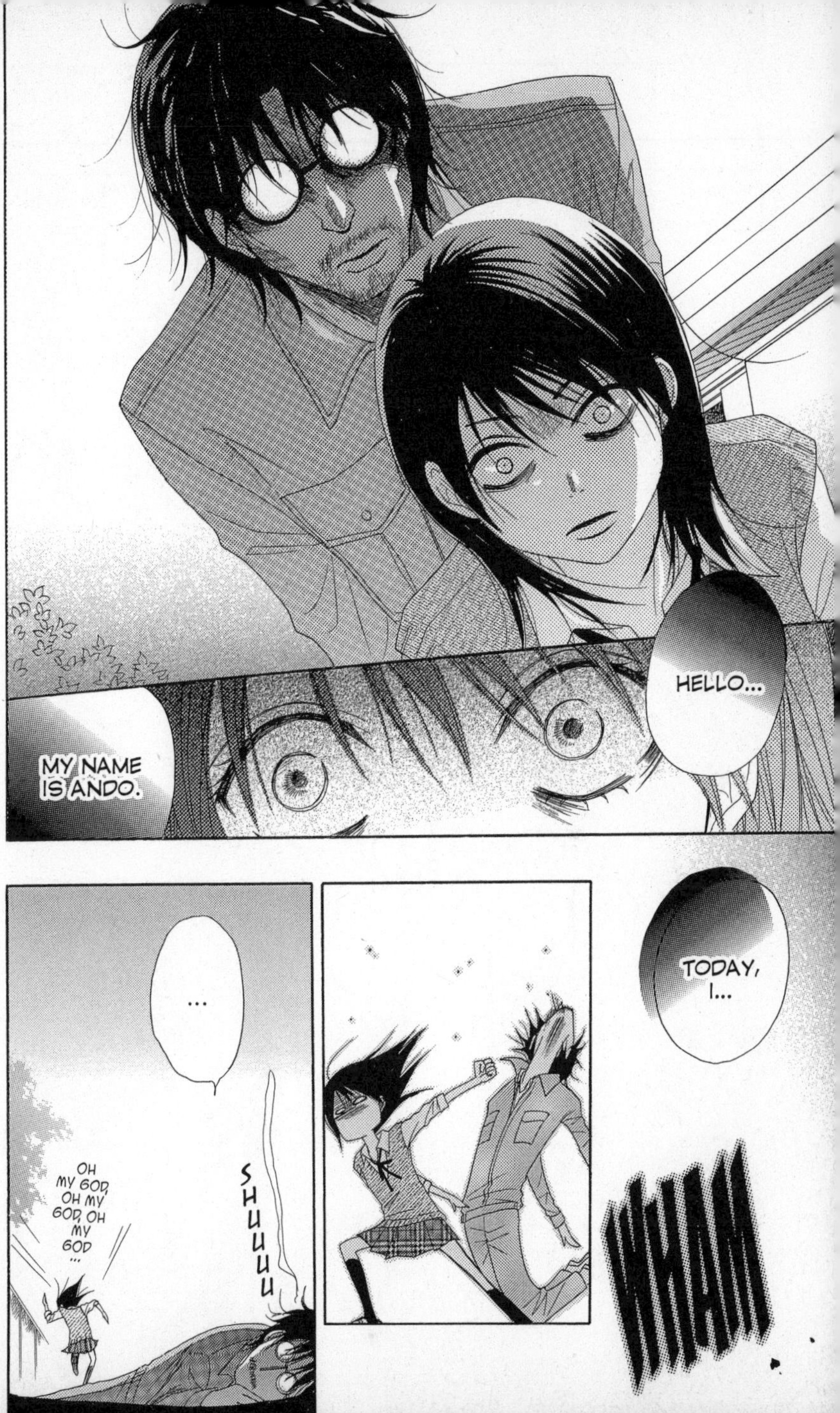
HELLO...
MY NAME IS ANDO.
TODAY, I...
WHAM
...
SHUUUUU
OH MY GOD, OH MY GOD, OH MY GOD...

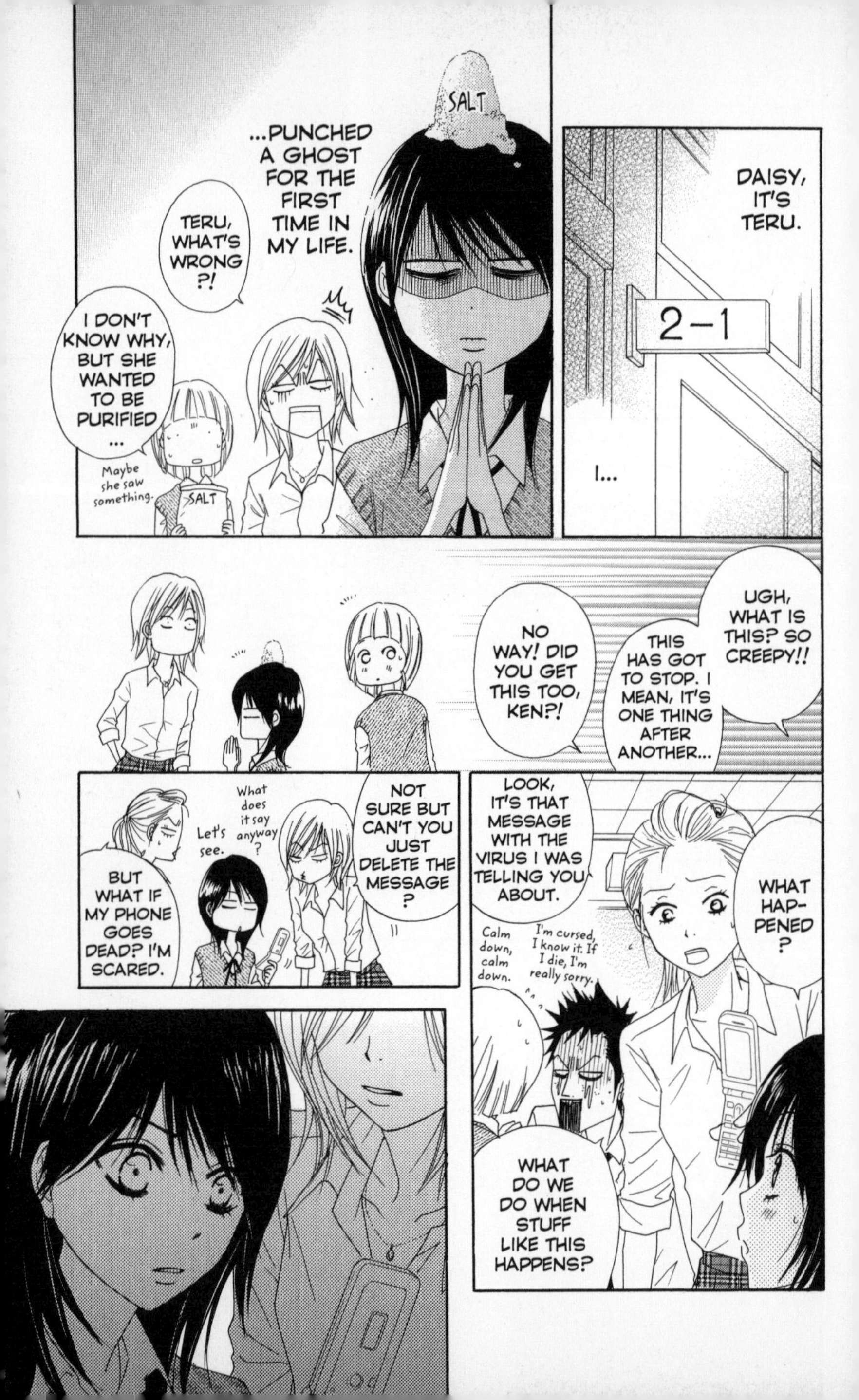
DAISY, IT'S TERU.
I...
SALT
...PUNCHED A GHOST FOR THE FIRST TIME IN MY LIFE.
TERU, WHAT'S WRONG?!
I DON'T KNOW WHY, BUT SHE WANTED TO BE PURIFIED...
Maybe she saw something.
SALT
UGH, WHAT IS THIS? SO CREEPY!!
THIS HAS GOT TO STOP. I MEAN, IT'S ONE THING AFTER ANOTHER...
NO WAY! DID YOU GET THIS TOO, KEN?!
WHAT HAPPENED?
LOOK, IT'S THAT MESSAGE WITH THE VIRUS I WAS TELLING YOU ABOUT.
I'm cursed, I know it. If I die, I'm really sorry.
Calm down, calm down.
WHAT DO WE DO WHEN STUFF LIKE THIS HAPPENS?
NOT SURE BUT CAN'T YOU JUST DELETE THE MESSAGE?
What does it say anyway?
Let's see.
BUT WHAT IF MY PHONE GOES DEAD? I'M SCARED.

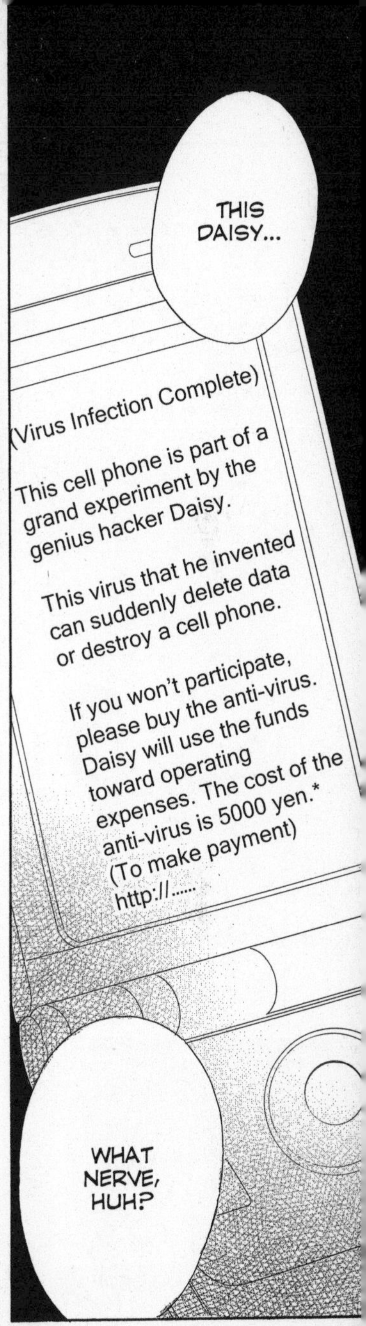
THIS DAISY...
(Virus Infection Complete)
This cell phone is part of a grand experiment by the genius hacker Daisy.
This virus that he invented can suddenly delete data or destroy a cell phone.
If you won't participate, please buy the anti-virus. Daisy will use the funds toward operating expenses. The cost of the anti-virus is 5000 yen.*
(To make payment
http://......
WHAT NERVE, HUH?

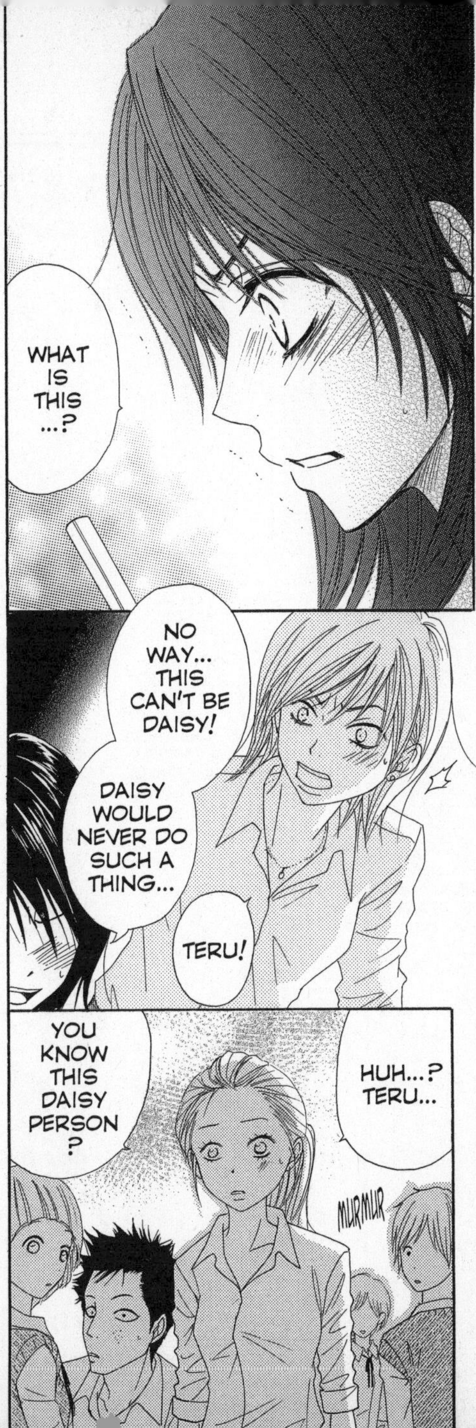
WHAT IS THIS ...?
NO WAY... THIS CAN'T BE DAISY!
DAISY WOULD NEVER DO SUCH A THING...
TERU!
HUH...? TERU...
YOU KNOW THIS DAISY PERSON ?
MURMUR

*ABOUT $61

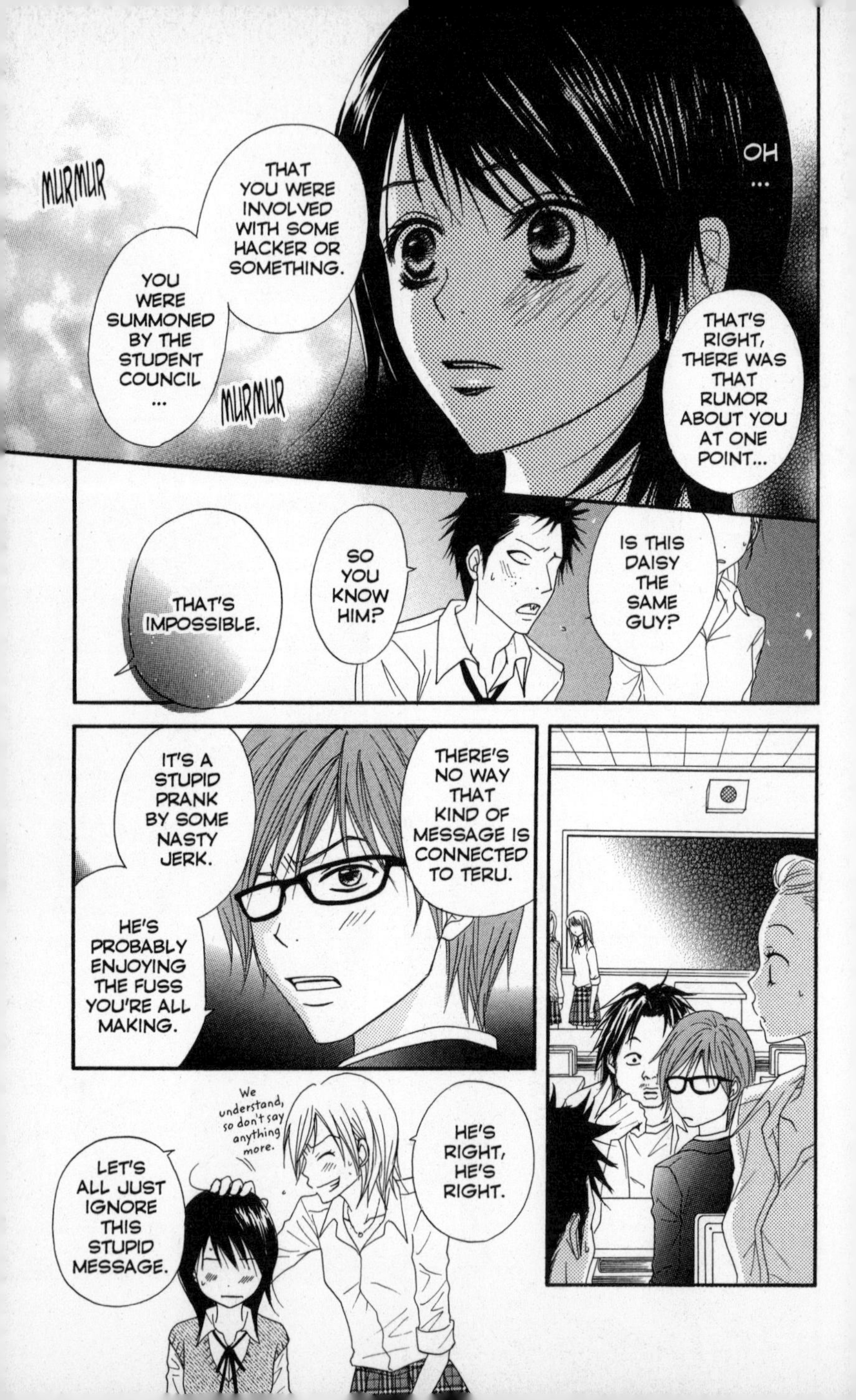
OH ...
THAT'S RIGHT, THERE WAS THAT RUMOR ABOUT YOU AT ONE POINT...
THAT YOU WERE INVOLVED WITH SOME HACKER OR SOMETHING.
MURMUR
YOU WERE SUMMONED BY THE STUDENT COUNCIL ...
MURMUR
IS THIS DAISY THE SAME GUY?
SO YOU KNOW HIM?
THAT'S IMPOSSIBLE.
THERE'S NO WAY THAT KIND OF MESSAGE IS CONNECTED TO TERU.
IT'S A STUPID PRANK BY SOME NASTY JERK.
HE'S PROBABLY ENJOYING THE FUSS YOU'RE ALL MAKING.
HE'S RIGHT, HE'S RIGHT.
We understand, so don't say anything more.
LET'S ALL JUST IGNORE THIS STUPID MESSAGE.

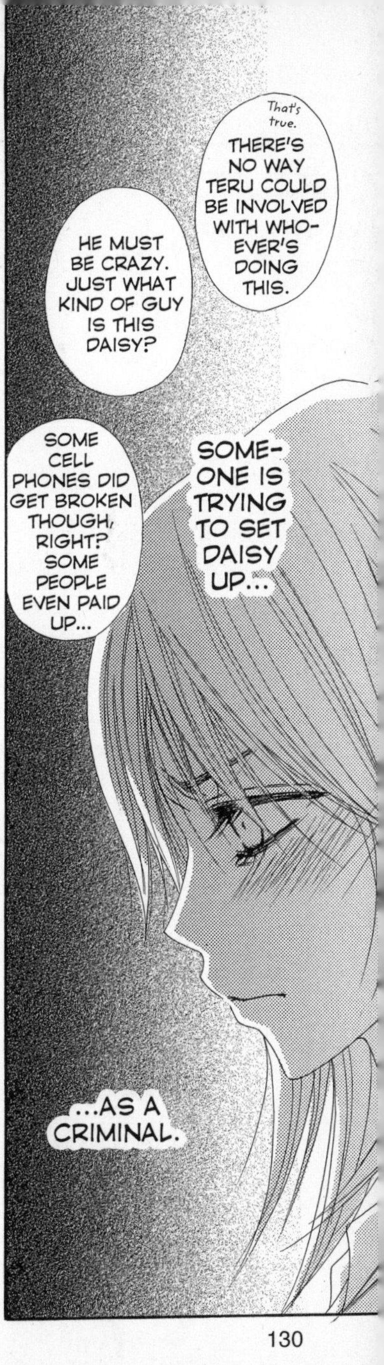
That's true.
THERE'S NO WAY TERU COULD BE INVOLVED WITH WHO-EVER'S DOING THIS.
HE MUST BE CRAZY. JUST WHAT KIND OF GUY IS THIS DAISY?
SOME-ONE IS TRYING TO SET DAISY UP...
SOME CELL PHONES DID GET BROKEN THOUGH, RIGHT? SOME PEOPLE EVEN PAID UP...
...AS A CRIMINAL.

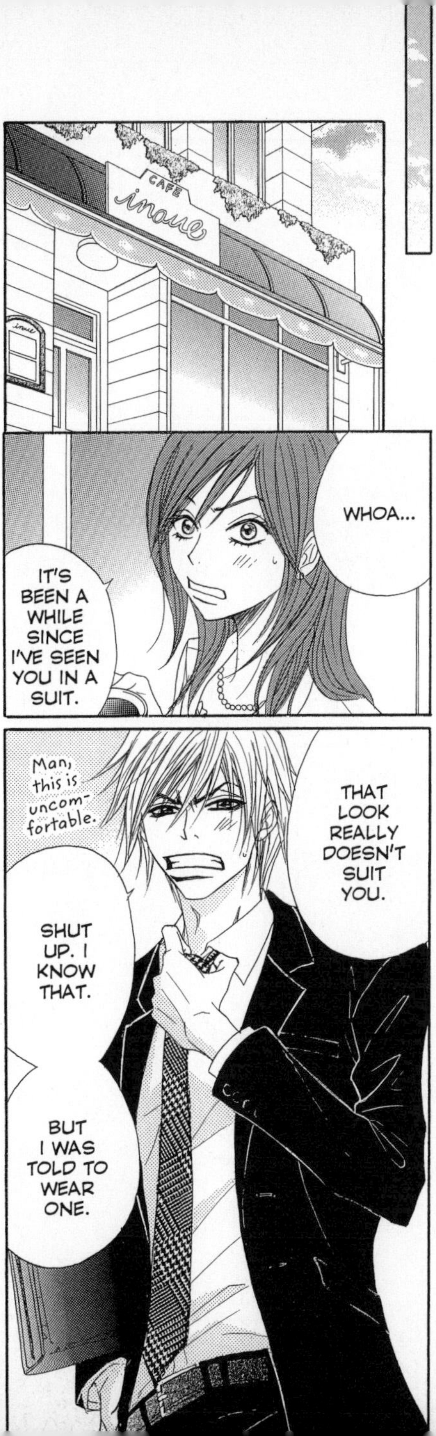
CAFE inoue
WHOA...
IT'S BEEN A WHILE SINCE I'VE SEEN YOU IN A SUIT.
THAT LOOK REALLY DOESN'T SUIT YOU.
Man, this is uncom-fortable.
SHUT UP. I KNOW THAT.
BUT I WAS TOLD TO WEAR ONE.

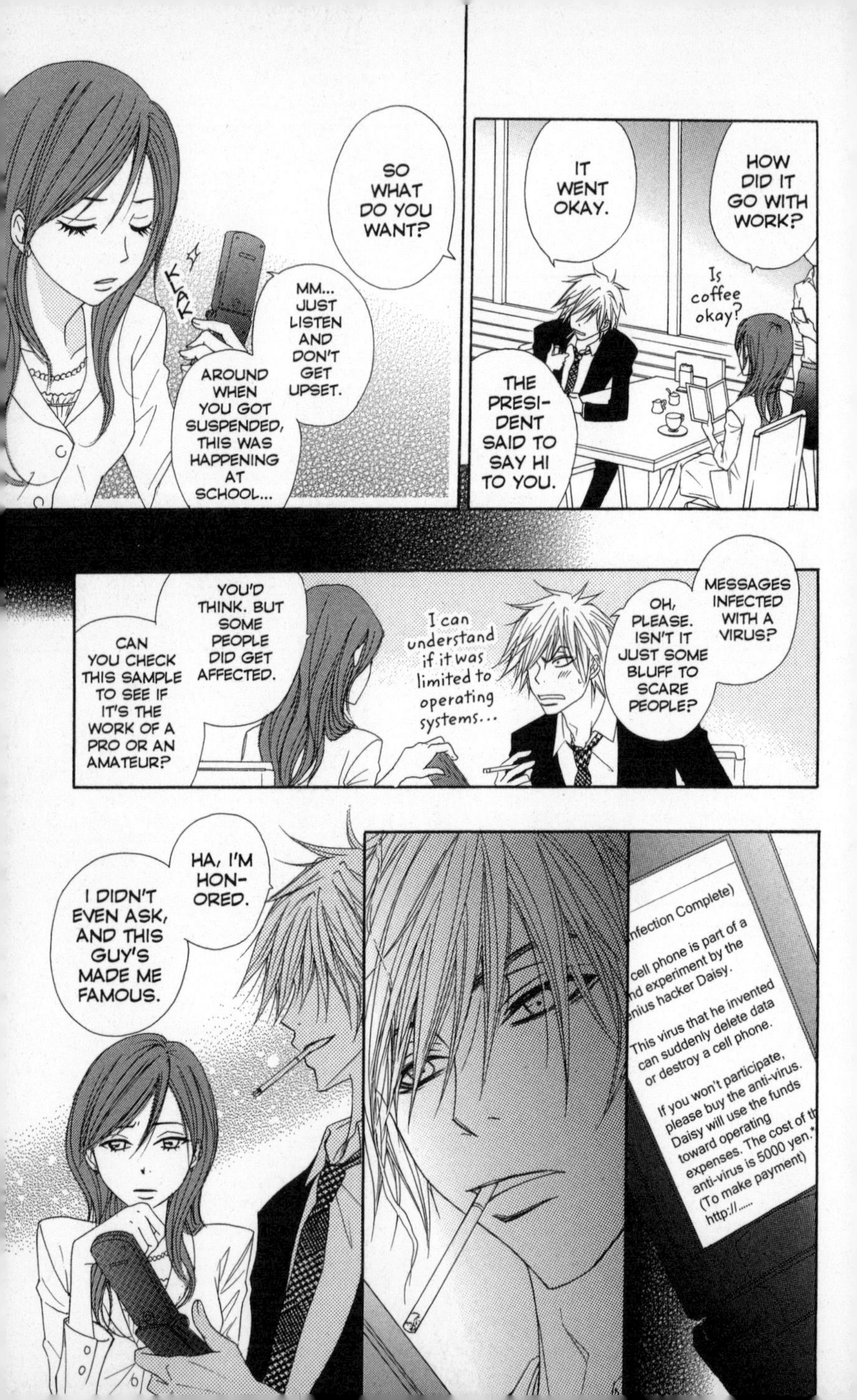
HOW DID IT GO WITH WORK?
Is coffee okay?
IT WENT OKAY.
THE PRESI-DENT SAID TO SAY HI TO YOU.
SO WHAT DO YOU WANT?
KLAK
MM... JUST LISTEN AND DON'T GET UPSET.
AROUND WHEN YOU GOT SUSPENDED, THIS WAS HAPPENING AT SCHOOL...
MESSAGES INFECTED WITH A VIRUS?
OH, PLEASE. ISN'T IT JUST SOME BLUFF TO SCARE PEOPLE?
I can understand if it was limited to operating systems...
YOU'D THINK. BUT SOME PEOPLE DID GET AFFECTED.
CAN YOU CHECK THIS SAMPLE TO SEE IF IT'S THE WORK OF A PRO OR AN AMATEUR?
nfection Complete)
cell phone is part of a
nd experiment by the
nius hacker Daisy.
This virus that he invented
can suddenly delete data
or destroy a cell phone.
If you won't participate,
please buy the anti-virus.
Daisy will use the funds
toward operating
expenses. The cost of th
anti-virus is 5000 yen.*
(To make payment)
http://......
HA, I'M HON-ORED.
I DIDN'T EVEN ASK, AND THIS GUY'S MADE ME FAMOUS.

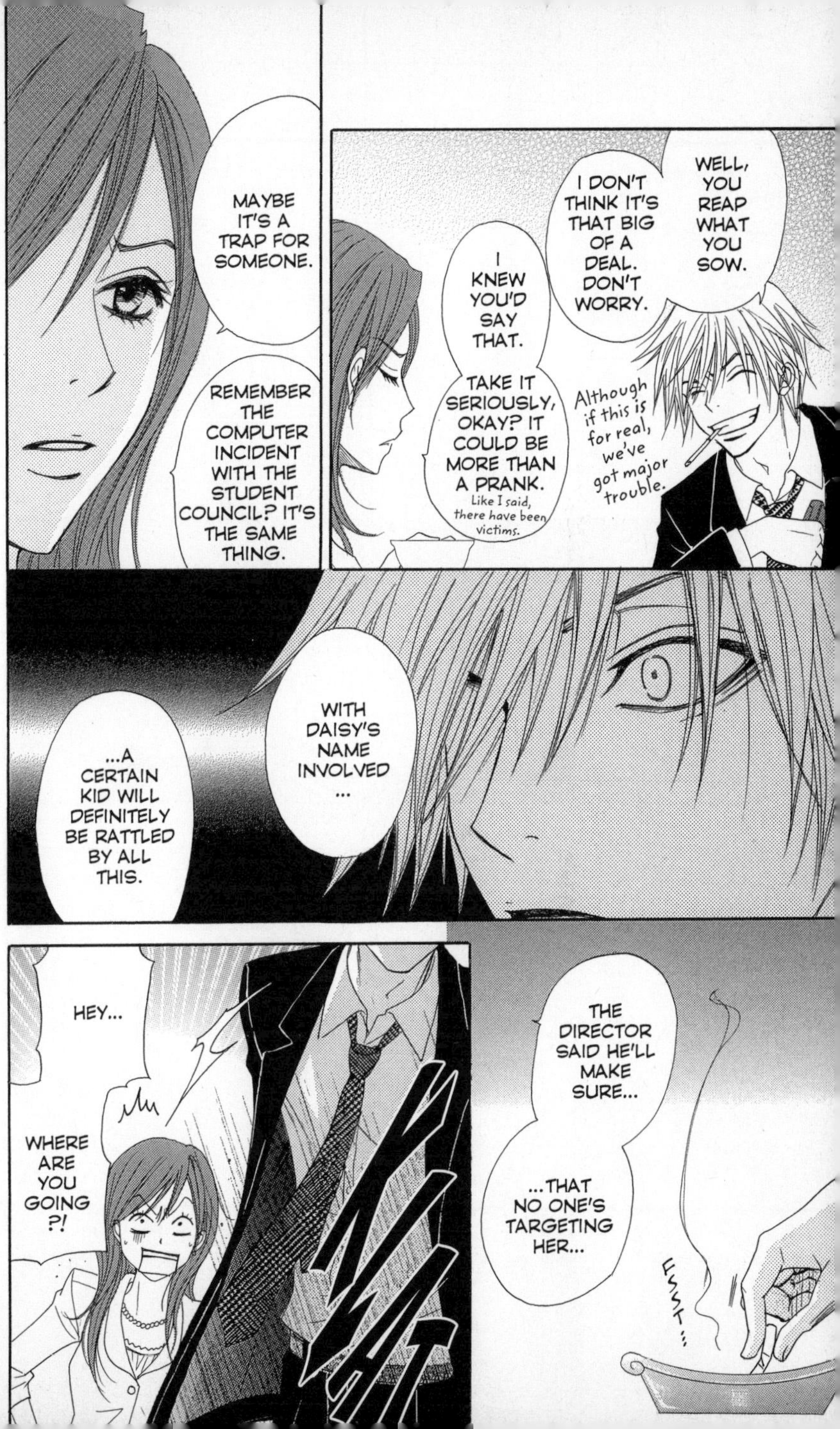
WELL, YOU REAP WHAT YOU SOW.
I DON'T THINK IT'S THAT BIG OF A DEAL. DON'T WORRY.
I KNEW YOU'D SAY THAT.
TAKE IT SERIOUSLY, OKAY? IT COULD BE MORE THAN A PRANK.
Like I said, there have been victims.
Although if this is for real, we've got major trouble.
MAYBE IT'S A TRAP FOR SOMEONE.
REMEMBER THE COMPUTER INCIDENT WITH THE STUDENT COUNCIL? IT'S THE SAME THING.
WITH DAISY'S NAME INVOLVED...
...A CERTAIN KID WILL DEFINITELY BE RATTLED BY ALL THIS.
THE DIRECTOR SAID HE'LL MAKE SURE...
...THAT NO ONE'S TARGETING HER...
FSST...
HEY...
WHERE ARE YOU GOING?!

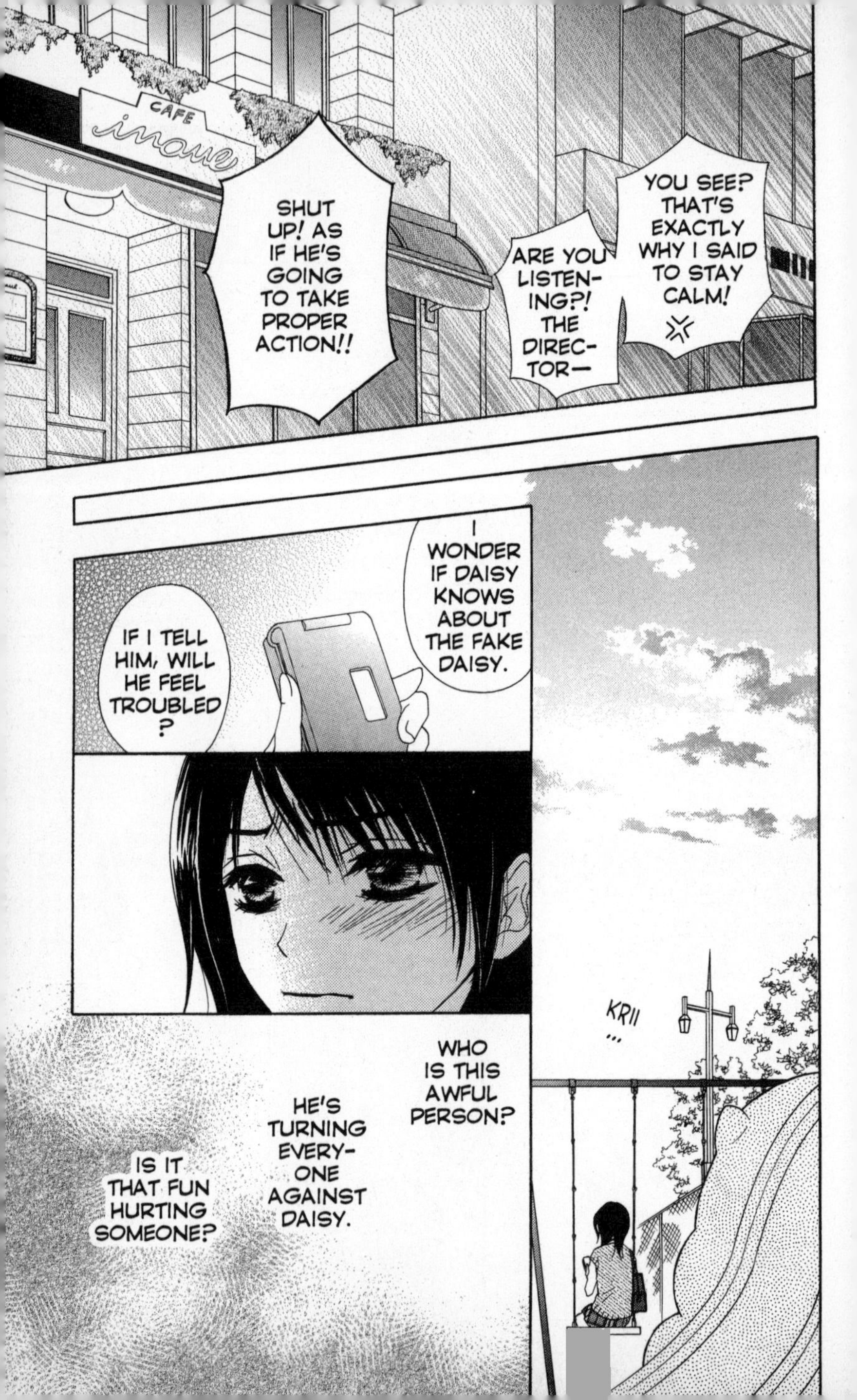
CAFE inoue
YOU SEE? THAT'S EXACTLY WHY I SAID TO STAY CALM!
ARE YOU LISTENING?! THE DIRECTOR—
SHUT UP! AS IF HE'S GOING TO TAKE PROPER ACTION!!
KRII...
I WONDER IF DAISY KNOWS ABOUT THE FAKE DAISY.
IF I TELL HIM, WILL HE FEEL TROUBLED?
WHO IS THIS AWFUL PERSON?
HE'S TURNING EVERYONE AGAINST DAISY.
IS IT THAT FUN HURTING SOMEONE?

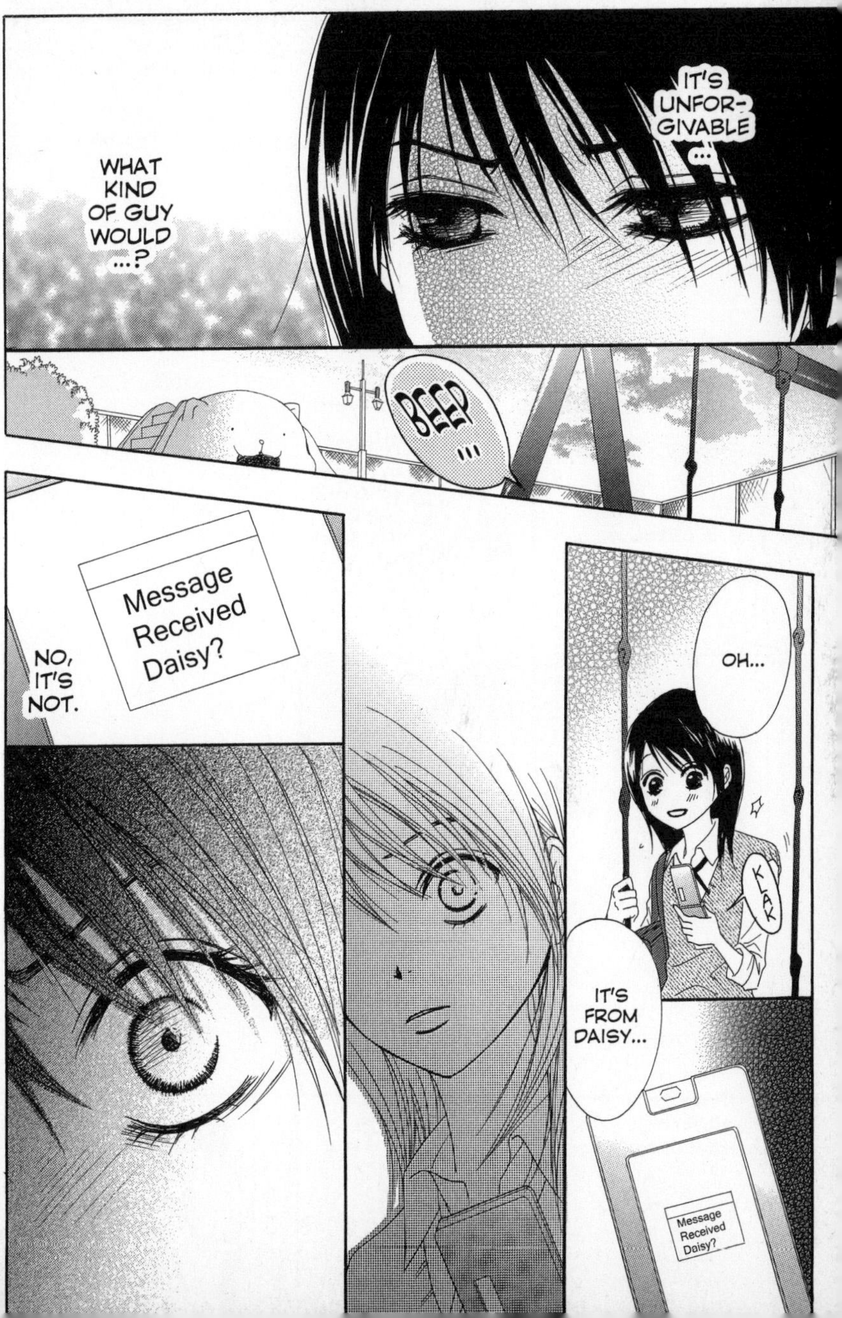
IT'S UNFOR-GIVABLE ...
WHAT KIND OF GUY WOULD ...?
BEEP ...
OH...
KLAK
IT'S FROM DAISY...
Message Received Daisy?
Message Received Daisy?
NO, IT'S NOT.

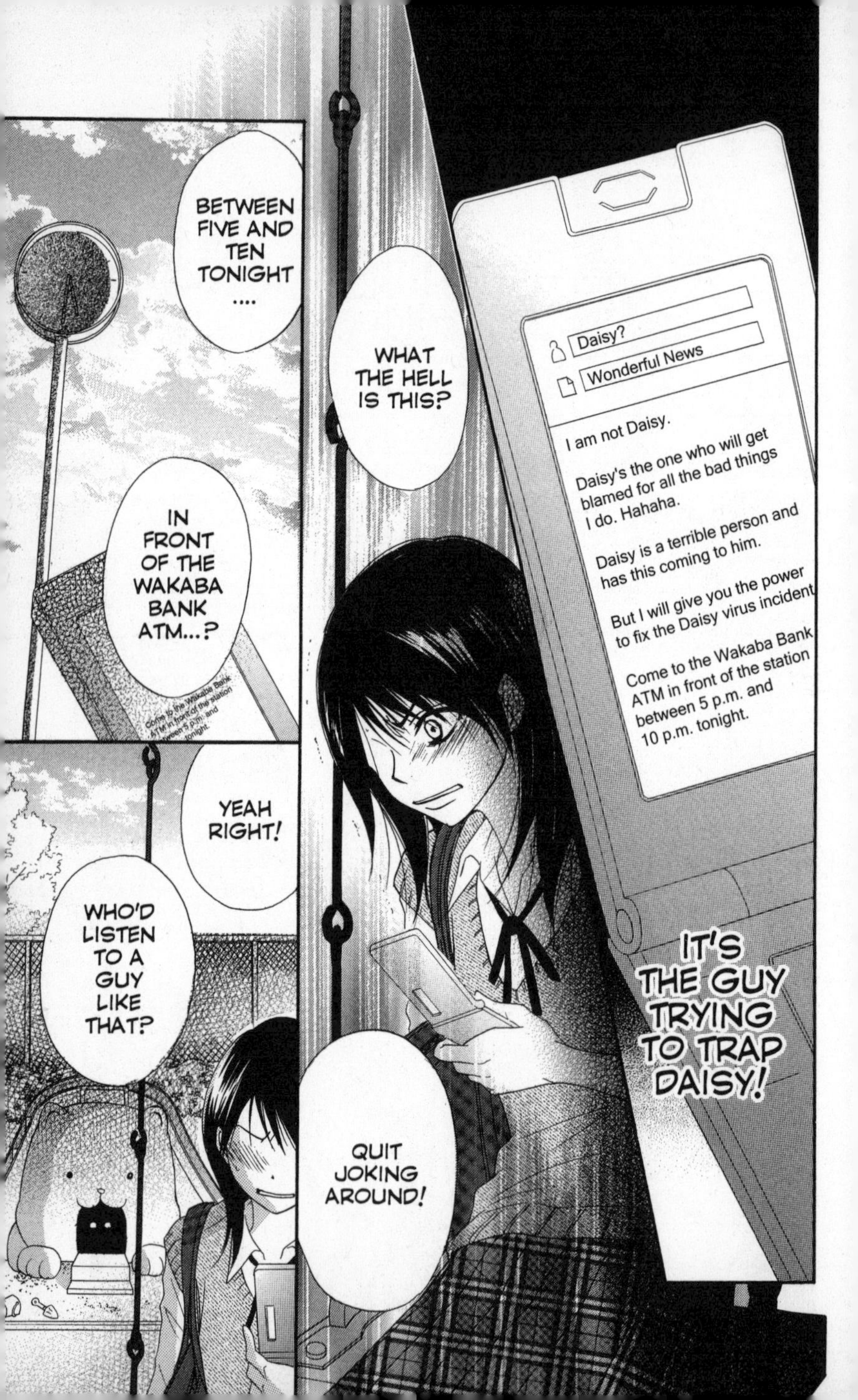
Daisy?
Wonderful News
I am not Daisy.
Daisy's the one who will get blamed for all the bad things I do. Hahaha.
Daisy is a terrible person and has this coming to him.
But I will give you the power to fix the Daisy virus incident
Come to the Wakaba Bank ATM in front of the station between 5 p.m. and 10 p.m. tonight.
WHAT THE HELL IS THIS?
IT'S THE GUY TRYING TO TRAP DAISY!
QUIT JOKING AROUND!
BETWEEN FIVE AND TEN TONIGHT....
IN FRONT OF THE WAKABA BANK ATM...?
YEAH RIGHT!
WHO'D LISTEN TO A GUY LIKE THAT?

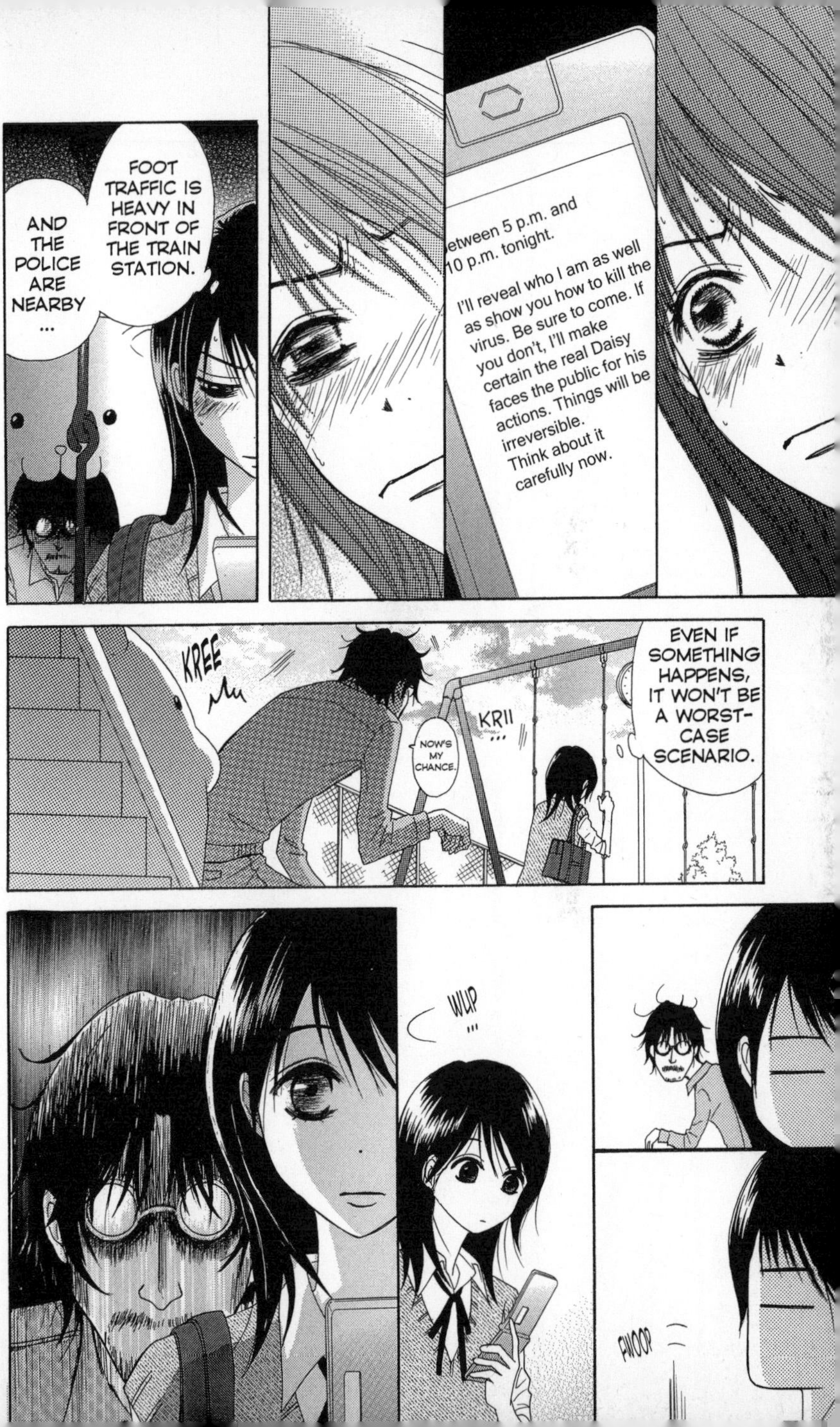
etween 5 p.m. and
10 p.m. tonight.
I'll reveal who I am as well as show you how to kill the virus. Be sure to come. If you don't, I'll make certain the real Daisy faces the public for his actions. Things will be irreversible.
Think about it carefully now.
FOOT TRAFFIC IS HEAVY IN FRONT OF THE TRAIN STATION.
AND THE POLICE ARE NEARBY...
EVEN IF SOMETHING HAPPENS, IT WON'T BE A WORST-CASE SCENARIO.
KRII...
NOW'S MY CHANCE.
KREE
FWOOP
WUP...

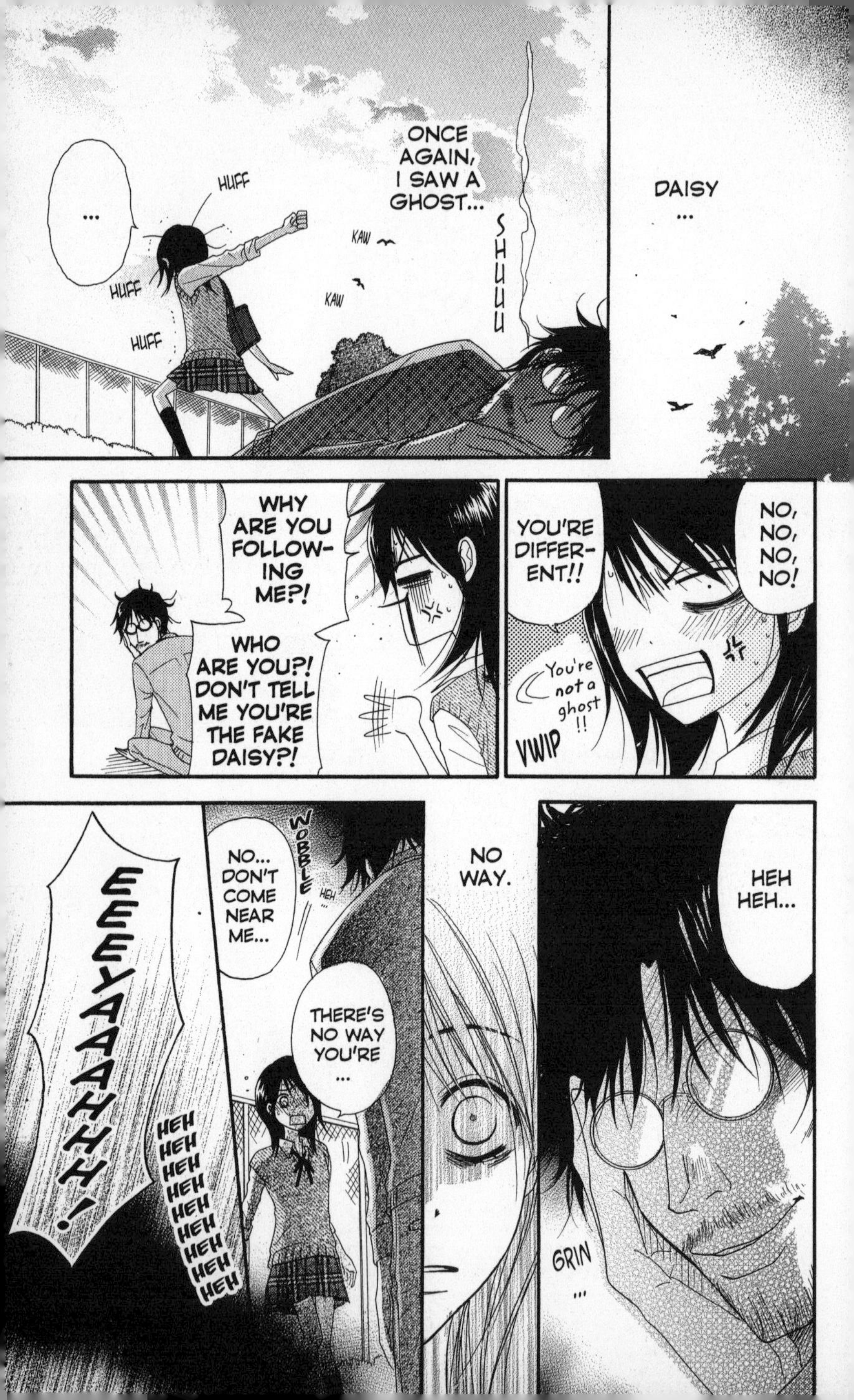
DAISY ...
ONCE AGAIN, I SAW A GHOST...
SHUUUU
HUFF
KAW
KAW
...
HUFF
HUFF
NO, NO, NO, NO!
YOU'RE DIFFER-ENT!!
You're not a ghost!!
VWIP
WHY ARE YOU FOLLOW-ING ME?!
WHO ARE YOU?! DON'T TELL ME YOU'RE THE FAKE DAISY?!
HEH HEH...
GRIN ...
NO WAY.
WOBBLE
HEH ...
NO... DON'T COME NEAR ME...
THERE'S NO WAY YOU'RE ...
EEEYAAAAHHH!
HEH HEH HEH HEH HEH HEH HEH HEH HEH

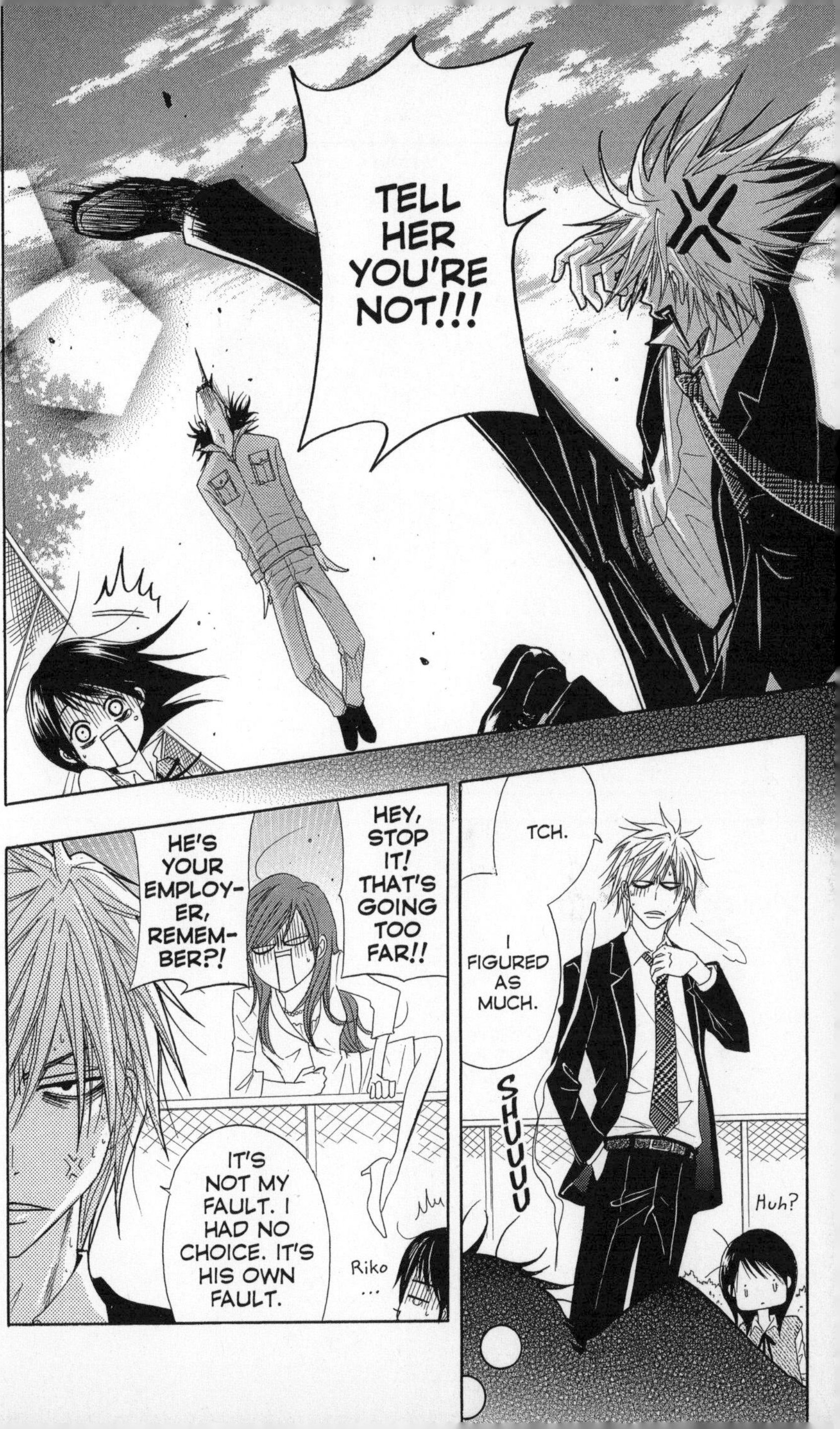
TELL HER YOU'RE NOT!!!
TCH.
I FIGURED AS MUCH.
SHUUUU
Huh?
HEY, STOP IT! THAT'S GOING TOO FAR!!
HE'S YOUR EMPLOYER, REMEMBER?!
IT'S NOT MY FAULT. I HAD NO CHOICE. IT'S HIS OWN FAULT.
Riko ...

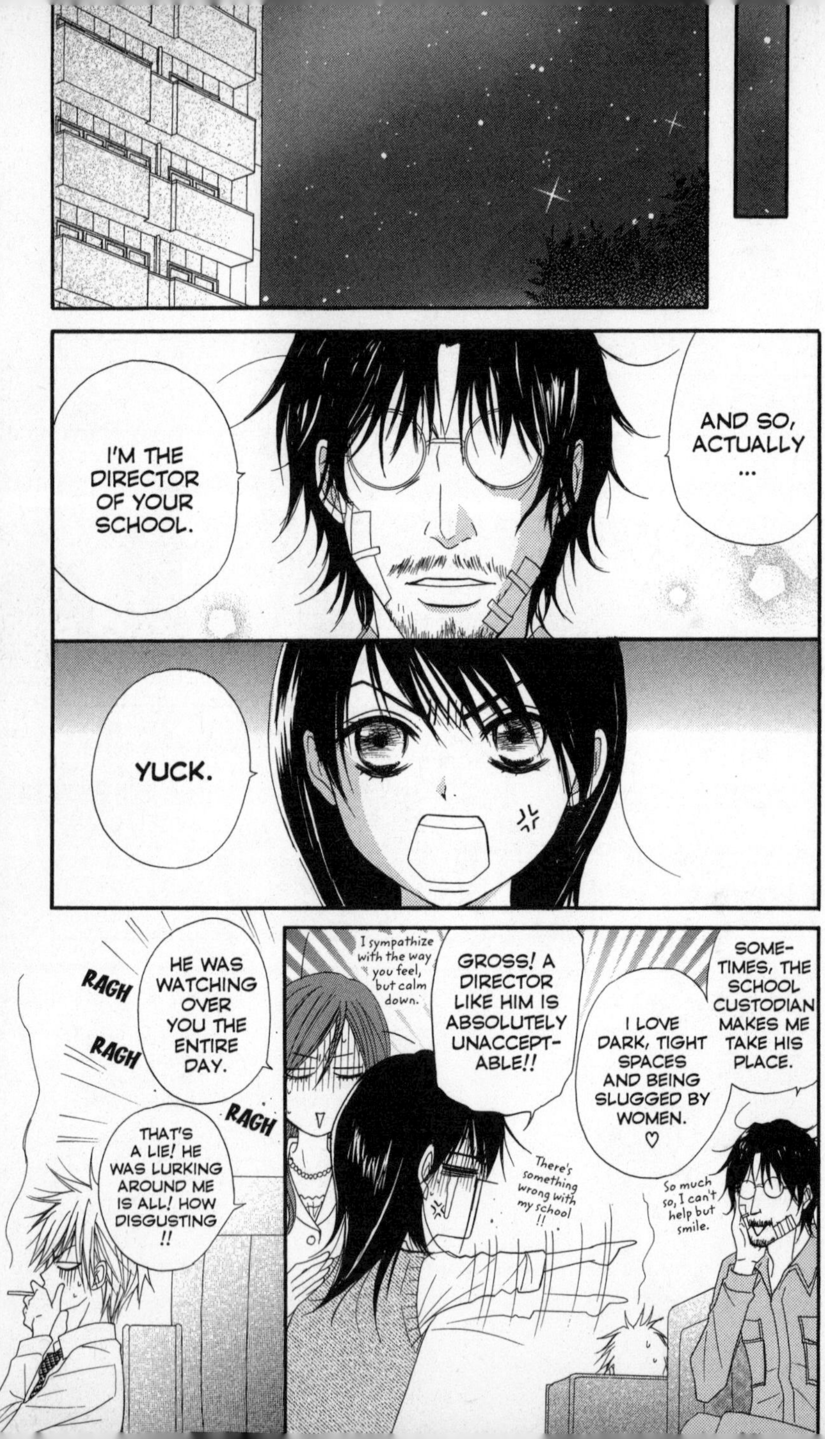
AND SO, ACTUALLY ...
I'M THE DIRECTOR OF YOUR SCHOOL.
YUCK.
SOME-TIMES, THE SCHOOL CUSTODIAN MAKES ME TAKE HIS PLACE.
I LOVE DARK, TIGHT SPACES AND BEING SLUGGED BY WOMEN. ♡
GROSS! A DIRECTOR LIKE HIM IS ABSOLUTELY UNACCEPT-ABLE!!
I sympathize with the way you feel, but calm down.
So much so, I can't help but smile.
There's something wrong with my school!!
HE WAS WATCHING OVER YOU THE ENTIRE DAY.
RAGH
RAGH
RAGH
THAT'S A LIE! HE WAS LURKING AROUND ME IS ALL! HOW DISGUSTING!!

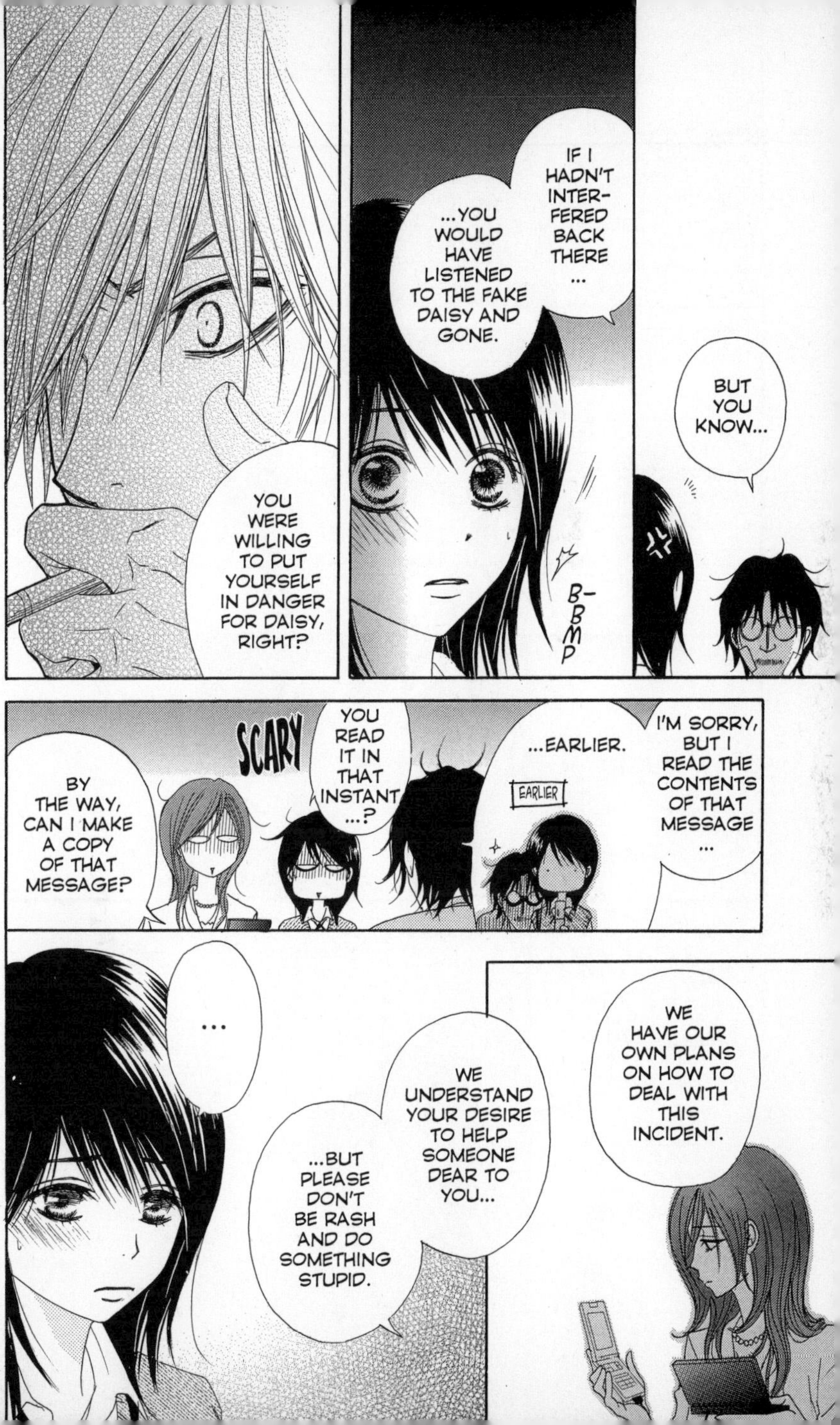
BUT YOU KNOW...
IF I HADN'T INTERFERED BACK THERE...
...YOU WOULD HAVE LISTENED TO THE FAKE DAISY AND GONE.
B-BBMP
YOU WERE WILLING TO PUT YOURSELF IN DANGER FOR DAISY, RIGHT?
I'M SORRY, BUT I READ THE CONTENTS OF THAT MESSAGE...
...EARLIER.
EARLIER
YOU READ IT IN THAT INSTANT...?
SCARY
BY THE WAY, CAN I MAKE A COPY OF THAT MESSAGE?
WE HAVE OUR OWN PLANS ON HOW TO DEAL WITH THIS INCIDENT.
WE UNDERSTAND YOUR DESIRE TO HELP SOMEONE DEAR TO YOU...
...BUT PLEASE DON'T BE RASH AND DO SOMETHING STUPID.
...

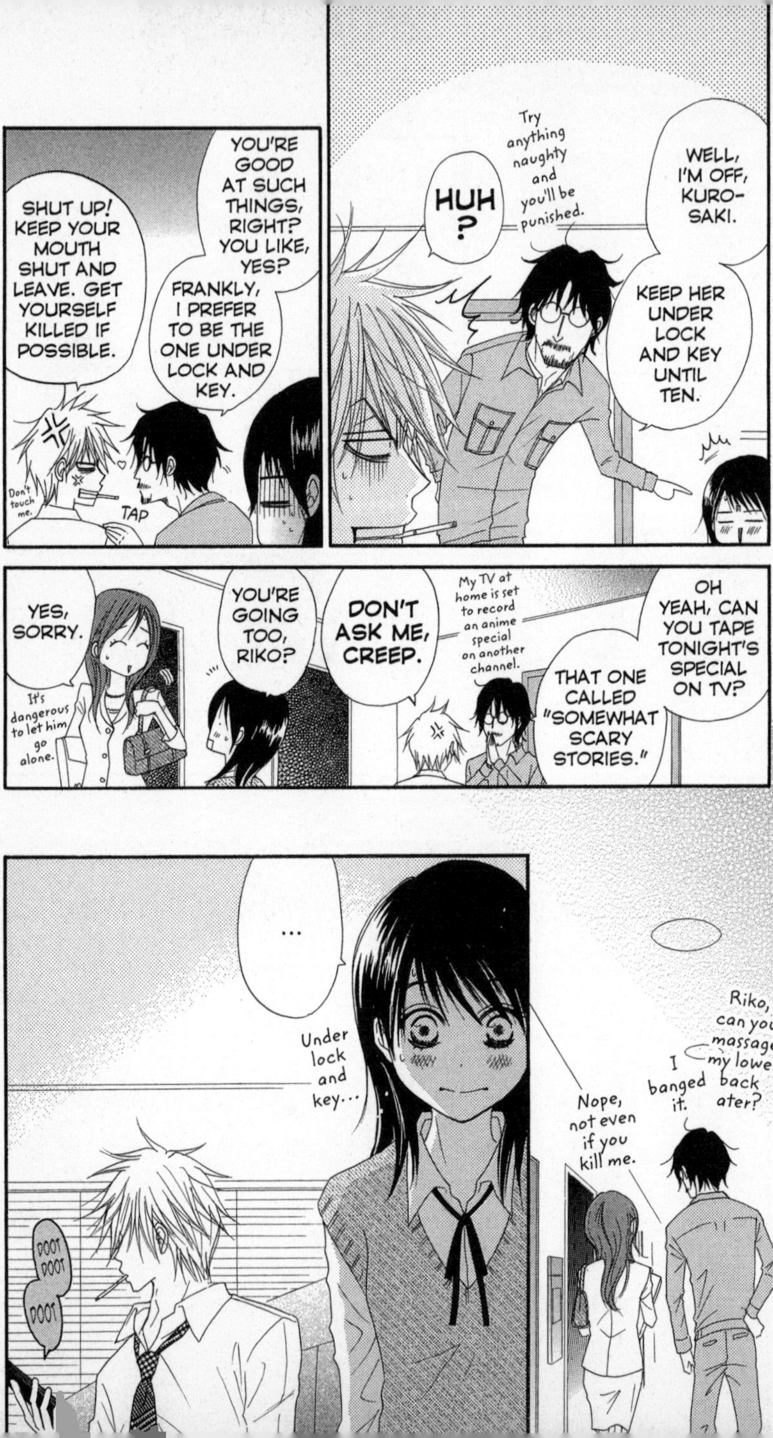
WELL, I'M OFF, KURO-SAKI.
KEEP HER UNDER LOCK AND KEY UNTIL TEN.
Try anything naughty and you'll be punished.
HUH?
YOU'RE GOOD AT SUCH THINGS, RIGHT? YOU LIKE, YES?
FRANKLY, I PREFER TO BE THE ONE UNDER LOCK AND KEY.
SHUT UP! KEEP YOUR MOUTH SHUT AND LEAVE. GET YOURSELF KILLED IF POSSIBLE.
Don't touch me.
TAP
OH YEAH, CAN YOU TAPE TONIGHT'S SPECIAL ON TV?
THAT ONE CALLED "SOMEWHAT SCARY STORIES."
My TV at home is set to record an anime special on another channel.
DON'T ASK ME, CREEP.
YOU'RE GOING TOO, RIKO?
YES, SORRY.
It's dangerous to let him go alone.
Riko, can you massage my lower back ater?
I banged it.
Nope, not even if you kill me.
...
Under lock and key...
DOOT DOOT
DOOT

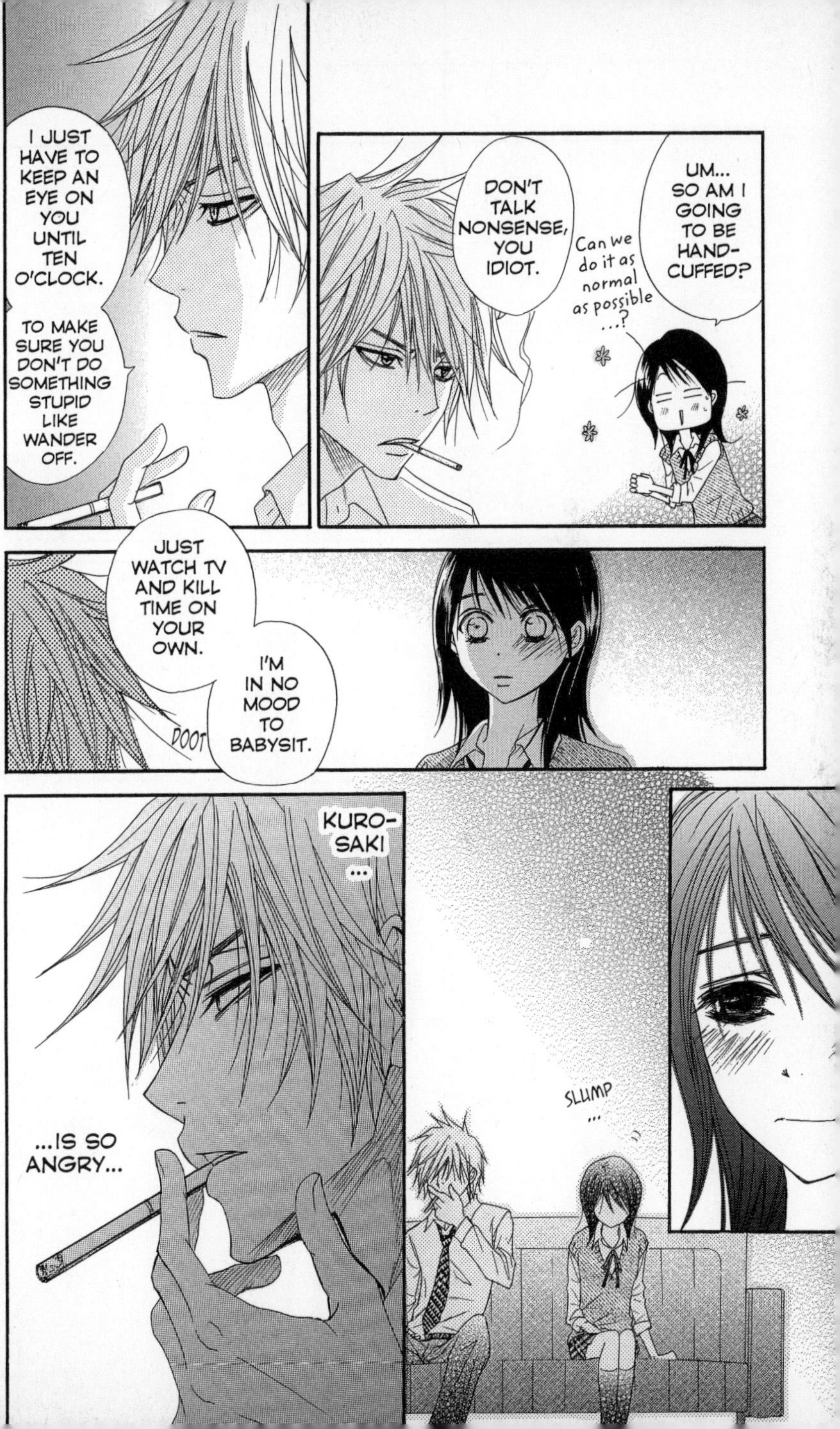
UM... SO AM I GOING TO BE HAND-CUFFED?
Can we do it as normal as possible ...?
DON'T TALK NONSENSE, YOU IDIOT.
I JUST HAVE TO KEEP AN EYE ON YOU UNTIL TEN O'CLOCK.
TO MAKE SURE YOU DON'T DO SOMETHING STUPID LIKE WANDER OFF.
JUST WATCH TV AND KILL TIME ON YOUR OWN.
I'M IN NO MOOD TO BABYSIT.
DOOT
SLUMP ...
KURO-SAKI ...
...IS SO ANGRY...

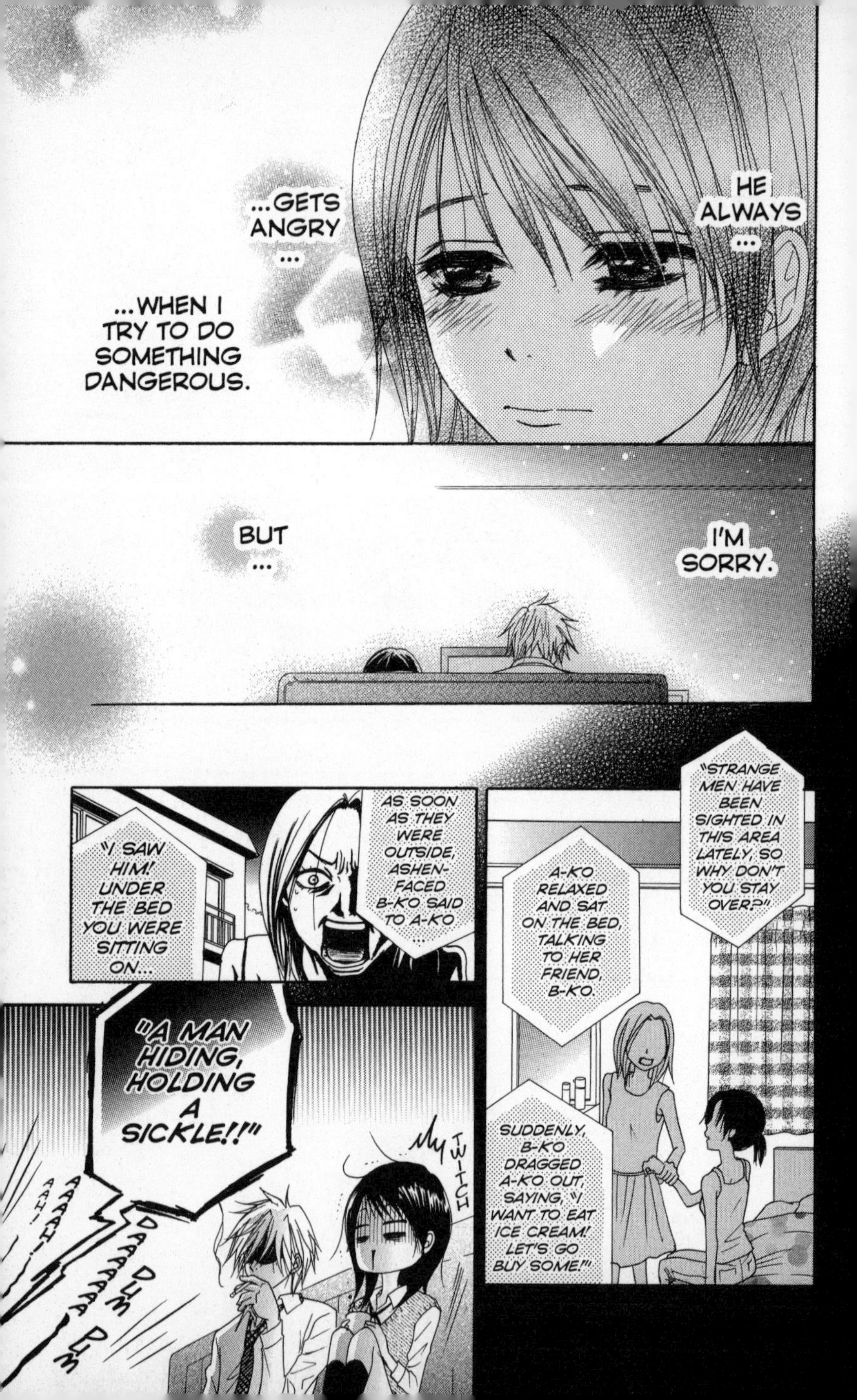
HE ALWAYS ...
...GETS ANGRY ...
...WHEN I TRY TO DO SOMETHING DANGEROUS.
I'M SORRY.
BUT ...
"STRANGE MEN HAVE BEEN SIGHTED IN THIS AREA LATELY, SO WHY DON'T YOU STAY OVER?"
A-KO RELAXED AND SAT ON THE BED, TALKING TO HER FRIEND, B-KO.
SUDDENLY, B-KO DRAGGED A-KO OUT, SAYING, "I WANT TO EAT ICE CREAM! LET'S GO BUY SOME!"
AS SOON AS THEY WERE OUTSIDE, ASHEN-FACED B-KO SAID TO A-KO ...
"I SAW HIM! UNDER THE BED YOU WERE SITTING ON...
"A MAN HIDING, HOLDING A SICKLE!!"
TWITCH
DAAAA DUM DAAAAAAA DUM
AAAAAAAH!

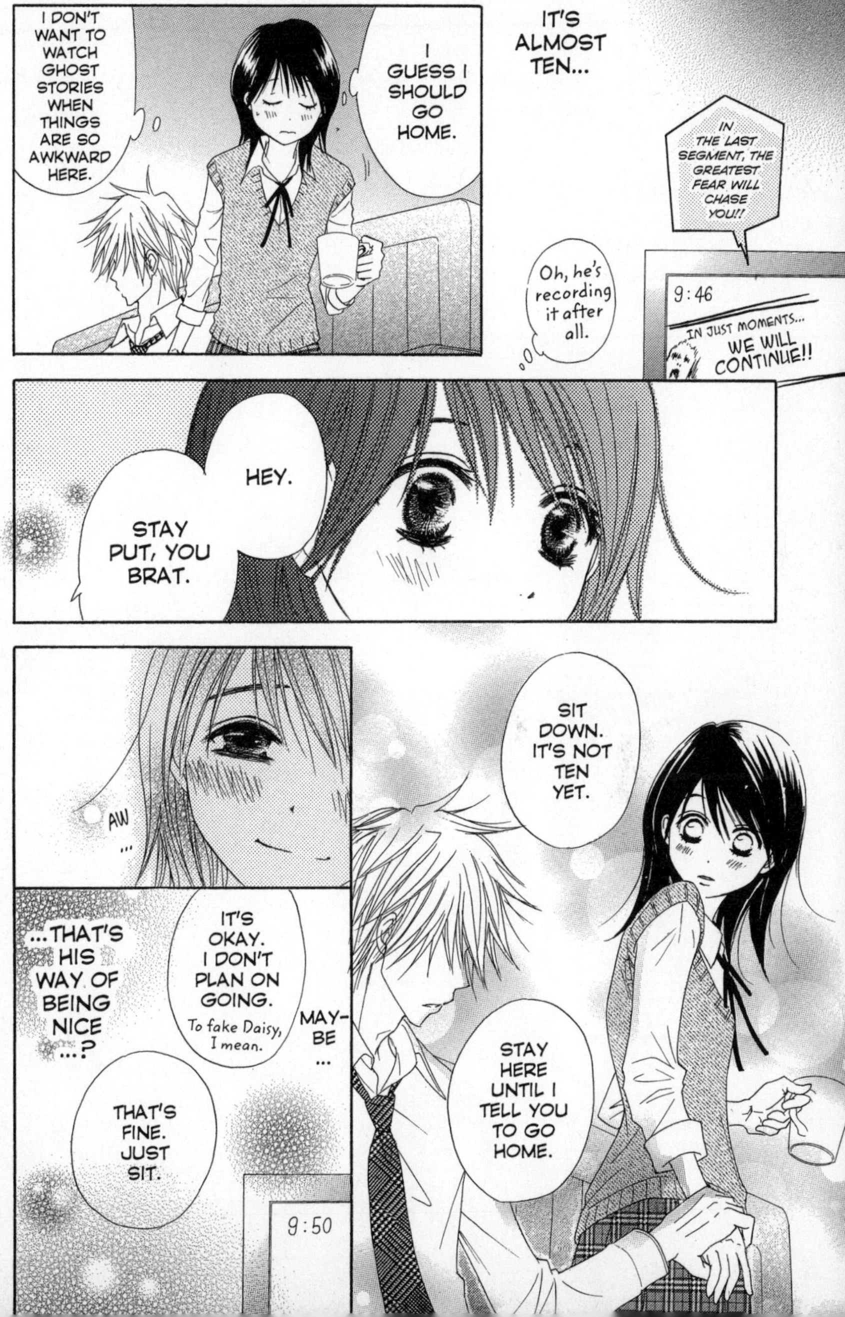
IT'S ALMOST TEN...
IN THE LAST SEGMENT, THE GREATEST FEAR WILL CHASE YOU!!
Oh, he's recording it after all.
9:46
IN JUST MOMENTS... WE WILL CONTINUE!!
I GUESS I SHOULD GO HOME.
I DON'T WANT TO WATCH GHOST STORIES WHEN THINGS ARE SO AWKWARD HERE.
HEY.
STAY PUT, YOU BRAT.
SIT DOWN. IT'S NOT TEN YET.
STAY HERE UNTIL I TELL YOU TO GO HOME.
AW...
IT'S OKAY. I DON'T PLAN ON GOING.
To fake Daisy, I mean.
MAY-BE...
...THAT'S HIS WAY OF BEING NICE...?
THAT'S FINE. JUST SIT.
9:50

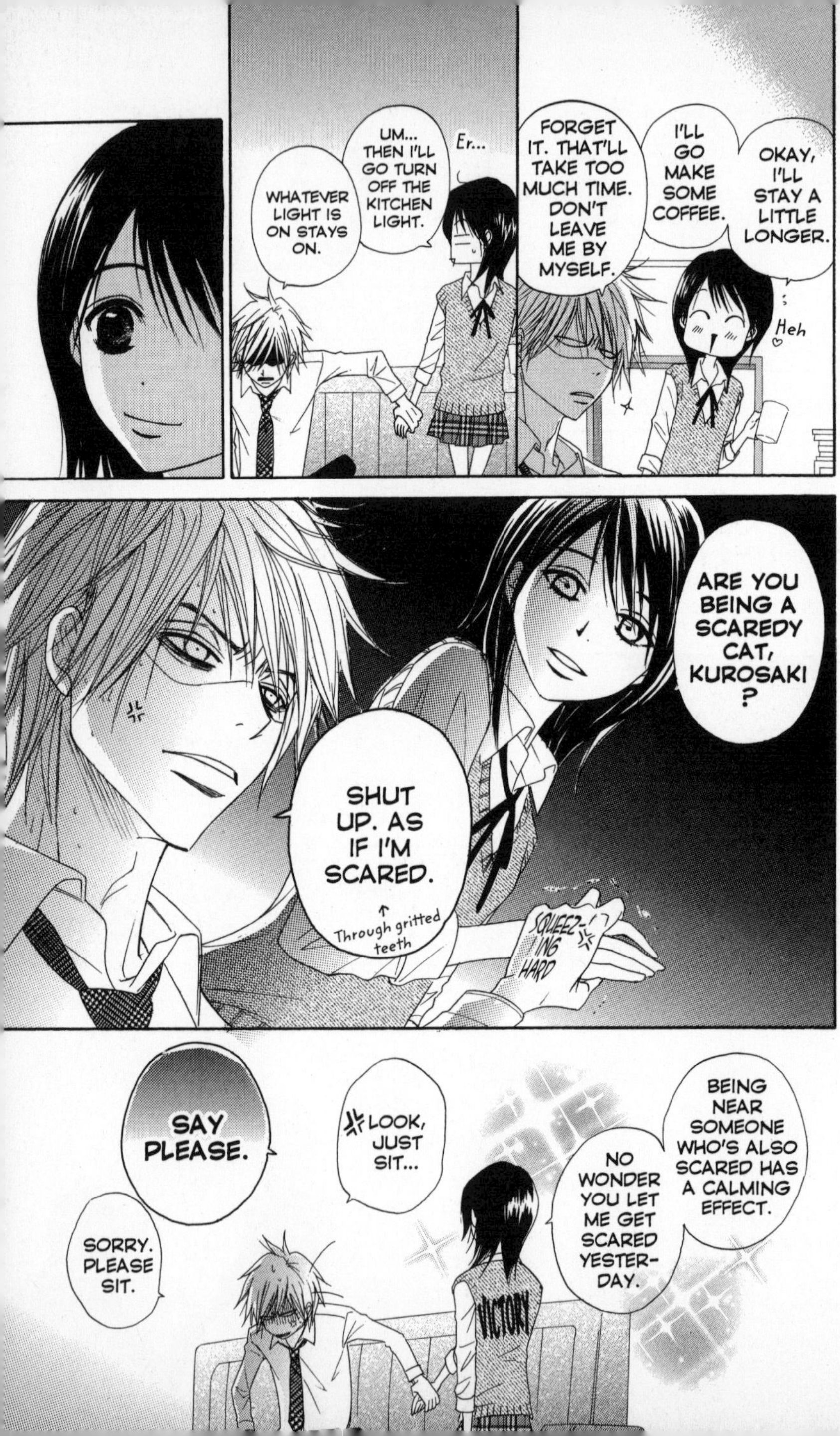
OKAY, I'LL STAY A LITTLE LONGER.
Heh
I'LL GO MAKE SOME COFFEE.
FORGET IT. THAT'LL TAKE TOO MUCH TIME. DON'T LEAVE ME BY MYSELF.
Er...
UM... THEN I'LL GO TURN OFF THE KITCHEN LIGHT.
WHATEVER LIGHT IS ON STAYS ON.
ARE YOU BEING A SCAREDY CAT, KUROSAKI?
SHUT UP. AS IF I'M SCARED.
Through gritted teeth
SQUEEZ-ING HARD
BEING NEAR SOMEONE WHO'S ALSO SCARED HAS A CALMING EFFECT.
NO WONDER YOU LET ME GET SCARED YESTER-DAY.
LOOK, JUST SIT...
SAY PLEASE.
SORRY. PLEASE SIT.
VICTORY

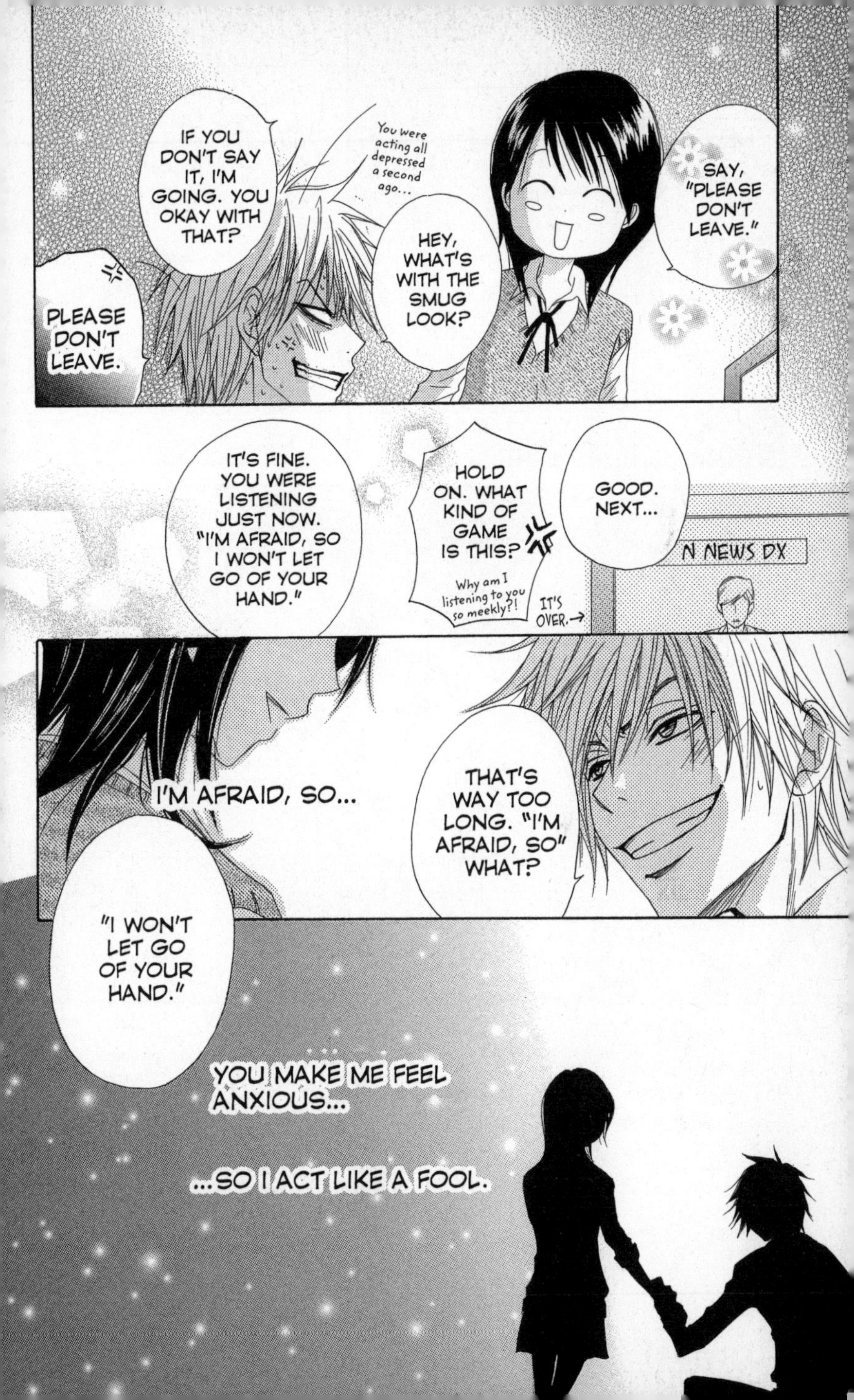
SAY, "PLEASE DON'T LEAVE."
HEY, WHAT'S WITH THE SMUG LOOK?
You were acting all depressed a second ago...
IF YOU DON'T SAY IT, I'M GOING. YOU OKAY WITH THAT?
PLEASE DON'T LEAVE.
GOOD. NEXT...
N NEWS DX
IT'S OVER.
HOLD ON. WHAT KIND OF GAME IS THIS?
Why am I listening to you so meekly?!
IT'S FINE. YOU WERE LISTENING JUST NOW. "I'M AFRAID, SO I WON'T LET GO OF YOUR HAND."
THAT'S WAY TOO LONG. "I'M AFRAID, SO" WHAT?
I'M AFRAID, SO...
"I WON'T LET GO OF YOUR HAND."
YOU MAKE ME FEEL ANXIOUS...
...SO I ACT LIKE A FOOL.

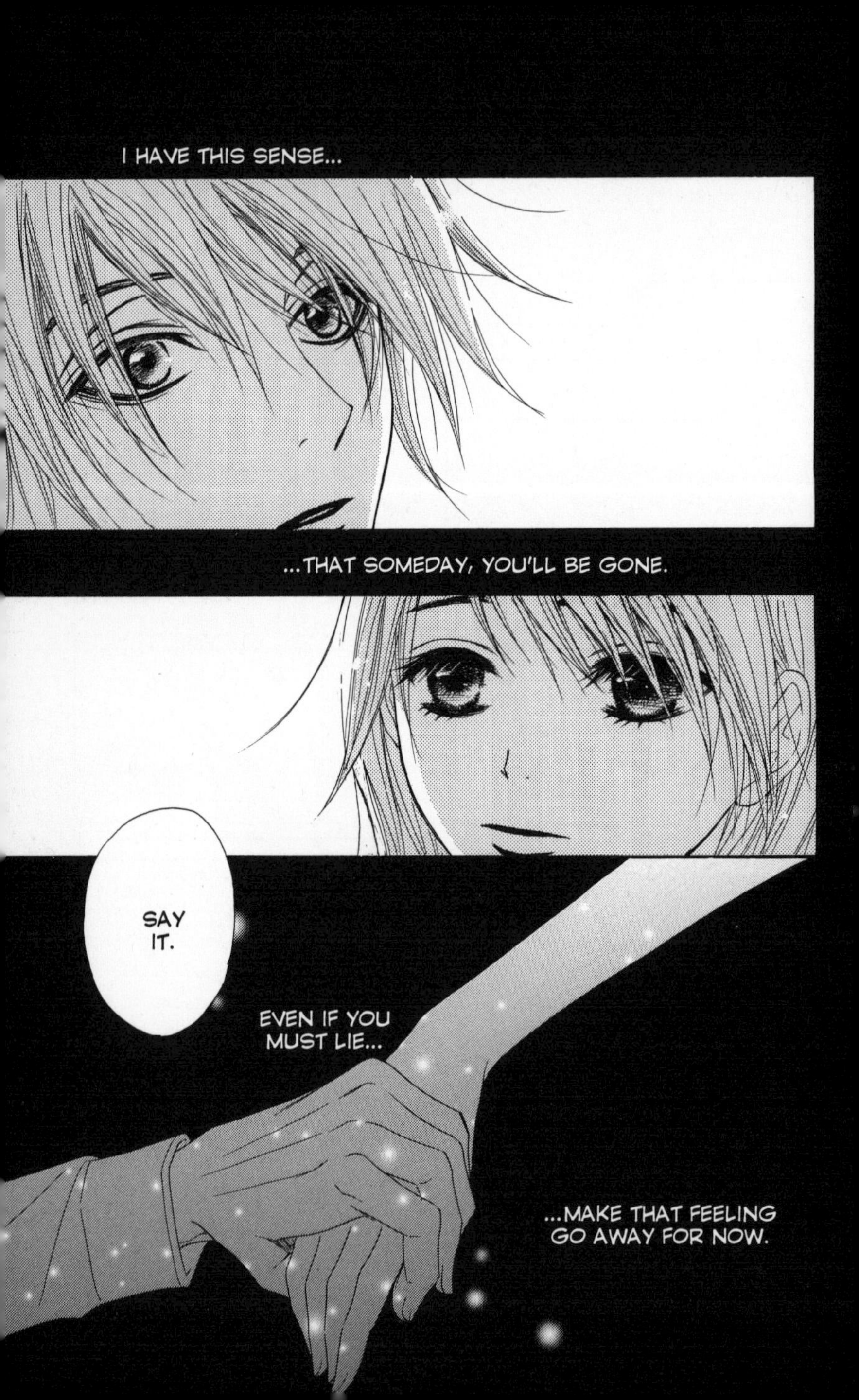
I HAVE THIS SENSE...
...THAT SOMEDAY, YOU'LL BE GONE.
SAY IT.
EVEN IF YOU MUST LIE...
...MAKE THAT FEELING GO AWAY FOR NOW.

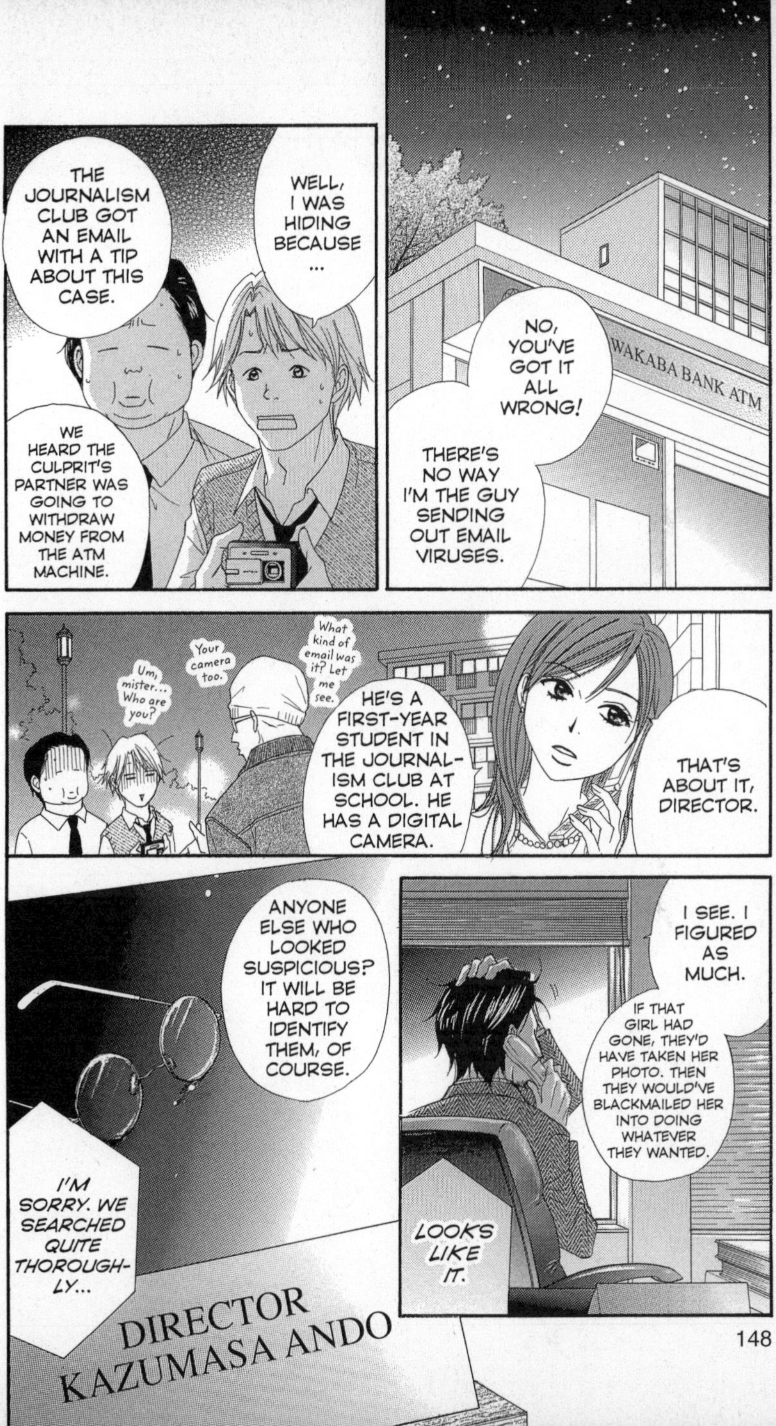
WAKABA BANK ATM
NO, YOU'VE GOT IT ALL WRONG!
THERE'S NO WAY I'M THE GUY SENDING OUT EMAIL VIRUSES.
WELL, I WAS HIDING BECAUSE ...
THE JOURNALISM CLUB GOT AN EMAIL WITH A TIP ABOUT THIS CASE.
WE HEARD THE CULPRIT'S PARTNER WAS GOING TO WITHDRAW MONEY FROM THE ATM MACHINE.
THAT'S ABOUT IT, DIRECTOR.
HE'S A FIRST-YEAR STUDENT IN THE JOURNAL-ISM CLUB AT SCHOOL. HE HAS A DIGITAL CAMERA.
What kind of email was it? Let me see.
Your camera too.
Um, mister... Who are you?
I SEE. I FIGURED AS MUCH.
IF THAT GIRL HAD GONE, THEY'D HAVE TAKEN HER PHOTO. THEN THEY WOULD'VE BLACKMAILED HER INTO DOING WHATEVER THEY WANTED.
LOOKS LIKE IT.
ANYONE ELSE WHO LOOKED SUSPICIOUS? IT WILL BE HARD TO IDENTIFY THEM, OF COURSE.
I'M SORRY. WE SEARCHED QUITE THOROUGH-LY...
DIRECTOR KAZUMASA ANDO

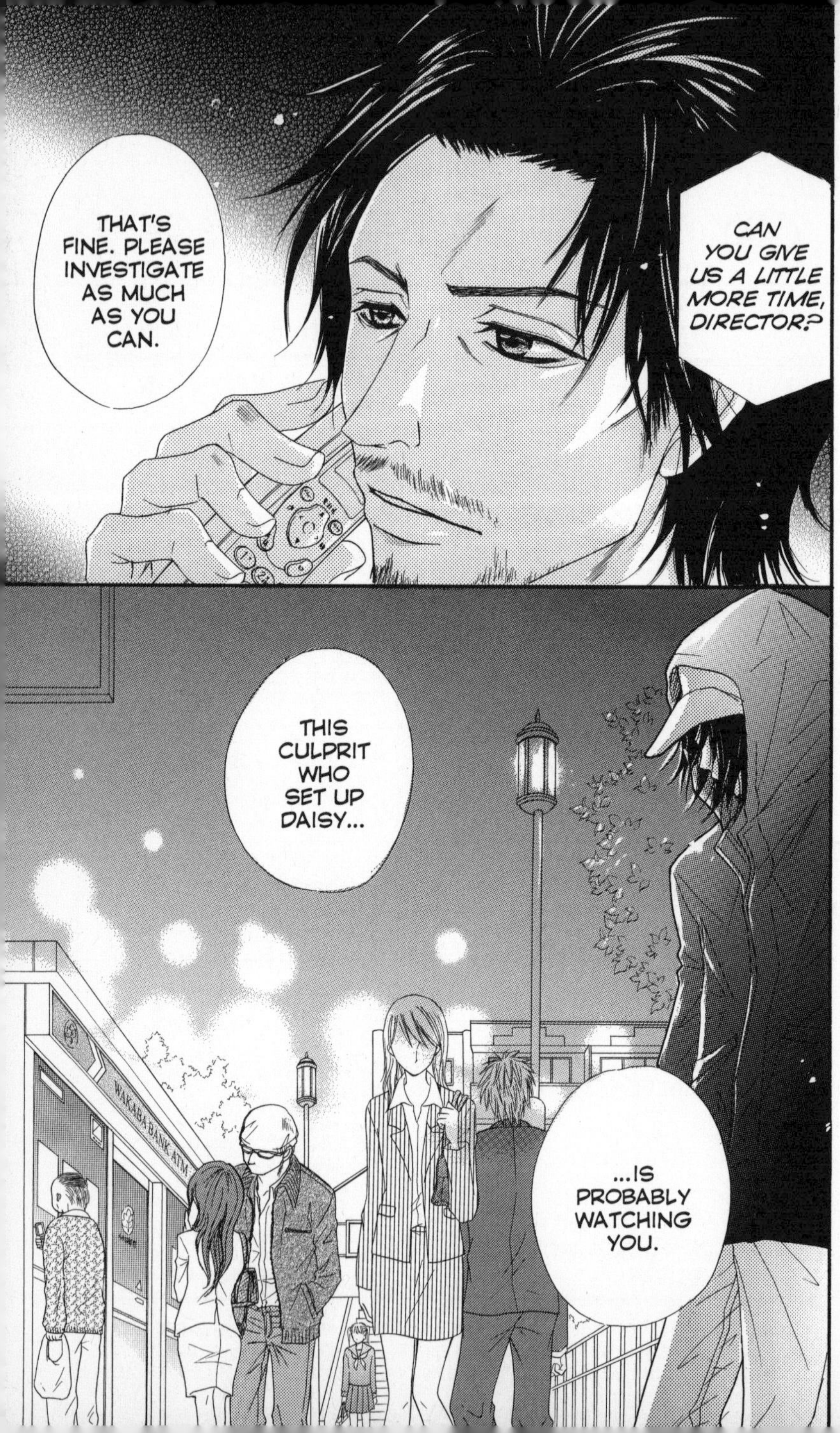
CAN YOU GIVE US A LITTLE MORE TIME, DIRECTOR?
THAT'S FINE. PLEASE INVESTIGATE AS MUCH AS YOU CAN.
THIS CULPRIT WHO SET UP DAISY...
WAKABA BANK ATM
...IS PROBABLY WATCHING YOU.

DENGEKI DAISY
COMMENTS FROM THE LAST PAGE
THAT CANNOT BE MISSED
~THE HISTORY OF THE GENIUS K-TANI ~

ON THE LAST PAGE OF THE CHAPTER SERIALIZATIONS IN *BETSUCOMI*,
THERE ARE CAPTIONS NEXT TO THE "TO BE CONTINUED IN..." LINE
THAT WRAP UP THE CHAPTER AND GIVE HINTS TO THE UPCOMING
CHAPTER. THE GENIUS EDITOR, K-TANI, IS FROM AN EDITORIAL
COMPANY AND IS IN CHARGE OF THIS. IT WOULD BE A SHAME NOT TO
SHOW HOW K-TANI IS LIKE GENIUS BA○○BON...!!

EVEN IF IT'S REJECTED, DON'T GIVE UP, K-TANI!!!

CH. 15	WILL TERU DECIDE TO WEAR HER HAIR WITH HER EARS EXPOSED, AS ADVISED?! NEXT TIME, PAY CLOSE ATTENTION TO TERU'S EARS!!	REJEC-TED	THE LAST PANEL HAD SO MUCH DIALOGUE, THERE WAS NO SPACE, UNFORTUNATELY. AND STARTING WITH THE FOLLOWING CHAPTER, TERU DOES EXPOSE HER EARS.
CH. 16	WHAT IS IT THAT KUROSAKI REALLY WANTS HER TO TAKE OFF...?! EXCITEMENT GOES UP *200%* NEXT TIME!!		"EXCITEMENT GOES UP *200%*" IS A PHRASE THAT SHOWS A DEEP UNDERSTANDING OF EDITING SHOJO MANGA.
CH. 17	LEANING ON YOUR BACK... ARF ♡♡ NEXT TIME: THE MAN STANDING IN FRONT OF THE TWO IS...?!		THIS IS THE BEST OF THE CAPTIONS THAT PASSED. BUT THAT "ARF" PART SURE SPOILED THE MOOD.
CH. 18	THE ONE IN THE BACK IS... SUMIRE-CHAN?!	REJEC-TED	THERE WAS CONCERN THAT SOME PEOPLE MIGHT REALLY BELIEVE IT'S SUMIRE, SO IT WAS REJECTED. BY THE WAY, THE BEGINNING OF THIS CHAPTER ALSO HAD A CAPTION IN THE MAGAZINE. "I WANT TO BE THIS CUSHION... A VOICE SEEMS TO BE SAYING THAT FROM SOMEWHERE...?!" (BETTER IGNORED)
CH. 19	• THE SCREEN IS RED... • HOW MANY HP (HIT POINTS) DOES KUROSAKI HAVE LEFT?!	REJEC-TED REJEC-TED	THERE WERE TWO OPTIONS, BUT BOTH WERE REJECTED SUPPOSEDLY BECAUSE THEY SEEMED LIKE GAME-RELATED REFERENCES. HOWEVER, THE FACT THAT "...ON YOUR BACK... ARF" MADE IT WHILE THESE DIDN'T MAKES ONE QUESTION THE EDITORIAL DEPARTMENT.

IF YOU WANT TO READ MORE OF K-TANI'S GREAT WORK, PLEASE CHECK
OUT *BETSUCOMI*. THE FAN PAGE "THE SECRET SCHOOL CUSTODIAN OFFICE" IN
THERE IS ALSO HANDLED BY K-TANI. IT'S CRAZIER THAN ANY OTHER FAN PAGE.

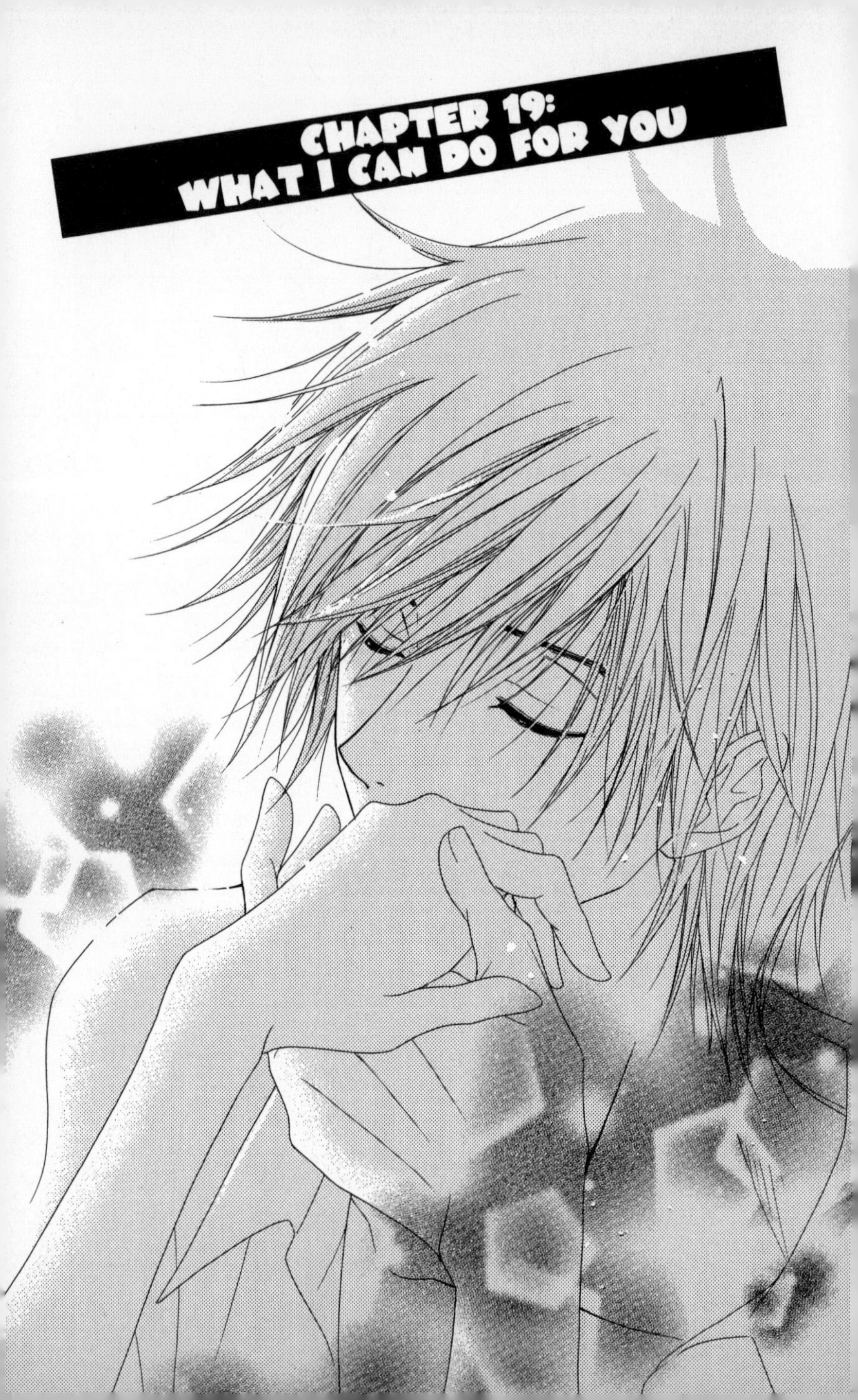
CHAPTER 19:
WHAT I CAN DO FOR YOU

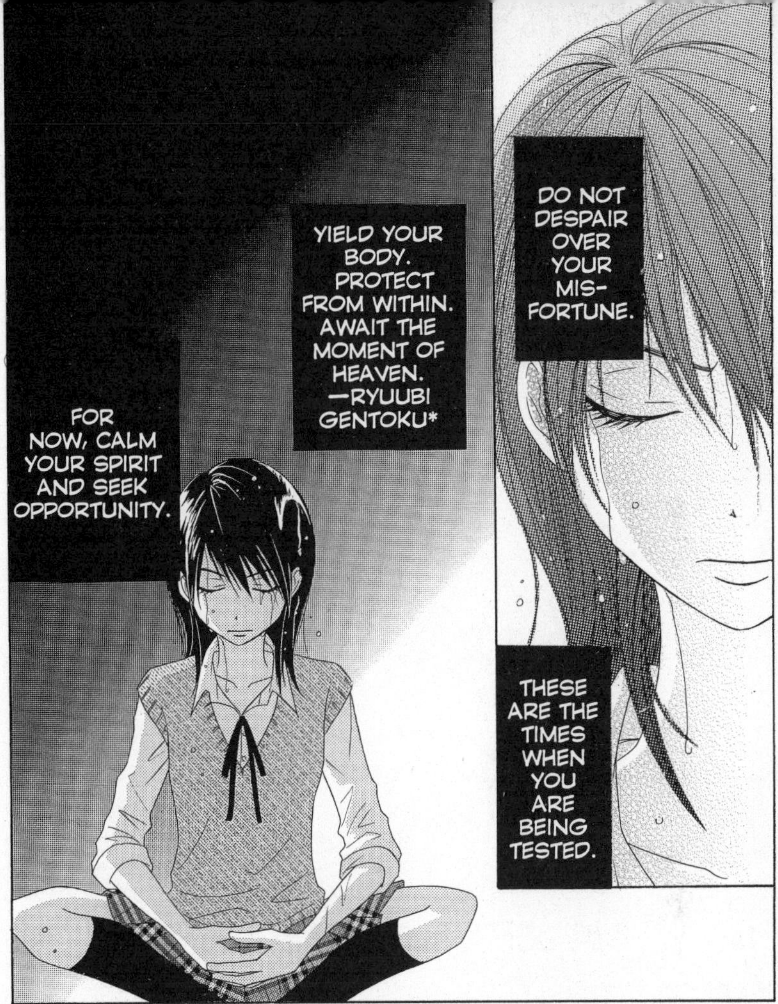
DO NOT DESPAIR OVER YOUR MIS-FORTUNE.
THESE ARE THE TIMES WHEN YOU ARE BEING TESTED.
YIELD YOUR BODY. PROTECT FROM WITHIN. AWAIT THE MOMENT OF HEAVEN. —RYUUBI GENTOKU*
FOR NOW, CALM YOUR SPIRIT AND SEEK OPPORTUNITY.

*A LEADER OF A MARTIAL ARTS SCHOOL IN THE ANIME *IKKI TOUSEN*

IT APPEARS AGAIN... GLASSES.

I HATE TO DRAW GLASSES, BUT THIS MANGA SEEMS TO HAVE AN UNUSUALLY HIGH OCCURRENCE OF THEM.

OH, IT'S NOT THAT I DON'T LIKE PEOPLE WITH GLASSES. I JUST CAN'T DRAW GLASSES VERY WELL.

ON THE COVER PAGE OF CHAPTER 17, I PUT GLASSES ON KUROSAKI EVEN THOUGH IT WAS A PAIN TO DRAW. I GOT QUITE A POSITIVE REACTION (ESPECIALLY FROM EDITOR J-KO). THUS, I LEARNED THE STRANGE PHENOMENON OF HOW GLASSES CAN INCREASE A PERSON'S APPEAL.

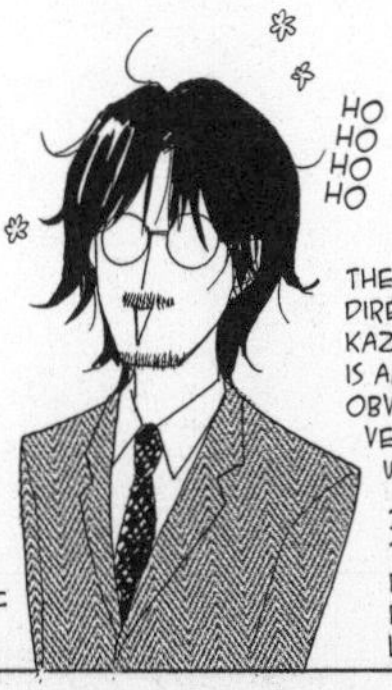
HO HO HO HO

THE FACT THAT DIRECTOR KAZUMASA ANDO IS ANDY WAS OBVIOUS FROM THE VERY START. WHY WAS THAT?

I'VE ONLY SEEN TWO PEOPLE IN REAL LIFE WEAR ROUND GLASSES LIKE HIS.

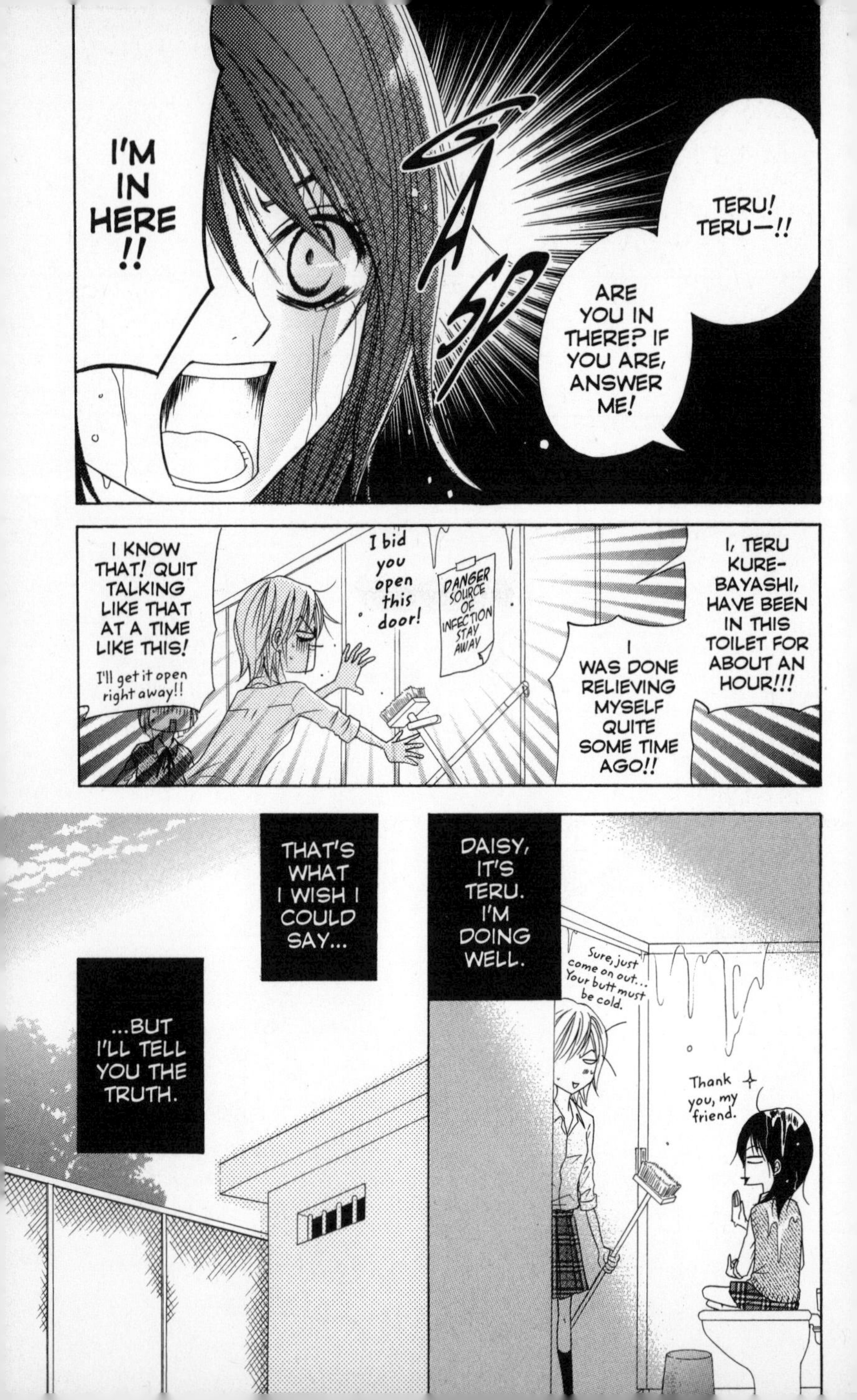
TERU! TERU—!!
ARE YOU IN THERE? IF YOU ARE, ANSWER ME!
GASP
I'M IN HERE!!
I, TERU KURE-BAYASHI, HAVE BEEN IN THIS TOILET FOR ABOUT AN HOUR!!!
I WAS DONE RELIEVING MYSELF QUITE SOME TIME AGO!!
I bid you open this door!
DANGER SOURCE OF INFECTION STAY AWAY
I KNOW THAT! QUIT TALKING LIKE THAT AT A TIME LIKE THIS!
I'll get it open right away!!
DAISY, IT'S TERU. I'M DOING WELL.
Sure, just come on out... Your butt must be cold.
Thank you, my friend.
THAT'S WHAT I WISH I COULD SAY...
...BUT I'LL TELL YOU THE TRUTH.

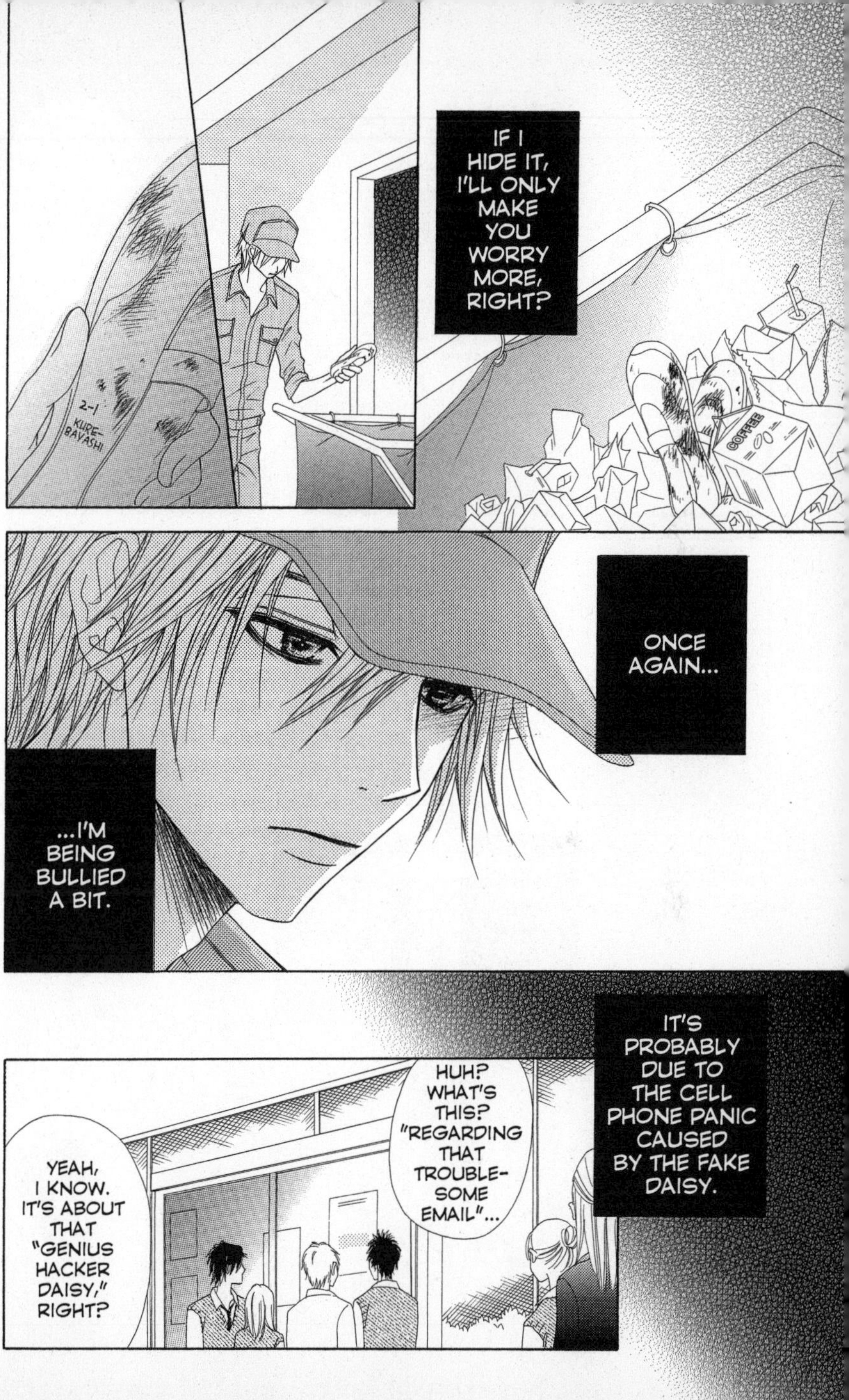
IF I HIDE IT, I'LL ONLY MAKE YOU WORRY MORE, RIGHT?
2-1 KURE-BAYASHI
ONCE AGAIN...
...I'M BEING BULLIED A BIT.
IT'S PROBABLY DUE TO THE CELL PHONE PANIC CAUSED BY THE FAKE DAISY.
HUH? WHAT'S THIS? "REGARDING THAT TROUBLE-SOME EMAIL"...
YEAH, I KNOW. IT'S ABOUT THAT "GENIUS HACKER DAISY," RIGHT?

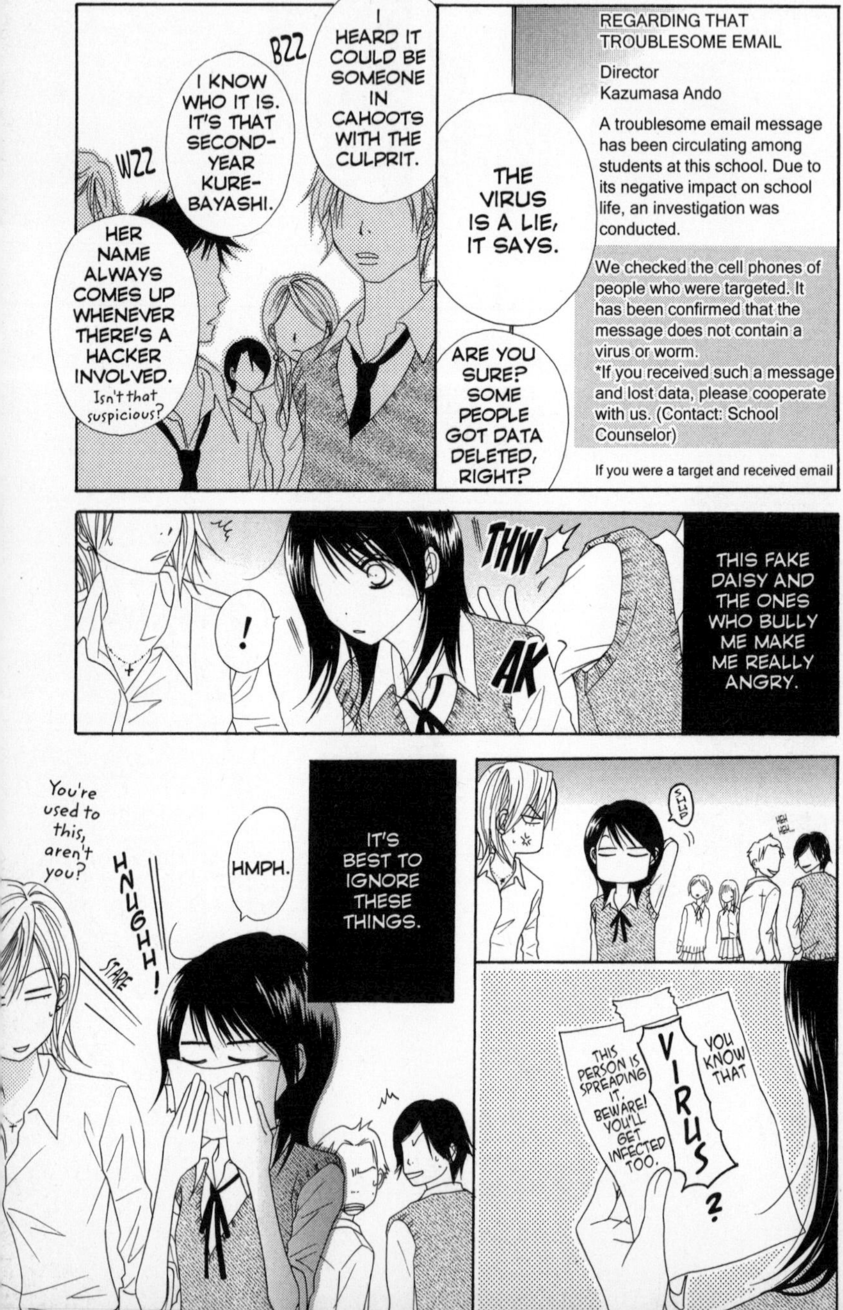
REGARDING THAT TROUBLESOME EMAIL
Director
Kazumasa Ando
A troublesome email message has been circulating among students at this school. Due to its negative impact on school life, an investigation was conducted.
We checked the cell phones of people who were targeted. It has been confirmed that the message does not contain a virus or worm.
*If you received such a message and lost data, please cooperate with us. (Contact: School Counselor)
If you were a target and received email
THE VIRUS IS A LIE, IT SAYS.
ARE YOU SURE? SOME PEOPLE GOT DATA DELETED, RIGHT?
I HEARD IT COULD BE SOMEONE IN CAHOOTS WITH THE CULPRIT.
BZZ
I KNOW WHO IT IS. IT'S THAT SECOND-YEAR KURE-BAYASHI.
WZZ
HER NAME ALWAYS COMES UP WHENEVER THERE'S A HACKER INVOLVED.
Isn't that suspicious?
THIS FAKE DAISY AND THE ONES WHO BULLY ME MAKE ME REALLY ANGRY.
THWAK
!
SHUP
HEH HEH...
YOU KNOW THAT
VIRUS?
THIS PERSON IS SPREADING IT. BEWARE! YOU'LL GET INFECTED TOO.
IT'S BEST TO IGNORE THESE THINGS.
HMPH.
HNUGHH!
You're used to this, aren't you?
STARE

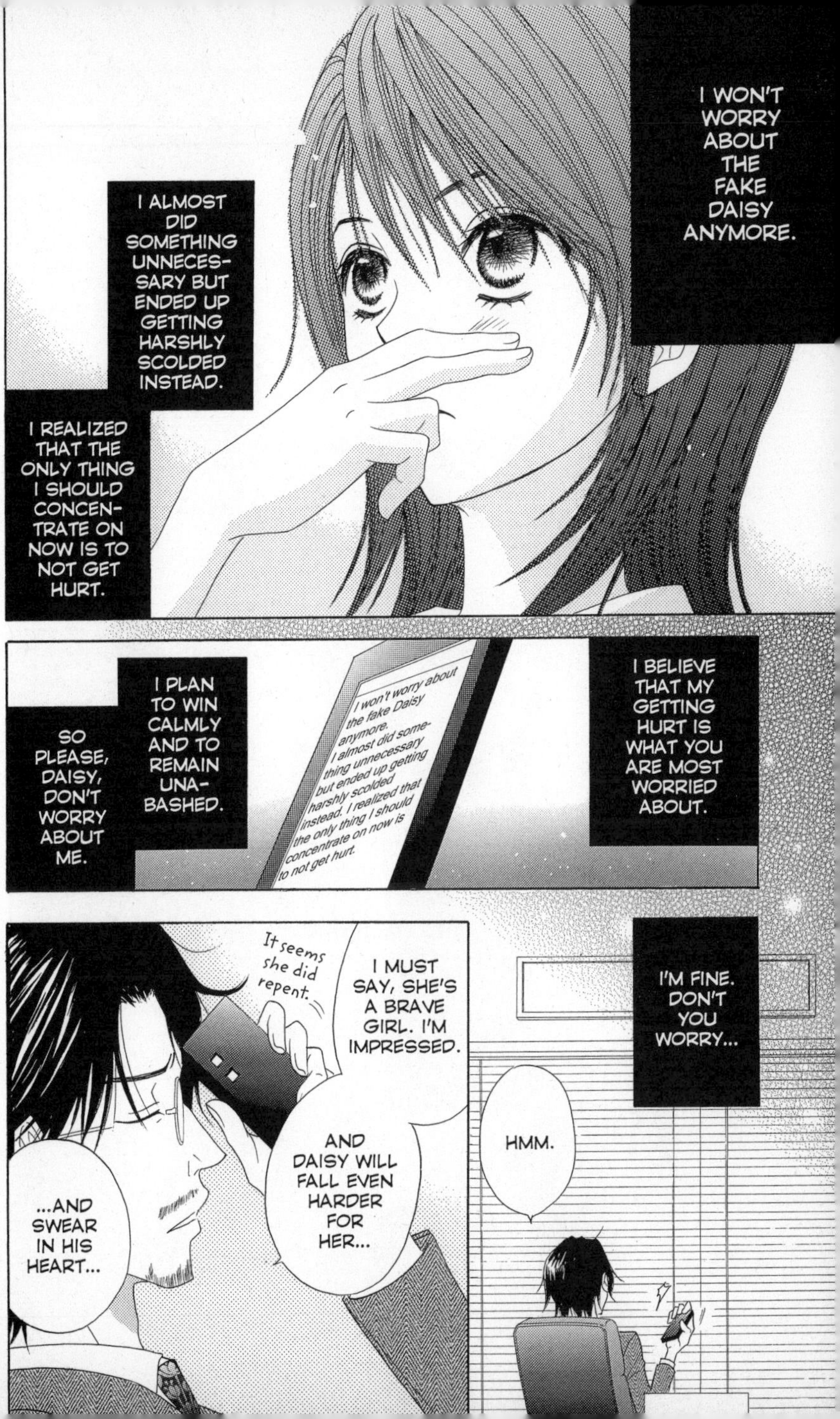
I WON'T WORRY ABOUT THE FAKE DAISY ANYMORE.
I ALMOST DID SOMETHING UNNECES-SARY BUT ENDED UP GETTING HARSHLY SCOLDED INSTEAD.
I REALIZED THAT THE ONLY THING I SHOULD CONCEN-TRATE ON NOW IS TO NOT GET HURT.
I BELIEVE THAT MY GETTING HURT IS WHAT YOU ARE MOST WORRIED ABOUT.
I won't worry about the fake Daisy anymore. I almost did some-thing unnecessary but ended up getting harshly scolded instead. I realized that the only thing I should concentrate on now is to not get hurt.
I PLAN TO WIN CALMLY AND TO REMAIN UNA-BASHED.
SO PLEASE, DAISY, DON'T WORRY ABOUT ME.
I'M FINE. DON'T YOU WORRY...
HMM.
I MUST SAY, SHE'S A BRAVE GIRL. I'M IMPRESSED.
It seems she did repent.
AND DAISY WILL FALL EVEN HARDER FOR HER...
...AND SWEAR IN HIS HEART...

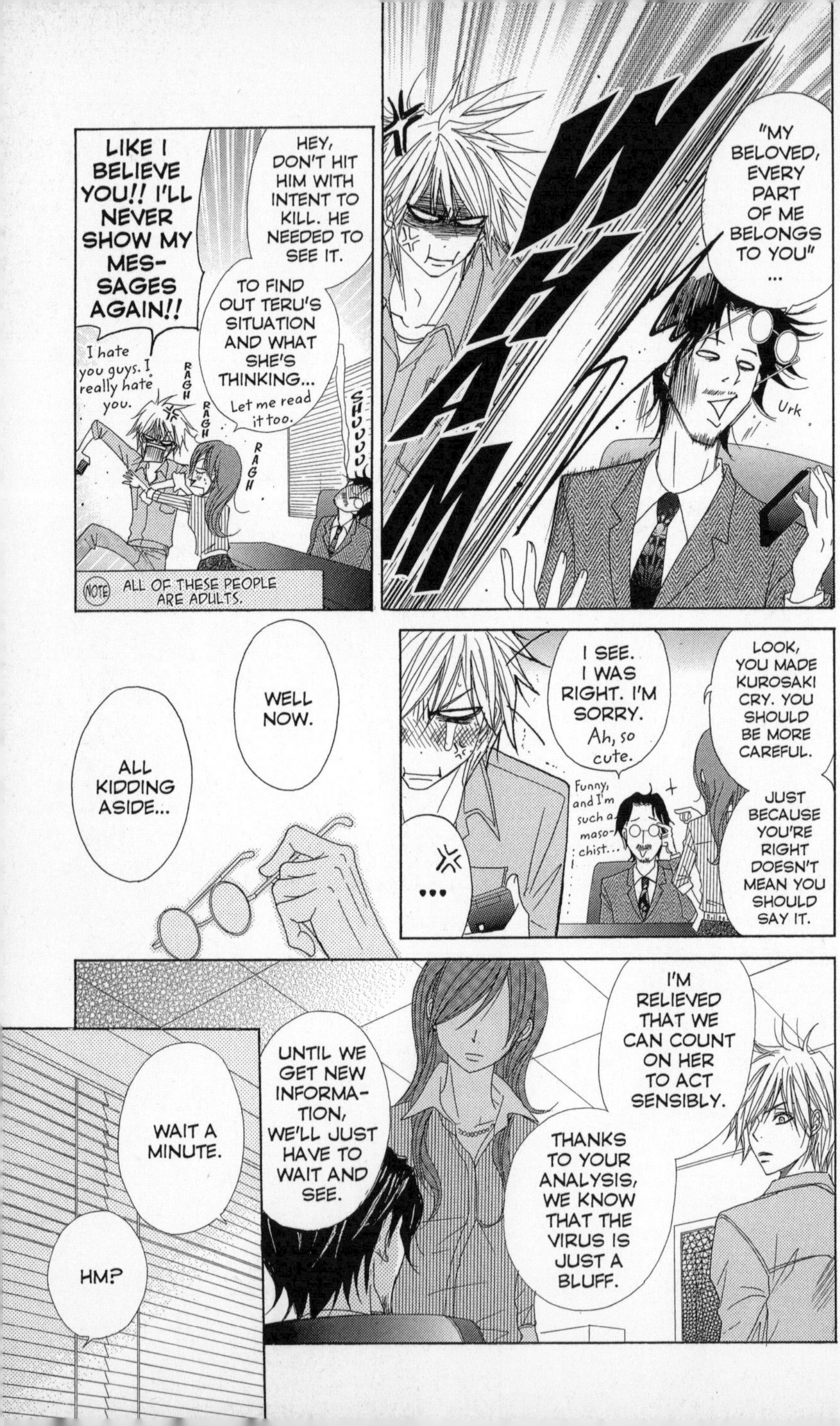
"MY BELOVED, EVERY PART OF ME BELONGS TO YOU"...
WHAM
Urk
HEY, DON'T HIT HIM WITH INTENT TO KILL. HE NEEDED TO SEE IT.
TO FIND OUT TERU'S SITUATION AND WHAT SHE'S THINKING...
LIKE I BELIEVE YOU!! I'LL NEVER SHOW MY MES-SAGES AGAIN!!
I hate you guys. I really hate you.
RAGH
RAGH
RAGH
Let me read it too.
SHUUUU
NOTE ALL OF THESE PEOPLE ARE ADULTS.
LOOK, YOU MADE KUROSAKI CRY. YOU SHOULD BE MORE CAREFUL.
I SEE. I WAS RIGHT. I'M SORRY.
Ah, so cute.
JUST BECAUSE YOU'RE RIGHT DOESN'T MEAN YOU SHOULD SAY IT.
Funny, and I'm such a maso-chist...
...
WELL NOW.
ALL KIDDING ASIDE...
I'M RELIEVED THAT WE CAN COUNT ON HER TO ACT SENSIBLY.
THANKS TO YOUR ANALYSIS, WE KNOW THAT THE VIRUS IS JUST A BLUFF.
UNTIL WE GET NEW INFORMA-TION, WE'LL JUST HAVE TO WAIT AND SEE.
WAIT A MINUTE.
HM?

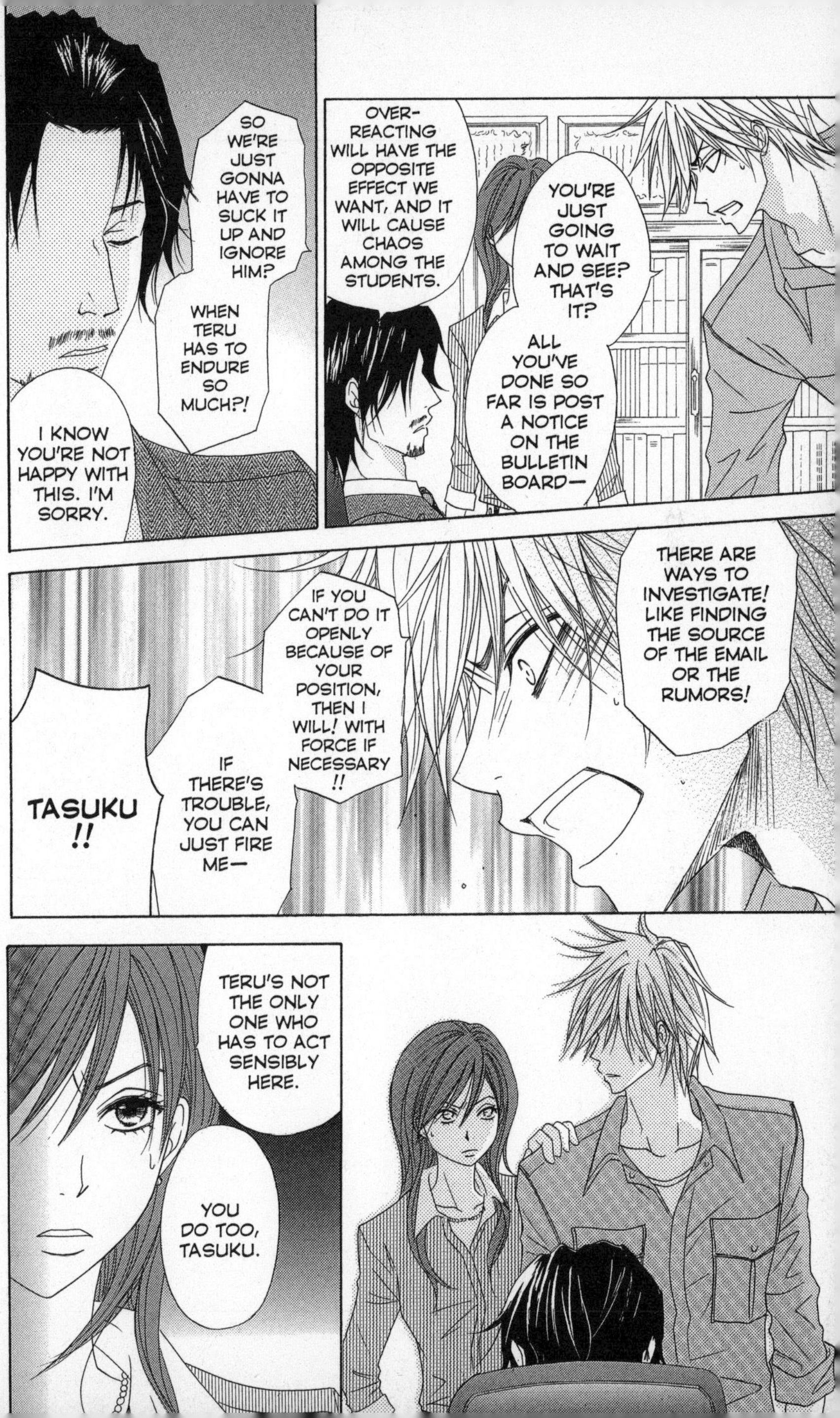
YOU'RE JUST GOING TO WAIT AND SEE? THAT'S IT?
ALL YOU'VE DONE SO FAR IS POST A NOTICE ON THE BULLETIN BOARD—
OVER-REACTING WILL HAVE THE OPPOSITE EFFECT WE WANT, AND IT WILL CAUSE CHAOS AMONG THE STUDENTS.
SO WE'RE JUST GONNA HAVE TO SUCK IT UP AND IGNORE HIM?
WHEN TERU HAS TO ENDURE SO MUCH?!
I KNOW YOU'RE NOT HAPPY WITH THIS. I'M SORRY.
THERE ARE WAYS TO INVESTIGATE! LIKE FINDING THE SOURCE OF THE EMAIL OR THE RUMORS!
IF YOU CAN'T DO IT OPENLY BECAUSE OF YOUR POSITION, THEN I WILL! WITH FORCE IF NECESSARY!!
IF THERE'S TROUBLE, YOU CAN JUST FIRE ME—
TASUKU!!
TERU'S NOT THE ONLY ONE WHO HAS TO ACT SENSIBLY HERE.
YOU DO TOO, TASUKU.

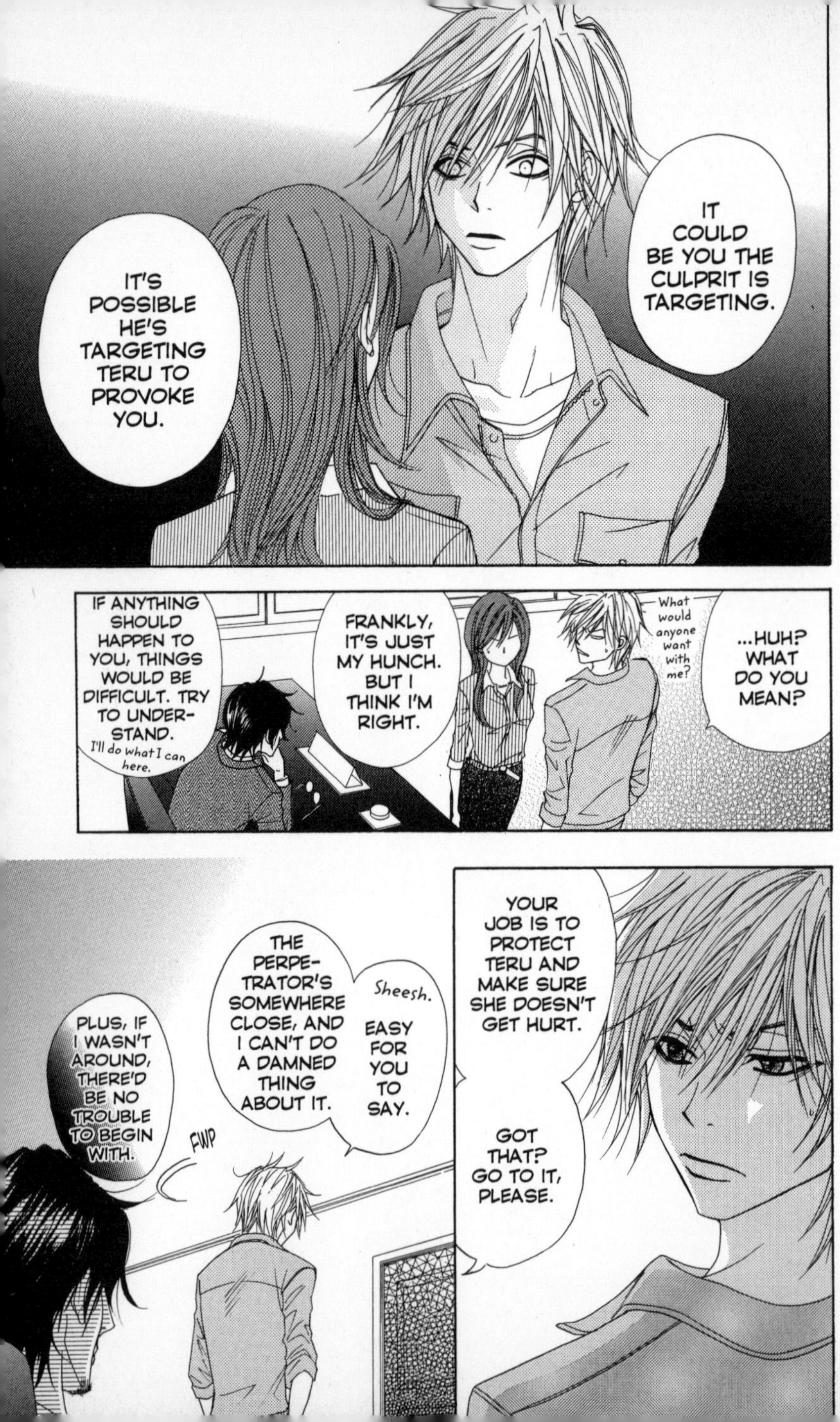
IT COULD BE YOU THE CULPRIT IS TARGETING.
IT'S POSSIBLE HE'S TARGETING TERU TO PROVOKE YOU.
...HUH? WHAT DO YOU MEAN?
What would anyone want with me?
FRANKLY, IT'S JUST MY HUNCH. BUT I THINK I'M RIGHT.
IF ANYTHING SHOULD HAPPEN TO YOU, THINGS WOULD BE DIFFICULT. TRY TO UNDER-STAND.
I'll do what I can here.
YOUR JOB IS TO PROTECT TERU AND MAKE SURE SHE DOESN'T GET HURT.
GOT THAT? GO TO IT, PLEASE.
EASY FOR YOU TO SAY.
Sheesh.
THE PERPE-TRATOR'S SOMEWHERE CLOSE, AND I CAN'T DO A DAMNED THING ABOUT IT.
PLUS, IF I WASN'T AROUND, THERE'D BE NO TROUBLE TO BEGIN WITH.
FWP

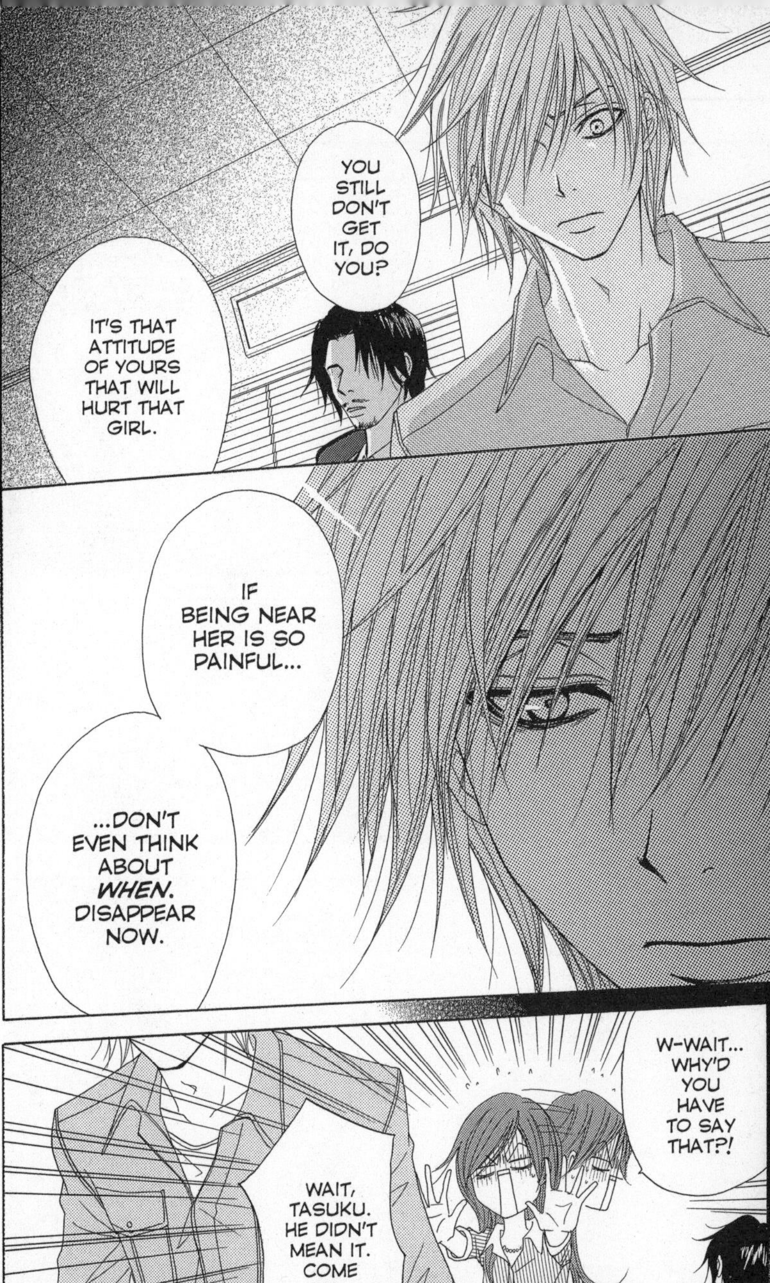
YOU STILL DON'T GET IT, DO YOU?
IT'S THAT ATTITUDE OF YOURS THAT WILL HURT THAT GIRL.
IF BEING NEAR HER IS SO PAINFUL...
...DON'T EVEN THINK ABOUT *WHEN*. DISAPPEAR NOW.
W-WAIT... WHY'D YOU HAVE TO SAY THAT?!
WAIT, TASUKU. HE DIDN'T MEAN IT. COME ON...

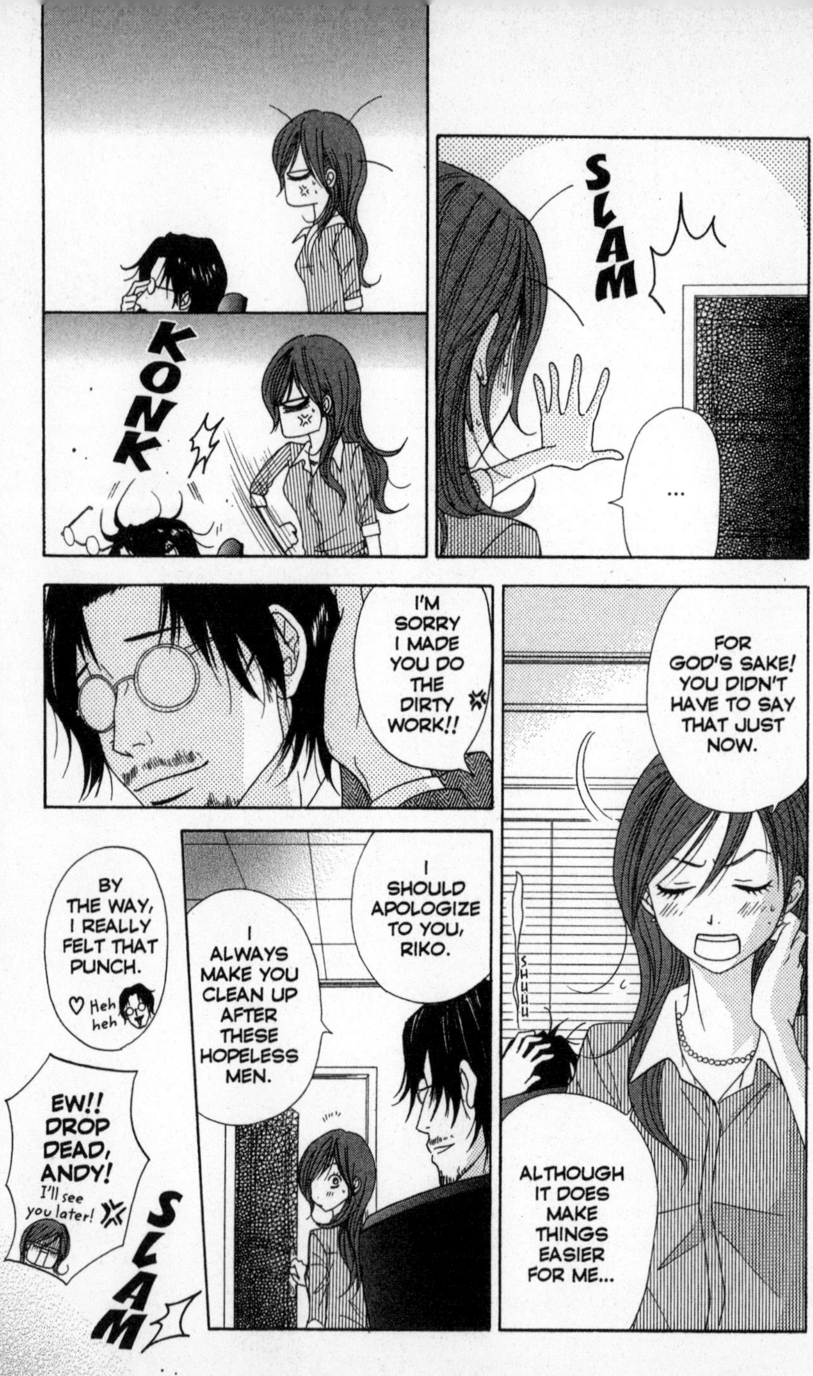
SLAM
...
KONK
FOR GOD'S SAKE! YOU DIDN'T HAVE TO SAY THAT JUST NOW.
SHUUU
ALTHOUGH IT DOES MAKE THINGS EASIER FOR ME...
I'M SORRY I MADE YOU DO THE DIRTY WORK!!
I SHOULD APOLOGIZE TO YOU, RIKO.
I ALWAYS MAKE YOU CLEAN UP AFTER THESE HOPELESS MEN.
BY THE WAY, I REALLY FELT THAT PUNCH.
♡ Heh heh
EW!! DROP DEAD, ANDY!
I'll see you later!
SLAM

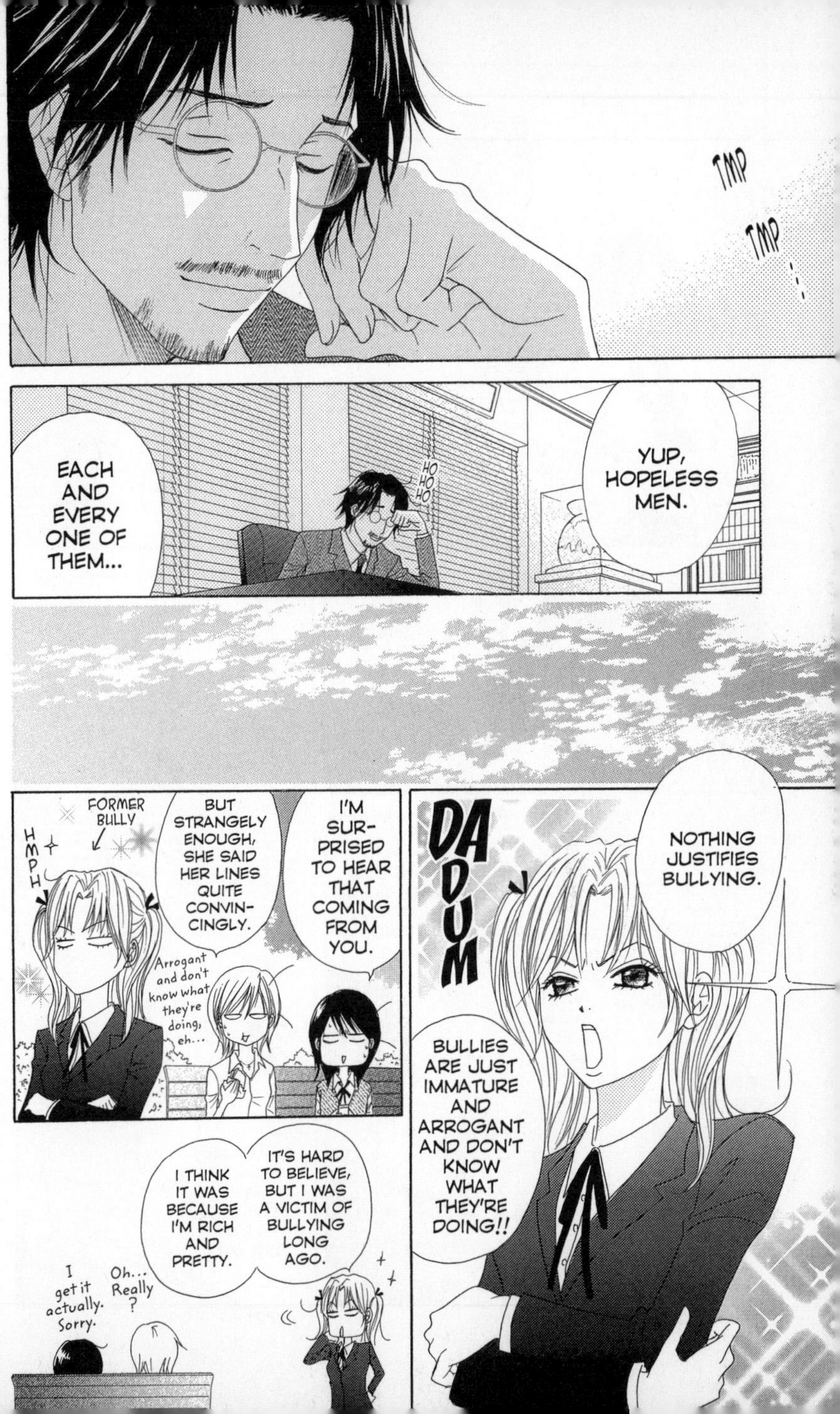
TMP
TMP
YUP, HOPELESS MEN.
HO HO HO
EACH AND EVERY ONE OF THEM...
DADUM
NOTHING JUSTIFIES BULLYING.
BULLIES ARE JUST IMMATURE AND ARROGANT AND DON'T KNOW WHAT THEY'RE DOING!!
I'M SURPRISED TO HEAR THAT COMING FROM YOU.
BUT STRANGELY ENOUGH, SHE SAID HER LINES QUITE CONVINCINGLY.
FORMER BULLY
HMPH
Arrogant and don't know what they're doing, eh...
IT'S HARD TO BELIEVE, BUT I WAS A VICTIM OF BULLYING LONG AGO.
I THINK IT WAS BECAUSE I'M RICH AND PRETTY.
Oh... Really?
I get it actually. Sorry.

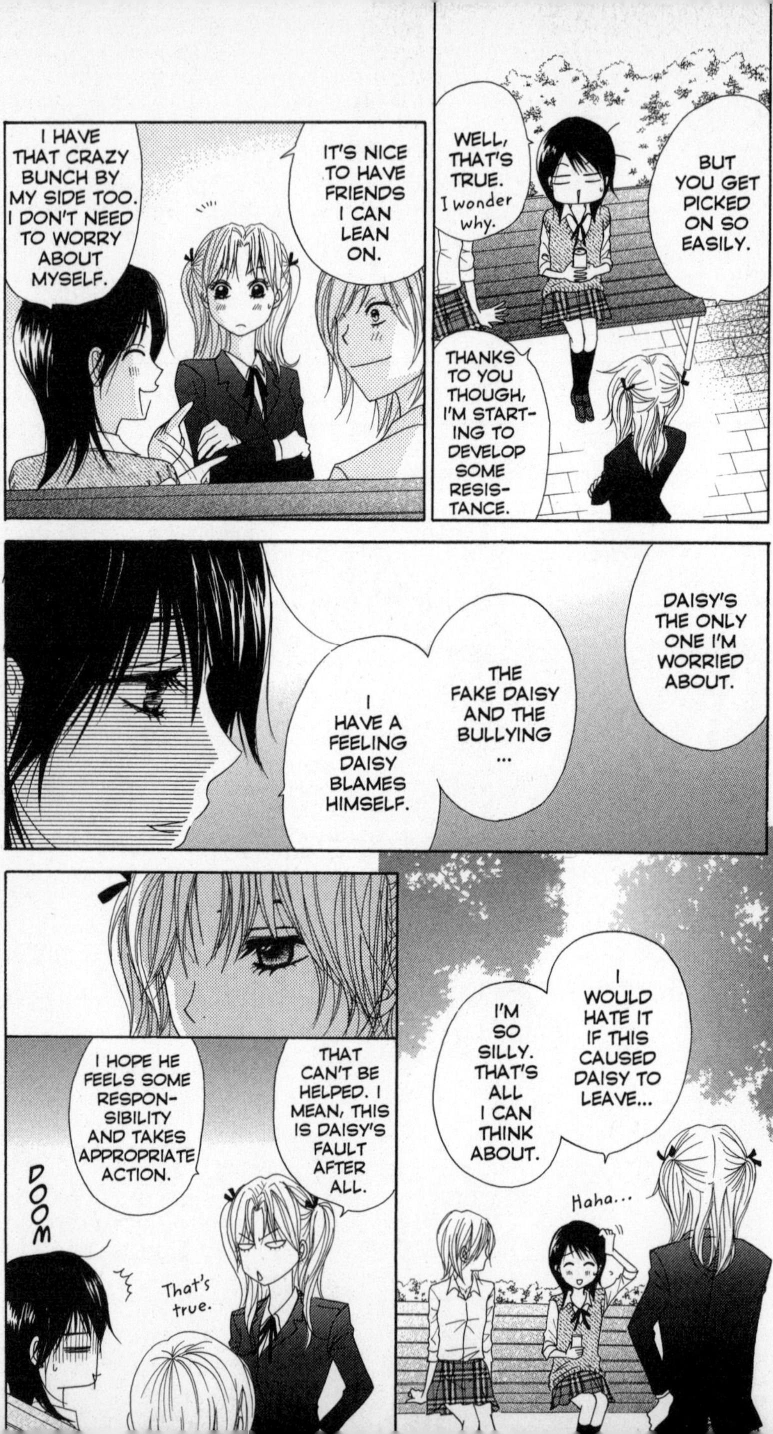
BUT YOU GET PICKED ON SO EASILY.
WELL, THAT'S TRUE. I wonder why.
THANKS TO YOU THOUGH, I'M START-ING TO DEVELOP SOME RESIS-TANCE.
IT'S NICE TO HAVE FRIENDS I CAN LEAN ON.
I HAVE THAT CRAZY BUNCH BY MY SIDE TOO. I DON'T NEED TO WORRY ABOUT MYSELF.
DAISY'S THE ONLY ONE I'M WORRIED ABOUT.
THE FAKE DAISY AND THE BULLYING ...
I HAVE A FEELING DAISY BLAMES HIMSELF.
I WOULD HATE IT IF THIS CAUSED DAISY TO LEAVE...
I'M SO SILLY. THAT'S ALL I CAN THINK ABOUT.
Haha...
THAT CAN'T BE HELPED. I MEAN, THIS IS DAISY'S FAULT AFTER ALL.
I HOPE HE FEELS SOME RESPON-SIBILITY AND TAKES APPROPRIATE ACTION.
That's true.
DOOM

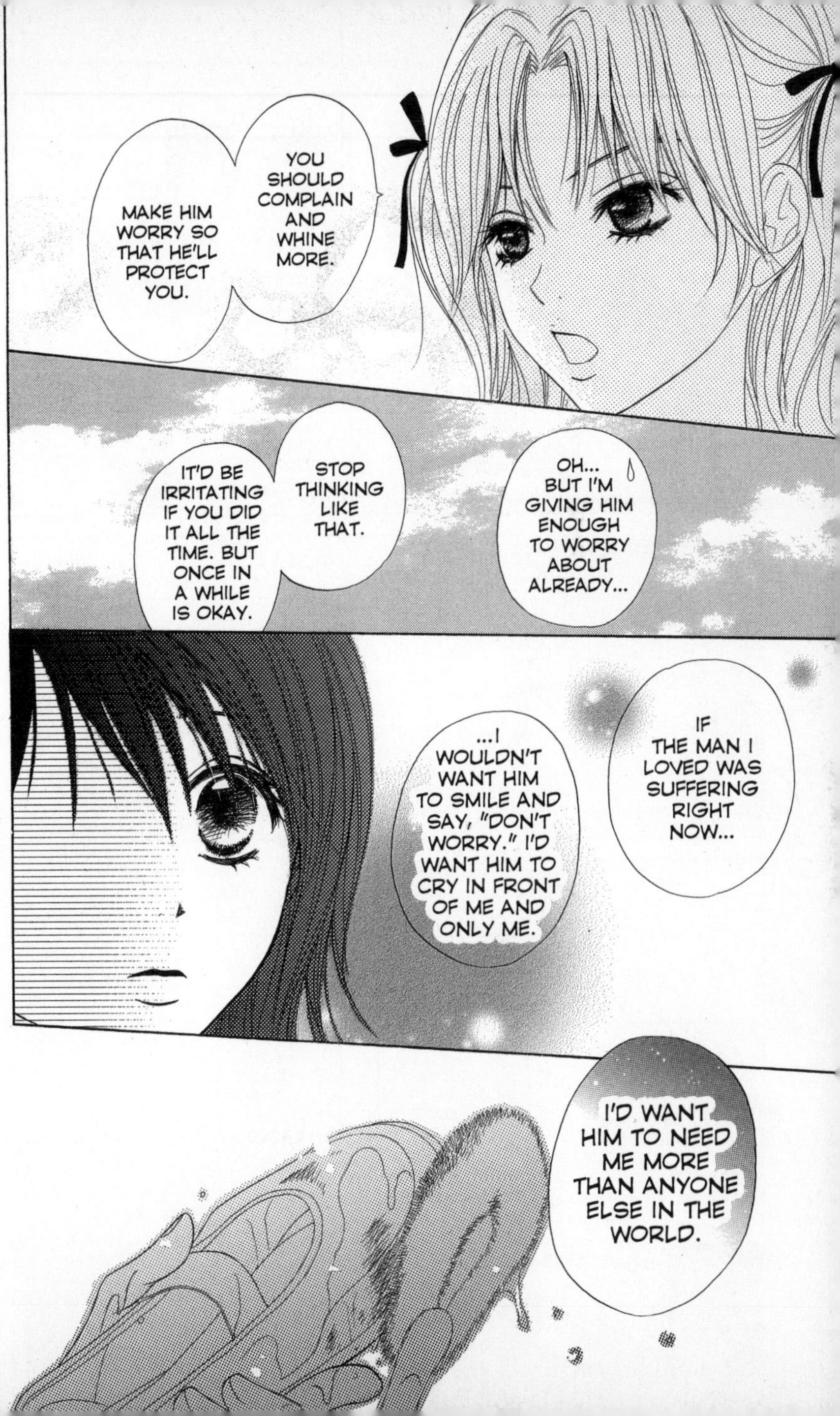
YOU SHOULD COMPLAIN AND WHINE MORE.
MAKE HIM WORRY SO THAT HE'LL PROTECT YOU.
OH... BUT I'M GIVING HIM ENOUGH TO WORRY ABOUT ALREADY...
STOP THINKING LIKE THAT.
IT'D BE IRRITATING IF YOU DID IT ALL THE TIME. BUT ONCE IN A WHILE IS OKAY.
IF THE MAN I LOVED WAS SUFFERING RIGHT NOW...
...I WOULDN'T WANT HIM TO SMILE AND SAY, "DON'T WORRY." I'D WANT HIM TO CRY IN FRONT OF ME AND ONLY ME.
I'D WANT HIM TO NEED ME MORE THAN ANYONE ELSE IN THE WORLD.

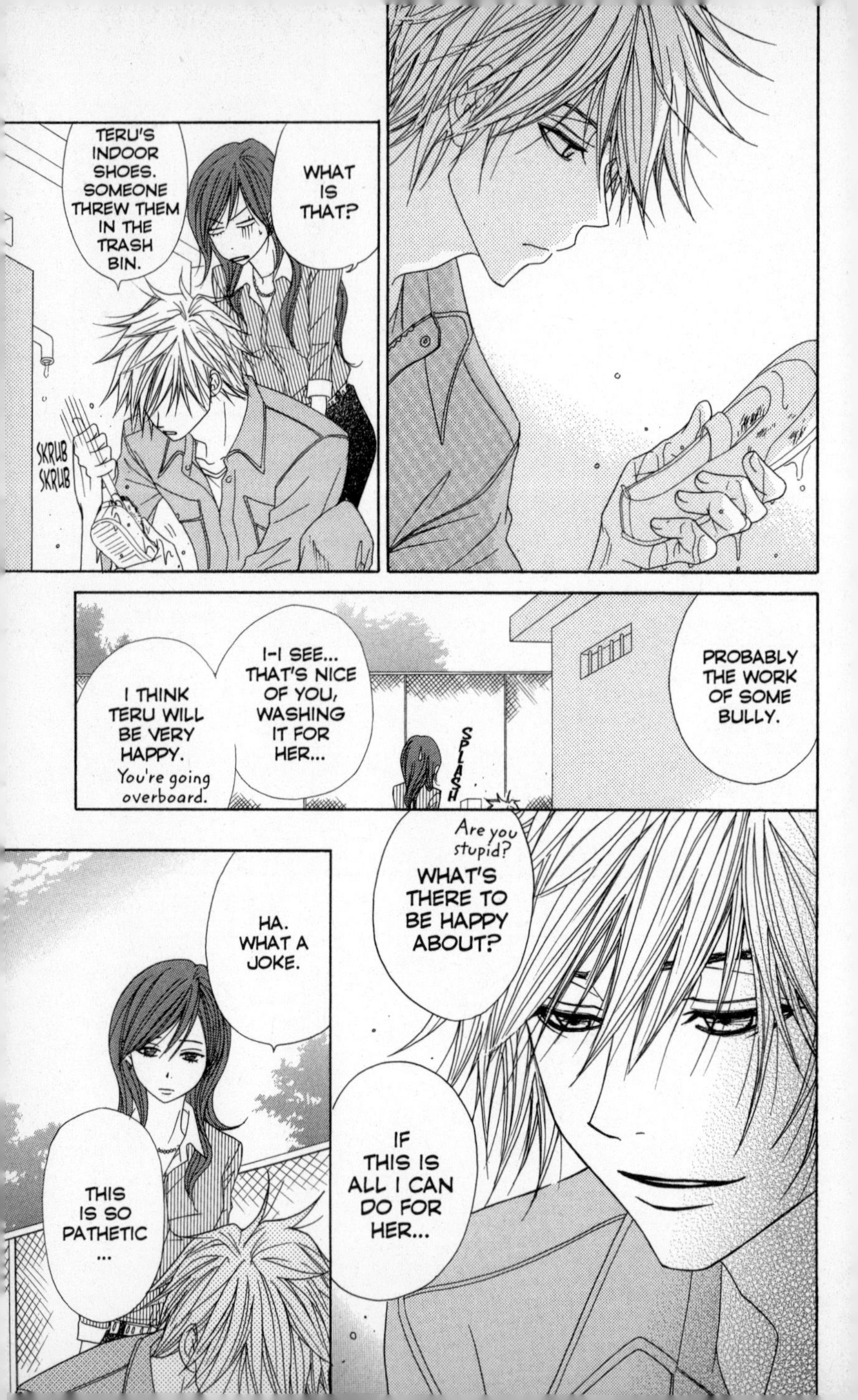
WHAT IS THAT?
TERU'S INDOOR SHOES. SOMEONE THREW THEM IN THE TRASH BIN.
SKRUB SKRUB
PROBABLY THE WORK OF SOME BULLY.
SPLASH
I-I SEE... THAT'S NICE OF YOU, WASHING IT FOR HER...
I THINK TERU WILL BE VERY HAPPY.
You're going overboard.
Are you stupid?
WHAT'S THERE TO BE HAPPY ABOUT?
IF THIS IS ALL I CAN DO FOR HER...
HA. WHAT A JOKE.
THIS IS SO PATHETIC ...

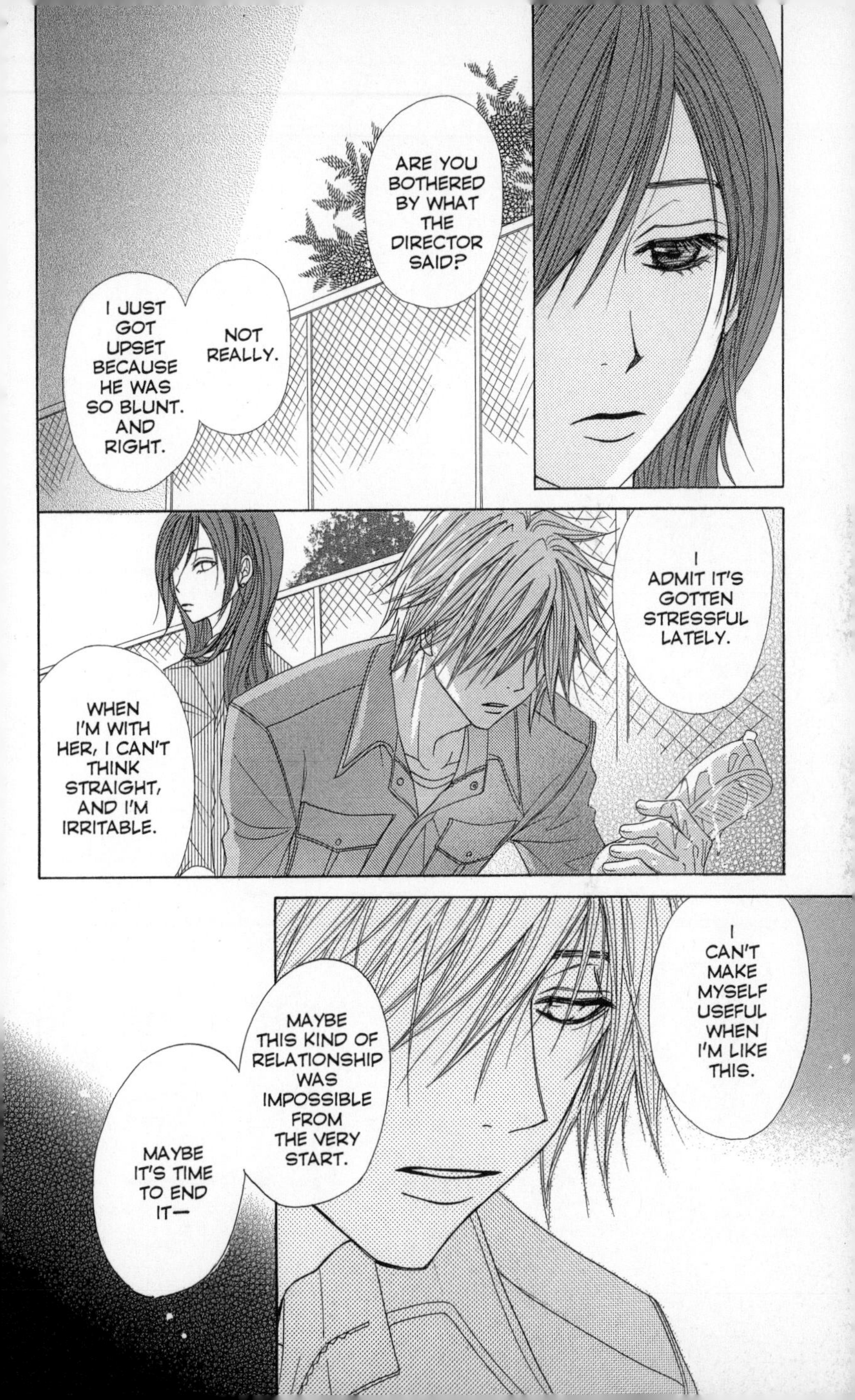
ARE YOU BOTHERED BY WHAT THE DIRECTOR SAID?
NOT REALLY.
I JUST GOT UPSET BECAUSE HE WAS SO BLUNT. AND RIGHT.
I ADMIT IT'S GOTTEN STRESSFUL LATELY.
WHEN I'M WITH HER, I CAN'T THINK STRAIGHT, AND I'M IRRITABLE.
I CAN'T MAKE MYSELF USEFUL WHEN I'M LIKE THIS.
MAYBE THIS KIND OF RELATIONSHIP WAS IMPOSSIBLE FROM THE VERY START.
MAYBE IT'S TIME TO END IT—

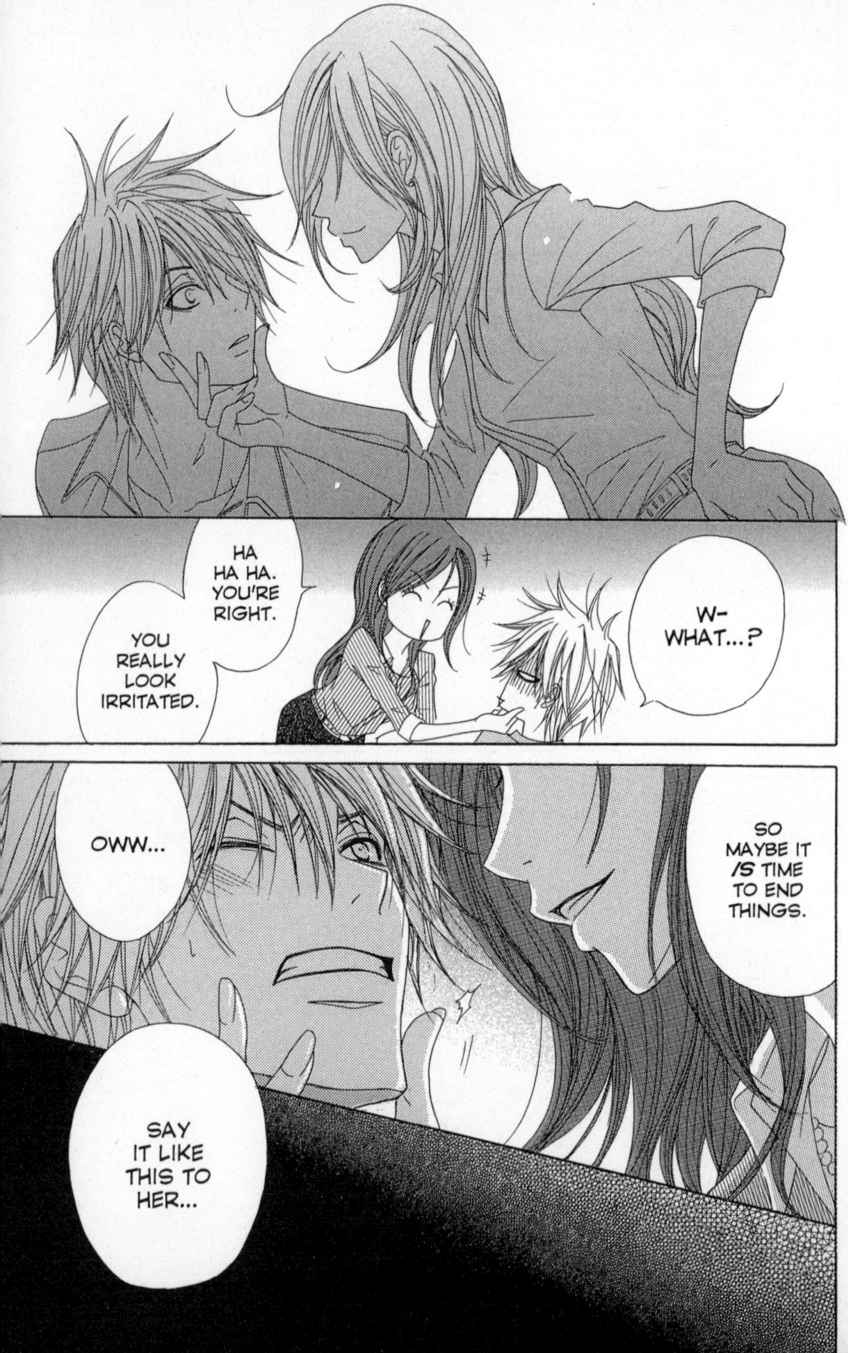
W- WHAT...?
HA HA HA. YOU'RE RIGHT.
YOU REALLY LOOK IRRITATED.
SO MAYBE IT *IS* TIME TO END THINGS.
OWW...
SAY IT LIKE THIS TO HER...

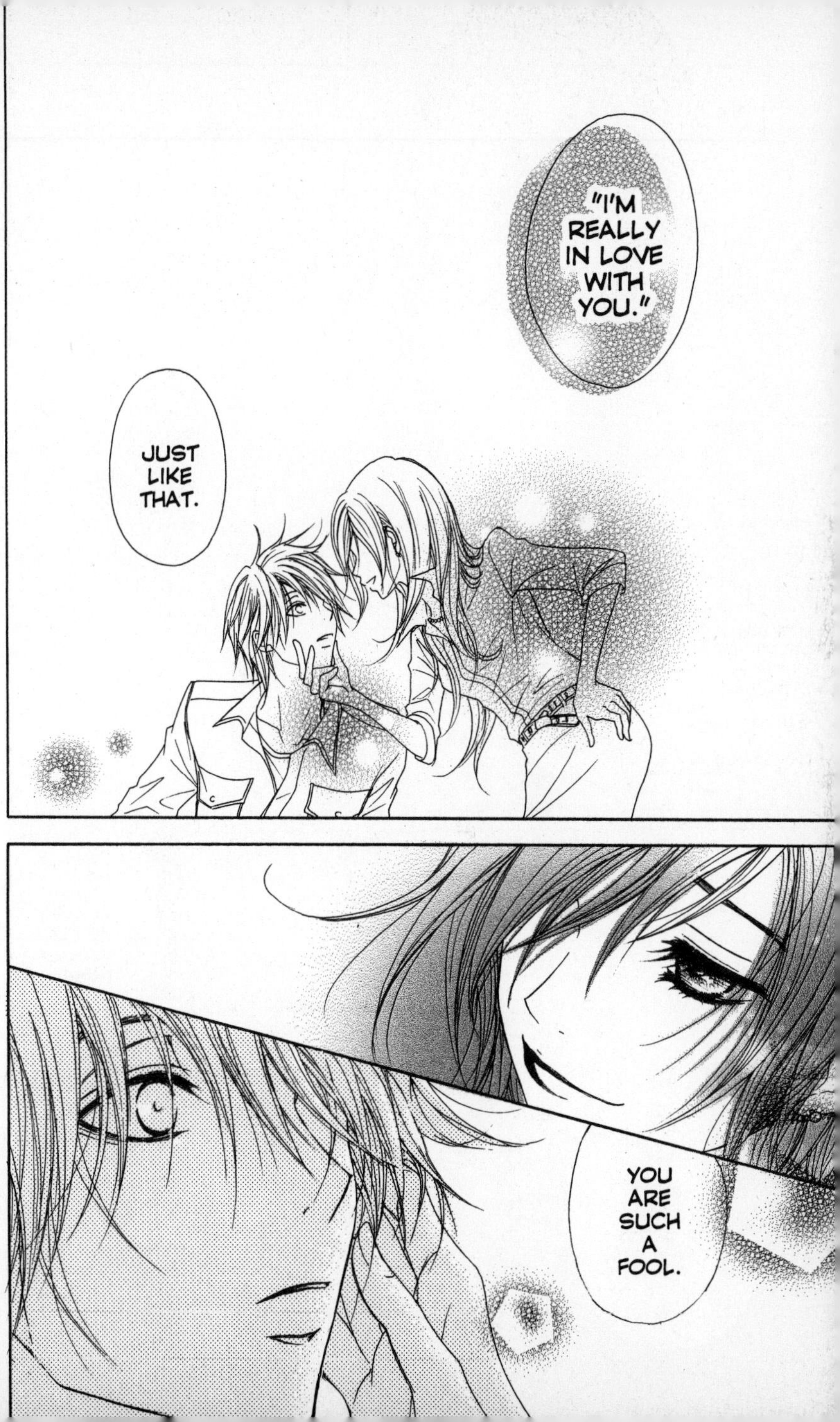
"I'M REALLY IN LOVE WITH YOU."
JUST LIKE THAT.
YOU ARE SUCH A FOOL.

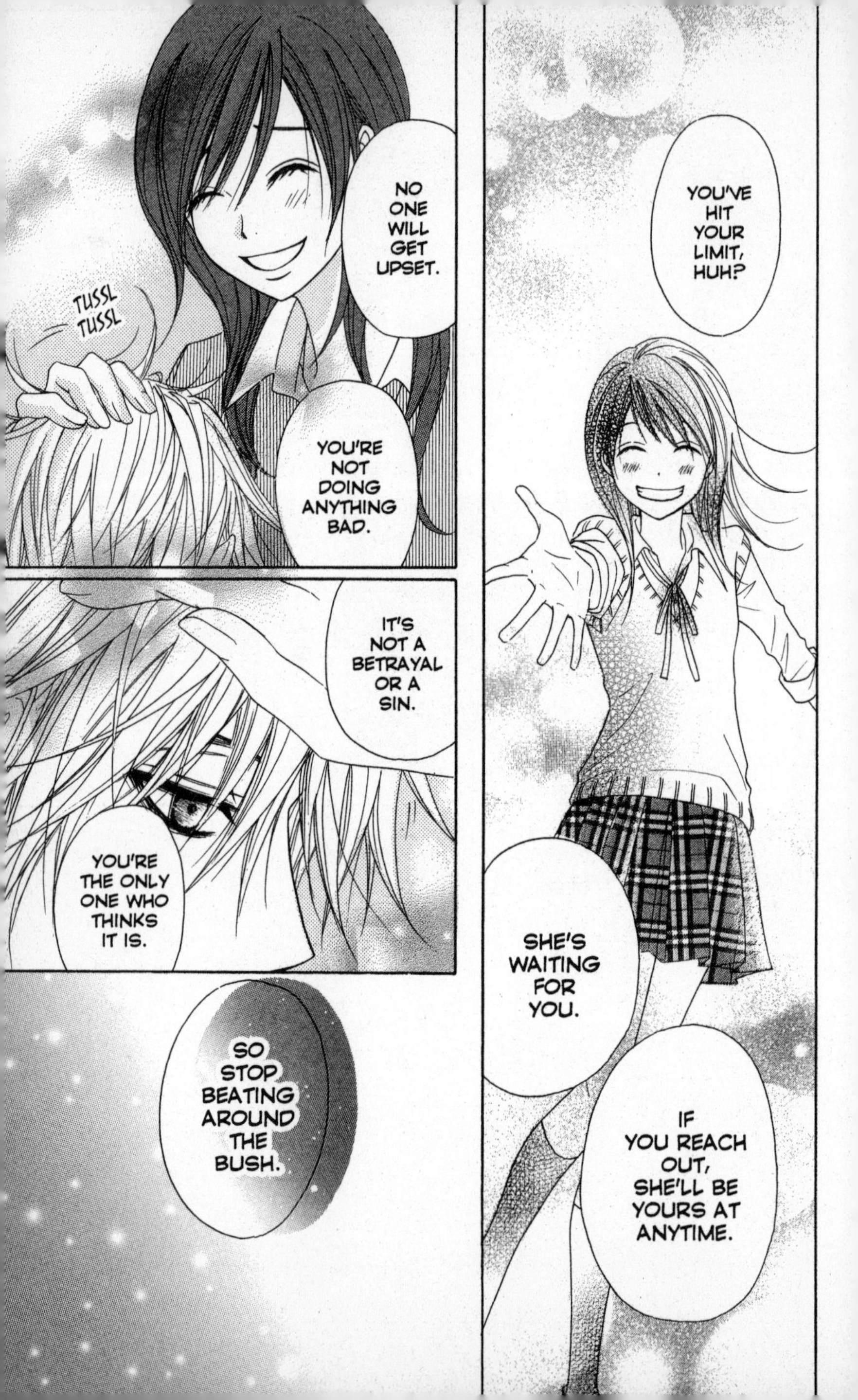
YOU'VE HIT YOUR LIMIT, HUH?
SHE'S WAITING FOR YOU.
IF YOU REACH OUT, SHE'LL BE YOURS AT ANYTIME.
NO ONE WILL GET UPSET.
TUSSL TUSSL
YOU'RE NOT DOING ANYTHING BAD.
IT'S NOT A BETRAYAL OR A SIN.
YOU'RE THE ONLY ONE WHO THINKS IT IS.
SO STOP BEATING AROUND THE BUSH.

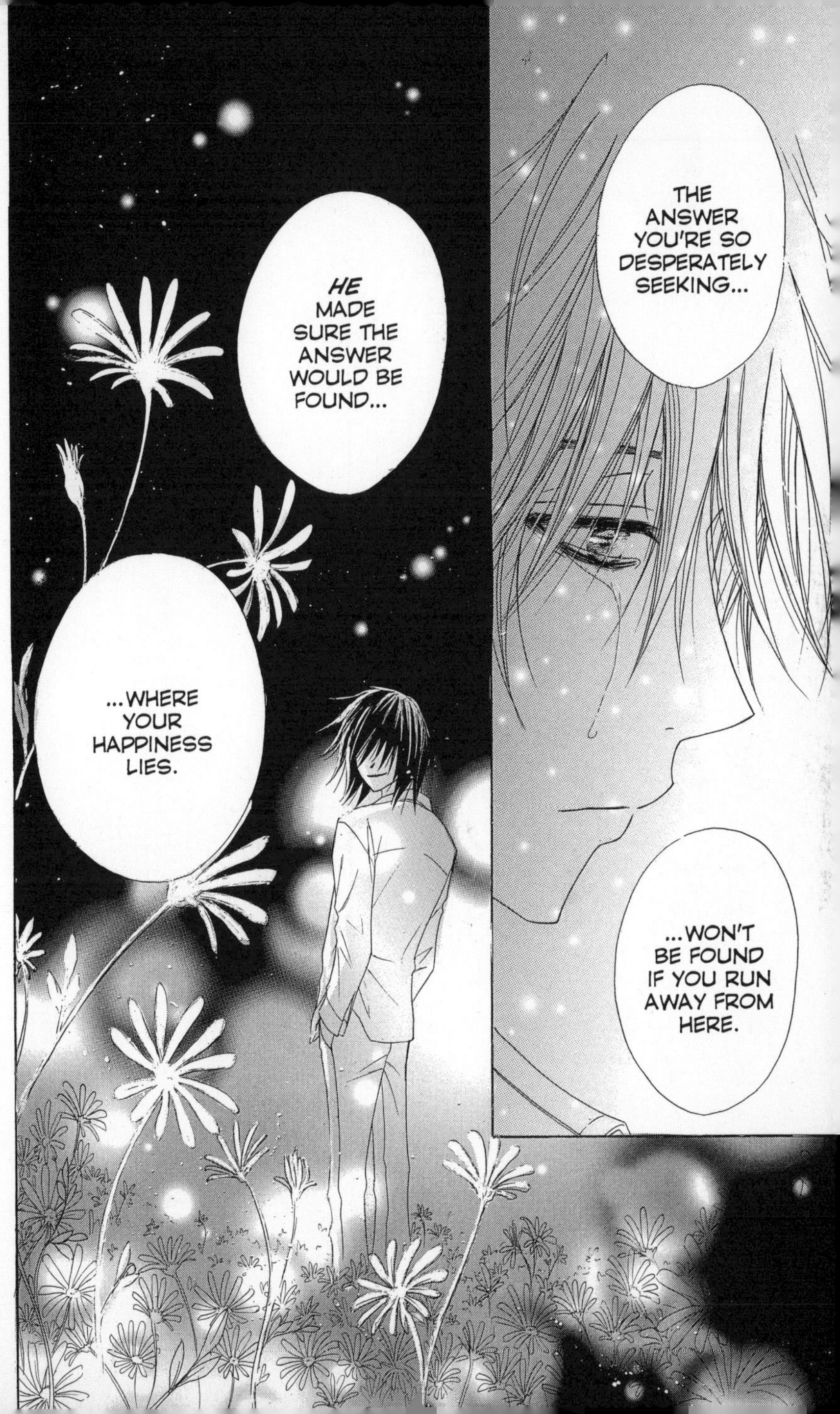
THE ANSWER YOU'RE SO DESPERATELY SEEKING...
...WON'T BE FOUND IF YOU RUN AWAY FROM HERE.
HE MADE SURE THE ANSWER WOULD BE FOUND...
...WHERE YOUR HAPPINESS LIES.

VIZ MEDIA
ATTN: DENGEKI DAISY
QUESTION CORNER
(TEMPORARY)
P.O. BOX 77010
SAN FRANCISCO, CA
94107

↑
PLEASE SEND YOUR CORRESPONDENCE TO THIS ADDRESS. (THE NAME OF THE CORNER IS BORING, AND I'LL THINK OF A DIFFERENT NAME IN TIME.)

ANY KIND OF QUESTION OR COMMENT IS FINE. IN FACT, THE SILLIER, THE BETTER. QUESTIONS LIKE "DOES KUROSAKI PREFER *TSUBUAN* MASHED RED BEAN JAM OR *KOSHIAN* STRAINED RED BEAN JAM?" WOULD BE GOOD.

QUESTIONS RELATED TO THE HEART OF THE STORY WOULD REVEAL HOW EMPTY IT IS, SO I'D APPRECIATE IF YOU DIDN'T ASK SUCH QUESTIONS.

ANYWAY, THANK YOU VERY MUCH FOR YOUR SUPPORT.

• BY THE WAY...

KUROSAKI → STRAINED RED BEAN JAM
TERU → HARD TO FIGURE OUT, BUT AFTER 30 MINUTES OF THOUGHT; MASHED RED BEAN JAM
RIKO → STRAINED RED BEAN JAM
BOSS → MASHED RED BEAN JAM
KIYOSHI → MASHED RED BEAN JAM
ANDY → STRAINED RED BEAN JAM
HARUKA → MASHED RED BEAN JAM
YOSHI (TERU'S PLUMP FRIEND) → MASHED RED BEAN JAM
TAKEDA → STRAINED RED BEAN JAM
RENA → MASHED PEA JAM (DOESN'T LISTEN TO PEOPLE)
SOICHIRO → TERU (SAME)

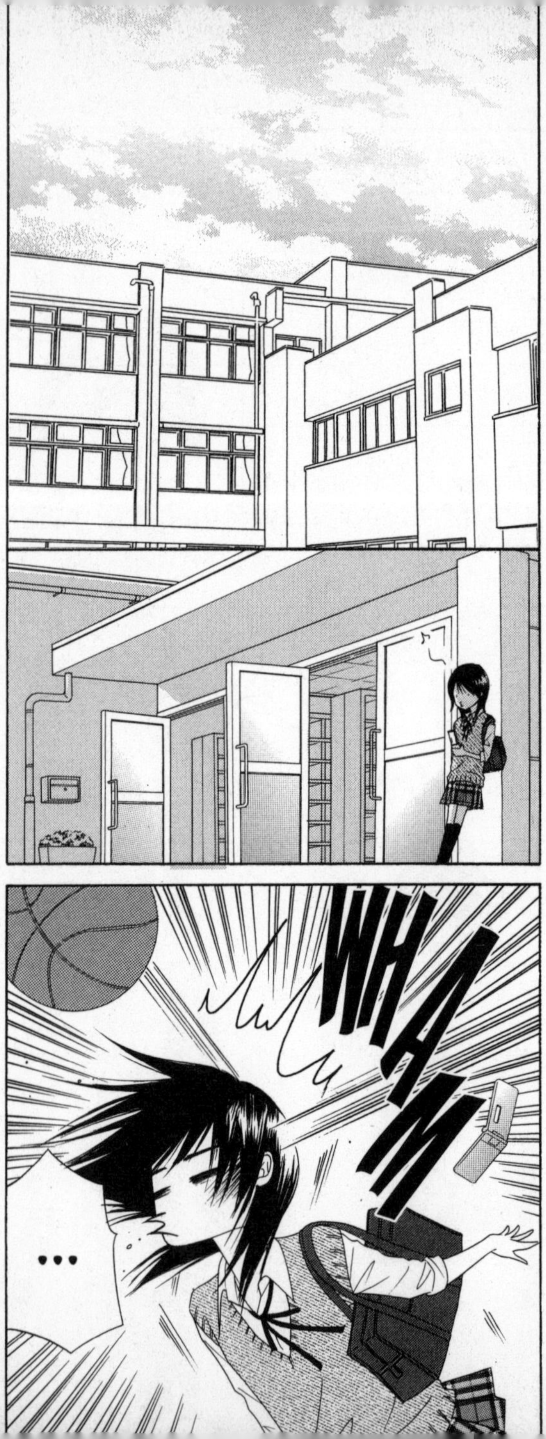
WHAM
...

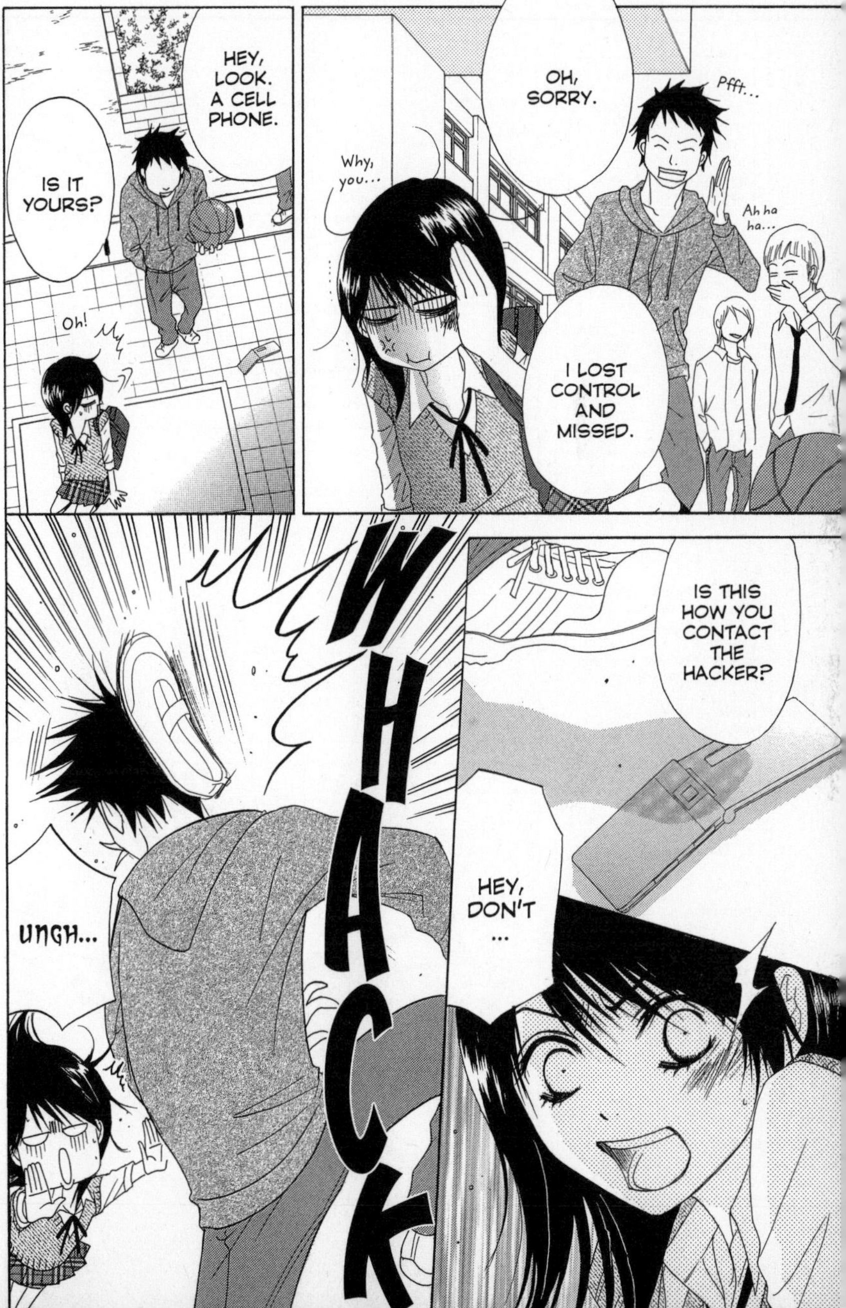
Pfft...
OH, SORRY.
Ah ha ha...
Why, you...
I LOST CONTROL AND MISSED.
HEY, LOOK. A CELL PHONE.
IS IT YOURS?
Oh!
IS THIS HOW YOU CONTACT THE HACKER?
HEY, DON'T ...
WHACK
UNGH...

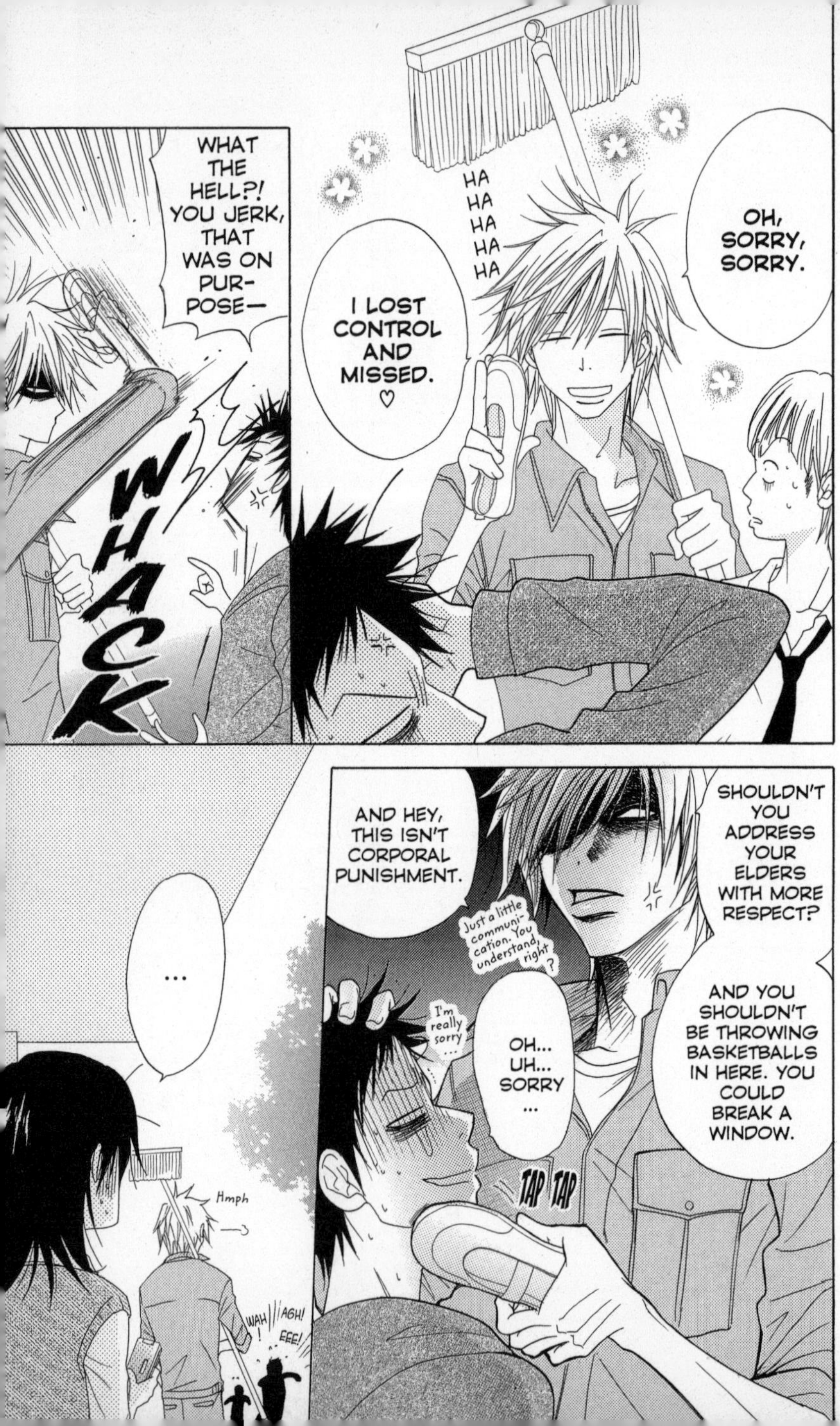
OH, SORRY, SORRY.
HA HA HA HA HA
I LOST CONTROL AND MISSED. ♡
WHAT THE HELL?! YOU JERK, THAT WAS ON PUR-POSE—
WHACK
SHOULDN'T YOU ADDRESS YOUR ELDERS WITH MORE RESPECT?
AND YOU SHOULDN'T BE THROWING BASKETBALLS IN HERE. YOU COULD BREAK A WINDOW.
AND HEY, THIS ISN'T CORPORAL PUNISHMENT.
Just a little communi-cation. You understand, right?
OH... UH... SORRY...
I'm really sorry...
TAP TAP
...
Hmph
AGH!
WAH!
EEE!

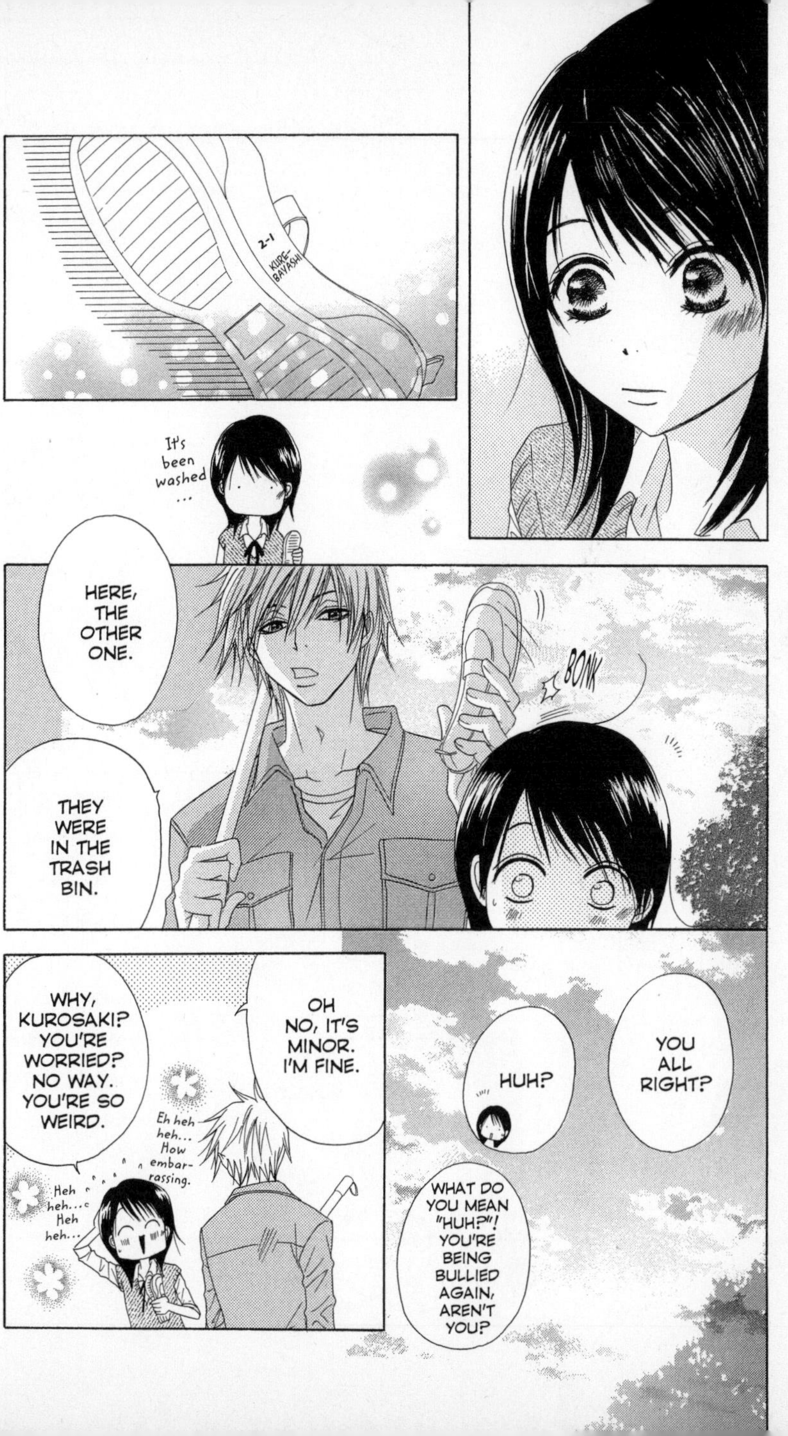
2-1
KURE-BAYASHI
It's been washed...
HERE, THE OTHER ONE.
BONK
THEY WERE IN THE TRASH BIN.
YOU ALL RIGHT?
HUH?
WHAT DO YOU MEAN "HUH?"! YOU'RE BEING BULLIED AGAIN, AREN'T YOU?
OH NO, IT'S MINOR. I'M FINE.
WHY, KUROSAKI? YOU'RE WORRIED? NO WAY. YOU'RE SO WEIRD.
Eh heh heh... How embarrassing.
Heh heh... Heh heh...

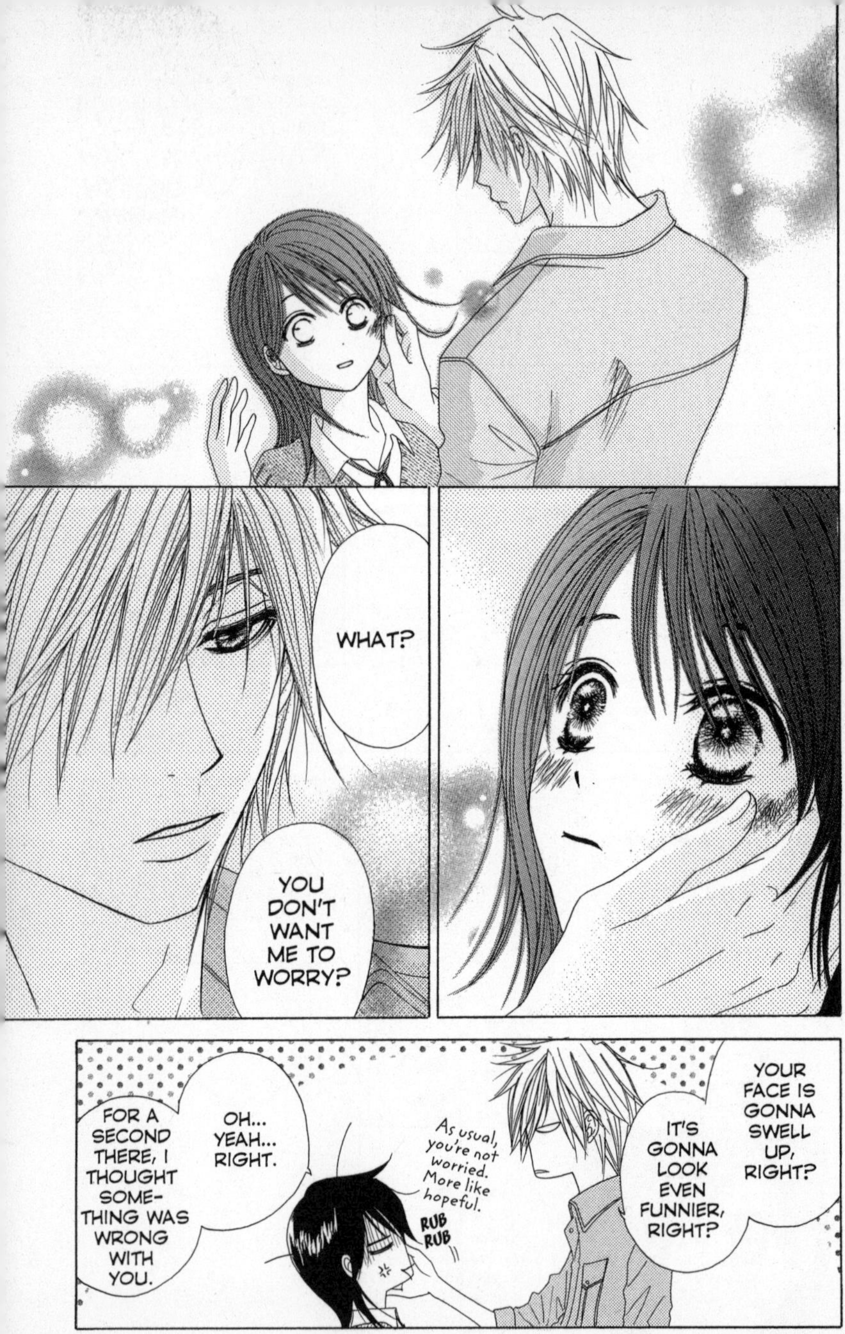
WHAT?
YOU DON'T WANT ME TO WORRY?
YOUR FACE IS GONNA SWELL UP, RIGHT?
IT'S GONNA LOOK EVEN FUNNIER, RIGHT?
As usual, you're not worried. More like hopeful.
RUB RUB
OH... YEAH... RIGHT.
FOR A SECOND THERE, I THOUGHT SOME-THING WAS WRONG WITH YOU.

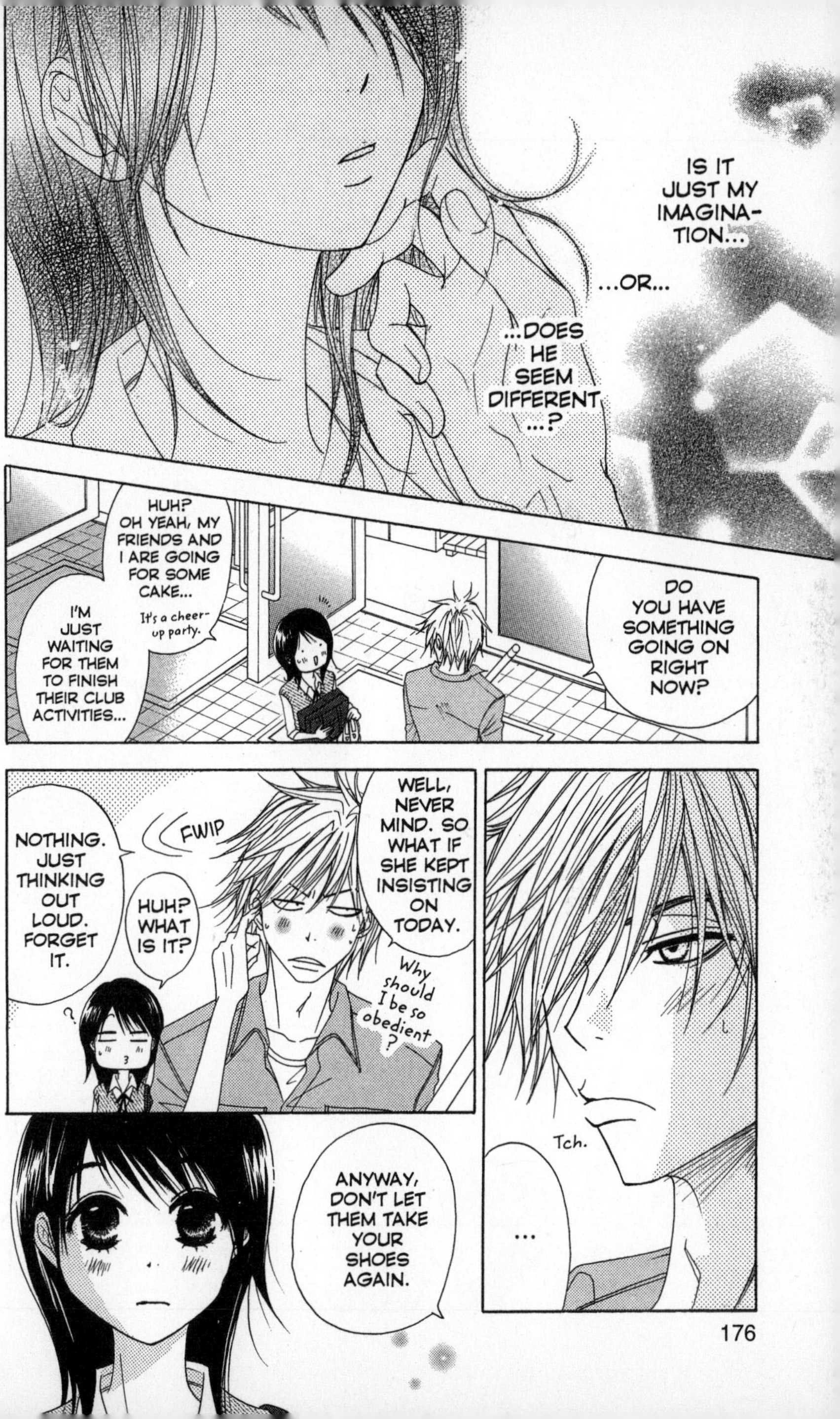

IS IT JUST MY IMAGINA-TION...
...OR...
...DOES HE SEEM DIFFERENT ...?
DO YOU HAVE SOMETHING GOING ON RIGHT NOW?
HUH? OH YEAH, MY FRIENDS AND I ARE GOING FOR SOME CAKE...
It's a cheer-up party.
I'M JUST WAITING FOR THEM TO FINISH THEIR CLUB ACTIVITIES...
Tch.
...
WELL, NEVER MIND. SO WHAT IF SHE KEPT INSISTING ON TODAY.
Why should I be so obedient?
FWIP
HUH? WHAT IS IT?
NOTHING. JUST THINKING OUT LOUD. FORGET IT.
ANYWAY, DON'T LET THEM TAKE YOUR SHOES AGAIN.

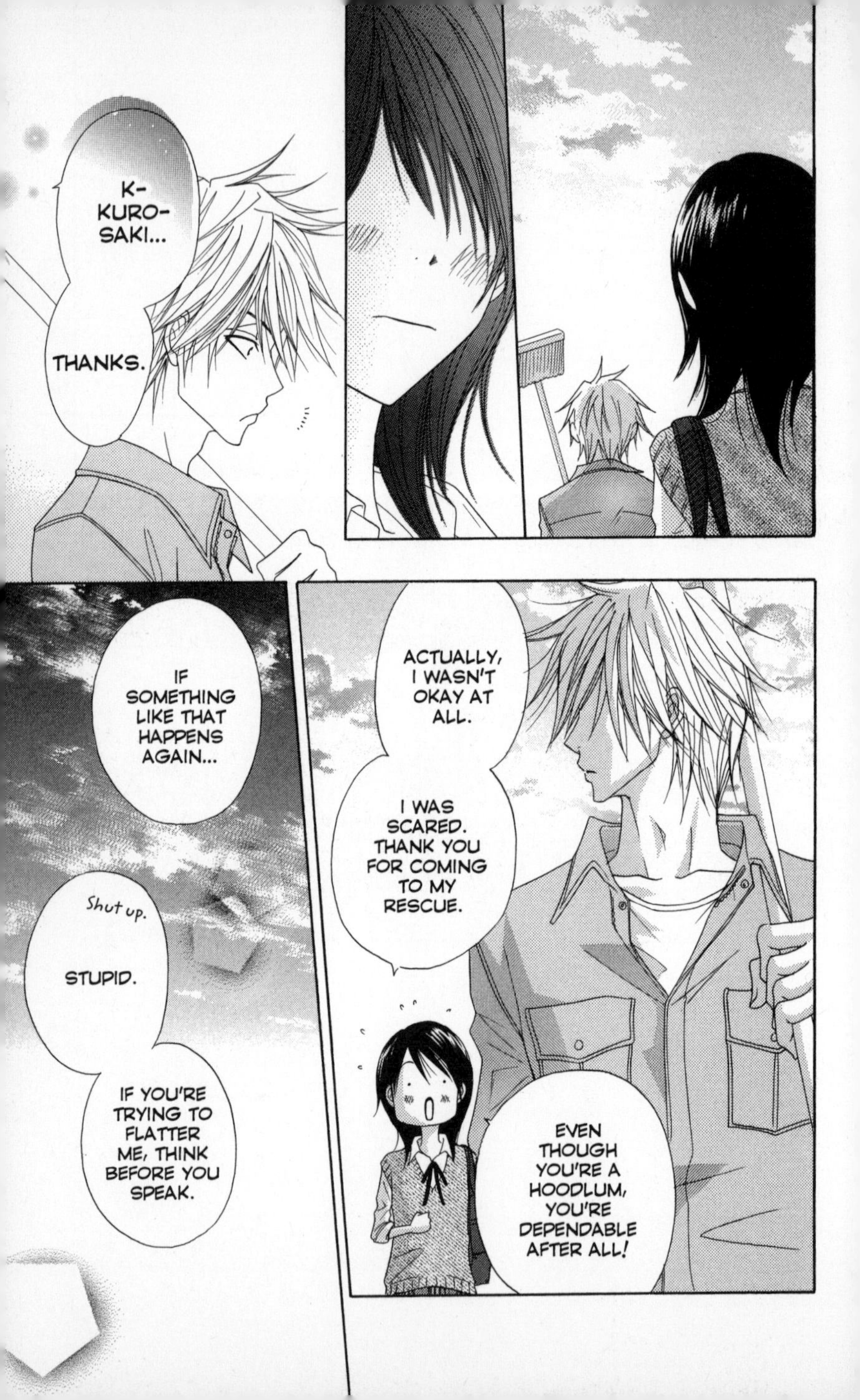
K-KURO-SAKI...
THANKS.
ACTUALLY, I WASN'T OKAY AT ALL.
I WAS SCARED. THANK YOU FOR COMING TO MY RESCUE.
EVEN THOUGH YOU'RE A HOODLUM, YOU'RE DEPENDABLE AFTER ALL!
IF SOMETHING LIKE THAT HAPPENS AGAIN...
Shut up.
STUPID.
IF YOU'RE TRYING TO FLATTER ME, THINK BEFORE YOU SPEAK.

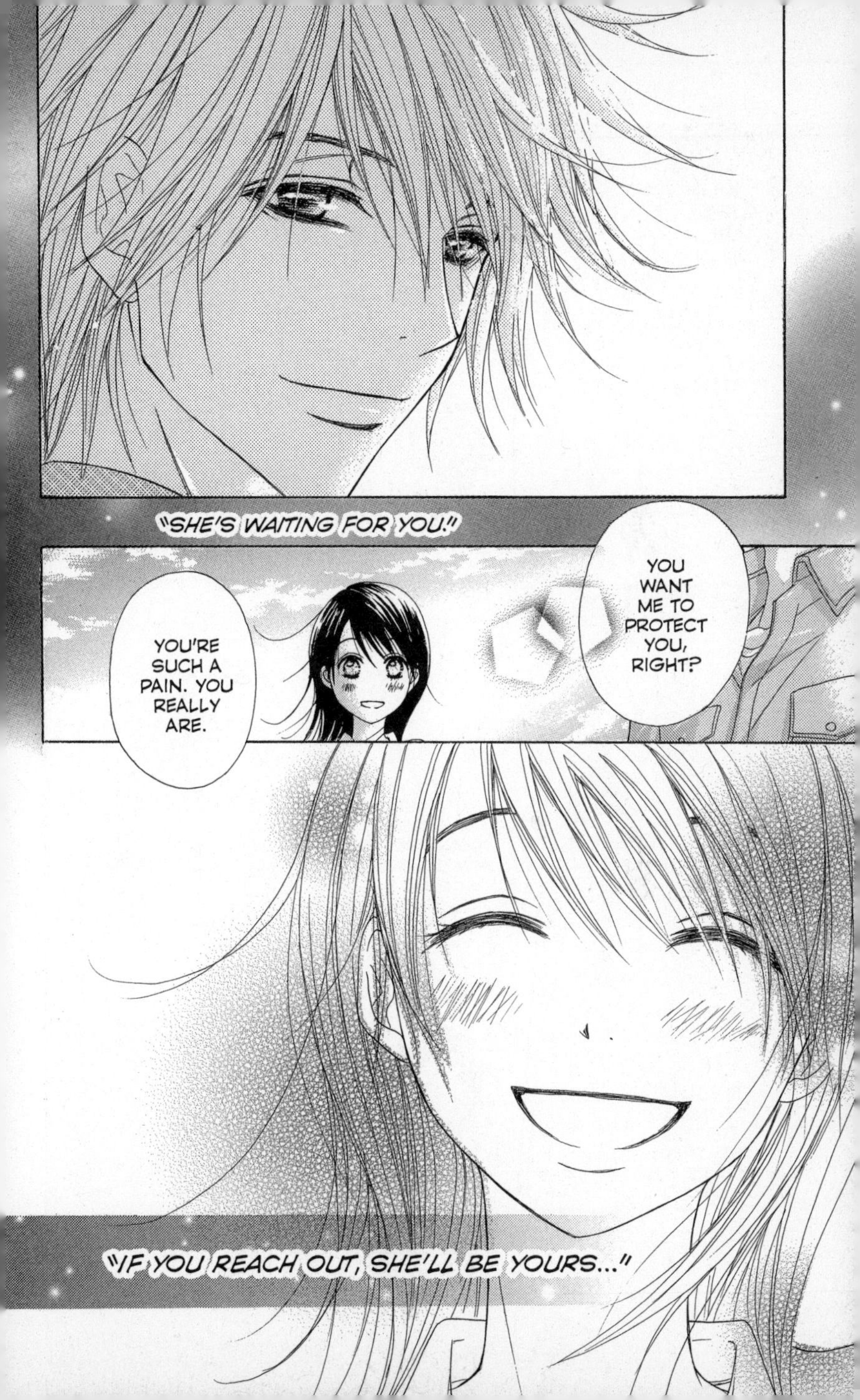
"SHE'S WAITING FOR YOU."
YOU WANT ME TO PROTECT YOU, RIGHT?
YOU'RE SUCH A PAIN. YOU REALLY ARE.
"IF YOU REACH OUT, SHE'LL BE YOURS..."

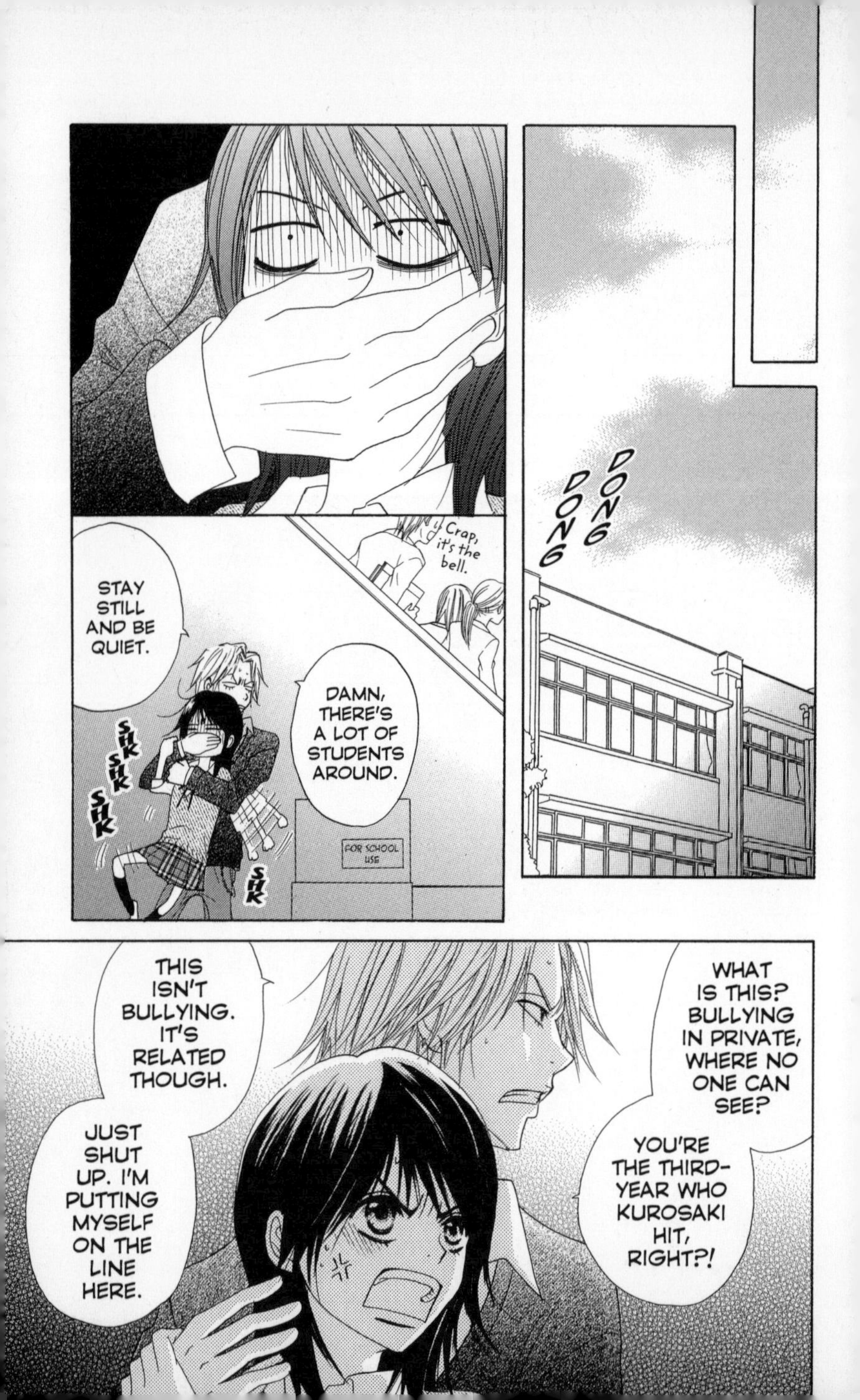
DONG DONG
Crap, it's the bell.
DAMN, THERE'S A LOT OF STUDENTS AROUND.
STAY STILL AND BE QUIET.
SHK
SHK SHK SHK
FOR SCHOOL USE
WHAT IS THIS? BULLYING IN PRIVATE, WHERE NO ONE CAN SEE?
YOU'RE THE THIRD-YEAR WHO KUROSAKI HIT, RIGHT?!
THIS ISN'T BULLYING. IT'S RELATED THOUGH.
JUST SHUT UP. I'M PUTTING MYSELF ON THE LINE HERE.

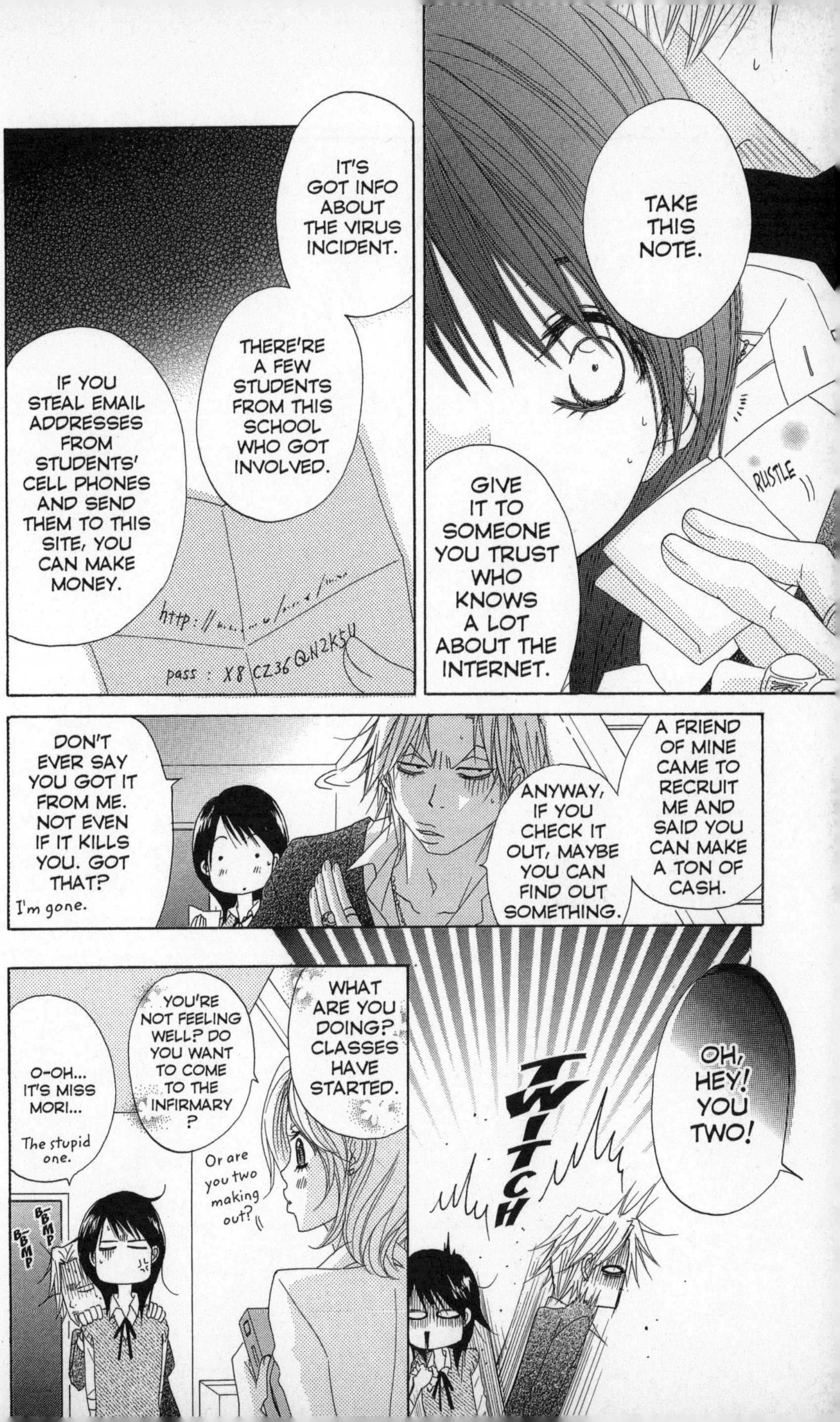
TAKE THIS NOTE.
RUSTLE
GIVE IT TO SOMEONE YOU TRUST WHO KNOWS A LOT ABOUT THE INTERNET.
IT'S GOT INFO ABOUT THE VIRUS INCIDENT.
THERE'RE A FEW STUDENTS FROM THIS SCHOOL WHO GOT INVOLVED.
IF YOU STEAL EMAIL ADDRESSES FROM STUDENTS' CELL PHONES AND SEND THEM TO THIS SITE, YOU CAN MAKE MONEY.
pass : X8CZ36QN2K5U
A FRIEND OF MINE CAME TO RECRUIT ME AND SAID YOU CAN MAKE A TON OF CASH.
ANYWAY, IF YOU CHECK IT OUT, MAYBE YOU CAN FIND OUT SOMETHING.
DON'T EVER SAY YOU GOT IT FROM ME. NOT EVEN IF IT KILLS YOU. GOT THAT?
I'm gone.
OH, HEY! YOU TWO!
TWITCH
WHAT ARE YOU DOING? CLASSES HAVE STARTED.
YOU'RE NOT FEELING WELL? DO YOU WANT TO COME TO THE INFIRMARY?
Or are you two making out?
O-OH... IT'S MISS MORI...
The stupid one.
B-BMP
B-BMP

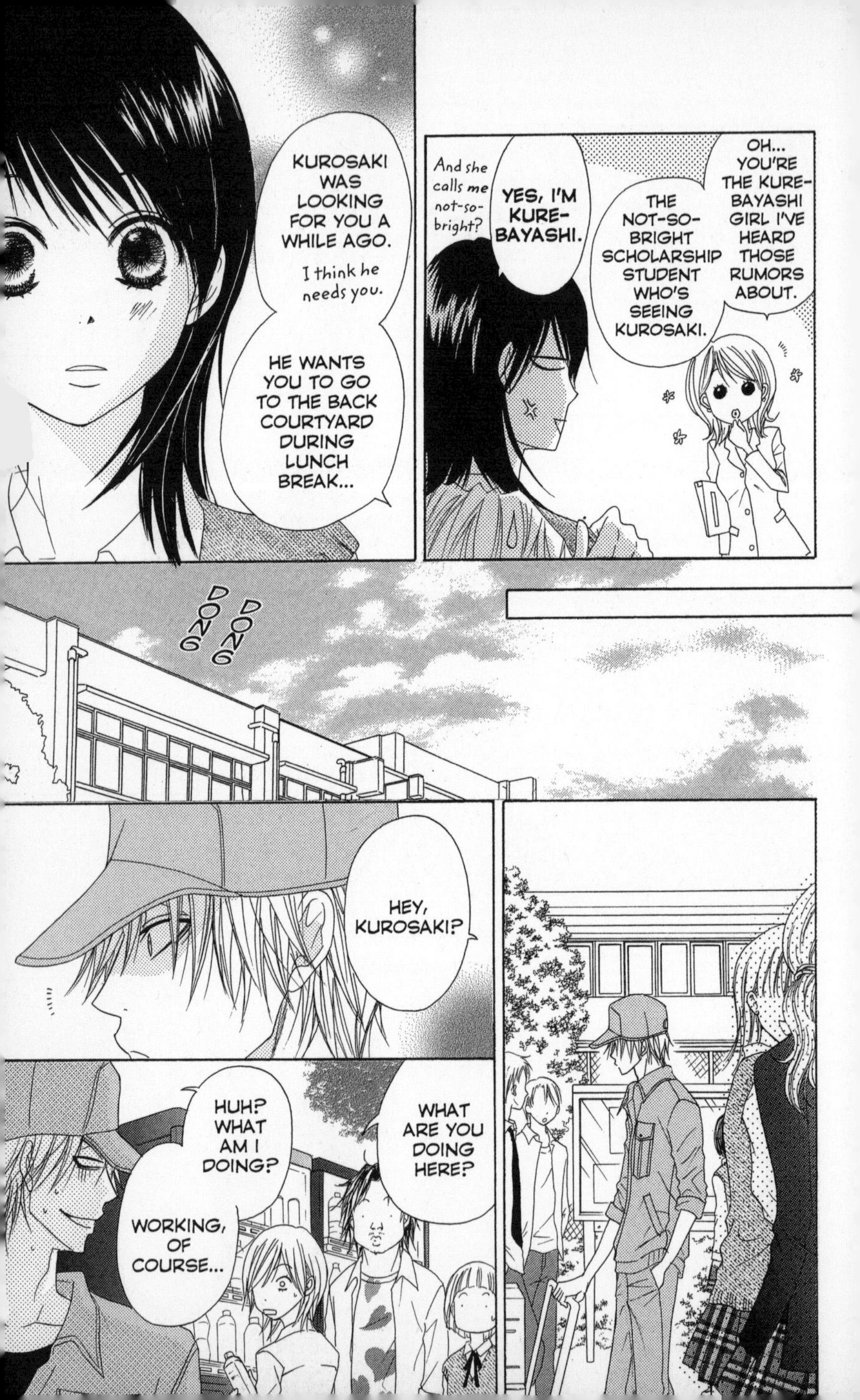
OH... YOU'RE THE KURE-BAYASHI GIRL I'VE HEARD THOSE RUMORS ABOUT.
THE NOT-SO-BRIGHT SCHOLARSHIP STUDENT WHO'S SEEING KUROSAKI.
YES, I'M KURE-BAYASHI.
And she calls me not-so-bright?
KUROSAKI WAS LOOKING FOR YOU A WHILE AGO.
I think he needs you.
HE WANTS YOU TO GO TO THE BACK COURTYARD DURING LUNCH BREAK...
DONG DONG
HEY, KUROSAKI?
WHAT ARE YOU DOING HERE?
HUH? WHAT AM I DOING?
WORKING, OF COURSE...

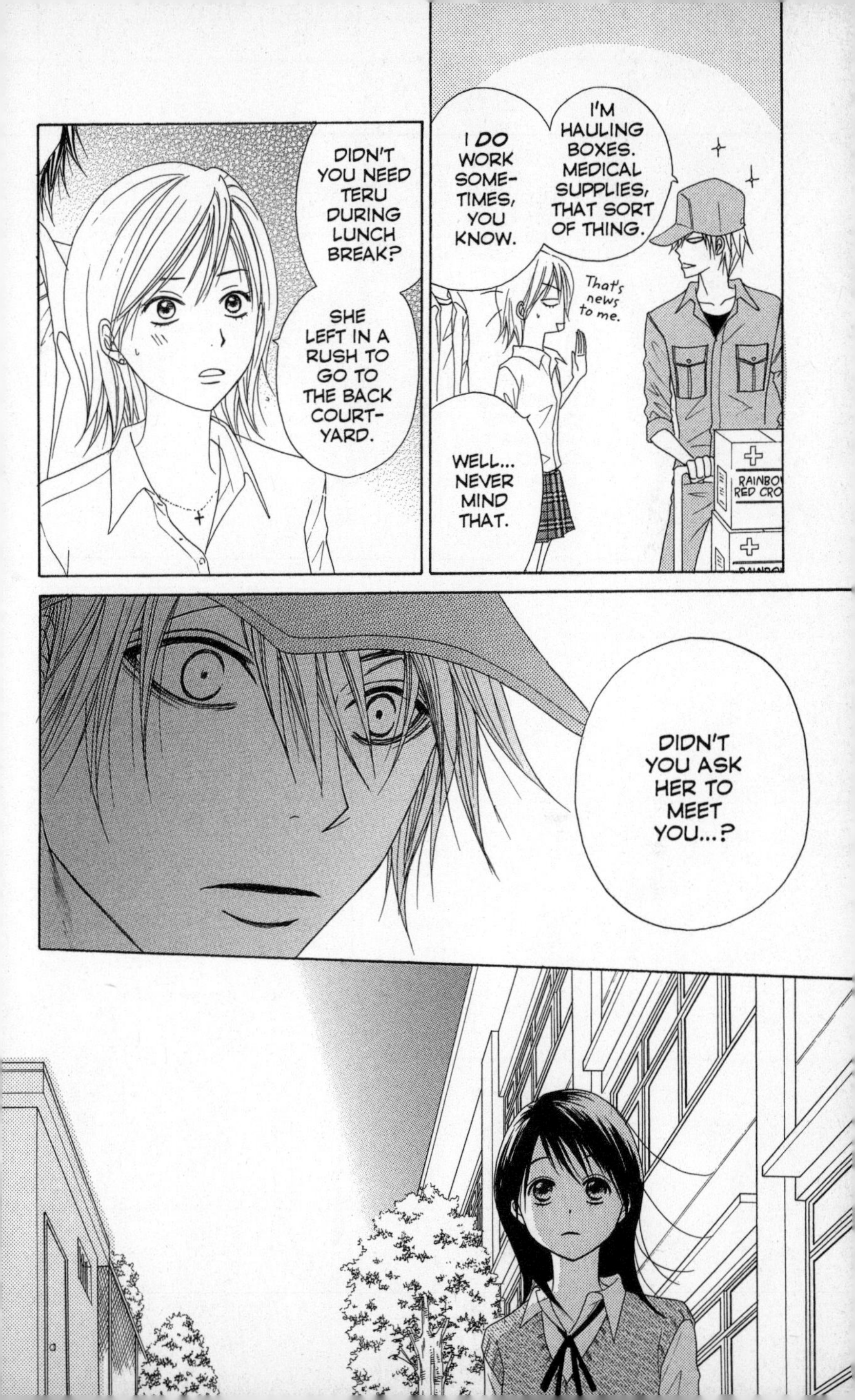
I'M HAULING BOXES. MEDICAL SUPPLIES, THAT SORT OF THING.
I *DO* WORK SOME-TIMES, YOU KNOW.
That's news to me.
WELL... NEVER MIND THAT.
DIDN'T YOU NEED TERU DURING LUNCH BREAK?
SHE LEFT IN A RUSH TO GO TO THE BACK COURT-YARD.
DIDN'T YOU ASK HER TO MEET YOU...?

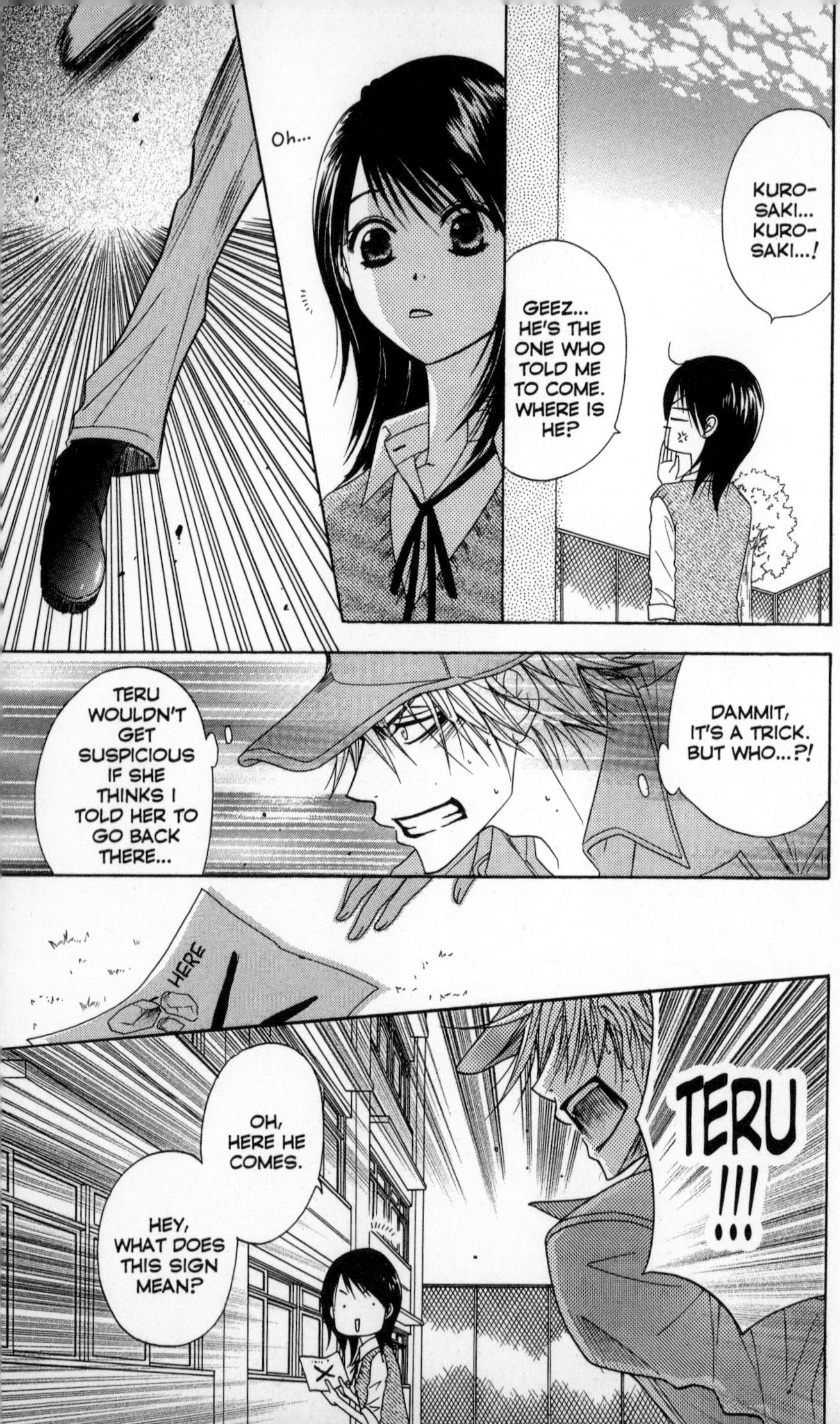
KURO-SAKI... KURO-SAKI...!
GEEZ... HE'S THE ONE WHO TOLD ME TO COME. WHERE IS HE?
Oh...
DAMMIT, IT'S A TRICK. BUT WHO...?!
TERU WOULDN'T GET SUSPICIOUS IF SHE THINKS I TOLD HER TO GO BACK THERE...
HERE
TERU!!!
OH, HERE HE COMES.
HEY, WHAT DOES THIS SIGN MEAN?

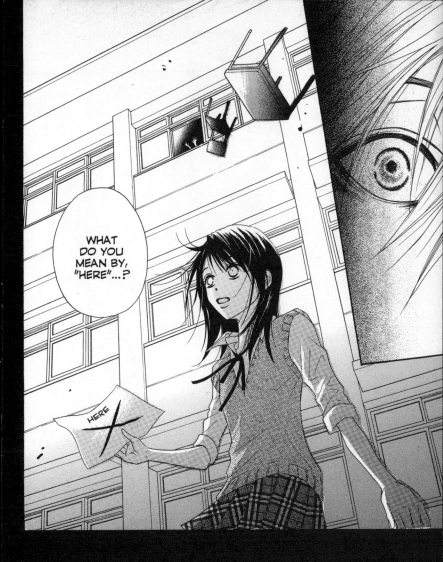

WHAT DO YOU MEAN BY, "HERE"...?

"IF YOU REACH OUT, SHE'LL BE—"

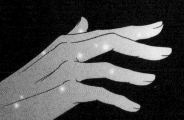

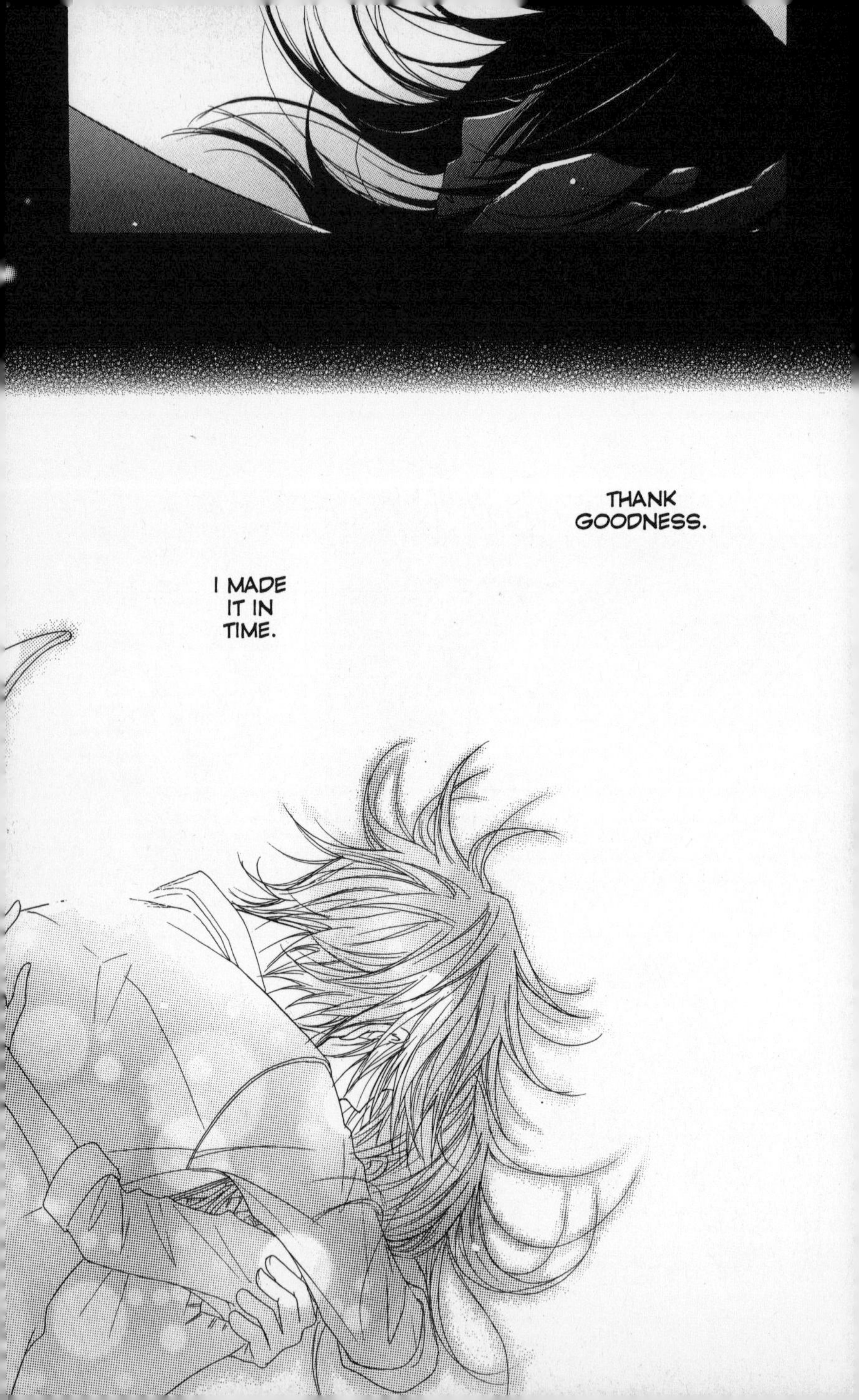
THANK GOODNESS.
I MADE IT IN TIME.

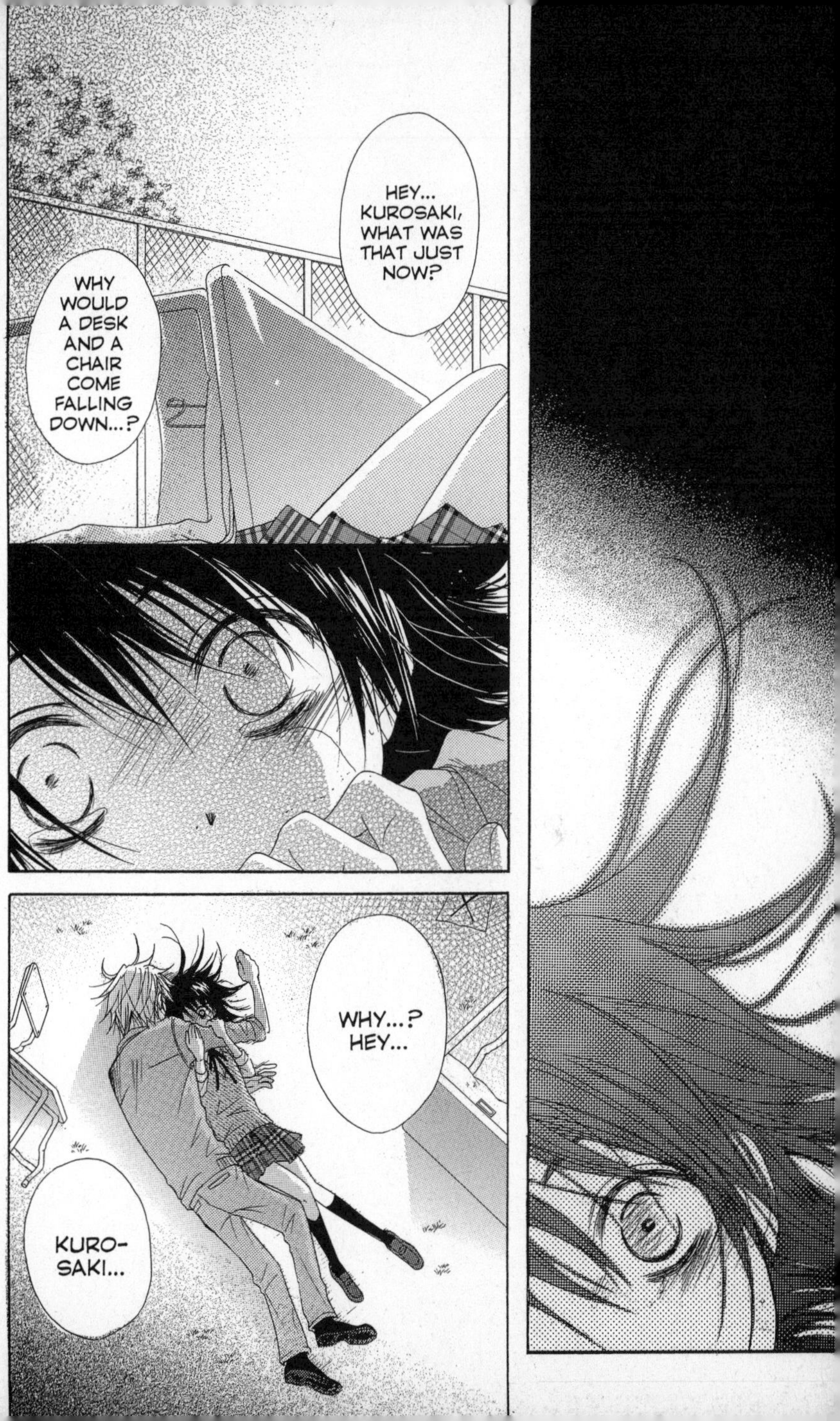
HEY... KUROSAKI, WHAT WAS THAT JUST NOW?
WHY WOULD A DESK AND A CHAIR COME FALLING DOWN...?
WHY...? HEY...
KURO-SAKI...

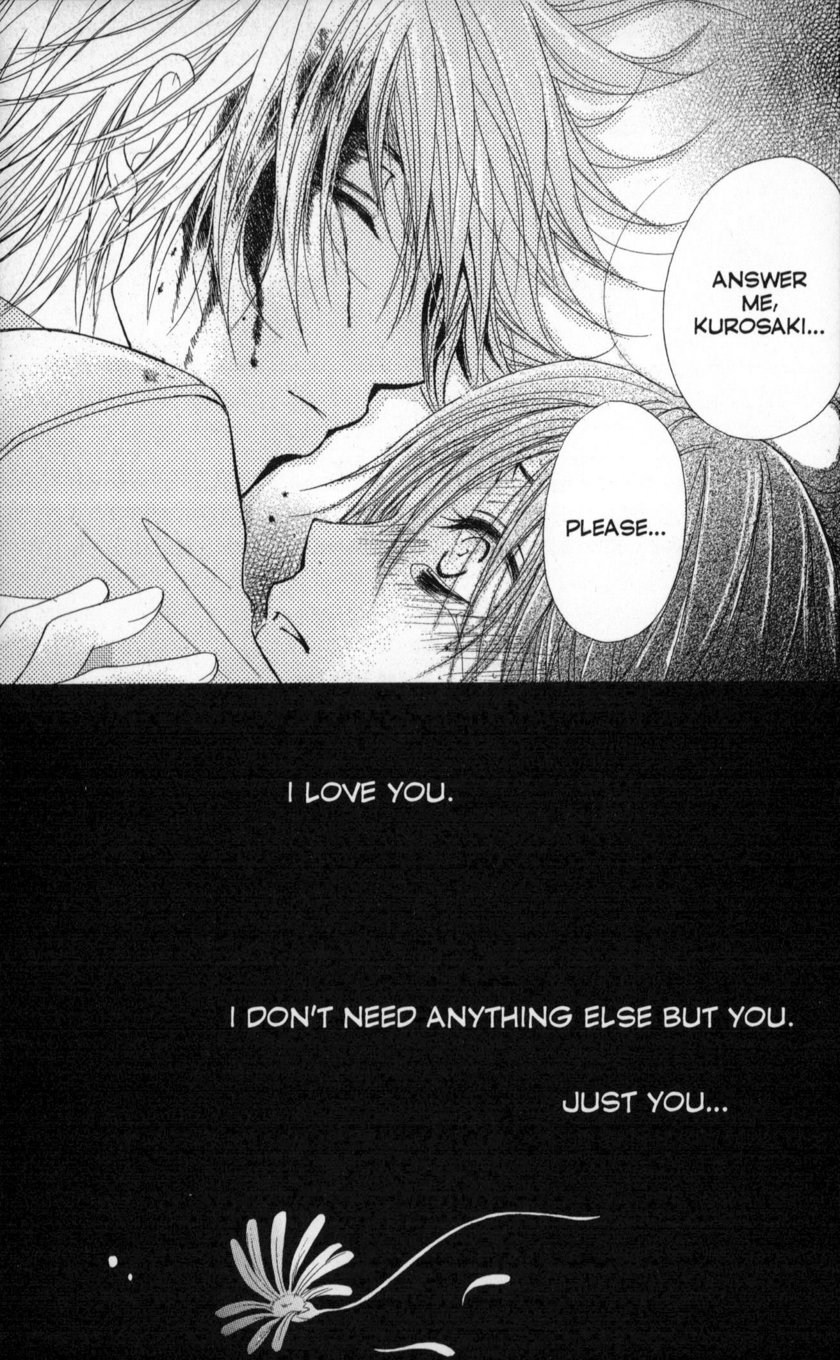
ANSWER ME, KUROSAKI...
PLEASE...
I LOVE YOU.
I DON'T NEED ANYTHING ELSE BUT YOU.
JUST YOU...

AFTERWORD

AND SO, THIS CONCLUDES *DENGEKI DAISY* VOLUME 4.
THANK YOU FOR READING IT UNTIL THE VERY END!

WELL, WELL. I MADE IT TO VOLUME 4. I'M SPEECHLESS.
AND IT'S ALL THANKS TO READERS LIKE YOU. I'M FILLED
WITH GRATITUDE.

NOW THEN, WITH THE CLOSE OF VOLUME 4, IS KUROSAKI
ALIVE OR IS HE DEAD? AS LONG AS I, KYOUSUKE MOTOMI,
AM NOT OVERWHELMED BY THE HELL OF DEADLINES AND
SURVIVE THIS BATTLE, THERE IS A GOOD CHANCE THAT
VOLUME 5 WILL BE PUBLISHED.

SO I WILL DO MY BEST. I'M LOOKING FORWARD TO
MEETING YOU ALL AGAIN. THANK YOU. ♡

最富キョウスケ
KYOUSUKE MOTOMI

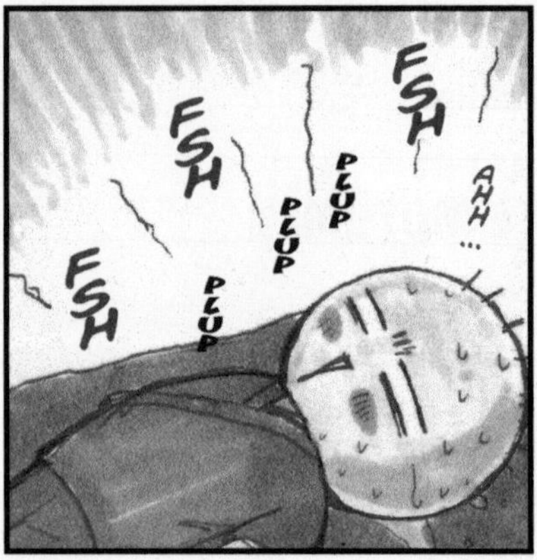
FSH
AHH...
PLUP
PLUP
FSH
FSH
PLUP

Lately, I have so little physical strength that even doing radio calisthenics makes my muscles ache, so I've become interested in ways to stay healthy that aren't too strenuous (what a cop-out). I really enjoy stone saunas. I become drenched in sweat. Almost as much as when I'm facing my deadlines.

-Kyousuke Motomi

Born on August 1, Kyousuke Motomi debuted in *Deluxe Betsucomi* with *Hetakuso Kyupiddo* (No-Good Cupid) in 2002. She is the creator of *Otokomae! Biizu Kurabu* (Handsome! Beads Club), and her latest work, *Dengeki Daisy,* is currently being serialized in *Betsucomi.* Motomi enjoys sleeping, tea ceremonies and reading Haruki Murakami.

DENGEKI DAISY

VOL. 4
Shojo Beat Edition

STORY AND ART BY
KYOUSUKE MOTOMI

© 2007 Kyousuke MOTOMI/Shogakukan
All rights reserved.
Original Japanese edition "DENGEKI DAISY"
published by SHOGAKUKAN Inc.

Translation & Adaptation/JN Productions
Touch-up Art & Lettering/Rina Mapa
Cover Design/Yukiko Whitley
Interior Design/Nozomi Akashi
Editor/Amy Yu

Printed in the U.S.A.

Published by VIZ Media, LLC
P.O. Box 77010
San Francisco, CA 94107

10 9 8 7 6 5 4 3 2
First printing, April 2011
Second printing, November 2012

www.viz.com

www.shojobeat.com

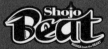

This is the last page.

In keeping with the original Japanese comic format, this book reads from right to left—so action, sound effects, and word balloons are completely reversed. This preserves the orientation of the original artwork—plus, it's fun! Check out the diagram shown here to get the hang of things, and then turn to the other side of the book to get started!